Introduction To
Security and
Crime Prevention
Surveys

Introduction to Security and Crime Prevention Surveys

By

ARTHUR A. KINGSBURY, B.S., M.S.

Chairman
Public Service Departments
Macomb County Community College
Mount Clemens, Michigan
Formerly, Assistant Director
Department of Criminal Justice
University of Wisconsin, Platteville, Wisconsin
United States Treasury Agent
United States Army Counterintelligence Officer

With a Foreword by

Wilbur Rykert

Director
National Crime Prevention Institute
University of Louisville
Louisville, Kentucky

CHARLES C THOMAS · PUBLISHER
Springfield · Illinois · U.S.A.

Published and Distributed Throughout the World by
CHARLES C THOMAS • PUBLISHER
BANNERSTONE HOUSE
301-327 East Lawrence Avenue, Springfield, Illinois, U.S.A.

© *1973, by* CHARLES C THOMAS • PUBLISHER
ISBN 0-398-02836-2
Library of Congress Catalog Card Number: 73-218

With THOMAS BOOKS *careful attention is given to all details of manufacturing and design. It is the Publisher's desire to present books that are satisfactory as to their physical qualities and artistic possibilities and appropriate for their particular use.* THOMAS BOOKS *will be true to those laws of quality that assure a good name and good will.*

Library of Congress Cataloging in Publication Data

Kingsbury, Arthur A.
    Introduction to security and crime prevention surveys.

    Bibliography: p.
    1. Crime prevention surveys. 2. Crime prevention. 3. Retail trade—Security measures. 4. Industry—Security measures. I. Title.
HV7431.K47   364.4'07'23   73-218
ISBN 0-398-02836-2

Printed in the United States of America
N-1

To MARY DELL

FOREWORD

Security—that age old need for protecting oneself against the elements of nature and against other men—has in the last two years been rediscovered in the United States under the term of *crime prevention*. Indeed, *crime prevention* appears to be the rallying point around which police departments can take renewed interest in their service role by providing valuable information to citizens as to the means by which they may protect themselves from crime. While sociologists and criminologists debate the various so-called methods of crime prevention, one thing is becoming increasingly clear, and that is the need to directly prevent crime from occurring. It is therefore necessary for potential victims to be properly informed of methods available for their defense. While the police in the United States are still relatively new to the process of developing security recommendations, the necessity for such programs are no longer open for speculation. However, before police officers can undertake comprehensive surveys and make recommendations to their citizen clients, they must receive specialized training heretofore unavailable in the United States.

At the National Crime Prevention Institute, we find police officers are gaining a new spirit of service, as they become involved in discussion with their fellow officers about locking devices and alarm systems, public information campaigns and all the broad aspects of crime prevention. But in spite of the more glamorous aspects of crime prevention, the security survey remains the backbone of any police crime prevention effort.

Professor Kingsbury has been a member of the Institute's consulting staff from the time of its inception and funding by the Law Enforcement Assistance Administrtation, and every student graduating from the school has benefited from his instruction in the art of security surveys. I have spent many, many midnight sessions with him in attempting to come up with the "great model security check list." Each time it becomes more and more evident that each and every security survey, particularly business surveys, develops from a unique set of circumstances and therefore must be designed specifically for the client. Many officers attending the Institute have expressed the need for a day-to-day manual containing various suggested surveys to assist them in structuring surveys to clients' needs.

This volume on crime prevention surveys is a much needed practical tool for the police crime prevention officer as well as the professional security consultant. Because of its practical aspects, crime prevention officers will use it as a daily reference much as an officer would his traffic code or criminal law manual. This book can be used in conjunction with other books on a more philosophical plane and yet standing alone, it will provide the everyday foundation for a police department's crime prevention activities. It is very gratifying to have worked with Professor Kingsbury as he developed material for this book. With the publication of this volume, he has indeed contributed substantially to the future success of crime prevention officers in the United States.

WILBUR RYKERT

PREFACE

IN THE TOTAL environment of security and crime prevention the one single method for *recognizing, appraising,* and *anticipating* loss is centered in the technique known as surveying or risk analysis. The key factor in many security or crime prevention survey programs is the surveyor's ability to identify risk or the physical opportunity for crime, and the preparation of recommendations. Based on the preceding assumption, the surveyor will, by necessity, need to have an indepth background combining security experience, training, and education.

It is the objective of this book to present an overview reflecting the predominant methods and techniques utilized by security and crime prevention specialists in the security, audit, risk or crime prevention surveys. Thus, this manual deals with the techniques of information collection as they relate to crime risk identification (physical opportunity for crime) and the preparation of recommendations to alleviate crime risk. Since every profession has unique fundamental principles or procedures which distinguish it from related professions, this book then will be an attempt to suggest some basic guidelines in crime prevention and security surveying. In this framework the security or crime prevention survey reflects the method that most security or crime prevention risk identifiers use to reduce criminal opportunity.

The previously written materials dealing with security surveys have traditionally been published by the government or privately owned companies. No effort has really been made to collect and present a group of selections which reflect the major methods utilized by security and crime prevention specialists in surveying.

This book is designed to be used as a basic manual and guide for:

1. Police crime prevention officers,
2. Security personnel,
3. A supplemental text in Loss Prevention and Physical Security college courses.

The framework for security surveying as outlined in this book has been presented as a guide to supplement the security or crime prevention specialist's knowledge in surveying and to better meet his responsibilities in the area of risk identification or physical opportunity for crime. The book has been organized to aid the surveyor in his (a) planning, (b) identification of priorities, (c) formulation of a survey program, (d) development of a model security or crime prevention survey instrument, (e) implementation of the survey, and (f) making recommendations and evaluation of the total security for the organization or site.

The appendices of this book include examples of specific recommendations classified by type of security violations and areas of loss.

This book has been based on the generally accepted premise that the identification of a problem/hazard (risk) and the formulation of recommendations to modify this existing or potential weakness in an organization, public or private, is the first step in developing a comprehensive and secure environment.

ACKNOWLEDGMENTS

I GRATEFULLY ACKNOWLEDGE the assistance of the following individuals who so kindly gave of their time and professional expertise in making this procedural book a reality.

Carl Carter
Assistant Vice President
Director of Security
National Bank of Detroit

Inspector Ronald Dawson
Detective Chief Inspector
Home Office Crime Prevention Centre
Stafford, England

Dr. Daniel Kennedy
Account Executive
Campbell-Ewald

Dr. John Krnacik
Chairman, Communications
Macomb County Community College

O. P. Norton
Executive Director
American Society for Industrial Security

Eric Oliver
Corporate Security Director
Unilever Limited
London, England

Jack Penland
Security Manager
Michigan Bell Telephone Company

H. S. Seaford
Home Office, Horseferry House
London, England

Jack Seitzinger
Director, Criminal Justice Center
Macomb County Community College

My special thanks and appreciation to the following three individuals who allowed me the opportunity to seek their professional advice many times prior to the completion of the manuscript.

Dr. Dale Bartch
Vice-President of Operations
Suter Incorporated
Orlando, Florida

Jon Howington
Professor
Law Enforcement
Macomb County Community College

Dr. Vern Rich
Associate Professor
Center for the Study of Crime, Delinquency,
and Correction
Southern Illinois University

The encouragement and assistance of my wife, Mary Dell, who has written more about security than most people realize, is sincerely appreciated. My special appreciation to Sylvia Polowniak, whose helpful suggestions and staff assistance did much to make this project a reality, and my thanks also to James Clark, for his constructive advice and aid in the final preparation of this text.

CONTENTS

Introduction To
Security and
Crime Prevention
Surveys

PART I

RATIONALE FOR SURVEYS

CHAPTER 1

INTRODUCTION

THIS BOOK IS A collection of security works concerned with crime risk identification (physical opportunity for crime). The selections included have been chosen to reflect the predominant methods utilized by security and crime prevention specialists in regard to the traditional problems of risk identification and reduction, and the techniques known as *security surveys*.

The *surveys* are collected into one volume primarily with a view of the fact that they all deal with one problem: the problem of the relation between *loss* vs. *security* (risk identification and reduction). The subject matter of the following *surveys* may be said to fall within the province of the procedure (technique) as it relates to a concept—security.

Contributions to the field of security, risk management, loss prevention, risk accountability, etc. are beginning to be processed more and more in the form of formal writings. Historically, the security or crime prevention field has had a limited amount of scholarly contributions. This text is not intended to create a conceptual or theoretical contribution to the field of security but mainly to collect a body of knowledge in the form of security surveys and present them in such a manner that the practitioner, using this book as a guide, might more effectively accomplish his responsibilities in the area of risk identification. In essence the reader will be able to create his own survey instrument specifically suited to his own unique requirements. The following sequence is presented so as to allow the reader an opportunity to review a complete system for surveying. This framework will aid the individual in visualizing the total approach to security surveying. In the succeeding chapters each area in the planning and implementation of a survey will be discussed in detail.

Sequential Planning and Implementation of a Crime Prevention or Security Survey

1. Planning and designing survey procedures—Developing and writing survey objectives both for the instrument and survey (Chapter 2).
2. Designing a survey instrument outline—Major categories to be considered (Chapter 3).
3. Implementation of a survey—Type and kind of survey instrument to be used (Chapters 3 and 4).

4. Preparation of recommendations— (Chapters 5 and 6, Appendices) .
5. Presentation of survey findings— (Chapters 5 and 6, Appendices) .

It is important to understand that the key factors in any physical security or crime prevention survey program are to identify risk or the physical opportunity for crime, and to propose recommendations to alleviate these weaknesses.

BASIS FOR SECURITY SURVEY

Major requirements to justify security measures at any one location are:
1. An awareness of the problems,
2. An appreciation of the problems,
3. The ability to do something about the problems.

The security survey is primarily concerned with the first two items listed. These items are identified as (a) the actual survey stage, and (b) the recommendations stage. The third area listed is generally the responsibility of the individual who is the recipient of the survey.

DEFINING SURVEYS

A security survey is a critical on-site examination and analysis of an industrial plant, business, home, public or private institution, to ascertain the present security status, to identify deficiencies or excesses, to determine the protection needed, and to make recommendations to improve the overall security.*

It is interesting to note that a definition of crime prevention as outlined by the British Home Office Crime Prevention Program—"the anticipation, recognition and appraisal of a crime risk and the initiation of action to remove or reduce it"—could, in fact, be an excellent definition of a security survey. The only difference, of course, is that a survey generally does not become the "action" as such but rather a basis for recommendations for action.

This definition can be divided into five component parts and analyzed so that its implications can be applied to the development of a working foundation for the security *surveyor*.

The Anticipation. How does the anticipation of a crime risk (weakness) become important to the security or crime prevention surveyor? Obviously, one of the primary objectives of a survey is the anticipation or prevention aspects of a given situation—the *pre-* or *before* concept. Thus an individual who keeps anticipation in the proper perspective would be maintaining a

---

*Raymond M. Momboisse, *Industrial Security for Strikes, Riots, and Disasters* (Springfield, Thomas, 1968) p. 13.

proper balance in the total spectrum of security surveying. In other words, the anticipatory stage could be considered a prognosis of further action.

Recognition. What means will provide an individual who is conducting a survey the relationships between anticipation and appraisal? Primarily the ability to recognize and interpret what he perceives to be a crime risk becomes one of the important skills a security surveyor acquires and develops.

Appraisal. The responsibility to develop, suggest, and communicate recommendations is certainly a hallmark of any security survey.

Crime Risk. This, as defined in this text, is the *opportunity for crime.* The total elimination of opportunity is most difficult, if not most improbable. Thus, the cost of protection is measured in

1. Protection in depth,
2. Delay time.

Obviously, the implementation of the recommendation should not exceed the total (original/replacement) cost of the item(s) to be protected. An exception to this rule would be human life.

The Initiation of Action To Remove or Reduce a Crime Risk. This section indicates the phase of a survey in which the recipient of the recommendations will make a decision to act, based on the suggestions (recommendations) set forth by the surveyor. In some cases the identification of a security risk is made early in a survey and it is advisable to act upon the recommendation prior to the completion of the survey. The responsibility to initiate action based on recommendations is the sole duty of the recipient of the survey. This is to suggest that the individual who receives the final evaluation and survey will be the individual who has commensurate responsibility and authority to act.

RATIONALE FOR A SURVEY SYSTEM

Establishing objectives within an environment of criminal opportunity (high risk area) is at best a difficult task. There are many influences both external and internal to the *installation or site,** that constrain the ability of the surveyor to act. Both physical constraints as well as constraints imposed through budgeting limitations, legal and/or public opinions are major considerations. Examples of such constraints would be floodlights, high fences, dogs, etc., to secure a modest home in a rather quiet neighborhood. Whether or not constraints exist may be academic, but the continued task of greater accountability of time, manpower, and finances in the area of loss prevention and specifically in security surveying is a reality. Demands on the security surveyor for planning and attaining appreciable measures

---

Installation or site refers to public and private buildings, homes, business and other related physical objects.

of output by the individual citizen or corporate representative appear to be a reality born of necessity. Thus, it appears that various conditions influence and/or limit the ability of security or crime prevention personnel to act.

In the past, security has been valued for itself. Both publicly and privately, the mystique of *total security* has worn off. Security can no longer afford to be an enterprise that encompasses unlimited numbers of nonmeasurable objectives.† The present resources are too limited and the demands are expanding too fast. What is needed is a system or approach which will allow both the clients and practitioners alike a relative measure of success or product. The product as such will be the *recommendations* ascertained via a survey and the measure of success will be the reduction of loss for the individual, home, business, building, etc.

A second criterion for a workable security survey system is the provision for the orderly planning and growth of the *installation or site*. In other words, too many restraints may not be justified or they conceivably may destroy the existing organization. Consequently, a planning system must include the total management system of the surveyed organization or site. This can be accomplished by good communications and well conceived plans of action which should be understood by all parties involved. It is important to reconfirm the objectives of the survey to the various units or individuals who will be affected by the actual survey. In the initial planning of a survey, a good technique is to *install* a system of self-evaluation and a mechanism for the acceptability of new processes by the individual surveyor. No two surveys are the same, and innovation must be a concept mastered by a successful security or crime prevention surveyor.

A security surveying system, to help remedy some of the deficiencies apparent in the *organization* or *site*, must aim for the following:

1. To provide a result-oriented system.
2. To provide a system for orderly growth and planning of the surveyed site.
3. To provide a framework for judging *risk accountability*.
4. To provide a security *system* that is responsive to programs and outputs. (This is not to imply a need in every case for security personnel, but to provide a system of loss control in the broadest sense.)
5. To provide a security interest that stimulates innovation. (Have people want to contribute to the security of the installation or site.)
6. To provide a system for selecting critical areas for further examination.

The security *system* or establishment of objectives is only a tool or technique

---

†Jim Blanzy and Dale Bartch, *Rationale for a Management System in Higher Education* (Mount Clemens, Macomb County Community College, Center Campus Management System, 1972).

that will assist the person to do the job that he wants to accomplish. The techniques of security surveying are and will be a means of risk identification and risk reduction, and the overall reducing of criminal opportunity as it relates to a physical object, building, home, etc.

CHAPTER 2

PLANNING SURVEY PROCEDURES

A N UNDERSTANDING OF the planning process prior to and during a survey will be necessary to successfully conclude the project. General management planning processes will have to be considered in preparing a workable survey instrument or model. The traditional steps in planning should be understood, including:

1. Recognizing a need,
2. Stating objectives,
3. Gathering significant/relevant data,
4. Developing alternatives,
5. Preparing a course of action,
6. Analyzing capabilities,
7. Reviewing the plan,
8. Implementing the plan.

PLANNING SEQUENCE

The establishment of a chronological sequence prior to the actual initiation of a survey will be most beneficial and is highly recommended. Thus, utilizing the major areas of planning, we can establish a working model.

Step 1. Recognizing a Need

How does a *need* for a security survey become apparent? The circumstances that warrant a survey include:

A. When a new store, home, business is opened.
B. The reactivation of an old business (changes may have taken place and new risk features may have been introduced).
C. When a business, building, home, or related physical installation has undergone a substantial change (there may be a building expansion program, or reduction in size, personnel, etc.).
D. If there is evidence of weakness in the existing security program (this generally applies to the private security area).
E. When there is no record of a previous survey.

F. If there is an unusual amount of loss taking place.

G. Changes in external conditions (demographical considerations) .

Step 2. Stating Objectives

Why consider criteria for objectives and be concerned with the whole spectrum of the development of objectives? Long-range practical and economic benefits will be derived if this part of the survey process is performed. In many cases this area of planning will be the most difficult, in that little methodology exists to aid the security surveyor in this operational task. With few exceptions, productivity will increase in the final analysis if specific objectives are formed.

The following example is presented in a simplified format to aid the surveyor in preparing goals.

PREPARING GOALS AND OBJECTIVES

There are two objectives in goal planning:

1. Understand and identify results,
2. Identify resources.

Phase 1 *GOALS:* State general goals.

Phase 2 *BEHAVIOR:* Anticipate behavior of surveyor and action of survey recipient.

Phase 3 *CRITERIA:* Develop criteria (performance levels) .

Phase 4 *TIME:* Time to be allocated to project.

Phase 5 *CONDITIONS:* What obstructions will be faced by surveyor (lack of information, budget restrictions, etc.) .

Phase 6 *REVIEW OBJECTIVES:* Review objectives as they relate to the actual implementation of the survey.

Again, in establishing objectives, to reach any stated goals two major areas should be considered:

1. To understand and identify results to be produced,
2. To identify resources to be used.

Phase 1. General Goal Statement. The general intent of performance goals (preparing objectives) , i.e. a brief synopsis of the expected results of the venture.

Topics to consider prior to implementing project.

1. What is the end result expected of the program?
2. How will the planning for a successful completion of the survey consider principle obstacles?
3. What other approaches are proposed or are already used in this area? (What other examples of surveying exist?)

4. Wherein is the program (survey) flexible enough to meet changing needs?
5. Will more than one feature of the survey serve more than one major objective?
6. Assess the value which successful results will create. (Is a survey really necessary?)
7. Will the survey reduce subsequent loss, or is this simply a technique to gain financial or other rewards?
8. What are the consequences of disapproval of this survey? (If the survey is not done well, will this be detrimental to the organization, and if the survey is completed but rejected, what responsibility does the surveyor bear?)

Phase 2. Behavior. In this phase of the setting of objectives the surveyor should consider the action of the receiver: i.e. what performance will be necessary to elicit desired results from the organization or site surveyed? In other words, how can you make a survey more successful by anticipating the survey recipient's action? If this individual does not accept the survey, have you really reviewed all the facets? This is not to imply a survey should downgrade itself to the total wishes of the recipient, but rather be a truly objective project.

Phase 3. Criteria. The level of performance of the surveyor should be considered. This area of concentration deals with the amount of effort to be placed in the project and a consideration of the final goal; a set of objective recommendations to aid the survey recipient to better identify and reduce his risk areas. The task to be performed should be considered in this phase.

Phase 4. Time. How much time will be allocated to the project?

Phase 5. Conditions. What materials (information) will be given or withheld from the surveyor? (Much depends on the full cooperation of all individuals involved; misinterpretation of goals can limit the efficiency of the survey.)

Phase 6. Reviewing Objectives. Review the objectives as they relate to actual implementation of the survey.

Step 3. Gathering Significant/Relevant Data

How important is the gathering of facts and what are the best sources for references? Regardless of the specific purposes, form, or context, the survey is essentially a method of collecting information and translating this information into recommendations. The nature of the information sought varies widely depending on the circumstances surrounding the particular survey. Five basic criteria should be considered in selecting a method of data gathering*:

1. Accessibility of data.
2. Economy (Will there be a charge for the information?)
3. Accuracy (Objectivity is the key to a good survey.)
4. Relevance (Much time can be wasted relying on false information and, needless to say, recommendations may be affected.)
5. Verification.

1. Recorded data. (Building blueprints, etc.) 2. The installation or facility itself 3. People (personnel).	CONSTRAINTS EXTERNAL & INTERNAL

The following list includes recorded data sources that may be most helpful to the planning and implementing of a security or crime prevention survey.

SOURCES OF INFORMATION*†

A. Federal Sources of Information: It should not be assumed that all of the agencies listed here will readily reveal their records to the investigator. Some of them supply only limited information. The reputation of the various departments and men who are working on special cases will determine the amount of information you will receive.

1. Alcohol Tax and Firearms Division—Treasury Department: License and various information concerning addresses and information relative to known rackets on liquor transportation, and firearms.
2. Bureau of Customs—Treasury Department: Identity of stolen property or property which has entered the country illegally.
3. Bureau of Narcotics and Dangerous Drugs—Justice Department: Information concerning the trade in narcotics and those regularly engaged in such trade.
4. Civil Service Commission
5. Coast Guard
6. Federal Communications Commission

---

*Stephen A. Richardson, et al., *Interviewing* (New York: Basic Books, 1965).
*While not commonly realized, the following agencies provide much information on legal aspects pertaining to controls, approach and techniques in noncriminal matters. The surveyor should also be cognizant of new legal ramifications in securing data. (Ex. Menard v. Mitchell, 430 F. 2d 486, 1970).
†Charles E. O'Hara, *Fundamentals of Criminal Investigation* (Springfield: C C Thomas, 1970) pp. 162-165.

    7. Federal Compensation Offices
    8. Federal Unemployment Offices
    9. Immigration and Naturalization Service—Justice Department
  10. Intelligence Division—Treasury Department
  11. Internal Revenue Service—Treasury Department
  12. Federal Bureau of Investigation:
      a. Criminal files
      b. Single fingerprint section
      c. Regular prints
      d. Noncriminal files
      e. Information concerning suspects and subversives
  13. Maritime Commission—Commerce Department
  14. Navy Department
  15. Post Office Department
  16. Post Offices—generally
  17. Probation Bureaus
  18. Provost Marshal's Offices
  19. Secret Service—Treasury Department
  20. Selective Service Administration
  21. Veterans Administration
  22. Defense Department
  23. Government Printing Office

B. State Sources of Information
  1. State Police
     a. All arrest records of convicted felons (many photographs and practically all fingerprints of these subjects)
     b. Pawn shop records (registered firearms)
     c. Laundry marks
     d. Records bureau: Names of persons involved in auto accidents or persons who otherwise come to the attention of the police.
     e. Accident investigation reports
     f. Gun permit file
     g. Special investigation bureau or file for commercial gambling and racketeering
  2. State Attorney's Office: Special investigations
  3. Labor bureaus
  4. Correction department
  5. Probation and parole records
  6. Assessor's Office (usually for county services)
  7. State Department of Records

8. Liquor Control Commission
   a. Files of applications for licenses
   b. Complaints concerning certain establishments
   c. Violations of liquor laws
9. State Law Library
10. Secretary of State
    a. State Archives
    b. Election offices (ballot petitions)
    c. Articles of incorporation
11. Department of Motor Vehicles (in most states)
12. Conservation Commission (game and fish laws)
13. Judges—Justices of Peace
14. Blue Book (in some states)
15. Old Age Pension Offices
16. Penal agencies
17. Probation and parole bureaus
18. Public Welfare and Social Service
19. Department of Agriculture
20. State Tax Commissioner or Collector
21. Workman's Compensation
22. Treasurer's Office
23. State Health Department
    a. Birth records (Bureau of Vital Statistics) —Death records
    b. Beauty and barber shop licenses
    c. Marriage records
24. Civil Service Commission: Background information concerning state employees
25. State Insurance Departments
26. State Banking Commission: Information concerning banks—cooperates in bank robberies
27. Mental hospitals (employees)

C. County Sources of Information
   1. Police Records
      a. General index files (arrests, charges, convictions, sentences, addresses, and description)
      b. FBI returns—information of previous arrests
      c. MO files
      d. Permit files
      e. Fraudulent check files
   2. County Records Files
      a. Sheriff's Department—Police records and jail records

   b. Local Draft Board
   c. County Clerk
      (1) Information concerning
          (a) Judgments
          (b) Liens
          (c) Mortgages
          (d) Deeds
          (e) Divorces
          (f) Marriages
          (g) Vital statistics
          (h) Testimony of court cases
          (i) Inheritance taxes
          (j) Board of Election's proceedings
          (k) School records
   d. Circuit Clerk's Office: All records of the Circuit Court
   e. Health Bureau
   f. Welfare Commission
   g. County Hospital
   h. County Prosecutor

3. Others
   a. City Clerk and License Bureau
      (1) Pet registration
      (2) Bicycle registration
      (3) City auto registration
      (4) City voting registration
   b. Bureau of Weights and Measures
   c. License of Clerks: Licensing not done by city clerk—eating establishment license
   d. City relief and welfare agencies
   e. Private and social organizations and agencies
   f. Photography (commercial)
   g. Register and recorder
   h. Building and construction records
   i. Local unions

4. Commercial agencies
   a. Insurance
   b. Credit
   c. Finance

5. Newspapers
   a. Morgue
   b. Reference books (Back copies of newspapers)

6. City Directory
   a. Cross-indexed by name and street address
   b. Occupations, marital status, home owner, etc.
7. Telephone directory
8. *Who's Who*
9. Law dictionaries
10. Medical associations: Private medical agencies (Blue Cross, etc.)

D. Private Sources of Information
   1. Airlines
   2. American Red Cross
   3. Banks
   4. Bonding companies
   5. Brokerage offices
   6. Commercial investigative agencies
   7. Contractors
   8. Credit bureaus
   9. Fraternal organizations
   10. Hotels
   11. Income records
   12. Industrial organizations
   13. Insurance companies
   14. Loan and finance companies
   15. Mortgage, debt, and lien records
   16. Real estate agencies
   17. Railroad companies
   18. Public utility offices
   19. Rental agencies
   20. Steamship companies
   21. Storage companies
   22. Trade union records
   23. Transportation companies
   24. Water, electric, and gas companies

E. Directories: The following are among the publications which will be found to contain useful information.
   1. Telephone directory: Local and out-of-town directories are available at central branch libraries. Geographical telephone lists are available to the police.
   2. City directories: A number of cities still publish listings of residents by name, address, and occupation.
   3. *Who's Who in America*
   4. *Who Knows What:* Listing of experts in various fields

5. *American Medical Directory*
6. *Specialist in Medicine*
7. *Who's Who in Engineering*
8. *American Men of Science*
9. *Martindale-Hubbel Law Directory*
10. *Leaders in Education* and school directories—Local, County, and State.
11. *Polk's Bank Directory:* A listing of bank officials, brokers, and bank examiners.
12. *Polk's Motor Vehicle Directory:* A listing of ownership of approximately thirty million passenger car and truck owners.
13. *U.S. Postal Guide*
14. *Insurance Directory*
15. *Dunn and Bradstreet*

Step 4. Developing Alternatives

A single course of action could be detrimental to a survey. Rigid standards cannot fit all surveys in all circumstances. Thus, you cannot choose the best way of getting something done until you have considered where you want to go. This means you will have to refer to your objectives and consider alternatives.

The process of developing alternatives is part of the decision-making process. Thus, decision making is the process of choosing between various ways of getting a job done. This involves first the development of a standard of comparison, which is the list of objectives to be achieved by the action contemplated. Against this standard, each alternative is measured and one is chosen according to the manager's (surveyor's) best judgment. Before acting on this choice, he looks for possible adverse consequences, balancing advantages against disadvantages. A systematic decision is the product of a great many small judgments, organized and summarized.*

In summarizing the major stages of decision making, *seven* specific yet interrelated considerations exist:†

1. Establishing objectives,
2. Classifying objectives according to importance,
3. Developing alternatives from which to choose,
4. Evaluating the alternatives against the objectives to make a choice,
5. Choosing the best alternative as a tentative decision,
6. Assessing the adverse consequences of the tentative decision,

---

*Charles H. Kepner and Benjamin B. Tregoe, *The Rational Manager—A Systematic Approach to Problem Solving and Decision Making* (New York: McGraw-Hill, 1965) p. 172.
†*Ibid.*

7. Controlling effects of the final decision by preventing adverse consequences and by follow-up.

Step 5. Preparing Course of Action

This developmental stage of the security survey process refers to the previous considerations: recognizing a need, stating objectives, etc. The setting of priorities and specifying the division of labor is finalized during this stage.

Step 6. Analyzing Capabilities

The ability to recognize individual strengths and weaknesses is most important. In analyzing and recognizing these capabilities, the individual surveyor may bypass potential problems. If weakness (professional incapability) exists, take preventive action to remove the causes. To minimize this potential problem consult other colleagues, attend training courses, utilize research literature, employ consultants, etc.

Step 7. Reviewing Plan

If a systematic approach is taken in preparation of the implementation of a survey, the survey will be more successful. All processes related to the survey should be continuously updated and reviewed. A major responsibility of the surveyor is the anticipation of potential problems and the successful completion of a security or crime survey.

Step 8. Implementing Plan

The action taken here will be contingent upon a successful plan of attack and continuous evaluation of all survey procedures. A comprehensive security survey will be continuously:

1. Collecting information,
2. Evaluating information,
3. Disseminating information.

As such, the techniques of surveying will at all times be oriented to utilizing these three steps to eventually set forth a series of recommendations which will ultimately identify and reduce:

1. Man-made and environmental *hazards* in an organization
2. *Loss* (fire, theft, etc.)

The preceding pages have presented a greatly detailed plan for the initiation of survey procedures. The complete process of survey planning can be summarized in terms of a cycle involving *six* basic steps:*

---

*Desmund Cook, *An Introduction to Pert* (Columbus: Ohio State University Educational Program Management Center).

1. The first step is the determination and statement of survey objectives.
2. The second step includes the development of a plan of action for the accomplishment of the objectives.
3. The third step is the translation of the plan into a schedule using available or allowable resources.
4. The fourth step is the evaluation of progress.
5. The fifth step is the making of decisions or actions in view of the evaluation.
6. The last step is the evaluation of the total process and adding new or modified decisions and actions.

PART II

COMPONENTS OF SURVEYS

CHAPTER 3

MODEL SECURITY SURVEY

Tʜɪs ᴘᴏʀᴛɪᴏɴ ᴏꜰ the text deals with the methodology used in developing a survey instrument. The major categories in preparing a survey are chronologically ordered so as to aid the individual in his survey planning. The distinction between an example survey model and an *accepted* survey, though clear-cut in some instances, often proves to be superficial. What is called an example or model survey may have significant practical uses, whereas the *traditional survey* may not be applicable. Thus, it is important for the surveyor to have the ability to develop from different resources a workable format so as to guide him through an actual survey. As in many professions, certain techniques are considered the *optimal* way of doing things. Needless to say, in security or crime prevention surveying, there is no one best way to accomplish a given goal, but rather a combination of many techniques and ideas to achieve the desired objectives.

FLOW CHART OF A SURVEY

The sequence of the tasks involved in carrying out the actual design of a model survey, from the first stages of planning to the preparation of the final report, is presented in this section.

In preparing a model security or crime prevention survey instrument, the material in Chapter 2 (Planning Survey Procedures) must be taken into consideration and applied to the development of a survey sample or model. The time considerations are presented as a general guide, thus each survey model prepared will vary in preparation and implementation time.

The four major categories in developing the total crime prevention and security survey process include *three alternatives* and *four developmental stages:*

Alternatives

A. Priorities
B. Time Line
C. Considerations

Developmental Stages

1. Initiating

2. Establishing Priorities
3. Formulating Program
4. Implementation

Table I: DEVELOPMENTAL STAGES OF THE SECURITY SURVEY PROCESS

DEVELOPMENTAL STAGES

ALTERNATIVES:	INITIATING		ESTABLISHING PRIORITIES		
A. PRIORITIES:	RECOGNIZING A NEED — NEED IDENTIFIED BY PERSON — ORGANIZATION— SITE.	PREPARING OBJECTIVES	GATHER DATA	DEVELOP ALTERNATIVES	PREPARE COURSE OF ACTION
B. TIME LINE: *	VARIABLE	4 HOURS	VARIABLE	2 HOURS	2 HOURS
C. CONSIDERATIONS:	SOME ORGANIZATIONS ARE NOT AWARE THEY NEED A SURVEY.	1. UNDERSTAND AND IDENTIFY RESULTS. 2. IDENTIFY RESOURCES.	ACCESSIBILITY AND AVAILABILITY OF SOURCES.	A SYSTEMATIC DECISION MAKING PROCESS WILL TAKE PLACE DURING THIS STAGE.	THE DIVISION OF LABOR AND RESOURCES TAKES PLACE DURING THIS STAGE.

*The expressed times are predicated on a complete and extensive survey of a given premise by one surveyor. If the surveyor uses a simple checklist, the on-site time for a 2,000 sq. ft. private home may be reduced to only twenty to thirty minutes. This, of course, refers to the intended goals and objectives of the survey, individual, or department conducting any given survey.

DEVELOPMENTAL STAGES

FORMULATING PROGRAM		IMPLEMENTATION	
ALYZE ABILITIES	REVIEW PLAN	IMPLEMENT SURVEY	EVALUATE

1 HOUR	1 HOUR	VARIABLE	VARIABLE
VIEW IVIDUAL AND RVEY STAFF ERTISE.	REVIEW PRECEDING CONSIDERATIONS.	1. INFORMAL MEETING WITH SUBJECT. 2. REVIEW PHYSICAL LAYOUT OF INSTALLATION. 3. CONSIDER SOCIAL RAMIFICATIONS. 4. REVIEW COURSE OF ACTION WITH SURVEY STAFF. 5. FORMAL MEETING WITH SUBJECT. 6. IMPLEMENT SURVEY. THE SIZE, COMPREHENSIVENESS, COST, DESIRED GOALS (BOTH INDIVIDUAL AND ORGANIZATIONAL) HAVE TO BE CONSIDERED. EXAMPLES: (ON SITE—NOT INCLUDING PREPARATION, WRITING, AND FINAL EVALUATION TIME.) 2000 SQ. FT. PRIVATE HOME – 3 HOURS. 3000 SQ. FT. SMALL BUSINESS – 4 HOURS. (2 EMPLOYEES, ETC.)	1. DURING AND AFTER SURVEY PREPARE RECOMMENDATIONS. 2. STAFF (INDIVIDUAL) REVIEW RECOMMENDATIONS. 3. EVALUATION OF SURVEY BY STAFF. 4. TYPE AND BIND SURVEY. 5. FORMAL PRESENTATION OF SURVEY TO RECIPIENT. 6. EVALUATION OF SURVEY WITH APPROPRIATE REPRESENTATIVE. 7. CLARIFICATION OF SURVEY WITH RECIPIENT.

PRELIMINARY PLANNING

The method of determining the correct course of action to take in any given situation often refers to the notion of *scientific procedure*. In paraphrasing the scientific method, distinct steps are present. It will be noted that the scientific method has been tailored to the particular problems of the security survey.

Scientific Methodology	*Survey Methodology*
1. Observation	General consideration of all factors that will influence the survey
2. Record selected data	Collect data based on observation
3. Problem	Define the problem
4. Hypothesis	Consider tentative alternatives
5. Experiment	Compare with similar situations (Simulation techniques)
6. Evaluation and interpretation	Formulate recommendations

Observation. The first step of the scientific method begins with the observation of the subject. By this we mean the site to be surveyed and all possible factors that may influence the subject: Objective observation is a most difficult art.

Record. The second phase of the scientific method is the recording and verifying of data obtained from the observation.

Problem. The third step of the scientific method is the defining of the problem. Take nothing for granted and ask questions to supplement your own observations. The difficulty is that it is often very hard to tell in advance whether a question is relevant or irrelevant. Portions of the six interrogatives are important at this stage: *Who, what, when, where, how,* and *why.* However, *why* falls into the untestable category, and thus may not elicit an answer.

Hypothesis. The definition of hypothesis as expressed in *The American Heritage Dictionary,* considers tentative alternatives. "A premise from which a conclusion is drawn. A conjecture that accounts, within a theory or ideational framework, for a set of facts and that can be used as a basis for further investigation. An assumption used as a basis for action.*

Experiment. This step can be considered the application of basic criminal or scientific investigation techniques, the actual collection of evidence vs. the emotional hunch.

A decision must be made regarding the survey sample: (a) what the area of the survey is to cover; i.e. geographical (buildings, houses, apartments, small business, etc.), personnel (background, etc.), organizational and administrative structures (management systems, etc.), or a combination of all three; and (b) the size and design of the sample survey. Will a brief questionnaire be utilized, or a complex set of survey instruments? After these decisions are made, the actual drawing of the sample unit(s) can be prepared.

Evaluation and Interpretation. Clear knowledge of the scientific method does not in itself make for a good security or crime prevention survey. Surveying techniques are essentially an art and require a sensitivity of eye and of mind. Imagination and keen inventiveness would always be a major attribute of the surveyor. The intelligence gathered in the experimental stage is evaluated and interpreted in light of security risk. Based upon this information, recommendations are formulated based on possible or actual security violations.

DESIGNING A SAMPLE SURVEY MODEL

A major requirement of developing a survey instrument is the preparing

---

*William Morris (Ed.), *The American Heritage Dictionary of the English Language* (New York: American Heritage, 1969) p. 649.

of a topical outline depicting the major areas of concentration. Subject areas of interest or topics to be surveyed should be listed under three major categories. The basis for each major category, (physical, personnel, information security, etc.) is based on the individual installation to be surveyed.

Physical Security. Protective device against security hazards; physical measures designed to safeguard personnel and to prevent' unauthorized access to facilities, materials, and documents.

Personnel Security (Government). Measures taken to ensure thorough and careful selection of personnel for employment who may have access to or use of classified information or devices.

Information Security. Safeguarding all information, ideas, correspondence, etc., which have been printed, written, or verbalized by a person, organization, or government.

TOPICS TO CONSIDER

Major considerations or topics to be aware of during the development of a survey instrument fall into four general areas of consideration: (a) planning (purpose), (b) responsibilities, (c) area (duties), and (d) issues (policy—procedure). A proper balance in each area listed is the responsibility of each survey model designer.

A. Planning (Purpose) : What and how much security?—*Degree*
   1. Physical security (property, etc.)
   2. Personnel (background, etc.)
   3. Information (files, records, etc.)
   4. Security survey/consultant

B. Responsibilities: Who?
   1. Administrative authority (Vice President level, etc.) —security organization
   2. Budget/scheduling

C. Area (Duties) : Where will the security emphasis be placed?
   1. Parking
   2. Visitor control
   3. Hazards (man-made and environmental)
   4. Employee pilferage
   5. Outside losses
   6. Disaster planning/civil disturbance
   7. Fire/safety responsibility
   8. Special events

D. Issues (Policy—Procedure) : When? Why?
   1. Legal basis

2. Education/training
3. Manuals (general/specific)
4. Intelligence gathering
5. Contract guard vs. in-house
6. Side arms vs. none
7. Extra chores
   (a) Escort
   (b) Lock-up
   (c) Room checks
   (d) Protect transfer of monies
8. Guard force vs. hardware
9. Uniform vs. nonuniform
10. Contract with local law enforcement
11. Security cadets
12. Consultant (outside)
13. Consultant (staff member) —contract guard

The use of more than one individual in preparing and implementing a security or crime prevention survey is recommended. This approach employs the expertise of more than one individual which is conducive to new and varied viewpoints. This criterion could engender a more solid and objective survey.

SECURITY SURVEY OUTLINE

Every organization or facility is unique and different from all others. Thus it is most difficult to establish a universal checklist.* The following brief topical outline depicts only an example of categories. Detailed surveys are found in Chapter 4. The designer of a survey instrument is encouraged to review the examples and supplement the areas of interest to each individual survey.

A. GENERAL
   1. The purpose of the survey
   2. Name of the plant/organization
   3. Location (street address, city, county, state)
   4. Jurisdiction (city, county, federal)
   5. Security responsibility (private or governmental agency)
   6. Names of the principal officers and their duties. (Attach as an exhibit an official roster of the installation if readily available.)
   7. Type of business

---

*Raymond M. Momboisse, *Industrial Security for Strikes, Riots, and Disasters* (Springfield: C C Thomas, 1968) p. 15.

8. Product or service rendered
9. Brief history of plant and products
10. Size and physical characteristics of the plant and labor force
11. Statement of hazards caused by type of industry, neighborhood and terrain
12. Previous surveys, including the date and conducting agency, and a statement of the corrective action taken[†]

B. SOCIOPOLITICAL CONSIDERATION
   1. Radical or reactionary groups
   2. Local power structures
   3. Primary political opinions
   4. Economic progress of area

C. PHYSICAL SECURITY
   1. Perimeter barriers
      (a) Natural barriers
      (b) Structural barriers
      (c) Human barriers
      (d) Animal barriers
      (e) Energy barriers
   2. Protective lighting
   3. Alarm procedures
   4. Entrances
      (a) Vehicle
      (b) Personnel

D. PERSONNEL SECURITY
   1. Key personnel
   2. Security clearances of employee (if applicable)
   3. Disaster and emergency plans
   4. Morale (employees)

E. INFORMATION SECURITY
   1. Classified information available (if applicable)
   2. Areas where important documents are kept
      (a) Safes
      (b) Cash registers, etc.
   3. Destruction of documents
      (a) Employee payroll records
      (b) Cancelled checks, etc.
   4. Transmission of documents from one place to another

---

†*Ibid.*, p. 13.

F. SECURITY EDUCATION
   1. How much security education?
   2. Who receives security education?
   3. How often given?

G. FIRE FIGHTING FACILITIES
   1. Personnel
   2. Equipment
   3. Alarms

IMPLEMENTING A SURVEY

The implementation of a survey should follow a smooth course of action.
   1. Design survey model procedures: Objectives, etc.
   2. Design survey model: Major categories to be considered and the inclusion of a checklist
   3. Informal meeting with subject: The recipient of the survey should be appraised of the intent of the survey prior to implementation. The surveyor should be sensitive to employee attitudes toward the potential survey.
   4. Review physical layout of installation: Refer to any blueprints, photos, etc., that may be available
   5. Consider social ramifications: Areas of political and social ramifications
   6. Review course of action with survey staff: Approach to be taken and techniques to be used
   7. Formal meeting with subject: Explain course of action with appropriate installation representative.
   8. Implement survey: Use type and kind of survey instrument appropriate to the individual survey.
   9. During and after completion of survey prepare recommendations: Recommendations should generally be written as each security violation is considered.
   10. Recommendations should be brief and concise, to include all pertinent data regarding the identified risk: See Table II which depicts examples of location and placement of recommendations in the final report.
   11. The final writing of the survey findings by staff
   12. Evaluation of survey by staff members: This may include another visit to the premises where the survey took place.
   13. Formal presentation of the survey findings to appropriate recipient
   14. Evaluation of the survey recommendations with the appropriate representative (survey recipient)

15. Clarification (with survey recipient) regarding all aspects of the survey
16. If necessary and appropriate, a follow-up inspection at a later date may take place to aid (the survey recipient) in instituting previous recommendations.
17. Consider each survey as privileged information and attempt not to disseminate any information regarding survey to unauthorized persons.

The implementation of a survey should be considered one of the most important tasks a security or crime prevention representative will ever undertake. This is based on the fact that the first step in any security, crime prevention, risk identification, or loss control program will be the evaluation of the present state of affairs. This of course means a thorough and objective survey. The critical on-site examination and analysis of any installation or site will, in effect, dictate the future course of action regarding the *security* of the surveyed organization (home, business, etc.) .

CHAPTER 4

SELECTED SURVEY EXAMPLES

THE PREPARATION OF ANY ONE SURVEY will of necessity have to consider existing examples of different surveys. The techniques used for selection and modification of each survey will be based partially on the goals, finances, manpower, time, type, and size of the installation or site to be surveyed.

A random sampling of checklists, surveys and related survey considerations are outlined in this chapter so as to aid the surveyor in his preparation design and implementation of his survey model.

The design of a survey model should and must be the ability to consider all the ramifications and techniques associated with survey writing.

Some survey models may be based on a point system as depicted in the examples found in Chapter 4, or the often-used checklist type. Whichever example or technique is utilized, it is imperative to the surveying team or member to be objective in his recommendations and thorough in his investigations.

The selected examples presented in this section have been chosen for the individual qualities, and are not to be construed as the only method of surveying in any one situation. The successful surveyor will develop and record his own survey instrument for given situations and modify his survey techniques and procedure as situations, organizations, sites or other changes occur.

It is again emphasized that the following surveys are a guide only, and should not be interpreted as the only technique to accomplish a given goal.

CLASSIFICATION OF SURVEYS BY TYPE

The major categories listed have been selected to facilitate the identification and selection of survey examples by organization or site. The techniques which accompany any one given survey example may be found to exist in other survey examples, e.g. techniques for a home security survey may have much in common with those of a small business establishment.

The emphasis is again made that this collection of selected surveys is an example and that each surveyor should utilize it as a guide to prepare his own survey instrument or model.

Specific Survey Examples by Major Category

1. Plant/Manufacturing Companies
2. Small Business
3. Government
4. Home
5. Apartment
6. Fire
7. Transportation
8. General

PLANT/MANUFACTURING COMPANIES

1. Industrial Emergency Plan Outline Against Civil Disorders
2. Sample Survey: Proprietary
3. Surveying Buildings for Security
4. Security Survey Checklist
5. Plant Security
6. Physical Security Check List
7. Plant Closing Check List
8. Performance Evaluation Program

Industrial Emergency Plan Outline Against Civil Disorders*

I. Purpose: The following items should be included in the purpose of the plan:
   A. Orderly and efficient transition from normal to emergency operations
   B. Delegate emergency authority
   C. Assign emergency responsibilities
   D. Assure continuity of operations
   E. Indicate authority by company exectives for actions contained in the plan
II. Execution Instructions: This should include the elements of who, what, when, where and how for executing the plan
   A. Individual(s) having authority to execute the plan
   B. Conditions under which the plan may be partially executed
   C. Conditions under which the plan may be fully executed
   D. Coordination between all responsible individuals to assure an efficient sequence of execution
III. Command Control Center: The command control center is the plant command post. The focal point for directing all emergency actions. If

---

*Reprinted with permission from *A Checklist for Plant Security*. National Association of Manufacturers, pp. 5-8.

more than one control center is established, for decentralized operations, all emergency actions should be coordinated through the central control center

A. Location: The primary location should be in a well-protected area of the plant where access can be controlled with a minimum of manpower. An alternate location, also well protected, should be selected in the event of damage or inaccessibility to the primary location.
   1. Primary
   2. Alternate

B. Chain of Command: Assure the legal continuity of leadership and direction. Prepare a management succession list to assure leadership and supervision in the event executive and administrative personnel and key employees are incapacitated or unable to report to work. Assure that management continuity and other emergency modifications of the organization are in accord with state corporate laws and the charter or by-laws of the company.
   1. Emergency organization
   2. Continuity of management and key employees
   3. Designation of successors
   4. Pre-published company orders constituting emergency authority
   5. Establish in accordance with state corporate laws and charter or by-laws of the company

C. Planning coordination and liaison: This element of the plan is designed to assure mutual planning approaches and objectives. It also provides a means of keeping you abreast of the social climate and receiving advance warning of the imminence and possible magnitude of a disturbance. Coordination and liaison should be maintained with
   1. Local and state officials
   2. Fire departments
   3. Adjacent plants and business firms
   4. Local utilities
   5. Employee union officials
   6. Local news media for news release policy

D. Communications: Internal and external for command control units
   1. Internal
      a. Adequate coverage of plant area
      b. Complement primary system with two-way radios, walkie-talkies, field telephones, or megaphones (bull-horns)

c. Controlled usage

2. External: Local and state law enforcement agencies (consider police radio monitor)

   a. Fire departments

   b. Hospitals

   c. Adjacent plants and business firms

   d. Management and key employees

   e. Train switchboard operators in emergency procedures

E. Maintain a log of all emergency actions taken

IV. Personnel: An inventory should be made of employee secondary skills

   1. Apply secondary skills to possible emergency requirements based on emergency organization

   2. Determine degree of competence

   3. Develop accelerated training where necessary

B. Availability: Keep switchboards open and operators available. Designate male operators as alternates for female operators who may not report. The cascade system of notification is very effective. This is accomplished by having the switchboard operator, or whatever means are available, notify two or more key persons—they in turn will notify a designated number of employees, who in turn will notify others until all employees have been notified.

   1. System of notification (cascade system)

      a. Recall to work

      b. Reporting instructions

   2. Rendezvous or reporting points: Central assembly points for employees should be pre-selected, if possible, in areas of relative safety. Employees should be informed of the location of these areas and instructed to report to them if routes to the plant are inaccessible. Transportation, i.e. busses, trucks, should be provided from assembly points to the plant.

      a. Primary—out of emergency area

      b. Secondary—alternate for primary

      c. Inform employees of location(s)

   3. Transportation

      a. Company-owned

      b. Contract needs

      c. Mutual needs with other plants

      d. Escort by law enforcement agencies

      e. Pre-selected routes from reporting points to and from the plant (Plan for escort of female personnel—car pools should be considered)

4. Training
   a. Emergency functions
      (1) Primary and/or secondary skills (related to inventory of secondary skills)
      (2) Immediate emergency repairs
         (a) Internal
         (b) External
   b. Situation briefings: Employees should be briefed daily as to the impact of the riot on the plant and the overall status of the community. These briefings must be factual in order to dispel rumors and speculation.
   (1) Pre-emergency
   (2) During the emergency
      (a) Reacting to crowd pressure: Employees should be prepared psychologically to remain on the job. They should be advised that management needs their loyalty. Self restraint must be emphasized—don't irritate the mob—don't associate with rioters—in essence "ignore the overtures of the mob." Act only upon and as directed by management or local law enforcement officials. The pressures of the mob may be overwhelming—thus this type of training is essential.
         1. Psychological preparation
         2. Self-restraint
         3. Act only upon direction of management or law enforcement officials
         4. Report all rumors to supervisor
         5. Loyalty to the organization
   (3) Post-emergency
      (a) Recognition of exemplary performance
      (b) Impact of emergency on plant
      (c) Employment continuity

V. Evacuation Routes: Predesignated routes to evacuate buildings and/or the plant should be included. All employees should be informed of these routes and procedures for evacuation.
   A. Buildings
      1. Evacuate by departments if practicable
      2. Exits
         a. Primaries
         b. Alternates

B. Plant
   1. Primary—away from emergency area
   2. Alternates—away from emergency area

VI. Electric Power: Coordinate this portion of the plan with local electric power companies
   A. Transmission lines
      1. Location of transformer banks
      2. Availability of alternate distribution lines
   B. Emergency power: An auxiliary source for providing sufficient emergency power for lighting and other essentials. This should not be construed to mean a stand-by capability to continue full production operations. The following items are suggested:
      1. Generators
         a. Show size and location
         b. Fuel supply
         c. Operators
      2. Battery-powered equipment
         a. Flashlights
         b. Lanterns
         c. Other battery-powered sources of illumination

VII. Plant Security: Detailed information pertaining to plant physical security is contained in Appendix I to this outline. The essential elements of this portion of the plan are:
   A. Organizational plans
      1. Develop plant security organization
      2. Put security plans and procedures in writing
      3. Provide for reporting promptly to the FBI any actual or suspected acts of espionage or sabotage
      4. Liaison with the local and state law enforcement agencies
      5. Have supervisory personnel attend plant protection training courses.
   B. Guard Force
      1. Organize the guard force
      2. Prescribe qualification standards
      3. Insure that guards are
         a. Trained
         b. Uniformed
         c. Armed (Examine the authority and legal liability during civil disturbances. Check with local officials)
         d. Deputized (if necessary)
      4. Assure that the guard force is on duty at all times

5. Issue written orders to the guard force
6. Have an internal communications system for the exclusive use of the guard force
7. Plan for an auxiliary guard force for use in an emergency. (This may be accomplished by designating and training company employees. If contract guards are to be used, advance arrangements should be made.)

C. Perimeter Barriers
  1. Check the facility security fence (or other perimeter barriers) to insure that it is:
     a. Properly maintained
     b. Inspected regularly
  2. Vehicle parking should be located outside of the security fence or wall. (This reduces the fire potential from gasoline in vehicle tanks and minimizes the hazard of explosives and incendiary devices which are easily concealed in a vehicle.)
  3. There should be adequate protective lighting to illuminate critical areas
  4. Intrusion detection devices may also be used

D. Control of Entry
  1. Develop procedures for positive identification and control of employees. (Samples of identification media should be given to local law enforcement officials. This is essential for getting through police lines and during times of curfew.)
     a. Identification cards (sample to police)
     b. Badges (sample to police)
     c. Personal recognition (may be used for routine admission of employees to plants with less than 30 employees per shift)
  2. Develop procedures for control of visitors
  3. Admittance to the facility should be controlled by the guard force
  4. Exercise control over movement and parking of vehicles

E. Protection of Critical Areas: Identify and list critical areas within the plant
  1. Enclose critical areas with physical barriers
  2. Designate specific personnel who are to have access to critical areas
  3. Admittance to critical areas should be controlled by:
     a. The guard force, or
     b. Supervisory personnel
  4. Protect unattended critical areas by:

        a. Locks (Locks should be rotated upon notification of impending civil disorder or other emergency)

        b. Intrusion detection devices

    5. Develop a key control system

    6. Develop package and material control procedures

    7. Institute procedures to protect gasoline pumps and other dispensers of flammable material. (Disconnect power source to electrically-operated pumps.)

F. Arms Rooms

    1. Keep arms rooms

        a. Locked

        b. Under 24-hour surveillance

    2. Ammunition

        a. Stored in locked separate location

        b. Under 24-hour surveillance

G. Personnel Security

    1. Conduct pre-employment investigations of applicants

    2. Make personnel checks of persons who are authorized access to critical areas

    3. Brief employees regarding the importance of plant security and the need for exercising vigilance

VIII. Fire Prevention: Additional information pertaining to fire prevention is contained in Appendix II to this outline. These measures are of utmost importance in preventing or minimizing fire damage resulting from civil disorders.

A. Post and enforce fire prevention regulations

B. Extend fire alarm system to all areas of the facility

C. Determine whether the municipal fire department can arrive at the facility within:

    1. Five minutes after the report of an alarm

    2. Ten minutes after the report of an alarm

D. Have a secondary water supply system for fire protection

E. Have facility fire protection equipment on-site and insure that it is properly maintained

F. Determine from local fire department the feasibility of using mesh wire or other screening material to protect roofs from fire bombs, molotov cocktails, or other incendiary devices

G. Organize employees into fire fighting brigades and rescue squads

H. Store combustible material in a well-protected area

I. Instruct employees in the use of fire extinguishers

J. Conduct fire drills periodically

K. Maintain good housekeeping standards

    L. Implement recommendations in the latest fire insurance inspection report

  IX. Vital Records Protection: Develop procedures for classification and protection of vital corporate records and protection of cash and other valuable items.

   X. Property and Liability Insurance: Review property and liability insurance against potential loss or obligation resulting from riots and other destructive acts

  XI. Emergency Requirements: These requirements should be based on estimated needs for the duration of the emergency. These items should be prestocked because conditions may preclude their procurement during the emergency. Unused portions can be carried over for post-emergency use.

    A. Food
    B. Water
    C. Medical Supplies
    D. Quarters
      1. Sleeping
      2. Separate male and female employees
    E. Sanitation
    F. Administrative supplies (office equipment)
    G. Emergency repair tools and equipment
    H. Develop procedures for employees to purchase gasoline from plant supply in case local stations are closed.

  XII. Testing the Plan: Frequent testing and correcting the plan will improve its effectiveness upon implementation under actual conditions. An emergency plan, like a chain, is no stronger than its weakest link.

    A. Types of Tests
      1. Partial—testing individual segments of the plan
      2. Complete—testing entire plan
    B. Tests should be unannounced
    C. Weaknesses should be noted and the plan revised to include corrective actions

Sample Survey: Proprietary*
(To Be Used for Survey Purposes Only)

A. Physical plant
  1. Critical service areas
    a. How are key plant facilities protected from unauthorized entry

---

*Reprinted with permission from Richard S. Post and Arthur Kingsbury, *Security Administration: An Introduction* (Springfield: C C Thomas, 1970) pp. 243-247.

and described physical means of protection, including exterior lighting. What services are outside fenceline?

switchgear or power plant	boiler room
transformer bank	incoming electric power
fire protection equipment	water towers
fire pump	post indicator valves
water valves and lines	emergency generator
gas meter house and gas lines	Tel switching equipment
oil storage tanks	computer tapes
computer facilities	

   b. Comments

2. Buildings
    a. Type of construction? Door construction?
    b. Leased or owned? Details if leased.
    c. Guardhouse construction and location.
    d. Comments
3. Perimeter security: Describe
    a. Terrain?
    b. Type of fence?
        (1) Height of fence?
        (2) Distance from buildings?
        (3) Cleared area both sides of fence?
        (4) Accessible for viewing during patrols?
        (5) Other
    c. Gates and their use? Control of gates?
    d. Patrols and their frequency?
    e. Barbed wire on top of fence? How installed?
    f. Are there any overpasses or subterranean passageways near the fence?
    g. Height of windows from ground?
        (1) Are windows located at perimeters?
        (2) Critical operations opposite windows?
    h. Are windows locked? Screened?
    i. How are entrances controlled? Day? Night?
4. Parking areas
    a. What type of fences are used? Are cars parked abutting interior fences? Describe.
    b. Are gates closed during work periods?
    c. Are unauthorized visits made to parking lot?
    d. Do employees have access to cars during their standard shift?
    e. Vehicle passes or decals?

    f. Are guards involved in traffic control?

    g. Are employees parking areas separated from company buildings?

    h. How are visitors' cars handled?

    i. What controls are in effect for vehicles parked within interior fence?

    j. Comments

5. Perimeter lighting

    a. Is the lighting provided adequate for the area?
       Foot candles on horizontal at ground level?
       (Estimate if possible)

    b. Is there a system of emergency lights that will automatically take over?

    c. Are doorways given sufficient light?

    d. Is lighting in use during all night hours?

    e. Is lighting directed toward perimeter? Can lighting hamper guard surveillance?

    f. Comments

6. Interior lighting

    a. Is the lighting provided during the day adequate?

    b. Is the light at night adequate?

    c. Is there a system of emergency lights?

    d. Is the night lighting sufficient for good surveillance by the night guard (or by municipal law enforcement agents) ?

    e. Are guard shelter areas properly illuminated?

    f. Comments

B. Interior operations

1. Key control

    a. Is a master key system in use?

    b. Does local security organization control or keep informed on lock installation and key distribution?

    c. Are the key locker and record files in order and current? Are issued keys cross-referenced?

    d. How long since the last visual inventory?

    e. Who is responsible for ascertaining the possession of keys?

    f. Have locks been changed when keys were lost?

    g. Are the holders of master keys authorized?

    h. Is locksmith's cage on master key system? If so, why?

2. Safeguarding cash

    a. How much cash is maintained on the premises?

    b. What is the location and type of the repository? What protection? Is location of teller's area acceptable?

c. What protective measures are taken when a money delivery is made?

d. Burglar alarm devices? Describe. Tone controls?

e. Employee background checks? Are tellers instructed in security measures?

f. How are blank employee checks handled? Blank bonds? Blank airline tickets? Travelers checks?

g. Comments

3. Shipping and receiving

   a. Supervision in attendance at all times? Guard checks?

   b. Are materials promptly removed from dock area?

   c. Are truck drivers allowed to wander about the area? Is there a waiting area outside a company office? Are there toilet facilities nearby? Water cooler? Pay telephone?

   d. Are truck court doors used by persons arriving and leaving their jobs?

   e. Are attractive items removed from the dock immediately? Storage area at platforms? Are there paperwork controls?

   f. Can each area be separately secured? Are they physically separated? Are they secured during lunch and break periods?

   g. Are shipping and receiving offices fully enclosed? How are they secured?

   h. What type seals are in use? Are they tamper-proof? How are seals controlled?

   i. Are truck interiors checked?

   j. Comments

4. Scrap operations

   a. What physical controls are available for area? Can area be secured?

   b. What type checks are made?

   c. How is station equipment scrap controlled?

   d. How is scrap contractor controlled?

5. Rubbish operations

   a. What are the physical controls?

   b. What type checks are being made?

   c. How is contractor controlled?

   d. What are hours of pickup?

6. Proprietary information

   a. Is management aware of need for protecting private information?

   b. How is this information handled?

   c. What are the safeguards for paper waste and how is it collected and destroyed?

C. Guards and company employees
  1. Guards
     a. How many are on the force?
     b. Are shifts arranged to provide adequate coverage at shift change?
     c. Is guard force own or contract?
     d. Review guard patrols and frequency. Is there complete penetration of all areas? Are yard areas reviewed?
     e. Are all clock stations being recorded? How?
     f. What are other duties?
     g. What reports do they make out? Follow up?
     h. Do they make adequate checks of parcels and lunch boxes being carried out of the building? Carried into the building?
     i. Are the guards alert and capable of carrying out their duties?
     j. Weapons carried? Are guards trained when to use weapons?
     k. Are instructions issued on weapon use?
     l. Does location have written instructions for guards?
     m. Do guards receive training? What type of training?
     n. How much training?
     o. Comments
  2. Employee credentials and passes
     a. Do employees have passes for identification purposes?
     b. Is it serially numbered and recorded? How are blanks stored?
     c. What are the routines for lost passes? What approval required to replace?
     d. How frequently are passes checked?
     e. What is the frequency of lost passes at termination? What measures can be taken to insure receipt of pass?
     f. Visitor credentials?
     g. Personal and company property passes?
     h. Comments

D. Alarm system
  1. Specific type
     a. Is it owned or leased?
     b. Is it tied to outside agencies or does it report to an in-plant local board?
     c. What types of alarms are in the system? Electrical? Mechanical? Photoelectric? Capacitance? Other?
     d. Is this a full time system or part time? Describe.
     e. What is the response time? (Minutes) (Seconds) Which device tested?
     f. Do vulnerable areas have special alarm devices? Type?

g. Are electrical or mechanical alarms given frequent checks or tests?

h. Comments

E. General

1. No. of employees? On each shift?
2. Male? Female?
3. Security Administration
4. Responsibility for location's security?

Name _____

Department Chief   Section Chief

Surveying Buildings for Security*

A security survey is a critical analysis of a facility for the purpose of determining its present physical security status and for making recommendations to improve security.

So, we offer a security survey questionnaire which has been designed to assist you in determining the security status of your buildings. The general instructions under each outline heading should aid you with the mechanics of the survey.

Because of the variances in design, size, location, and use of major buildings, no two security situations will be identical. Therefore, you probably will have to adjust the survey outline to your particular needs.

Good security may be compared with good housekeeping. A thorough survey should reveal the status of security housekeeping in your building and provide a logical basis upon which you may recommend meaningful and economically justified security improvements.

Section I of this outline should assist you in assessing your problem. Section II can aid you in preparing a logical series of recommendations based upon the security hazards found while assessing the problem.

Office Building Security Survey Questionnaire

I. Assessing the problem

A. Identification of office building

Date of Survey:

Name of Building:

Address of Building:

Persons Conducting Survey:

1.
2.

---

*Reprinted with permission from Bernard M. Ptacek, *Surveying Buildings for Security*, Industrial Security, June 1967, p. 10.

B. Physical control of property
   1. Prevention of unauthorized entry
      a. Area surrounding facility: north, south, east, west. Define the area on all four sides. What are the observable security hazards created by neighboring facilities?
      b. Perimeter barrier (doors, windows, fire escapes, access routes to roof and basements). Determine each exterior accessible opening in the building walls and roof through which an intruder might readily gain unauthorized entry To accomplish this the surveying person must mentally place himself in the role of an intruder and trace out and test the accessibility and vulnerability of these openings. Can door hinges or pins be easily removed? Can the locks be compromised? Can a door panel be easily broken? Could a window be smashed out with little fear of detection? Do attic ventilators, elevator houses and stairwells on the roof offer easy access into the building?
      An intruder fears detection, and he generally will attempt entry through an opening which is somewhat secluded from public view. Therefore, side, rear, and roof openings are usually more subject to attack than front openings. Once a particular opening is determined to be vulnerable, continue to trace the intruder's probable route inside the building and note what valuable materials or data he might take or what other sinister objective he could accomplish. Determine where all stairs lead, particularly noting where and how and with what case an intruder might gain egress from the building. This is important, because an intruder not only plans how he will enter a building, but also where he will make a quick exit should he be detected. If possible, make egress as difficult as ingress.
      c. Locks and keys
      The adage that "a burglar-proof lock has never been built" is probably true. However, many adequate locks are available and they certainly are definite deterrents to unauthorized entry. On each building opening requiring a lock (doors, windows, gate, roof scuttles, etc.) test the lock for adequacy. Can a door lock be easily compromised by pressing the latch backward with a piece of thin metal; is the deadlocking latch functioning; is it possible to twist a knob lock off with a pipe wrench; can an adjacent glass panel be broken out and the inside lock handle reached and operated; does the door lock

bolt or latch fit snuggly into the jamb or can the jamb be easily pried away from the bolt? Are the padlock shackles soft metal or case-hardened; can the padlock hinge hasps be easily unscrewed or unbolted from the building while the padlock is engaged; are rolling or solid overhead doors securely chained and pinned or padlocked from the inside? The list is almost endless. Each lock must be critically analyzed. Additionally, when were the locks last changed? Who has keys? Is it possible that unauthorized persons have keys?

d. Lighting

Thieves and other intruders *do not like light.* It is obvious that darkness is the ally of an intruder. Lighting partially restores the protection naturally provided during daylight hours. Check the nighttime level of light, especially in alleys, near entrances, lower fire escape termini, ground level windows, etc. Is there enough light to enable a policeman, guard, or passer-by to readily detect an intruder attempting unauthorized entry? Night lighting inside the building is also helpful in silhouetting an intruder climbing through a window or door or detecting his presence inside.

Lighting is a deterrent only if it is used. Determine who turns on the manually controlled portion of nightime lighting and which portions are automatically turned on by time clocks or photocells. Be certain that low-mounted external lighting cannot be compromised by easily unscrewing a bulb, etc.

e. Intrusion detection devices

If your facility is equipped with these devices, become familiar with the entire system and assess to what degree it protects the facility. How could an intruder circumvent the system? What changes in the system would improve its effectiveness?

f. Employee vigilance

Employees, especially elevator operators and maintenance personnel, are often in a position to detect persons of questionable character who frequent large public buildings. Determine which employees of your facility are in this category. To what extent do they enhance security? What are their instructions if an intruder is detected? Make as many employees as possible a part of your security team.

g. History of unauthorized entry

Obviously a study of the history of unauthorized entry to a particular building will tend to reveal the weaknesses in physical security and will assist you in justifying necessary improvements to deter unauthorized entry.

2. Control of authorized entry
   a. Identification of employees

   Where large groups of employees are involved, it is usually desirable that they have some positive means of identification, preferably company-issued identification cards. A guard or elevator starter can then readily determine the right of an individual's presence in a building particularly at night.

   b. Employee parking

   Where do employees park their private automobiles? If they park in the building garage, do they have access to company vehicle supplies (spark plugs and other parts)? Would it be easy for an employee to take an office machine down quickly into the garage and hide it in his vehicle, etc.? Do you have a procedure to authorize removing equipment?

   c. Contractors, vendors, repairmen, janitors

   Contractors, vendors, repairmen, and janitors who regularly work in large buildings often become very familiar with the operations of the building and are able to locate the storage areas of valuable supplies, money, and machines. They also are in an excellent position to "case" the alarm system, telephone systems, and frequency of guard tours, etc. In short, *they are outsiders with a reason to be inside.* Any of these persons is in an excellent position to steal, "set up a burglary," or perform acts of espionage. Know who these people are and determine to what extent they are supervised at your facility. Be particularly thorough when checking into the activities of janitorial personnel. Remember, they usually have a legitimate reason to be in any part of the building. Possibly they could be bribed into cooperating with a burglar or industrial spy.

3. Guards

   If your facility employs guards, review their instructions as to their proposed action should they detect an intruder, a fire, or a dishonest employee. Be certain their "clock tours" are arranged to cover the most vulnerable portions of the building. Do they vary their routes and times, or could an intruder observe their activities for a short interval and thus avoid detection? Are they observers or do they just walk from one to the next clock point?

C. Critical security areas

Up to this point in the survey, the broad aspects of the building security have been considered. The amount of time and money necessary to totally secure a large public building against the unauthorized entry of the most clever intruder may not be justified; therefore, the surveying person must identify and isolate areas within the building which require special security. Too much security may be costly in loss of time by personnel who must comply.

Some examples are listed below.

1. Company records

   The nature of the business being conducted in your particular facility will dictate the degree of emphasis you should place on this category of the survey. If the building is occupied by various private tenants, you may wish to consult with them regarding the degree of security needed. Determine what records, computer tapes, correspondence, plans, original source documents, models, etc., might be subject to theft or prying eyes, especially at night. If a particular record were taken or copied by an intruder, what might be the ultimate consequences? What security controls are now in force? What, if any, improvements in security could logically be made? During your assessment of records security, don't forget to check the trash. An industrial spy can learn many interesting things about a company from reviewing discarded letters and other data. Plan security in accordance with need.

2. Mail

   Many large buildings having mailing departments through which flow volumes of correspondence and sometimes cash payments. The day-to-day recorded activities of the company pass through the "mailman's" hands. Aside from the need for good physical security in the mail room, the honesty and integrity of the mail personnel is most important, whether they are company employees or are employed by a private mail delivery service. Investigate the operational procedures of the mailing department. How is the mail handled? When are the mail bags delivered, by whom, and where are the bags left—in the hall or a locked room? Who has the key? How secure is the room? What provision has been made in the company for the special handling of confidential correspondence, to prevent its unauthorized interception in the building?

3. Medical supplies

   Every day many doctors' offices and other sources of medical supplies are entered by unauthorized persons, and narcotics and other drugs are stolen. Very strict controls are necessary in the storage and dispensing of these supplies. A survey of this situation, in cooperation with the medical staff of your organization, should reveal the controls presently exercised and what, if any, additional control might be advisable.

4. Money

Any business which daily receives cash from customers and stores the cash in the building at night is subject to being burglarized or the cashiers robbed. The security measures enforced in banks are of a specialized nature, and attempt is made here to suggest that bank-type security should be practiced in all firms receiving money from the public. Transfer as much of the incoming money to your bank as often as practical each working day and provide reasonable protection for the remainder.

a. Safes and vaults

Some considerations in analyzing safes are: What type is it; location; is it pinned to the floor or can it be rolled away; could it be torched or otherwise broken open easily; who has the combination; how often is the combination changed; is the combination written on calendar pads, on the wall, over the safe, or stored in an unlocked drawer; how much cash is stored overnight; is there a night light over the safe?

b. Cashiers

Is the cashier's counter under observation of other employees? What type of cash drawers; what are the cashier's instructions as to the maximum amount of cash to be accumulated before it is removed to a safer location; are large amounts of cash counted in public view at balancing time; what, if any, instructions have the cashier and other employees been given in case of a robbery or a burglary? If more than one cashier works out of a single drawer, you lose accountability.

c. Bank messenger

Who makes the trip; is he accompanied; distance to bank; is time and route varied; how is cash carried; how much and how often; does the carrying bag make its contents obvious?

d. Fire protection

The adequacy of fire protection equipment definitely has a bearing on the basic overall security of a particular facility. It is, however, a separate study and is mentioned here primarily as a reminder to be certain that qualified persons periodically inspect the facility. You should be alert to any areas you might feel are inadequately protected.

E. Security organization

1. Delegated responsibility for security

Determine responsibility for various phases of security and make an overall assessment of the performance of the persons involved. As personnel are reassigned, is the replacement given the security assignment?

2. Liaison with law enforcement

What law enforcement agency has jurisdiction; do employees know the telephone numbers; is the number posted in appropriate locations; what are the instructions for protecting the scene of a crime?

3. Communications

What type of and how much communication equipment is in the building? Telephone trunk lines, two-way radios, teletypes, etc? What security regulations are in force concerning this equipment.

II. General comments and recommendations

All the previous security analyses were designed to reveal many of the weak points in the security of your building. In this section of the survey you should recapitulate those weaknesses and set forth recommendations to eliminate or reduce their potential hazards. As a practical matter, recommendations to improve security ordinarily should not seriously restrict the operation of the facility. Excessive restrictions on the movements of employees could result in an economic loss to your company greater than the savings which might result from increased security. Too much security can cause personnel to rebel. If security is in accord with need and the personnel are informed, they will usually comply. Therefore, each recommendation should be carefully weighed. Listed below are some basic considerations which may be helpful in improving security deterring potential intruders, and reducing the probability of a "runaway loss." A word of caution—*any physical change made in the openings of your building should not be in conflict with local building, fire, or safety regulations.*

III. Basic security considerations

A. Exterior doors

1. Should be as formidable as aesthetically possible.

2. Removable exterior hinge pins should be made fast by welding or inserting a set screw which locks the hinge to the pin and which screw is not accessible from outside the door.

3. Removable exterior hinge leaves should be secured to the door with bolts which cannot be disassembled from the outside.

4. Rear and side doors opening into alleys or other secluded areas and roof doors to stairwells and elevator houses should be resistant

to lock picking, drilling sawing or breakage. Windowless metal doors are preferable. Lightweight paneled wood doors not of solid core construction should be clad with metal or replaced by metal doors. Glass panel exceeding 8" x 12" or over 96 square inches in area in "secluded" doors should be replaced with a metal panel, or covered with a network of iron bars or with heavy gauge screening, none of which can be easily removed from the otuside. Door louvers should be similarly secured.

B. Accessible exterior windows
1. If unnecessary and not aesthetically required, eliminate the window or "brick in" the opening.
2. All windows not regularly monitored by an employee should be kept locked
3. If there are no valid countervailing considerations, all side and rear windows next to secluded outside areas should be barred or covered with heavy gauge screening.
4. Any side or rear glass transoms or the windows of a rooftop elevator house should be similarly secured.

C. Roof openings
1. All roof openings, skylights, attic ventilators, air ducts, etc., (over 96 square inches) should be barred or covered with heavy-gauge screening. It is usually best to install these security devices on the inside of the opening.
2. Ideally, hatchway (scuttle) covers should be constructed of metal and have no exterior accessible hinges or locks. Presently installed wooden covers can be improved by installing expanded metal plates on the inside of the cover and by installing concealed hinges. The cover should be locked in place from the inside (consult local building and fire regulations). In refurbishing the cover, carriage (round head) bolts should be used (rather than screws), with the round head placed outside.
3. Louvered openings should be secured with bars or heavy-gauge screening.

D. Fire escapes
External fire escapes often provide an intruder with the means to reach at least one building opening of each floor and many of the roof openings. Internal fire escapes (usually stairwells) often assist him in gaining access to many other portions of the building. Because of the public safety considerations involved, it can only be suggested here that fire escapes should permit quick exit but difficult entry. This should not deter you from investigating your particular fire escape system to determine feasible methods of restrict-

ing the ready use of the system by a person to gain unauthorized entry.

E. Locks

In general, building locks, *especially on accessible exterior openings,* should be of reasonably high quality. With the important exception of fire exits which must be fitted with locks permitting rapid exit, all other exterior accessible doors should have locks which are equally difficult to circumvent from the interior or exterior. An intruder always wants a quick way out, and interior turn knobs permit him to quickly unlock the door. Also, he might break an adjacent glass panel from the outside and reach inside and unlock the door. Therefore, if permitted, door locks should be keyed on both sides. All doors should fit into their jambs as tightly as possible commensurate with freedom of operation.

1. Dead-bolt cylinder locks

Dead-bolt cylinder locks usually are more difficult to circumvent than other standard types and should be used whenever possible. On double swinging doors, the "long-throw" laminated dead bolt is preferable. The laminated bolt is more resistant to sawing. The "short-throw" dead bolts sometimes can be pried out of the jamb of a loose fitting door. The "inactive leaf" of double swinging doors should be fitted with flush bolts at the head and foot. Thieves frequently use automobile jacks to pry door casings apart.

2. Knob locks

"Knob locks" often do not incorporate a deadlocking latch, or if installed, the deadlocking latch mechanism is inoperative. In this instance, an intruder is often able to push back the "unguarded" latch and gain entry, even though the lock is engaged. *Be certain that knob locks have operable dead-latching mechanisms.*

3. Padlocks

The effectiveness of padlocks is often compromised by an intruder by breaking the lock with a heavy object or prying it apart with a bar or by cutting the shackle with "bolt cutters." Sometimes the hinge-hasp hardware is pried off the door or wall or the hinges are removed by merely removing the screws or bolts holding the hinge to the wall or door. Therefore, padlocks should have qualities which will resist prying or breaking and have casehardened shackles to resist cutting. The hinge-hasp hardware should be as heavy as is practical and should be mounted with bolts which cannot be easily disassembled from the outside. If possible, the hinge leaf should be mounted so that when closed it will cover the heads of the mounting bolts. Padlocks should be locked in place during the day to prevent their being taken to a locksmith and duplicate keys made.

4. Miscellaneous locks

Overhead doors, sliding doors, metal accordion doors, etc., may be locked by various means, and each installation requires close scrutiny. These doors usually are installed at vehicle entrances. If possible, it is usually advisable to lock these doors from the inside so that the locking devices are not readily accessible to an intruder outside. Some of the previously set-out suggestions on pedestrian door locks also apply to vehicle doors, particularly regarding padlocks. If the doors are electrically operated, be certain that the electrical controls are not readily available to an intruder. If possible, lock the switch in the "off" position after the door is closed at night. Appropriately secure crank-operated doors. Be certain that any sidewalk opening covers are securely locked from the inside.

When special security is needed against unauthorized entry of a rear pedestrian door, heavy iron or wooden bars may be installed across the inside of the door and jamb. After the bar is hung in place on its supporting brackets, it is a good practice to drill holes horizontally into the brackets and bar and insert metal pins which keep the bar in place. This reduces the probability that the bar could be dislodged from outside by an intruder.

5. Key control

Because of the probability that keys to the locks of your facility might be duplicated by unauthorized persons, it is a good practice to change the lock combinations periodically. Additionally, a log should be maintained of all facility keys which have been issued to various persons having a realistic need for a key. Facility keys should always be "picked up" when a person (employee, contractor, vendor, tenant) no longer has need for the key, particularly in the case of a disgruntled employee who has been discharged.

F. Lighting

Thieves do not like light. Be certain that there is sufficient nighttime security lighting both inside and outside your building to be a definite deterrent to an intruder. Also be certain that the lighting is turned on by competent personnel or by automatic devices and that the lighting cannot be easily compromised by the intruder. Substantially made lighting fixtures deter criminals seeking an easy means to eliminate light.

G. Intrusion detective devices

Specialized assistance is usually necessary to determine the advisability and cost of installing these devices. All such devices tend to increase the level of security in a building.

H. Employee vigilance

Be certain to have your employees share the burden of security. Enlist the aid of your employees by tactfully letting it be known that you (the management) are interested in security, which security is beneficial to both management and employees. "The key to a successful security program is the security-conscious employee." In a large building, elevator operators and maintenance personnel are particularly helpful. Employees are glad to know that you are protecting their working facilities.

I. Contractors, vendors, repairmen, and janitors

These people are "outsiders with a reason to be inside." Many of them could have (or surreptitiously establish) a reason to be in the sanctums of the building. Dishonest persons could steal, obtain intelligence information, or otherwise compromise the security of the building and business being conducted therein. Know who these people are and establish reasonable controls of their movements. Know the critical security areas of your building.

J. Guards

Know your guards' background and character. Establish positive instructions and regulations concerning their duties. Be certain their tours are designed to provide the most security per man-hour spent. If applicable, establish "sign-in" procedures for "off-hour" employees or tenants. Hire guards, not merely "warm bodies." Give them responsibilities—you'll get more for your money. They're happier with something to do.

K. Critical security areas

Previously in this survey the areas of records, mail, medical supplies, and money were given as examples of critical security areas. You may have even more important security areas. Identify the areas and provide as much special security as is warranted. Because these areas are special, it probably would serve no useful purpose to list various and sundry security "do's and don'ts." Therefore, only a few general suggestions applicable to most businesses are set out below.

1. Safes and vaults
   a. Determine the degree to which the safe or vault will resist the efforts of a burglar. If justified, purchase a more suitable safe or vault.

    b. Safes should be "pinned" to the floor.

    c. Combinations should be changed periodically and given only to employees having a definite need for the combination.

    d. Combinations should not be written on the wall or calendar pads or stored in desks or other insecure places.

    e. How much cash is stored overnight? If practical, reduce this amount by more frequent trips to the bank.

    f. Store cash stubs separately from the cash. If stolen, these records sometimes are potentially more valuable than the cash.

2. Cashiers

Only enough cash should be kept in cash drawers to enable the cashier to make change. Periodically, "bleed" the excess cash from the drawers and remove it to a safer location and as soon as practical to the bank. Cash should not be counted in full view of the public. This "tips off" a potential robber to the amount of money he might be able to steal. Instruct cashier and employees not to attempt to physically resist a robber. Teach them to be good witnesses and to obtain a good physical description of peculiarities of the robber which could lead to his identification. Instruct all employees not to disturb the scene of a burglary, in order to maintain the evidence for the police.

3. Bank messengers

Bank messengers should carry the cash in the most inconspicuous manner possible. They should vary the times of their trips and routes taken. It is usually best to walk on the side of the street opposing traffic. Money bags only advertise the mission of the messenger. If possible, men should carry the cash in their inside coat pockets and women should use ordinary purses.

4. Confidential trash

Be certain that discarded sensitive records, correspondence, and other data are kept separate from the regular trash. Paper shredders are valuable for destroying sensitive material.

L. Security organization

As the caption implies, organize your security program and be certain that delegated responsibilities are being carried out by designated employees. Maintain good relations with local law enforcement and gain their assistance in planning your security program. Employees should know the telephone number of the police Establish appropriate security regulations regarding telephone and other communications rooms. Any repairman entering these rooms should be required to positively identify himself to responsible communications personnel.

Security Survey Check List*

Importance of Plant or Business
1. Is the produce or service vital to national defense or community?
2. Is any part of its operations or product of a classified nature?
3. How critical is the product?
    a. Demand for product
    b. Number of plants producing and/or personnel engaged in such production (ease of replacement or substitution)
4. Are the plants or business a probable target for espionage or sabotage?
    a. In peacetime?
    b. In wartime?

Physical Description of the Plant or Business and Surroundings
1. Layout of the installation. (Attach as exhibit maps, sketches or photographs showing the area, types and location of buildings, roads, railroad sidings and piers.)
2. Roads or highways passing or leading to the plant or business. Description of railroads in the vicinity (spurs to plant), nearby airports serving the plant, dock facilities and steamship lines.
3. Physical description of surrounding area, topographical features, adjoining plants or buildings, etc.
4. Area of plant premises. Type of boundary (fenced?).
5. Description of buildings and other facilities on the premises, including docks, roads, canals, loading platforms, sheds, storage areas, repair shops, motor pools, fuel pumps, warehouses, power plants, communication systems, transformer stations, laboratories, fire stations and fire fighting equipment, etc.

Identification of Critical Areas
1. Has management (owner) determined and identified critical and vulnerable areas, both manufacturing and non-manufacturing?
2. Is management's evaluation of critical and vulnerable areas up-to-date, considering changes in products, production processes, vulnerability factors, etc.?
3. Is management aware of the physical vulnerability of the facility in

---

*Reprinted with permission from Raymond M. Momboisse, *Industrial Security for Strikes, Riots and Disasters* (Springfield: C C Thomas, 1968) pp. 15-30.

terms of location, type of construction and equipment, degree of combustibility, etc.?

Security of Buildings

1. Type of construction (wood, steel, concrete). Are the buildings fireproof, earthquake proof, protected for lighting?
2. Are the buildings locked at night and on holidays and weekends when not in use? If so, are the doors, windows, and other openings adequately protected?
3. How often are the buildings checked during closing hours for fire, burglary, damage by storm, etc.?
4. Are the buildings equipped with burglar alarms? If so, are they local alarms or the central station type?
5. Is valuable or critical machinery or equipment stored in the buildings?
6. Do the buildings house critical or secret products, plans, formulas, etc.? If so, are extra precautionary measures taken?
7. Are those buildings or rooms which contain safes or valuables given extra attention by the guards or owner, etc.?

Restricted Areas

1. Number, size and location of restricted areas, i.e. cash area, air condition room, etc.
2. Degree of restriction in each.
3. Are restricted areas fenced independently? If so, what type of fencing is used?
4. Type of pass system used for admittance to restricted areas (if applicable).
5. Is an "access list" maintained of those authorized admittance?
6. Are electronic alarm or intrusion detection devices used?

Information and Material Handling

1. Have all personnel been properly cleared to handle the material with which they come in contact, i.e. cashiers, etc.?
2. Are safe combinations known only by cleared personnel? Are combinations changed every six months, or whenever anyone knowing the combination leaves the organization or changes jobs to another activity?

Receiving and Shipping

1. Are employees and visitors' packages checked at the entrance?
2. What examinations or spot checks are made of lunchboxes, toolboxes and packages?

3. Describe method of sealing mailed packages.
4. Are truck and rail shipments adequately braced, lashed, and delivered before movement?
5. Is the shipping and receiving area separated from the rest of the installation by a fence or other barrier? If so, is access through a controlled gate?
6. If there is storage area; is it open or covered?
7. What supervision is given the docks, wharves and loading platforms? Is it adequate?
8. Is the area open to visitors or loitering?
9. Is there guard protection for the area? Is it adequate? How could it be improved?
10. Is incoming and outgoing material handled quickly and efficiently, or is there a backlog of crates and boxes piled up on the dock or platform area? What is the loss experience from pilferage here? Is it excessive?
11. Are freight receivers, shippers and handlers supervised for possible conspiracy with truck drivers or others for theft of merchandise?

Perimeter Barriers

1. Type of barrier, including height and presence or absence of a top guard.
2. Do buildings or bodies of water form any part of the perimeter, and if so, what protective measures are employed?
3. Are utility openings and outside windows and doors properly secured?
4. Frequency of inspections by guard and maintenance personnel.
5. Are clear zones maintained on inside and outside of perimeter fence? If not, are they feasible?
6. Are electric or electronic alarm or intrusion detection devices used on the perimeter?
7. Are warning signs used on the perimeter? If so, give size and location?
8. Are there any unprotected areas?
9. Present condition of perimeter fence. Any holes, breaks, posts down, etc.?
10. Any holes or tunnels under fence?
11. Any lumber, boxes or refuse piled near fence?
12. Can vehicles drive up to fence? If so, at which points? Do vehicles park near fence? What is the relative ease of using vehicle near fence as a "stepladder" for climbing over?
13. Weak places in perimeter caused by railroad spur tracks, a stream or

body of water, sewer line, coal chute or other opening through which unauthorized persons could enter?

14. Are there roving guard patrols? What is the frequency of patrol route activity?

Entrances

1. Number, type and location of active gates, vehicle or pedestrian.
2. Railroad siding gates.
3. Hours gates are open.
4. Inactive gates, and occasions on which they are used.
5. Type of locking devices on gates.
6. Location of keys for the locking devices.
7. Is there an adequate key control system in effect?
8. When gates are not in use, are they securely locked?
9. Are entrance and exit gates designed so as to facilitate the proper checking of vehicles and credentials during rush periods?
10. Are gates guarded?

Alarm System

1. Is there a protective burglar alarm system for the premises. Is it an off-premises central station reporting system or a local reporting system which sends the alarm to personnel standing by on the premises?
2. Does the perimeter fence have an alarm system to detect trespassers?
3. Do the safes, vaults, or rooms containing valuable or vital information have adequate protective devices?
4. What specific protection is provided to prevent burglary, fire, robbery?
5. Following an alarm, are the communication and transportation facilities sufficient to insure a rapid follow-up by guards? By local police?

Lighting

1. Are there good power facilities available?
2. Are the protective lighting system and the working lighting system separate?
3. Is there an auxiliary power source for protective lighting?
4. Are the lights controlled by automatic timer or manually operated?
5. Are switchboxes and automatic timer boxes secured?
6. What emergency lighting is available?
7. Are the perimeter areas adequately floodlighted during hours of darkness?
8. Are the light sources directed to aid the guard and hinder the tres-

passer, i.e. into the face of the trespasser and leaving the guard in softer light or semishadow?

9. Are the entrance and exit gates sufficiently lighted?
10. Are lights at the gate arranged to light up the interior of vehicles entering and leaving?
11. Are buildings or areas which contain important material or valuable material well illuminated?
12. Are power stations, transformers and other critical machinery and equipment adequately lighted at night?

Guard Force

1. How many are on duty at any one time? Is this adequate for conditions?
2. How are guards selected? What are the qualifications for the job (age, physical, mental, education, background) ?
3. Are the requirements such as to bring good men into the job? If not, how should the qualification standards be revised?
4. Training. Is it sufficient for them to carry out their duties and responsibilities properly?
5. Is there a set of written rules and regulations for the night guard force? If so, is it adequate?
6. What specific instructions are given them pertaining to: their daily duties, identifying checks or personnel and visitors, vehicle checks, box car and train checks, package checks, personal searches, making arrests, handling drunks, handling mental cases, first aid, money escorts, etc.?
7. What are the working hours for guards?
8. What is the salary for guards? Is it high enough to attract qualified men? What salary is recommended?
9. Are the guards alert and efficient in carrying out their duties?
10. How is the morale of the guards? If inadequate, what recommendations can be made for improvements?
11. What type of firearms and other equipment do they carry? Are reserve firearms and emergency disaster equipment available?
12. If firearms and ammunition are issued, how are they accounted for?
13. What instructions and target practice are given guards before firearms are issued to them?
14. Are the guards thoroughly schooled as to when and under what circumstances they are to use their firearms? Do they understand the criminal and civil consequences of misuse of their firearms on another person?
15. System of supervision.

16. Communication system with civil agencies.
17. Number and location of guard posts, punch clock stations.
18. Number of patrols (foot and motor) and their frequency.
19. Is the guard communication system separate from other systems?

Control of Entry

1. Identification media for employed personnel.
2. How carefully are employees screened by the personnel department at the time of submitting their application? Is there close cooperation between the personnel department and the security department in the examination and clearance of questionable applicants?
3. Are all applicants' character references and previous employment history completely checked? If there are gaps or blanks in an applicant's previous employment record, are these carefully investigated?
4. Does the application questionnaire provide adequate information regarding the applicant's character, reliability, stability, honesty, etc.?
5. Parking lots: location? fenced? lighted? guarded?
6. What controls are maintained over salesmen, vendors and solicitors?
7. Are there restricted areas within the plant or business? If so, what additional controls are exercised over personnel entering these aeras? Are these controls adequate?

Key Control

1. Are building keys and gate keys maintained in a secure place when not actually in use?
2. Are all keys accounted for? Are they handled only by authorized personnel?
3. Is a record kept of all persons holding building or gate keys? Is this record reviewed periodically and kept up to date?
4. Is provision made for the replacement of locks when a key is lost?
5. Are master keys closely controlled?
6. Are the locks of a type which offer adequate protection for the purpose for which they are used?

Security Education

1. Are all newly assigned or employed personnel given a security orientation?
2. What follow-up security instruction is given?
3. Is the instruction applicable to various types of employment and degrees of responsibility?
4. What personnel give the instruction and what are their qualifications?

5. Are security signs and placards on display? Is any other media used?
6. Does the installation have a security operating plan, i.e. what to do in case of burglary, fire, etc.?

Theft Control

1. Is an effort made to interest employees and supervisors in reducing the amount of theft in the business?
2. How prompt and cooperative are employees in reporting thefts or suspicious incidents?
3. Are trash collectors properly supervised by security personnel?
4. Is the disposal or sale of scrap and salvage material frequently checked for honesty and accuracy?
5. Are janitors, maintenance men, and clean-up crews properly supervised for control of theft activity?
6. If there is a general lack of theft control? Inadequate accounting methods? Lack of supervision? Improper attitude of employees? Lack of interest on the part of management? Poor package pass control?
7. What type of theft is most prevalent? What is being done about it? Is it actually known how great the theft problem really is?
8. Is the tool checking system adequate? Are tool inventories made regularly? Are maintenance men checked by appropriate personnel when they leave the premises for jobs in other areas?

Fire Protection

1. Are there an adequate number of fire alarm boxes located throughout the premises or near by? Are they conspicuously located?
2. Is the type and number of fire extinguishers adequate? Are they frequently inspected to ascertain that they are in good working order, filled, sealed, etc.?
3. How far is it to the nearest public fire department? Have the firemen ever visited the business to study the layout of buildings and equipment, the location of fire doors, stairways, and the special problems involved in the plant?
4. Are the buildings equipped with automatic sprinkler systems? Are they equipped with automatic alarm systems for fire control?
5. Are the physical fire barriers in the buildings adequate; i.e. fire doors, etc.?
6. Are the fire doors installed where needed? Are they in proper working condition, with fusable fire links or automatic closing devices working properly and free of obstructions of any kind?
7. Is the housekeeping of the business well maintained? Are oily rags kept in covered metal containers? Are paper, lint and other inflam-

mable deposits frequently cleaned from floors and from the insides of exhausts, ventilators, air-conditioning ducts, ovens and from around heaters, conveyors and pipes?

8. Are the "No Smoking" rules enforced?
9. Are electric cords roped over nails or otherwise improperly placed? Are worn or defective electric cords immediately replaced?
10. Are electric fuses replaced by fuses of too high amperage, or by coins, wires, or nails?
11. Are proper measures taken to safeguard the storage and handling of gasoline, kerosene, alcohols, fuel oils and other explosive or toxic liquids and gases?

Emergency Plans

1. Are there separate emergency plans for fire, explosion, riots, mass civil disobedience, demonstrations, major accidents and air alert?
2. Is there a natural disaster emergency plan, if applicable?
3. Do the above plans provide for evacuation of the installation?
4. Have the plans for installation disaster been coordinated with the area civil defense plans?
5. Who is in charge of the operation of these plans during an emergency?
6. Are the emergency plans kept up to date with changing conditions and personnel?
7. What part do the employees play in an emergency situation? How are they notified of an emergency?
8. How are outside agencies such as the fire department, police department, Red Cross, doctors, ambulances, etc., notified in the event they are needed? Who is responsible for seeing that this is done?
9. Are there an adequate number of exits (doorway, fire escapes, etc.) in the buildings to meet an emergency situation? Are they kept clear of obstructions?
10. What instructions have been given the employees regarding their duties during emergencies in the plant?

Liaison with Police

1. Have contacts with local police been established?
2. Are the police advised of the business security plans?
3. Have arrangements been made for police aid in emergencies?
4. Have contact men been designated?
5. Is there an exchange of information relating to danger to the plant or a disturbance in the area?

Report and Recommendations

The concluding step in making the physical security survey is the preparation of a report. The report itemizes the conditions which are conducive to breaches of security, records the preventive measures currently in effect and, when required, makes specific, practical and reasonable recommendations to bring the physical security to the desired standard. The report may be in any form desired although normally the narrative form is used.

Plant Security*

1. Security Plan: Outline the emergency organization and responsibilities of the plant security force. The normal organization and responsibilities should be adapted to meet the requirements imposed by a civil disturbance, sabotage, bomb threat, unexploded ordnance or other hostile or destructive acts. The security plan should include all actions and techniques to be employed to protect personnel, materials, products or services, premises and process from hazards inherent in operations and other acts mentioned above. The security organization of a facility will depend almost entirely on the size, criticality and vulnerability of the facility.

2. Legal Rights and Restrictions: This is a most important element and must be understood by management and members of the security force. The facility legal counsel must coordinate with the city attorney, district attorney or other legal offices to determine the authority of the property owner, and his employees, in protecting property and life. Some factors to be considered are:
   a. What are the geographic limits within the authority of management?
   b. What are local laws and statutes concerning security force being armed? Their use of weapons?
   c. With what type weapons can they be armed?
   d. What actions can the security force take during a civil disturbance?
   e. How and under what conditions might they exercise "citizens arrest?"
   f. Under what conditions can force be used? How much force can be used?
   g. The advisability of deputizing the security force?
   h. Are the legal limits of authority the same for "normal" (day to day) conditions and "emergency" conditions?

3. Liaison and Coordination: List the names (positions), telephone numbers, law enforcement agencies, (local, State and Federal) with whom the plan has been coordinated and liaison should be maintained.

---

*Reprinted with permission from Industrial Defense Civil Disturbances, Bombings, Sabotage. *Plant Security*, Office of the Provost Marshal General—Department of the Army, pp. 13-19.

4. Security Force: The organization of the security force should be tailored to meet the requirements of a specific facility. The security force is the most effective and important element of security planning. It is the only in-house element capable of physically responding, utilizing judgment in an incident. The following factors should be considered relative to the security force.
   a. Qualification standards
      (1) Age
      (2) Loyalty
      (3) Intelligence
      (4) Physical Qualifications
      (5) Dependability
      (6) Cooperativeness
      (7) Ability to exercise good judgment; possess courage, alertness, self-reliance, tact and even temper
      (8) Security clearance may be required in some instances
   b. Training: These are basic essentials:
      (1) Discipline
      (2) Familiarization firing of weapons
      (3) Use and safe practices and maintenance of weapons
      (4) Legal limits of authority
      (5) Procedures for apprehension and restraint to include citizens arrest
      (6) Self-defense
      (7) Actions during civil disturbances
      (8) Actions in event of bomb threats
      (9) Actions upon discovery of unexploded ordnance
      (10) Elementary first aid and fire protection
      (11) Communications procedures
      (12) Report writing
      (13) Employee and public relations
      (14) Basic rescue techniques
   c. Uniforms: It is recommended that security personnel wear uniforms or clothing with distinctive markings. This facilitates identification and minimizes problems which could arise from lack of immediate recognition of the individual as a member of the security force.
   d. Weapons: The matter of arming the security force is quite controversal. The decision must be made by management. Consideration should be given to the mission of the security force. If the mission is to protect life and property, can this be accomplished without firearms? Will the presence of an armed security force deter the omission or commission of destructive acts? Will the presence of firearms

incite trouble? Management may decide not to arm the security force during normal operations, but rather to have weapons available to arm the force during an emergency. The following factors should be considered and included in the plan:

(1) Type of weapon
(2) Registration of firearms (check with local Internal Revenue Service, Alcohol, Tobacco, and Firearms Division)
(3) Procedures for issue and turn-in of weapons and ammunition
(4) Maintenance
(5) Inspections
(6) Frequency of familiarization firing (at least annually). If your security force is armed, the question is: What should their orders be?

First of all, armed security people must be thoroughly trained in the use of and when they are legally authorized to use the weapon with which they are armed. Even when they're proficient with weapons, be sure they know the consequences of firing. In all cases, the by-word is discretion. Minimum force should be standard; for instance, a member of the security force shoots an escaping felon who turns out to be 15 years old. He was still an escaping felon, but once it happens, he'll never again be known as anything but a defenseless, young boy. You'll have a case on your hands. If you even restrain a trespasser, you can be in trouble.

e. Organization: Security forces may be organized in any one or any combination of the following.
   (1) Regular force
      (a) Fixed post deployment
      (b) Patrol deployment
   (2) Auxiliary force: An auxiliary security force should be established to supplement the regular force during an emergency. Personnel should be selected from the employee population and trained in their emergency security function.

f. Shift changes: Show the times of shift changes and tours of duty. Shift change times should not be the same as the time for employee shift changes. It is well to consider establishing shift changes of the security force at least one hour in advance of or one hour after employee changes.

g. Communications: Adequate communications are essential to the effective operation of the security force during normal times and especially in the event of a civil disturbance or other emergency. Consideration should be given to a communication system for the exclusive use of the security force. The type and comprehensiveness of the system will vary with the size of the facility and the size of the force.

h. Limitations of security force functions: Members of the regular force should have no "fire fighting" or other duties. Cross training to provide an in-depth, dual capability is acceptable. Such emergencies offer an excellent diversion to cover the entrance of a saboteur or dissident groups. During such incidents the security force should be more than normally alert in the performance of its primary mission.

5. Perimeter Barriers: Fences and other anti-personnel barriers are the physical media by which the boundaries of a facility, or restricted area with a facility, are physically defined for protection and control. The fundamental purposes of such barriers are to define the area, impede access or intrusion, aid security personnel, channel the flow of personnel and vehicles, and provide a psychological deterrent.

   a. Types of barriers:

      (1) Natural (body of water, cliffs, canyons, or other terrain difficult to traverse)

      (2) Structural (buildings, chain link fence, barbed wire). Natural barriers should be reinforced by a structural system of barriers.

   b. Construction:

      (1) Chain link fence

         (a) Minimum height of chain link portion—7 feet

         (b) Mesh openings not larger than 2" square

         (c) Number 11 gauge or heavier wire

         (d) Twisted barbed selvage—top and bottom

         (e) Extend to within 2" of firm ground or below the surface if soil is sandy and easily wind-blown or shifted.

         (f) Fence mesh should be drawn taut and securely fastened to rigid metal posts set in concrete. Additional bracing, as necessary, should be placed at corners and gate openings.

         (g) Topped with a 45° outward and upward extending arm bearing 3 strands of barbed wire stretched taut and spaced to increase the vertical height of the fence by approximately 1 foot.

         (h) Provided with culverts, troughs, or other openings, where necessary, to prevent washouts in the barrier. If such openings are larger than 96 square inches in area they should be provided additional protection.

         (i) Checked (inspected) periodically for undergrowth, damage or deterioration.

      (2) Masonry walls when used as perimeter barriers should have a

minimum height of 7 feet and topped by a barbed wire guard as indicated, or have a minimum height of 8 feet and be topped by a layer of broken glass set on edge and cemented to the top surface.

(3) Building walls, floors, roofs, and dikes, when serving as perimeter barriers, should in general be of such construction and so arranged as to provide uniform protection equivalent to that provided by chain link fencing as specified. **If buildings form a part of the perimeter barrier—protective grill work or laminated shatter proof glass should be installed to increase the protection for windows, doors or other openings.**

(4) Bodies of water: If a lake or stream forms one side or any part of the perimeter, it in itself should not be considered an adequate perimeter barrier. Additional security measures must be provided for that portion of the perimeter, such as a fence or frequent guard patrol and flood lighting.

c. Posting. Post with "no trespass' signs in accordance with criminal laws of the state.

d. Protective lighting.

(1) Inspect the perimeter barrier to insure that it is properly maintained and properly lighted.

(2) Without doubt, lighting is the best security bargain available. Most riot and firebomb damage occurs after dark, and nothing discourages hit-and-run types like full coverage, glare lighting. They don't know whether a camera—or an armed guard—may be waiting beyond the glare. You may be able to reposition existing lighting for this purpose, but light the villain, not the target. And don't make the mistake of relying entirely on mercury protective lighting, because even a momentary power dip can mean several minutes of darkness.

(3) One solution is direct substitution of instant-starting combination incandescent mercury lamps for some of the straight mercuries. Light output and wattage remain essentially the same. Another is to use low-cost quartz iodine fixtures on weighted pedestals on the plant roof.

(4) Insure continuous lighting in parking lots and on ground floors.

(5) Use screening to protect lighting fixtures against rocks and other objects.

e. Vehicle parking: Vehicle parking should be located outside of the security fence or wall. (This reduces the fire potential from gasoline in vehicle tanks and minimizes the hazard of explosives and incendiary devices which are easily concealed in a vehicle.)

f. Intrusion detection devices: Anti-intrusion alarm devices are employed for the purpose of detecting and announcing proximity or intrusion which endangers or may endanger the security of a facility. These systems are utilized to accomplish one or more of the following purposes:

(1) To permit more economical and efficient use of manpower by substituting mobile responding security units for larger numbers of fixed security posts and/or patrols.

(2) To take the place of other necessary elements of plant security which cannot be used because of building layout, safety regulations, operating requirements, appearance, cost, or other reasons.

(3) To provide additional controls at vital areas as insurance against human or mechanical failure.

The advantage of a protective alarm is measurable reliability. While there is a wide range of complexity between the various alarm systems, each can be tested and evaluated to determine what degree of security can be expected from the device. Detection devices are usually designed to detect a single phenomenon. The choice of the type detection device to be employed is based upon what will be most readily detectable in the given situation. It may be desirable in some cases to employ more than one type of detection device to protect against all possible methods of entry. Usually, similar equipment is manufactured by several companies. Such equipment will operate on the same basic principles, but may well differ in refinements. These differences may, under certain circumstances, alter the degree of security provided.

The most common detection devices are:

a. *Electro-mechanical devices* are designed to effectively place a current carrying conductor between the intruder and the area to be protected. The most common in this category are foils, screens, contact switches and vibration detections which are damaged or disturbed by penetration (usually used for protection of doors, windows, ducts, and nonsubstantial walls or partitions).

b. *Photoelectric device,* whereby interruption of a virtually invisible beam of light is detected. This device is highly effective in detecting vehicular movement since it is impractical to move vehicles over or under the beam.

c. *Proximity detection device* operates by surrounding an object with an electrical field in usch a balance that, any disturbance of the field creates imbalance in the system that results in the initiation of an alarm. There are two different types of proximity alarms—electromagnetic and the capacitance. Both of these systems lend themselves to use as fence alarms and the capacitance device is also effective for interior use.

d. *Acoustic detection device* actuates by the sound or vibration made by the intruder during his approach or as a result of his attempt to gain entry. Environmental conditions must be carefully evaluated before applying these devices since peripheral noise will cause false alarms.

e. *Movement detection devices* are designed to create an alarm when there is movement of any sort within the established limits of the device. There are two types of movement detection devices: Ultrasonic and Radar.

   (1) Ultrasonic detects movement by the reflection of sound waves which causes electronic control units to trigger an alarm signal.

   (2) Radar detection is designed to serve any doppler shift in the frequency of transmitted signals. The movement of a human being within the sensitive detection field will generate an alarm signal.

The use of alarms in the protective program of a restricted area or facility may be required in certain instances because of the critical importance of the area or the facility and, in other instances, because of situations and conditions pertaining to the location or the layout of the area or facility. In some instances, their use may be justified as a more economical and efficient substitute for other necessary protective elements. In determining whether the use of alarms in a restricted area is essential or advisable, the various conditions and situations peculiar to the restricted area or facility will, of course, affect the ultimate decision. However, in general, the following criteria should form the basis for a determination of the use of alarms:

a. The critical importance and vulnerability of certain restricted areas or facilities require the additional control and insurance against human or mechanical failure which is provided by alarms systems. In this group are:

   (1) Restricted areas or facilities which, because of a concentration of vital components, materials, or data, are attractive, high-priority targets for sabotage, theft, espionage, or other criminal acts.

   (2) Critical processes and process controls.

   (3) Very important restricted areas or facilities where it is desirable to have admission controlled by both guards and operational employees, or where it is desirable for operators to deny access to guards.

b. In certain cases due to restrictions imposed by location, layout, or construction, alarms are necessary to take the place of the more usual protective elements such as fences, lighting, patrols, etc. Included in this group are:

(1) Restricted areas or facilities which, because of proximity to adjacent structures, activities, or property lines, require the use of alarms in lieu of physical barriers to limited or exclusion areas.

(2) Restricted areas or facilities which are difficult or impossible to protect effectively due to terrain conditions, personnel hazards, or atmospheric conditions, and where other types of protection are not effective or practicable.

(3) Restricted areas or facilities, or components which are small, or remote areas requiring more than safe and lock protection but not justifying a full-time guard.

c. Alarm systems, because of their cost, are justified only where their use results in a commensurate reduction or when need dictates a higher level of protection to include a more positive or fail-safe method of detecting unauthorized entry. In determining the advisability of substituting alarms for other protective elements, a careful comparison of relative costs is essential. This should include service and maintenance charges. In this connection, it should be borne in mind that many alarm systems have little salvage value and, consequently, the longevity of the activity being protected is an important consideration. The advice of a competent engineer from a reputable firm dealing in protective devices and signal alarms should be obtained when considering protective alarm systems.

To afford the required degree of protection and be acceptable as protective units, alarm installations should meet the following requirements:

a. The system should be so designed that the interval of time between the detection of activity and the achievement of the objective of such activity is sufficient to permit the application of necessary countermeasures.

b. Central station systems should be specified for all locations where security personnel are not continually in the immediate vicinity to pick up a local alarm signal and make adequate response.

c. All systems, materials, and equipment should meet the Underwriter's Laboratories, Inc. standards where applicable, for the purpose for which they are used.

Generally, it may be stated that there are two types of intrusion detection systems:

a. A central station system is one in which the operation of electrical protective circuits and devices is automatically signaled to a central station which has a trained response force and operators in attendance at all times. The central station monitors the signal end of the system, provides the response to a signal, and supervises the functioning of the system.

b. A local alarm system is one in which the protective circuits and devices are connected to a visual and/or audible signal element which is located at or in the immediate vicinity of the protected facility or component, and which is responded to by security personnel in the immediate vicinity.

6. Control of Entry: Develop procedures for positive identification and control of employees, visitors and vehicles. A positive means of identifying employees is the use of a photograph identification card. Samples of the identification media should be given to law enforcement officials. (This is essential for getting through police lines and during times of curfew.) Coordinate with the police the category of personnel essential to plant operations, i.e. engineer, maintenance, etc.

7. Protection of Critical Areas: Identify and list critical areas within the plant. (Refer to annex VIII.)

   a. Enclose critical areas with physical barriers.
   b. Designate specific personnel who are to have access to critical areas.
   c. Admittance to critical areas should be controlled by:
      (1) The guard force, or
      (2) Supervisory personnel
      (3) Where locks are used, they should be rotated upon notification of impending civil disorder or other emergency.
   d. Develop a key control system
   e. Develop package and material control procedures. (All packages and materials going into or out of critical areas should be checked.)
   f. Institute procedures to protect gasoline pumps and other dispensers of flammable material. Disconnect power source to electrically operated pumps.

8. Arms Rooms
   a. Keep arms rooms
      (1) Locked
      (2) Under 24-hour surveillance
   b. Ammunition
      (1) Stored in locked separate location
      (2) Under 24-hour surveillance

9. Personnel Security
   a. Conduct pre-employment check of applicants
      (1) State and local police
      (2) Former employers
      (3) References (not limited to those provided by applicant)

    (4) High schools (be watchful for falsification of education and background)

    (5) Colleges and universities

  b. Check Selective Service Classifications

    (1) Registration certificate

    (2) Notice of classification

    (3) Selective service number

    (4) Local selective service board number

  c. Military service and type discharge (have applicant show discharge papers)

  d. Make personnel checks of persons who are authorized access to critical areas.

  e. Brief employees regarding the importance of plant security and the need for exercising vigilance.

10. Reporting of Incidents: Show procedures as to how, when, where and to whom incidents will be reported.

11. Bomb Threats

12. Emergency Notification: Prepare an emergency notification list or chart of personnel to be notified in the event of civil disturbance, or other emergency. This list must be kept current.

13. Emergency Shutdown: Indicate procedures to be followed by security personnel during and after shutdown.

14. Safeguarding Classified Material: Specify procedures for safeguarding or removal of classified material. Security personnel should know how to contact custodians of classified material. They should also be advised of actions to be taken with regard to the Department of Defense Indutrial Security Cognizant Officer, if applicable.

Physical Security Check List*

Facility Location

1. Is the facility located in an area with high crime rates, whereby employees may be afraid to work at night?

2. Do surrounding buildings or properties present obvious security hazards?

3. Is the site available to fire fighting equipment? Approximately what time is needed for fire units to arrive on the scene?

4. Are areas and approaches around the building such that cruising police vehicles can observe activities? Is police protection readily available?

---

*Reprinted with permission from Charles F. Hemphill, Jr., *Security for Business and Industry* (Homewood: Dow Jones—Irwin, 1971) pp. 65-72.

Landscaping

1. Do large masses of shrubbery or trees provide "cover" for a burglar who may be attacking outside walls, doors, or windows? Or do they provide cover for armed robbery or personal attack?
2. Are trees or telephone poles located so close to outside building walls that they may furnish easy access to a burglar who wants to drill through the roof?
3. Are wooden skids or pallets allowed to accumulate around building walls to hide rear doors and windows? Does the brush need to be cut?

Fencing

1. Is the fence constructed of chain link or of wood? What is the height of the fence? (Is it controlled by city ordinance?)
2. Is construction of the fence such that it can be easily scaled by an intruder?
3. Is chain link fence topped by angle bars, projecting both inward and outward at 45° angles to form a "V"? Covered with barbed wire? Is the wire taut?
4. Are the gates as well-constructed as the fence itself? Topped with barbed wire?
5. Are gates secured by good padlocks and chains? Are padlocks on gates protected by a metal shield to prevent prying, etc.?
6. Are gates electrically controlled? If so, how vulnerable are the controls that activate gates?
7. Are decorative plastic or metal panels inserted in the openings of the chain link fence in such a manner that the view of cruising police cars is obstructed?

Exterior Lighting

1. Is it possible to take advantage of municipal lighting? If so, is it dependable?
2. Are night lights controlled by an automatic timer, so that they will be activated without the possibility of human error?
3. Are hours of night illumination varied to follow the hours of darkness?
4. Is outside night lighting good enough so that the subheads of a newspaper can be read?
5. Does management have a regular program for replacement of burned out or broken lights?
6. Is lighting adequate on parking lots or areas where company vehicles and/or cargos may be parked?
7. Are customer and employee parking lots lighted sufficiently to deter car prowling, robbery, and attack?

8. Are outside lights protected by wire mesh or comparable material to prevent breakage or theft of bulbs?
9. Is the outside lighting so located that good illumination will be had at warehouse and entrance doors and on warehouse docks?

Doors

1. Are all doors lockable from the inside, except the main entrance? Are these doors lockable, or merely "pinned"?
2. Is there some kind of a control, such as a time lock or silent alarm, on the main door so that unauthorized entry will be detected?
3. If doors must be open or openable for ventilation, are they properly protected?
4. Are doors themselves, locks, and hardware in good repair?
5. Are exterior doors as strong as aesthetically possible?
6. What kind of hardware is used on exterior doors? Are they padlocked? If so, where is the padlock retained during working hours? Is lock substitution possible? Has the serial number been removed?
7. Would exterior doors be more secure if faced with sheet metal? Heavy wire mesh over exposed glass surfaces?
8. Are door locks deadbolt type?
9. Can door frames be readily pried apart from the door, so as to release the bolt?
10. If warehouse overhead doors are operated electrically, are they also locked when not in use?
11. If warehouse overhead doors operate through rollers on a track, is the track sufficiently strong? Should they be reinforced?
12. Have warehouse doors been damaged seriously by battering from a forklift or trucks?

Windows

1. Are windows located at sufficient heights from the ground to afford protection?
2. Is safety glass used in any windows? Which?
3. Are windows removable, so that large objects may be passed through windows or so that cleaning people may not properly replace them in every instance?
4. Are windows permanently sealed or covered with heavy outside wire cages? Or can they be opened sufficiently to allow an outsider to open a lock?
5. Are steel bars or heavy wire mesh adequately protecting windows?
6. Is valuable merchandise readily visible through warehouse windows?

Should windows be painted to prevent persons passing by from observing merchandise?

7. Are windows connected with the alarm system? Contacts? Metallic foil?
8. If windows are not necessary, should they be bricked in or permanently sealed?

Key Control

1. What is the basis for the issuance of keys?
2. Is an adequate log maintained of all keys that are issued?
3. Are keys turned in during vacation periods? Are they turned in when employees leave or are transferred?
4. When security is breached, or employees transferred, are locks changed?
5. Unless a time lock is utilized on the main entrance, are keys and locks changed once a year, regardless of transfers or known violations of security?
6. Is an audit ever made, asking officials to actually produce keys, to ensure that they have not been loaned or lost?
7. Are key holders ever allowed to duplicate keys? Are keys marked "do not duplicate"?
8. Has a system been set up to provide submasters to supervisors and officials on a "need" basis, with facilities divided into different areas?
9. Is the key cabinet for duplicate keys regarded as an area of high security? Is the key to this cabinet maintained in a locked compartment or area of the safe?
10. If the building was recently constructed, did the contractor retain keys during the period when construction was being completed? Were locks changed since that time?

Roof Access to Buildings

1. Is the building located adjacent to other structures, so that access to an adjoining building will provide access to a roof burglar?
2. Are walls of the building so high that they hide visibility of roof areas?
3. What skylights, vents, fire escapes, and entrance areas to the roof are available to provide easy access? Are they adequately secured? Are they connected to a workable alarm system?
4. Are stepladders permanently attached to side walls of the facility? If so, are they adequately protected with a heavy wire mesh cage, etc.?
5. If other ladders are available on the premises, are they chained or locked inside in such a way that they will not be available to a burglar or thief?

Storage Areas Outside Buildings

1. It will often be observed that dangerous gases and chemicals, etc., are stored in outside areas protected by chain link fence. Are these areas adequate? Properly locked? Illuminated?

Company Equipment That May Be Available to Wrongdoer

1. Is an acetylene torch available in the company tool shop that may be turned to use against the company safe?
2. What about prybars? Cutting tools? Scaling ladders?
3. Is a forklift available so that it may be used to hoist a burglar onto the roof?
4. Are keys left in the forklift so that it may be available to a burglar with a truck for quick loading of heavy, valuable merchandise?

Railroad Spur Lines

1. Are there railroad spur tracks that actually enter the premises?
2. Is a chain link fence gate provided to close the yard after the boxcar is set on the company's siding? Is it lockable?
3. Are boxcars unloaded only after a responsible employee has recorded the seal number on the boxcar door at the time entry is made?
4. Are employees aware that cars should not be accepted or entered if the seal is broken prior to arrival, or the seal number does not correspond to the seal number listed on the shipping documents (bills of lading, shipping manifest, etc.) ?
5. Are claims filed for damaged, broken, or short material and railroad claims agents promptly contacted?
6. If the boxcar is not completely unloaded during the working day, is the remainder of the merchandise in the boxcar afforded overnight protection? Is the car padlocked with strong locks and keys properly controlled? In addition, is the boxcar door nailed shut?
7. Is merchandise properly received when it is removed from the boxcar? Completely and accurately counted?

Opening and Closing Procedures

1. Does the facility have set rules concerning opening and closing?
2. Must the key holder wait for some other employee before entering?
3. Does the employee entering relock the door behind himself, to make it imposisble for other individuals to sneak in when the employee goes to the back of the facility?
4. Are those areas and devices secured that should be secured upon opening? Is the safe opened immediately and left open with the possibility that it may be looted before regular employees arrive?

5. Are amounts of money and valuables on hand sufficient that a robbery could occur? Should the first employee entering give some kind of sign that premises are clear, so that a second employee can safely enter?
6. Is there a regular closing procedure? Does it entail use of a check list?

Employee Lockers

1. Are lockers provided to all employees?
2. Does the company retain a key and a written, signed agreement that allows the company to enter the lockers?
3. Are lockers located too close to valuable merchandise or products that might be secreted temporarily by employees in lockers?
4. Does the company have a printed policy for use of employee lockers? Can you obtain a copy of this list? Is the policy enforced?
5. Are regular, unscheduled inspections of lockers made by management?
6. What steps are taken by management if company property is found concealed therein?
7. Can employees steal from lockers of fellow employees? Are combination locks used? Padlocks furnished?

Outside Parking for Customers and Employees

1. Does any available guard come out to afford protection when female employees change shifts at night?
2. Is parking allowed immediately adjacent to a loading dock from which freight or merchandise may be stolen?
3. Are friends or family of employees allowed to park while waiting for an employee? Is such parking allowed in areas near production or receiving areas where property or merchandise may be available for the taking?
4. Should a fence be erected to protect the dock from parking areas?
5. Do available fences and barriers on parking areas provide protection to employees' cars on the parking lot?
6. Are race tracks, amusement parks, stadiums, etc. located nearby so that public use is made of parking areas?
7. Are parking areas patrolled?
8. On executive parking lots or areas, are personal key rings left in cars? If so, confidential business keys maintained on the same ring?

High Value Storage Bins, Cages, and Areas

1. Is the nature of the business such that special cages, bins, or rooms are needed for materials of high value?
2. What key control is in existence?

3. Is the cage equipped with a top, or is it merely a segregated area that could be climbed over by an intruder?
4. How are materials or property issued from this special area?

Company Vehicles

1. Are drivers allowed to leave keys in company vehicles?
2. Are vehicles used for deliveries capable of being locked?
3. Are keys retained on a locked board or container inside? Is the hood of the vehicle lockable, to protect against theft of batteries, etc.? Is a system used whereby the distributor cap is removed at night, especially where a diesel or large truck has no keys?
4. Does the forklift have a cage on top to protect the driver from serious injury? Does it have a fire extinguisher? Is it refueled inside the warehouse, or is it driven to an outside gas pump where there is less danger of serious fire?

Fire Protection

1. Have the premises ever been surveyed by an official of the fire department? Were his recommendations followed?
2. Is the company in compliance with the existing fire regulations and ordinances?
3. Are necesssary fire doors protected with panic bars and door alarms for emergency use?
4. Does the business have a program for fire protection? Is it in writing? Who is in charge?
5. Are employees aware of the location of fire extinguishers and available hoses? Are these locations marked in a distinctive manner, so that they may be found at a glance?
6. Have employees been given basic instructions as to the location of fire fighting equipment? Do they understand the difference in extinguishers to combat electrical fires?
7. Have employees actually utilized extinguishers in training?
8. Is the fire department number posted prominently near telephones?
9. Are packing boxes of excelsior and paper materials made of metal? Equipped with a lead link that will cause the lid to drop into place if heat is generated in the metal box?
10. If a sprinkler system is used, is merchandise stored in the warehouse to such heights that sprinklers are ineffective?
11. Is the valve to the sprinkler system regularly checked for pressure? Padlocked in an open position so that pressure may not be turned off accidentally or by sabotage?

Plant Closing Check List*

CHECK DAILY FOR SAFETY & SECURITY REASONS

DATE_____19_____

CHECK ALL ITEMS	CHECK ONE	
	OK	NO
PRODUCTION AREA		
Night Lights On		
Doors		
Windows		
Fans & Machinery Off		
Rest Rooms Empty—Lights Off		
Boiler Room Secure		
LOADING ROOM		
Rest Rooms Empty—Lights Off		
Fans and Machines Off—Chutes Locked		
Combustibles Watered Down		
Lights Out		
GARAGE		
Doors Secure—Vehicles Secure		
Windows Secure		
Fans—Motors—Engines Off		
Lights Off		
STOCK ROOM		
Stock Room Locked		
Fans—Machines Off		
Rest Rooms Empty—Lights Out		
Doors Secure—Windows Locked		
Lights Out		
OFFICE		
Safe Locked By———————————		
Windows & Blinds Secure		
Night Light On—Others Off		
Doors Secure		
BUILDING EXTERIOR		
Outside Lights On		
Outside Doors Locked		
Gates in Parking Area Locked		
GENERAL		
Cigarettes Out in all Departments		
No Cash Left Lying Out		
When in Doubt—Recheck		
Gas Pump Locked		

REMARKS:_____

_____

_____

_____

_____

Time Check Completed and Plant Locked_____

*Reprinted with permission from Charles F. Hemphill, Jr., *Security for Business and Industry* (Homewood: Dow Jones—Irwin, 1971) p. 286.

Performance Evaluation Program*

Audit Questionnaire Work Sheet

Location:_____
Division:_____
Date:_____
Auditor:_____

Plant Manager_____
Industrial Relations Manager_____
Security Supervisor_____

_____Shift Supervision   1   2   3
_____Name and Classification
_____Fire Protection Officer
(Fill out in advance and confirm)

Security Complement   _____
Security Complement   _____
Security Complement   _____

Theft Detection Record

Period	Total Cases Detected	Guard	Originated By: Sec. Sup.	Other
____	____	____	____	____
____	____	____	____	____
____	____	____	____	____
____	____	____	____	____

Location:_____
Date:_____

Security Assignments
(Weekdays)

	#1 Shift	#2 Shift	#3 Shift
Supervisor_____	____	____	____
Shift_____	____	____	____
FPO_____	____	____	____
Clerk_____	____	____	____

Guard Assignments

	#1 Shift	#2 Shift	#3 Shift
Console_____	____	____	____
Gate #_____	____	____	____
Gate #_____	____	____	____
Gate #_____	____	____	____
Gate #_____	____	____	____
Patrol ( )_____	____	____	____
Patrol ( )_____	____	____	____
RR Detail_____	____	____	____
Shipping & Receiving_____	____	____	____
Fire Detail_____	____	____	____
Scrap & Rubbish Detail_____	____	____	____
Relief & Special Assignment____	____	____	____
FCC (Passenger)_____	____	____	____
FCC (Trucks)_____	____	____	_/__
Other ( )_____	____	____	____
_____	____	____	____

_____
*Courtesy of Ford Motor Company, The American Road, Dearborn, Michigan.

_____
_____
Off Days_____
Total Per Shift

Total Complement_____
No. Shifts Scheduled
Overtime Per Week_____
Date:_____
Location:_____

Security Assignments For Week End Coverage
(Saturday)

	#1 Shift	#2 Shift	#3 Shift
Supervision			
Console			
Patrol ( )			
Patrol ( )			
Relief & Special Assignment			
Other_____			

Total Per Shift

(Sunday)

	#1 Shift	#2 Shift	#3 Shift
Supervision			
Console			
Patrol ( )			
Patrol ( )			
Relief & Special Assignment			
Other_____			

Total Per Shift

Plant Security
Performance Evaluation Program
Audit Questionnaire Work Sheet

Location: _____

Date: _____

GATES

Gate Nos.	Type	TIME OPEN			HOW IS GATE COVERED WHEN OPEN		
		No. 1	No. 2	No. 3	No. 1	No. 2	No. 3

PATROLS

Hours Covered

Daily	No. 1	No. 2	No. 3
Week End (Saturday)			
Week End (Sunday)			

Are Patrols Bi-Hourly?	Yes	No	If No, has approval been requested?	Yes	If No, explain

PEP AUDIT 19_____   LOCATION_____

DATE_____

I. ADMINISTRATION	Yes	No	S		SS		G	
			P	A	P	A	P	A
A. *Security Planning*								
1. Have new facilities been planned within past year?___								
a. If yes, explain what construction or modifications?___								
2. Were manual guidelines followed as to: ___								
Security Office___								
Outside gate houses___								
Truck gates___								
Perimeter fencing___								
Parking lots___								
Proprietary system ___								
If no to any of the above, explain___								
___								
___								
B. *Manpower Utilization*								
1. Does schedule show staggered starting?___								
2. Have personal and lunch relief assignments (except for console) been eliminated? ___								
3. Do guards advise security office when taking relief and return? ___								
4. Are non-security type functions being handled economically? ___								
Airport pick-up___								
Mail runs___								
Drives to bank___								
Medical drives___								
Pay check or parcel pick-up___								
Other___								
5. Are fractional duties combined?___								
6. Are routine duties scheduled mid-shift when possible? ___								
C. *Gate Coverage Alternatives*								
1. Are regular spot checks made at main employe entrances per operating shift?___								
2. Have employe and vehicle gates been combined where possible?___								
3. Have efficiencies been instituted at auxiliary employe gates where possible such as: ___								

PEP AUDIT 19_____   LOCATION_____

DATE_____

	Yes	No	S		SS		G	
I. ADMINISTRATION – Continued			P	A	P	A	P	A
o close gate_____								
o open only at shift change_____								
o checking on spot check basis_____								
o TV coverage_____								
o Identi-Card access_____								
o One-way stiles_____								
4. Has surveillance of salaried personnel to office areas been eliminated?_____								
D. *Communication Supplements*								
1. Are communication supplements used for efficiency and flexibility of operations (two-way radio, Pagemaster, PA system, other)?_____								
E. *Work Schedules*								
1. Are supporting assignments in response to operating hours?_____								
2. Are supervisors and leaders scheduled independently?_____								
3. Is there regular system for off-days, with minimum splits?_____								
4. Are assignments rotated as much as practicable?_____								
5. Is overtime equalized?_____								
6. Are above answers supported by:_____								
a. Form 1791*?_____								
b. Daily assignment sheets?_____								
c. Monthly schedules?_____								
d. Cumulative overtime record?_____								
F. *Observe Employe Performance*								
1. Are guards observed by supervision to assure that appearance and demeanor is proper and they understand assignment objectives?_____								
2. Is check of premises being made by supervisors?_____								
3. Are work reports reviewed daily by supervisors?_____								
4. Are duties performed confirmed by work and/or activity reports?_____								
G. *Reporting Activities*								
1. Is Daily Activity Register Form 1789, properly used?_____								
2. Do supervisors review and initial at start of each shift?_____								
3. Is Daily Report, Form 1787, properly utilized?_____								
4. Are guards reporting out-of-order and hazardous conditions?_____								
5. Is Incident Report, Form 1786, properly utilized and a file established?_____								

*Form 1791 (Ford own form)

PEP AUDIT 19_____　　　　　　　LOCATION_____

DATE

			S		S S		G	
	Yes	No	P	A	P	A	P	A
I. ADMINISTRATION – Continued								
6. Are spot checking assignments recorded in Log, Activity Register, or Shift Reports?_____								
H. *Security Equipment*								
1. Has the use of non-standard items of uniform been avoided?_____								
2. Are proper standards of appearance maintained?_____								
3. Have major items of specialized security equipment such as patrol car, motorized scooter, portable ladder for truck checking, been provided to afford efficiency and flexibility?_____								
4. Have minor items of specialized security equipment such as foul weather clothing, flashlight, and rubber stamp for shipping and receiving spot checks been provided for efficiency of operations?_____								
I. *Investigations*								
1. Are inquiries conducted immediately concerning fires, allegations of thefts, or breaches of Company rules?_____								
2. Is Investigations contacted immediately in cases of commercialized theft, bribery, or possible legal action against Company? _____								
J. *Lock and Key Control*								
1. Does Plant Security effectively control perimeter locks and keys?_____								
K. *Cooperation with Law Enforcement Agencies*								
1. Has the supervisor maintained liaison with top ranking law enforcement officers within last six months? _____								
L. *Internal Control*								
1. Does Supervisor participate in monthly meetings?_____								
II. GATES								
A. *Flow Analysis*								
1. Are traffic flow counts available?_____								
2. Do Supervisors review and analyze gate flows weekly?_____								
3. Do Shift Supervisors observe traffic flows daily? _____								
4. Do Supervisors use parked car gate surveillance technique?_____								
B. *Pedestrian Gates*								
1. Inbound								
a. Are inbound hourly employes spot checked for identification?_____								
b. Do the Shift Supervisors spot check this daily?_____								
c. Does the Supervisor spot check this at least weekly? _____								

PEP AUDIT 19_____   LOCATION_____

_____   DATE

	Yes	No	S P	S A	SS P	SS A	G P	G A
II. GATES – Continued								
d. Are employes questioned when entering mid-shift?___								
2. Outbound								
a. Do guards spot check employe egress daily?___								
b. Do guards stop employes carrying packages and see contents?___								
c. Do guards scan back and watch for deviation from normal behavior?___								
d. Are guards especially observant of bulges in clothing?___								
e. Do guards look at the backs of employes leaving the gate?___								
f. Do guards check stragglers more closely?___								
g. Are guards avoiding overly friendly contacts?___								
h. Are lunch boxes spot checked as to contents?___								
i. Are packages and clothing being carried thoroughly inspected?___								
j. Does Shift Supervisor spot check outbound surveillance daily?___								
k. Does Supervisor spot check outbound surveillance weekly?___								
C. *Truck Gate*								
1. Inbound – if gate is attended								
a. Is Form 1790 issued or each vehicle logged in delivering or making pick-ups?___								
b. Is cargo compartment inspected (except where sealed) and are accessories noted?___								
c. Does Shift Supervisor spot check operation daily?___								
2. Outbound – if gate is attended								
a. Does guard check interior of cab?___								
b. Does he examine the shipping papers?___								
c. Does guard look into cargo compartment and compare load with shipping papers?___								
d. Does he note accessories carried?___								
e. Does he examine undercarriage?___								
f. Are shipping papers secured and sent directly to Accounting?___								
g. Does Shift Supervisor spot check this job performance daily?___								

PEP AUDIT 19_____　　LOCATION_____

DATE

		Yes	No	S		S S		G	
				P	A	P	A	P	A
II. GATES – Continued									
	h. Does Supervisor spot check job performance weekly?_____								
3.	Inbound – if gate is *not* attended								
	a. Has a good permanent instructive sign been provided?____								
4.	Outbound – if gate is *not* attended								
	a. Has a good permanent instructive sign been provided?____								
	b. Has a locked ballot box been provided for deposit of shipping papers?____								
	c. Are regular unscheduled daily spot checks made of trucks or vehicles leaving gate?____								
D. *Vehicle Gate*									
1.	Inbound – if gate is attended								
	a. Are vehicles identified by Plant Security personnel?___								
	b. Are spot checks made of equipment and accessories carried?____								
	c. Are Visitors' Passes, Form 1042, issued when necessary?__								
2.	Outbound – if gate is attended								
	a. Are spot checks made?____								
	b. Do spot checks include trunk, glove box and engine compartment?____								
	c. Are spot checks made of equipment and accessories, with these listed for inbound comparison?____								
3.	Inbound – if gate is not attended								
	a. Has a good permanent instructive sign been provided?____								
4.	Outbound – if gate is not attended								
	a. Has a good permanent instructive sign been provided?____								
	b. Has a locked ballot box been provided for vehicle exit authorization papers?____								
	c. Are regular unscheduled daily spot checks made of vehicles leaving gate?____								
E. *Railroad Gate*									
1.	Inbound								
	a. Are railroad gates controlled by Company locks?____								
	b. Does Plant Security control train crew on the property?__								
2.	Outbound								
	a. Are outbound empties spot checked prior to leaving?____								
	b. Are outbound dunnage and "come-back" cars sealed?____								

PEP AUDIT 19_____   LOCATION_____

DATE_____

	Yes	No	S		SS		G	
II. GATES – Continued			P	A	P	A	P	A
c. Is railroad gate closed and locked after switch?_____								
III. PATROLS								
A. *Layout*								
1. Do Supervisor and F.P.O. lay out patrols and review as necessary consistent with operating conditions?_____								
2. Do patrols furnish compulsory coverage of high hazards?_____								
3. Are patrols bi-hourly?_____								
If not, what are plans for qualifications?_____								
B. *Performance*								
1. Does Supervisor walk patrols monthly?_____								
2. Do Shift Supervisors on non-operating shifts each walk a patrol daily?_____								
3. Do guards follow approved route and order of boxes?_____								
4. Does first patrol after occupancy cover highest hazards?_____								
5. Has poor housekeeping been reported?_____								
6. Do the guards check and remedy obstruction of fire doors?_____								
7. Do the guards check cribs for locked and secure conditions?_____								
8. Do guards report machinery left running after working hours?_____								
9. Does the first patrol check to see that safes and vaults are locked?_____								
10. Do the guards spot check trash containers for concealed parts?_____								
11. Are leaks and other out-of-order conditions reported?_____								
12. Do the guards check, particularly on first patrol, all building doors which would give access from outside the perimeter?_____								
C. *Console*								
1. Are patrols and fire signals monitored on a continuous basis?_____								
2. Does monitor perform other security and communications functions?_____								
3. Is patrol monitored by check-in list, in patrol box order?_____								
4. Are unusual conditions, including failures to ring, reported immediately to the supervisor on duty?_____								
5. Does supervisor or F.P.O. review and initial the check list and tapes?_____								
6. Are records retained for FIA inspection, and no longer?_____								

PEP AUDIT 19_____   LOCATION_____

DATE

IV. SHIPPING AND RECEIVING	Yes	No	S		SS		G	
			P	A	P	A	P	A
A. Shipping L.C.L.								
1. Are spot checks conducted daily?_____								
2. Do spot checks include a carton count?_____								
3. Do Shift Supervisors observe such checking daily?_____								
4. Does the Supervisor observe such checking weekly?_____								
5. Are records of all Shipping and Receiving spot checking maintained until audited by Finance personnel?_____								
6. Are waiting facilities and proper instruction signs provided for truck drivers?_____								
B. Trash & Rubbish								
1. Is trash and rubbish loading spot checked daily?_____								
2. Is trash and rubbish loading spot checked by Supervisor weekly?_____								
3. Are trucks hauling trash and rubbish followed to the dump on a nonscheduled basis and the loads spot checked?_____								
4. Does the Supervisor observe such checking monthly?_____								
C. Scrap and Salable Waste								
1. Is scrap loading 100 per cent checked?_____								
2. Are all serviceable parts mutilated?_____								
3. Are scrap trucks hauling to outside scale escorted by Security on a 100 per cent basis?_____								
4. Does the escort obtain the weight ticket at the scale, and is it forwarded directly to Accounting?_____								
5. Do Shift Supervisors accompany the escort weekly?_____								
6. Does the Supervisor accompany the escort at least monthly?_____								
7. Is the tare weight of each truck ascertained originally and confirmed on a spot-check basis by escort to the scale?_____								
8. If scrap is sold unmutilated, is a proper scrap warranty part of the sales agreement?_____								
9. Are surprise spot checks made of scrap yard where unmutilated scrap is sold to assure proper mutilation procedures are maintained?_____								
D. Receiving								
1. Are spot checks conducted daily?_____								
2. Do spot checks include a carton count?_____								
3. Do the Shift Supervisors observe spot checking weekly?_____								
4. Are records maintained of spot checks?_____								

PEP AUDIT 19_____   LOCATION_____

_____ DATE _____

IV. SHIPPING AND RECEIVING — Continued	Yes	No	S		SS		G	
			P	A	P	A	P	A
5. Are receivals checked, initialed, dated, and stamped?___								
V. SPECIAL ASSIGNMENTS								
A. *Fire Protection*								
1. Is training regularly furnished to guards by Shift Supervisor or F.P.O.?___								
2. Have fire brigades been organized and given monthly training?___								
3. Does Supervisor observe such training at least quarterly?___								
4. Does Plant Security handle normal requirements of:								
a. Fire extinguisher maintenance?___								
b. Cutting and welding standby?___								
c. Fire inspection program?___								
5. Has a disaster evacuation plan been drawn up and at least one drill held during past year?___								
B. *Parking Discipline*								
1. Is parking discipline spot checked daily?___								
2. Is Parking Violation Form 1792 used?___								
C. *Miscellaneous Functions*								
1. Do guards handling tours display basic elements needed?___								
2. Do security personnel answering plant telephone follow prescribed procedure for recording pertinent data?___								
VI. FINAL CAR CHECKING (Assembly Plants Only)								
A. *Vehicle Number Examination*								
1. Do the guards inspect and compare the vehicle numbers shown on the patent plate, the body/frame, and the invoice?___								
2. Does a supervisor observe the examination of these numbers daily?___								
3. Are discrepancies called to the attention of supervision?___								
B. *Security Inspection*								
1. Do the guards inspect each place on the car where accessories and premium equipment might be installed to locate such premium items?___								
2. Do the guards check from the car against the invoice to insure that all such items are billed?___								
3. Are discrepancies called to the attention of supervision?___								
4. Do the guards inspect the glove box, trunk, trunk lid, engine compartment, and under-seat areas for concealed material?___								

PEP AUDIT 19_____   LOCATION_____

DATE_____

VI. FINAL CAR CHECKING — Continued	Yes	No	S		SS		G	
			P	A	P	A	P	A
5. Do the Shift Supervisors observe the above inspections daily?_____								
6. Does the Supervisor observe this entire operation weekly?_____								
7. Does the Supervisor audit new units in the haulaway or outside storage lot monthly?_____								

SMALL BUSINESS

1. Offices: Security Checklist
2. Stores: Security Checklist
3. Armed Robbery and Burglary-Prevention
4. Exterior/Interior Protection
5. Burglary Prevention Checklist for Business Places
6. Credit Union—Risk Analysis
7. Crime Prevention Survey Report

Offices: Security Checklist*

1. Who is responsible for security?

Entrance(s)

2. Describe which
   a. are attended by a Receptionist/Commissionaire/Sec Officer.
   b. are unattended and at which entry can be obtained.
3. Can b. entrances be reduced without loss of efficiency?
4. Can they be fitted with springs and slam locks so as to be used for exit only?
5. Where the entrance is attended as above
   a. Are postal deliveries handled correctly?
   b. Is there a clear view from Receptionist's desk of entrance, stairs and lifts?
   c. Is there a notice posted requesting callers to go to Receptionist?
   d. Have instructions in writing been issued respecting the reception of callers?
   e. Where the receptionist is the telephone operator have instructions in writing been issued respecting the action required on the
      (1) Fire Alarm
      (2) Thief Alarm being heard?
   f. Have instructions been issued regarding the admittance of maintenance men, telephone operators, window cleaners, etc?

Security Officers/Commissionaires

6. Where they carry out additional security duties such as patrolling the premises on their closure, have the instructions been issued in the form of "Standing Orders"? Are they up to date?
7. In applicable instances is their concern associated with other(s) in a Mutual Aid Security scheme, or otherwise are any arrangements made

---

*Reprinted with permission from Eric Oliver and John Wilson, *Practical Security in Commerce and Industry* (London: Gower, 1968) pp. 393-396.

for the Security Officer to communicate at intervals with any security services company?

Employees

8. Is there a clause in the conditions of employment respecting the right of search, etc.?
9. Is their cloakroom located in a satisfactory position in relation to any entrances or exits?
10. Is a notice displayed in the cloakrooms disclaiming on behalf of the employer responsibility for losses?
11. Are notices displayed in toilets reminding users against leaving articles on the wash basins, jewellery, etc.?
12. If thefts are being experienced has the assistance of the local Crime Prevention Police Officer been sought?

Offices

13. Are all duplicate and other keys not in use kept under good security?
14. Has the cutting of extra keys been prohibited unless with proper permission by an authorized person?
15. When a safe is removed from use or transferred to another location are all keys accounted for?

Presigned Cheques

16. Are they kept in conditions recommended such as being under the protection of two separate locks, with the keys or codes held by two persons?
17. Are they counted daily by an independent person?

Coupons

18. Are they cancelled on receipt in a satisfactory manner?
19. Are remittances properly recorded, especially those from unidentifiable senders?
20. Are coupons destroyed in accordance with instructions and correct destruction certificates provided?

Contractors

21. Are contractors' employees subject to the same searching requirements as own employees?

Confidential Documents

22. Is security of vital information adequately protected?

Meetings/Conferences

23. Where specially advisable—
    a. Is secrecy of date, place and venue carried out?
    b. Are the times and venues changed at short notice?
    c. Can those attending be seen/overheard from outside?
    d. Are agendas, blotting paper and pads, and contents of waste paper baskets and ash trays destroyed immediately after the meeting?
    e. Is security coverage provided during intervals, e.g. for refreshments?

Fire

24. Have fire/security stewards been appointed on each floor/department?
25. Have they been issued with written instructions as to their duties?
26. Have replacements been made to account for leavings, transfers of stewards?
27. Are the stewards familiar with the handling of fire-fighting equipment?
28. Have notices been displayed instructing employees—
    a. What to do on discovering a fire?
    b. What to do on hearing the fire alarm?
    c. Which is the escape route they should take in event of alarm?
    d. Where they should assemble on leaving the building?
29. Are all Fire Exits correctly marked?
30. Are all Fire Exits unobstructed?
31. Are those on the ground floor fitted on the inside with breakable bolts?
32. Are they satisfactorily locked when the premises are vacated at close of business?

Locking Up Premises

33. Who is responsible for locking up the premises after ensuring no security risks exist, e.g. open doors, windows, electrical apparatus left switched on?
34. What happens to key(s)?
35. Who is the registered with police keyholder? Is this up to date?
36. Have door and safe keyholders been warned about the genuineness of requests to attend the premises when they are closed?

Security Check

37. When was the last *ad hoc* check up of security made, and by whom?
38. When was a complete check-up of security arrangements and their observation made, by whom and the result?
39. What weaknesses were discovered?
40. What was ordered to be done to improve them?

41. What is the present position?
42. If further weaknesses discovered what instructions have been given?

Stores: Security Checklist*

General

1. Who holds the keys in daily use and the duplicate(s)?
2. Is the protection of the windows adequate?
3. Is the lock satisfactory and any hasp of sufficient strength?
4. Has the store a service counter?
5. How are items obtained when store closed?
6. Is this under sufficient control?
7. What record is made of such withdrawals?
8. Are requisitions checked after being actioned to detect offences, and if so by whom?
9. What are the arrangements for the borrowing of tools by employees?
10. Are company tools of common description given a distinguishing mark?
11. Are the serial numbers, where available, of tools recorded?
12. Where is the burning/welding equipment kept?
13. Are the gas cylinders stored at some distance and near an exit?

Canteen

14. What arrangements are made for the security of the keys?
15. Are these satisfactory?
16. Are the arrangements for the security of wines, spirits, cigars and cigarettes satisfactory?

Armed Robbery and Burglary-Prevention†

Section A.	Yes	No	Does Not Apply	COMMENTS
1. Are counters sufficiently high and wide to keep cash drawers out of sight and out of reach? ..	Y	N	N/A	
2. Are robbery alarm actuators hidden from view? ..	Y	N	N/A	
3. Are locked doors or gates provided to protect against unauthorized entry into the teller's area?	Y	N	N/A	
4. Is a bundle of currency (listed serial numbers) placed in each teller's cash drawer and instructions given as to its purpose?	Y	N	N/A	
5. Is each teller's cash fund kept to a minimum at all times?	Y	N	N/A	

*Reprinted with permission from Eric Oliver and John Wilson, *Practical Security in Commerce and Industry* London: Gower, 1968) p. 397.

†Reprinted with permission from Loss Prevention Program Operational Security Analysis, *Armed Robbery and Burglary-Prevention.* Developed by the Risk Management Deaprtment of CUNA International, Inc., Filene House, Madison, Wisconsin.

	Yes	No	Does Not Apply	COMMENTS

6. Is the bulk cash locked in safe until needed? ......   Y   N   N/A

7. Does the head teller deliver additional amounts of cash to tellers periodically during business day (minimum amount in tellers' cash drawers)? .   Y   N   N/A

8. Does credit union have police/security guard protection when handling large sums of money? ..   Y   N   N/A

9. Are police notified concerning presence of suspicious characters in vicinity of credit union office? ......   Y   N   N/A

10. Are employees instructed not to be lured outside by unusual disturbances, leaving office unprotected? ..   Y   N   N/A

11. Are employees instructed to demand identification from strangers posing as messengers, police officers, or maintenance men? ..   Y   N   N/A

12. Do employees count large sums of money in area where they cannot be seen? ....   Y   N   N/A

13. When handling large sums of money, is more than one employee present at all times? ....   Y   N   N/A

14. Are all checks, money orders, and travelers' checks stamped "For Deposit Only" IMMEDIATELY upon receipt? ....   Y   N   N/A

15. Before opening the office each day, does an employee inspect the exterior for signs of forceable entry to avoid ambush from within? ....   Y   N   N/A

16. Does an employee then inspect interior of office before admitting other employees? ......   Y   N   N/A

17. Are lunch periods/coffee breaks staggered so that as many employees as possible will be on duty? ..   Y   N   N/A

Section B.

18. Does a guard accompany your bank messenger? ..   Y   N   N/A

19. Does the guard walk some distance behind to lessen the element of surprise? ....   Y   N   N/A

20. Does your messenger vary the type of conveyance, time, and route taken when transporting cash to or from the bank? ....   Y   N   N/A

21. Does your messenger disguise currency bags by wrapping them in plain paper or by placing them inside a brief case? ....   Y   N   N/A

22. Are your messengers instructed not to make other stops when transporting cash between the bank and the credit union? ....   Y   N   N/A

23. Do you retain a copy of your deposit slip in your credit union office while funds are in transit to the bank? ....   Y   N   N/A

24. Does your messenger avoid habits or routines that may be observed by criminals? ......   Y   N   N/A

25. Does credit union have cash delivered by armored car service? ....   Y   N   N/A

26. Does credit union have a training program for employees and officers to prepare them for the shock of an armed robbery? ....   Y   N   N/A

	Yes	No	Does Not Apply	COMMENTS

27. Does credit union have frequent refresher training sessions covering the precautions and procedures of the robbery program? .... Y N N/A
28. Does each officer and employee have a written copy of the above procedures? .... Y N N/A
29. Are officers and employees instructed not to discuss credit union affairs, especially cash handling procedures, in public? .. Y N N/A
30. Are officers and employees instructed NOT to play hero and offer direct resistance to criminals? . Y N N/A
31. Have employees been trained in how to identify criminals? .... Y N N/A
32. Have employees been instructed in procedures to follow if you are robbed? .... Y N N/A
33. Does credit union keep only enough cash on hand for the day's operation? .... Y N N/A
34. Are frequent deposits made? .... Y N N/A

Section C.

35. Does credit union keep large sums of cash overnight or over weekend? .... Y N N/A
36. Are large amounts of cash exposed on counters/desks? .... Y N N/A
37. Is the vault classification adequate? .... Y N N/A
38. Is an alarm actuator or telephone hidden from view inside vault? .... Y N N/A
39. Is an alarm actuator hidden from view inside rest rooms? .... Y N N/A
40. Can vault be unlocked from inside? .... Y N N/A
41. If the credit union handles cash, does it have a *torch and tool resistive** money safe? .... Y N N/A
42. Is the credit union safe anchored to the floor or wall? .... Y N N/A
43. Is the safe combination changed after people leave the credit union's employ? .... Y N N/A
44. Is a night light burning both within and without the credit union office during non-business hours? . Y N N/A
45. Do drapes remain open, especially during non-business hours? .... Y N N/A
46. Are "jimmy-proof" locks placed on all outside doors? .... Y N N/A
47. Are door locks changed every time a person *with access to the keys leaves the employ* of the credit union? .... Y N N/A
48. Are two persons assigned the responsibility of double checking to make sure that all safes, windows, and outside doors are locked at the end of each business day? .... Y N N/A
49. Are night depositories used to reduce the amount of cash kept in the safe? ...... Y N N/A

	Yes	No	Does Not Apply	COMMENTS
50. Is the safe or vault placed in an open area where it can be clearly seen from the outside?	Y	N	N/A	
51. Does the credit union have an AUDIBLE burglary alarm system to protect the office from unauthorized entry during non-business hours? ..	Y	N	N/A	
52. Does credit union have a SILENT alarm system as a protection against armed robbery?	Y	N	N/A	
53. Have the operating personnel received instructions regarding the use of the alarm system?	Y	N	N/A	
54. Are regular tests made (at least monthly) of the alarm system?	Y	N	N/Y	

Exterior/Interior Protection*

	Yes	No	Does Not Apply	COMMENTS
1. Weeds and/or tall grass in area of credit union office?	Y	N	N/A	
2. Incinerators a sufficient distance from building? ...	Y	N	N/A	
3. Parking lots free from dangerous conditions that may lead to injury?	Y	N	N/A	
4. Parking lots well-lighted?	Y	N	N/A	
5. Exit drives from parking lot to street marked with "stop" or "caution" signs?	Y	N	N/A	
6. Down spouts empty away from sidewalks, driveways, or parking lots?	Y	N	N/A	
7. Eave troughs and gutters over entrance or exit ways in good repair?	Y	N	N/A	
8. Sufficient space on landings outside of exit doors to reduce possibility that someone might be struck by the door or crowded off the landing by the door? ..	Y	N	N/A	
9. Automatic swinging doors properly guarded with rails and safety devices to prevent doors from striking bystanders?	Y	N	N/A	
10. Railings provided for protection?	Y	N	N/A	
11. Steps surfaced with anti-slip treads?	Y	N	N/A	
12. Doormats turned up at edges, or of a type that might catch a lady's high heel?	Y	N	N/A	
13. Entrances and exits to credit union office free of obstructions?	Y	N	N/A	
14. Doors provided with handles or pushbars?	Y	N	N/A	
15. Glass panels and glass doors marked at eye-level to indicate presence of glass?	Y	N	N/A	
16. Sidewalks and steps free of hazards?	Y	N	N/A	
17. Snow and ice removed from sidewalks and steps? ..	Y	N	N/A	

*Look for the Safe Manufacturers National Association label inside the door of your safe.

*Reprinted with permission from Loss Prevention Program Operational Security Analysis, *Exterior/Interior Protection*. Developed by the Risk Management Deaprtment of CUNA International, Inc., Filene House, Madison, Wisconsin.

	Yes	No	Does Not Apply	COMMENTS
18. Floors free of projections, cracks and debris?	Y	N	N/A	
19. Non-skid surface on floors?	Y	N	N/A	
20. Office furniture free of sharp edges, splinters, broken glass?	Y	N	N/A	
21. Filing cabinets evenly loaded in drawers and bolted together (or to the floor or wall) to prevent tipping?				
22. Office machine extension cords positioned in office in a manner that could prevent a fall by an employee or member?	Y	N	N/A	
23. Fire extinguishers checked annually and recorded on units?	Y	N	N/A	
24. Employees trained in proper use of fire extinguishers?	Y	N	N/A	
25. Sufficient circuits available for proper fusing to handle electrical load?	Y	N	N/A	
26. Master electrical control panel easily accessible (not in furnace room) ?	Y	N	N/A	
27. Safety valves regularly checked?	Y	N	N/A	
28. Guards on fans and/or ventilating equipment?	Y	N	N/A	
29. Vents on kitchen exhaust fans regularly cleaned? ..	Y	N	N/A	
30. Furnace rooms kept free of combustible materials?	Y	N	N/A	
31. Papers, cleaning materials, and other combustibles stored away from heat sources in approved containers and regularly removed from premises? ..	Y	N	N/A	

Burglary Prevention Checklist for Business Places

Reprinted with permission from Richard L. Holcomb, *Burglary Prevention Check list for Business Places* Iowa City: State University of Iowa, pp. 49-52, 1953.

EXTERIOR

1. Are all of the points where a breakin might occur lighted by street lights, signs or your own "burglar" lights? Yes ☐ No ☐
2. Have you protected blind alleys where a burglar might work unobserved? Yes ☐ No ☐
3. Are piles of stock, crates or merchandise placed so as not to give burglars hiding places? Yes ☐ No ☐
4. Are windows protected under loading docks or similar structures? Yes ☐ No ☐
5. Have the weeds or trash adjoining your building been cleared away? Yes ☐ No ☐
6. If a fence would help your protection, do you have one? Yes ☐ No ☐
7. Is your fence high enough or protected with barbed wire? Yes ☐ No ☐
8. Is your fence in good repair? Yes ☐ No ☐
9. Is your fence fixed so that an intruder cannot crawl under it? Yes ☐ No ☐
10. Are boxes, materials, etc., that might help a burglar over the fence placed a safe distance from the fence? Yes ☐ No ☐
11. Are the gates solid and in good repair? Yes ☐ No ☐
12. Are the gates properly locked? Yes ☐ No ☐
13. Are the gate hinges secure? Yes ☐ No ☐
14. Have you eliminated unused gates? Yes ☐ No ☐
15. Have you eliminated danger from poles or similar points OUTSIDE the fence that would help a burglar over? Yes ☐ No ☐
16. Have you protected solid brick or wood fences that a burglar could climb and then be shielded from view? Yes ☐ No ☐
17. Do you check regularly to see that your gates are locked? Yes ☐ No ☐
18. Do you regularly clean out trash or weeds on the outside of your fence where a burglar might be concealed? Yes ☐ No ☐

DOORS

19. Have you secured all unused doors? Yes ☐ No ☐
20. Are door panels strong enough and securely fastened in place? Yes ☐ No ☐
21. Is the glass in back doors and similar locations protected by wire or bars? Yes ☐ No ☐
22. Are all of your doors designed so that the lock cannot be reached by breaking out glass or a light-weight panel? Yes ☐ No ☐
23. Are the hinges so designed or located that the pins cannot be pulled? Yes ☐ No ☐
24. Is the lock bolt so designed or protected that it cannot be pushed back with a thin instrument? Yes ☐ No ☐
25. Is the lock so designed or the door frame built so that the door cannot be forced by spreading the frame? Yes ☐ No ☐
26. Is the bolt protected or constructed so that it cannot be cut? Yes ☐ No ☐
27. Is the lock firmly mounted so that it cannot be pried off? Yes ☐ No ☐
28. Is the lock a cylinder type? Yes ☐ No ☐
29. Are your locks in good working order? Yes ☐ No ☐
30. Are the set screws holding the cylinders firmly in place? Yes ☐ No ☐
31. Are your keys in the possession only of trusted persons? Yes ☐ No ☐
32. Do you have your keys issued only to persons who actually need them? Yes ☐ No ☐
33. Do your doors with panic locks have auxiliary locking mechanisms for use when the building is not occupied? Yes ☐ No ☐
34. Do you lock your padlocks in place when the door is unlocked? Yes ☐ No ☐
35. Are the padlock hasps installed so that the screws cannot be removed? Yes ☐ No ☐
36. Are the hasps heavy enough? Yes ☐ No ☐
37. Are they of a grade of steel that is difficult to cut? Yes ☐ No ☐
38. Are they mounted so that they cannot be pried or twisted off? Yes ☐ No ☐

WINDOWS

39. Are easily accessible windows protected by heavy screens or bars? Yes ☐ No ☐
40. Are unused windows permanently closed? Yes ☐ No ☐
41. Are your bars or screens mounted securely? Yes ☐ No ☐
42. Do you use the trick of piling heavy merchandise in front of windows not needed for light or ventilation? Yes ☐ No ☐
43. In the case of windows not protected by bars or alarms, do you keep the windows locked or shuttered? Yes ☐ No ☐

44. Are the window locks so designed or located that they cannot be opened by just breaking the glass?   Yes ☐   No ☐

45. Have you protected ALL of your seldom used windows, small windows or windows located in locations that you do not notice but that a burglar might?   Yes ☐   No ☐

46. If you leave valuable merchandise in display windows, do you protect it with grills or similar devices?   Yes ☐   No ☐

47. Do you remove valuable merchandise from unprotected display windows at night?   Yes ☐   No ☐

48. Have you considered the use of glass brick in place of some windows?   Yes ☐   No ☐

OTHER OPENINGS

49. Do you have a lock on manholes that give direct access to your building or to a door that a burglar could open easily?   Yes ☐   No ☐

50. Have you permanently closed manholes or similar openings that are no longer used?   Yes ☐   No ☐

51. Are your sidewalk doors or grates locked securely?   Yes ☐   No ☐

52. Are your sidewalk doors or grates securely in place so that the entire frame cannot be pried up?   Yes ☐   No ☐

53. Have you eliminated unnecessary skylights that are only a burglar hazard?   Yes ☐   No ☐

54. Are your accessible skylights protected with bars, net or burglar alarms?   Yes ☐   No ☐

55. Are your exposed roof hatches properly secured?   Yes ☐   No ☐

56. Are the doors to the roof or elevator penthouses strong, in good condition and securely locked?   Yes ☐   No ☐

57. Have you protected any ventilator shafts or fan openings through which a burglar might come?   Yes ☐   No ☐

58. If your transoms are large enough to admit even a small burglar, are they properly locked or protected with bars, screens or chains?   Yes ☐   No ☐

59. Have you eliminated the possibility of entrance through a sewer or a service tunnel?   Yes ☐   No ☐

60. Do your fire escapes comply with city and state fire regulations? (Remember that the protection of life is always more important than the protection of property.)   Yes ☐   No ☐

61. Are your fire exits and escapes so designed that a person can leave easily but would have difficulty in entering?   Yes ☐   No ☐

62. Do you check panic locks regularly to see that they are properly closed and in good working order?   Yes ☐   No ☐

WALLS

63. Are your walls actually as solid as they look; have you eliminated insecure openings in otherwise solid walls?   Yes ☐   No ☐

64. In checking walls, have you paid particular attention to points where a burglar can work unobserved?   Yes ☐   No ☐

65. Is your roof either secure or protected by an alarm system?   Yes ☐   No ☐

66. Have you eliminated weak points in your walls where entrance could be gained from an adjoining building?   Yes ☐   No ☐

SAFES

67. Is your safe designed for burglary protection as well as fire protection?   Yes ☐   No ☐

68. Is your safe approved by the Underwriters Laboratories?   Yes ☐   No ☐

69. If your safe weighs less than 750 pounds, is it fastened securely to the floor, the wall or set in concrete?   Yes ☐   No ☐

70. Is your safe located so the police can see it from outside?   Yes ☐   No ☐

71. Is your safe lighted at night?   Yes ☐   No ☐

72. If you have a vault, are the walls, as well as the door, secure?   Yes ☐   No ☐

73. Do you keep your money in your safe? (Some businessmen have sizeable amounts they don't.)   Yes ☐   No ☐

74. Do you keep your cash on hand at a minimum by banking regularly?   Yes ☐   No ☐

75. Do you SPIN the dial when you lock the safe?   Yes ☐   No ☐

76. Have you changed the combination if there are persons who have the combination, yet no longer need it?   Yes ☐   No ☐

77. Do you use care in working the combination so that you cannot be spied on?   Yes ☐   No ☐

78. Do you take the money out of your cash register at the close of business?   Yes ☐   No ☐
79. Do you leave your cash register open so a burglar will not damage it by forcing it open?   Yes ☐   No ☐

ALARMS

80. Have you investigated the use of a burglar alarm system?   Yes ☐   No ☐
81. If you have a system, is it fully approved by the Underwriters Laboratories?   Yes ☐   No ☐
82. Was it properly installed by competent workmen?   Yes ☐   No ☐
83. Is your burglar alarm system tested regularly?   Yes ☐   No ☐
84. Does the system cover your hazardous points fully?   Yes ☐   No. ☐
85. When your building was remodeled, was the burglar alarm system remodeled, too?   Yes ☐   No ☐

SECURITY OFFICER

86. Did you investigate your security officer when you hired him?   Yes ☐   No ☐
87. Has he received training?   Yes ☐   No ☐
88. If he is armed, does he have a good gun and does he know when he can use it and how to use it?   Yes ☐   No ☐
89. Is he supervised by use of a watchman's clock or some similar device?   Yes ☐   No ☐
90. If you have only one or two men, do they report in at regular intervals to a point outside of your building?   Yes ☐   No ☐
91. Does your security officer have plenty of time to perform his protection duties fully? (Or is he actually a maintenance man working at night?)   Yes ☐   No ☐
92. If you employ a commercial watch service, do you check to see if they really do what they claim to?   Yes ☐   No ☐

POLICE PROTECTION

93. Do you know the commanding officers in your police department? (In a large city, do you know the commanding officers in your police district?)   Yes ☐   No ☐
94. Do you know the police patrolmen who cover your area?   Yes ☐   No ☐
95. Do you assist in civic projects to support and improve your police?   Yes ☐   No ☐

MISCELLANEOUS

96. Do you lock up carefully at night, making certain the safe is properly closed, doors and windows locked, night lights on and that no one has hidden inside?   Yes ☐   No ☐
97. Do you have the serial numbers or descriptions of valuable merchandise?   Yes ☐   No ☐
98. Do you have the serial numbers or descriptions of your business equipment?   Yes ☐   No ☐
99. Do you keep records on large denomination bills, valuable papers, etc.?   Yes ☐   No ☐
100. Have you instructed your employees to leave the scene unchanged following a burglary and to call the police?   Yes ☐   No ☐

Credit Union—Risk Analysis*

I. Credit Union Property

	Yes	No	COMMENTS
1. Any occupants in building engaged in hazardous activities?	Y	N	
2. Electrical outlets overloaded?	Y	N	
3. Is fuse box warm to the touch?	Y	N	
4. Are NO SMOKING signs posted in storage areas?	Y	N	
5. Interior housekeeping adequate?	Y	N	
6. Adequate fire extinguishers and serviced regularly?	Y	N	
7. Sprinkler system?	Y	N	
8. Are records stored in fire resistive containers?	Y	N	

---

*Reprinted with permission from Loss Prevention Program Operational Security Analysis, *Credit Union—Risk Analysis*. Developed by the Risk Management Department of CUNA International, Inc., Filene House, Madison, Wisconsin.

	Yes	No	COMMENTS

9. Is record duplication system adequate?   Y   N

10. Are vital records removed from premises?   Y   N

11. Adequate Fire, Extended Coverage and
Vandalism Insurance?   Y   N

II. Liability

1. Are sidewalks, entrance ways, driveways and
parking areas in good repair?   Y   N

2. Are floors in good repair and free of tripping and
slipping hazards?   Y   N

3. Are stairways (inside and outside)
    a. Unobstructed and well maintained with nonslip
surface?   Y   N
    b. Hand rails provided?   Y   N

4. Exits clearly marked and free of obstacles?   Y   N

5. Machine and telephone cords properly arranged?   Y   N

6. Are filing cabinets securely anchored?   Y   N

7. Are outside signs attached FIRMLY to the
supporting structure?   Y   N

8. Does credit union
    a. Hold or sponsor any functions away from
credit union premises?   Y   N
    b. Serve food or refreshments at meetings or
functions?   Y   N
    c. Dispense promotional novelties?   Y   N

9. Does credit union
    a. Own or lease any vehicles?   Y   N
    b. Repossess collateral?   Y   N

10. Workmen's Compensation/Employers Liability
coverage adequate?   Y   N

11. Adequate Comprehensive General Liability?   Y   N

III. Robbery and Burglary

1. Individual lockable cash drawers provided for
each teller?   Y   N

2. Teller's cash fund kept to a minimum at all times?   Y   N

3. Checks, money orders and travelers checks stamped
"For Deposit Only" IMMEDIATELY upon receipt?   Y   N

4. Bait Money maintained?   Y   N

5. If travelers check, money order or credit card
service is provided, are controls adequate?   Y   N

6. Does credit union management instruct employees
on a regular basis regarding procedures in the
event of a burglary or holdup?   Y   N

7. Does credit union keep ONLY enough cash on hand
for daily operation (with excess deposited promptly)?   Y   N

8. Are firearms kept on premises?   Y   N

9. Does credit union have a torch and tool resistive
money safe?   Y   N

10. Is safe anchored to the floor or wall?   Y   N

11. Is safe or vault visible from outside?   Y   N

12. Check preparation adequate?   Y   N

	Yes	No	COMMENTS
13. Pre-numbered Cash Received and Disbursement Vouchers used properly?	Y	N	
14. Surveillance cameras used?	Y	N	
15. Cash handling procedures adequate (armored cars, field collectors, tellers) ?	Y	N	
16. Adequate exterior/interior lighting during nonbusiness hours?	Y	N	
17. Dead-bolt locks used on all doors?	Y	N	
18. Exterior doors hinged properly?	Y	N	
19. Window protection adequate?	Y	N	
20. Can entrance be gained to premises from:			
a. Fire escapes	Y	N	
b. Unlocked stairways	Y	N	
c. Roof (skylights, ventilation fans, etc.)	Y	N	
d. Elevator shaft openings	Y	N	
21. Does office have a recommended alarm system?	Y	N	
22. Alarm system tested on a regular basis?	Y	N	

Form No. 128

STAFFORDSHIRE COUNTY POLICE

CRIME PREVENTION SURVEY REPORT

CONFIDENTIAL

DIVISIONAL REFERENCE _____   HEADQUARTERS REFERENCE _____

DATE _____   POLICE STATION _____

TELEPHONE No. _____

REPORTING OFFICER:	Rank	No.	Name

1 (a) Name of Business (b) Address (c) Locality (i.e. type of area)	
2 (a) Owner of Business (b) Address or Head Office	
3 (a) Nature of Business (b) Nature and value of stock	
4 (a) Brief description of Premises (b) Details of Safe or Strongroom (c) Is Burglar Alarm fitted. (If so state type and make)	
5 (a) Date of survey (b) Un/solicited following crime) (c) Previous crimes (d) With whom Survey made	

6   SUMMARY OF RECOMMENDATIONS

*Delete as necessary   Continue overleaf

6 (continued)

Signature..

7   NOTE TO OWNERS

The recommendations contained in this report have been made with due regard to the risk involved and they are considered to be a minimum standard of security for your premises. Your co-operation in their implementation is urgently requested.

KEY SECURITY

1. Keys should not be left in doors. Such a procedure in the case of a locked door enables the criminal to manipulate the lock instead of having to force the door.

2. Keys should not be left hanging on a hook at the side of the door, for the reason given above.

3. Safe and Strongroom keys *must not* be left in drawers and desks or otherwise "hidden" in the premises. They must ALWAYS be kept in the personal possession of the keyholder.

4. The Police keep a Register of Keyholders to business premises. Please notify any change of keyholders immediately.

SAFES

The fitting of a modern safe is essential to good security. Many of those in use are now obsolete and not capable of resisting modern methods of criminal attack.

Any safe weighing less than one ton should be fixed to prevent removal.

Your local Crime Prevention Officer will advise on the suitability and security of your safe

CASH SECURITY

Never leave money on the premises at night, unless it is in a properly protected safe. Keep your cash holdings to a minimum by frequent banking. Empty all cash tills at night, leaving them unlocked and open. Ask your Crime Prevention Officer for a copy of the standard recommendations for the transportation of money.

DOORS

It is a fundamental requirement of good security that all external doors should be fitted with a locking device which is a security value not less than that obtained by the use of a good five lever mortice lock.

Doors may be additionally protected by lining with sheet metal. If this is necessary at your premises, ensure that the work is carried out strictly in accordance with the specification, which can be obtained from the Crime Prevention Officer.

MAKE SURE that all external doors are securely fastened and/locked when premises are closed at night.

WINDOWS

If the fitting of window bars is recommended, they should, wherever possible, be fitted internally and made of mild steel not less than ¾" thick and not more than 5" apart. Each bar should be sunk into the surrounding masonry for not less than 3" and, if the bars are more than 3 ft. long, a horizontal tie bar should be fixed to avoid forcing.

Window locks are now available for all types of windows and should always be fitted to ground floor windows and upper windows to which access can be gained by securing drainpipes or low roof. Make sure that all exterior windows are securely fastened and locked when premises are closed at night.

GENERAL

Your local Crime Prevention Officer will make a further visit in due course concerning the recommendations contained in this report, but if you require any further information concerning this or any other problem, you may contact him at any time at the Police Station named overleaf.

GOVERNMENT

1. Checklist Guide for Internal Crime Prevention Surveys
2. Total Loss Control Industry Security
3. Physical Security Plan
4. Physical Security Checklist
5. Checklist for Industrial Defense Against Civil Disturbances and Sabotage
6. Physical Security Inspection Checklists
   a. Unit Storage Facilities for Small Arms and Small Arms Ammunition
   b. Narcotics and Controlled Drugs
   c. Finance and Accounting Office
   d. U.S. Army Museums
   e. Quartermaster Cash Sales Store
   f. Post Exchange Activities
   g. Commissaries
   h. Open Mess Activities
   i. Warehouse Activities
   j. Motor Pools
   k. Unit Mailrooms
   l. General

Checklist Guide for Internal Crime Prevention Surveys*

Section I. General

1. Is there a record of criminal or disorderly conduct relative to the activity? If so, what is its nature? Is there a pattern in such occurrences?
2. Are operating cash funds, such as sale or entry fee collections, change banks, and petty cash funds, reasonably safeguarded from pilferage, violent theft, or other illegal taking?
3. Are stocks of goods for sale or use reasonably safeguarded from pilferage by physical location or procedural controls?
4. Is customer or user conduct readily observable by operating or supervising personnel?
5. Are safeguard procedures for storing, issue, and return of supplies, tools, and equipment being routinely applied fully?
6. Are safeguard procedures applicable to purchase or other initial or resupply actions for obtaining supplies and equipment being routinely fully adhered to in all details
7. In the disposal of unusable material, such as defective or obsolescent equipment and supplies, are safeguard procedures applicable to

---

*Reprinted with permission from *Army Crime Prevention Program*. Department of the Army Technical Bulletin—19, May 19, 1968, pp. 1-10.

determination of utility, value, means of disposal, or disposal price being routinely and fully followed?

8. Is the use of consumption goods such as gasoline, oil, and lubricants properly controlled?

9. Are the use of recreational facilities and areas and user conduct being adequately supervised or effectually observed by spot checks or other means of surveillance to prevent or deter criminal misuse or misconduct?

10. Are the equipment and physical arrangements of a facility adequate for intended user purposes, convenience, and comfort so as to deter an inclination toward criminal misuse, abuse, misappropriation, or other criminal misconduct?

11. Can goods or services readily be obtained and, where appropriate, readily paid for?

12. Are check-in facilities efficient and convenient for user return of equipment or excess materials?

13. Are waiting or toilet facilities available and adequate: Are they located in an area which permits their being used to smuggle out items?

14. Are operating personnel sufficient and attentive to user requirements so as to deter or preclude misappropriation or other criminal actions?

15. Where accounting and inventory procedures are in effect, are they proper, being used in the proper manner, and are personnel charged with fund and material accountability effectively supervised?

16. Are personnel charged with fund and material accountability free from background involving criminal acts? Supervisory personnel, and those directly involved with procurement activities should be checked at the Criminal Records Division, USAIRR, Fort Holabird, Md. 21219, and through other available police records resources to determine that they have a clear background.

Section II. Physical Security Aspects of Internal Crime Prevention Surveys (Normally conducted by Physical Security Specialists)

17. Perimeter Barriers
   a. Is the perimeter of the activity defined by a fence or other type physical barrier?
   b. If a fence is utilized as the perimeter barrier, does it meet the minimum specifications for security fencing?
      (1) Is it of chain link design?
      (2) Is it constructed of #11 gauge or heavier wire?
      (3) Is mesh opening no longer than two inches square?

(4) Is selvage twisted and barbed at top and bottom?

(5) Is bottom of fence within two inches of solid ground?

(6) Is the top guard strung with barbed wire and angled outward and upward at a 45° angle?

(7) Is it free from damage and deterioration?

c. If masonry wall is used, does it meet minimum specifications for security fencing? Is it at least seven feet high with a top guard similar to that required on a chain link fence or at least eight feet high with broken glass set on edge and cemented to top surfaces?

d. If building walls, floors, and roofs form a part of the perimeter barrier, do they provide security equivalent at least to that provided by chain link fence? Are all openings, with an area of 96 square inches or greater and located less than 18 feet above the level of the ground outside the perimeter barrier or less than 14 feet from uncontrolled structures outside the perimeter barrier, properly secured?

e. If a building forms a part of the perimeter barrier, does it present a hazard at the point of juncture with the perimeter fence? If so, is the fence height increased 100 percent at the point of juncture?

f. If a river, lake, or other body of water forms any part of the perimeter barrier, are additional security measures provided?

g. Are openings such as culverts, tunnels, manholes for sewers and utility access, and sidewalk elevators which permit access to the installation properly secured?

h. Are there sufficient entrances through the barrier?

i. Do the gates and/or other entrances in perimeters exceed the number required for safe and efficient operation?

j. Are all perimeter entrances equipped with secure locking devices and are they always locked when not in active use?

k. Are all perimeter gates of such material and installation as to provide protection equivalent to the perimeter barriers of which they are a part?

l. Are gates and/or other perimeter entrances which are not in active use frequently inspected by guards or other personnel?

m. Is the provost marshal (or security officer) responsible for security of keys to perimeter entrances?

n. Are keys to perimeter entrances issued to other than installation personnel?

o. Has any perimeter gate or entrance been newly established or permanently closed since the last survey?

p. Are all normally used pedestrian and vehicle gates and other perimeter entrances effectively and adequately lighted so as to assure
   (1) proper identification of individuals and examination of credentials?
   (2) that interiors of vehicles are clearly lighted?
   (3) that glare from luminaries is not in guard's eyes?

q. Are appropriate signs setting forth the provisions of entry conspicuously posted at all principal entrances? Are "No Trespassing" signs posted on or adjacent to perimeter barriers at such intervals that at least one sign is visible at any approach to the barrier for a minimum distance of 50 yards? Are signs worded in accordance with AR 380-20 and AR 420-70?

r. Are clear zones maintained on both sides of the perimeter barrier? Or if clear zone requirements cannot be met, are there additional security measures in use?

s. Are automobiles permitted to park against or too close to perimeter barrier?

t. Are lumber, boxes, or other material allowed to be stacked against, or in close proximity to, perimeter barrier?

u. Are frequent checks made by maintenance crews of condition of perimeter barriers and do guards patrol perimeter areas and report insecure factors related to perimeters barriers?

v. Are reports of inadequate perimeter security by maintenance crews or guards immediately acted upon and the necessary repairs made?

w. Is an interior all-weather road provided for the use of guard patrol cars? If so, what is its condition?

x. Are perimeters protected by intrusion alarm devices?

y. Does any relocated function, newly designated restricted area, physical expansion, or other like reason indicate necessity for installation of additional perimeter barriers or additional perimeter lighting?

18. Protective Lighting
   a. Where applicable, is the perimeter of the installation or activity protected by adequate lighting?
   b. Does protective lighting provide a means of continuing during the hours of darkness the same degree of protection available during daylight hours?
   c. Are the cones of illumination from lamps directed downward and outside the fence?
   d. Are lights mounted to provide a strip of light both inside and outside the fence?

e. Is perimeter lighting utilized so that guards remain in comparative darkness?

f. Are lights checked for proper operation prior to darkness?

g. Are repairs to lights and replacement of inoperative lamps made immediately?

h. Is there a system for replacing all lamps which have been in use approximately 80 percent of their rated life?

i. Do light beams overlap to provide coverage in case a bulb burns out?

j. Is additional lighting provided at active portals and points of possible intrusion?

k. Are gate guard boxes provided with proper illumination?

l. Are light finishes or stripes used on lower parts of buildings and structures to aid guard observation?

m. Does the installation or activity have a dependable source of power for its lighting system?

n. Does the installation or activity have a dependable auxiliary source of power?

o. Is the protective lighting system independent of the installation lighting or power system?

p. Is the power supply for lights adequately protected?

q. Is there provision for standby or emergency lighting? Is the standby or emergency equipment tested frequently? Is emergency equipment tested frequently?

r. Is wiring tested and inspected periodically to insure proper operation?

s. Is parallel circuit used in the wiring?

t. Are multiple circuits used? If so, are proper switching arrangements provided?

u. Is a closed loop used in multiple circuits?

v. Is wiring for protective lighting properly mounted?

   (1) Is it in tamper-resistant conduits?

   (2) Is it mounted underground?

   (3) If above ground, is it high enough to reduce possibility of tampering?

w. Are switches and controls properly located, controlled, and protected?

   (1) Are they weatherproof and tamper resistant?

   (2) Are they readily accessible to security personnel?

   (3) Are they located so that they are inaccessible from outside the perimeter barrier?

(4) Is there a centrally located switch to control protective lighting?

x. Is lighting system designed and location recorded that repairs could be made rapidly in an emergency?

y. Is adequate lighting for guard use provided on indoor routes?

z. Are materials and equipment in shipping and storage areas properly arranged to provide adequate lighting?

aa. If bodies of water form a part of the perimeter, is proper and adequate lighting provided?

19. Protective Alarms

a. Is an alarm system used on installation? What detection device is used?

(1) Is it a local alarm system?

(2) Is it a central station system?

(a) Is it connected to installation guard headquarters?

(b) Is it connected directly to a headquarters outside the installation proper? Is it a private protection service? Police station? Fire station?

b. Is there any inherent weakness in the system itself?

c. Is the system backed up by properly trained, alert guards?

d. Is the alarm system for active areas of structures turned off during operational hours?

e. Is the system tested prior to activating it for nonoperational periods?

f. Is the alarm system inspected regularly?

g. Is the system tamper resistant? Weatherproof?

h. Is an alternate alarm system provided for use in the event of failure of the primary system?

i. Is an alternate or independent source of power available for use on the system in the event of power failure?

j. Is the emergency power source designed to cut in and operate automatically?

k. Is the alarm system properly maintained by trained personnel?

l. Are properly cleared personnel utilized in maintenance of alarm systems?

m. Are frequent tests conducted to determine the adequacy and promptness of response to alarm signals?

n. Are records kept of all alarm signals received to include time, date, location, action taken, and cause for alarm?

20. Security Communications

a. Is the security communication system adequate?

b. What means of communication are used?

(1) Telephone
  (a) Is it a commercial switchboard system? Independent switchboard?
    1. Is it maintained by properly cleared personnel?
    2. Are the operations properly cleared?
  (b) Is it restricted for guard use only?
  (c) Are switchboards adequately guarded?
  (d) Are call boxes conveniently located? Weatherproof and tamper resistant?
  (e) Are open wires, terminal boxes, cables, etc., frequently inspected for sabotage and wiretapping?
  (f) Are personnel cautioned about disussing classified matter over the telephone?
(2) Radio
  (a) Is proper radio procedure practiced?
  (b) Is an effective routine code being used? Duress code?
  (c) Is proper authentication required?
  (d) Is the equipment maintained properly?
(3) Messenger
(4) Telegraph
(5) Teletype
(6) Public address system
(7) Visual signals. Do all guards know the signals?

c. Is security communication equipment in use capable of transmitting instructions to all key posts simultaneously?

d. Is the equipment in use sufficient for guards to communicate with guard headquarters with minimum delay?

e. Is there more than one system of security communication available for exclusive use of security personnel?

f. Does one of these systems have an alternate or independent source of power?

g. Is there more than one system of communication restricted to security use available for communicating with outside protective agencies?

h. Does one of these systems have an alternate or independent source of power?

i. Has the communication center been provided with adequate security safeguards?

21. Personnel Identification and Control
  a. Is an identification card or badge used to identify all personnel within the confines of the installation?

b. Is the identification medium designed in compliance with AR 606–5 to provide the desired degree of security?

c. Does the identification and control system include arrangements for the following?

    (1) Protection of coded or printed components of badges and passes as CONFIDENTIAL, modified handling authorized.

    (2) Designation of the various areas requiring special control measures.

    (3) Controlled issue of identification media.

    (4) Description of the various identification media involved and the authorization and limitations placed upon the bearer.

    (5) Mechanics of identification at time of entering and leaving each area, as applied to both employees and visitors.

    (6) Details of where, when and how badges shall be worn.

    (7) Procedures to be followed in case of loss or damage to identification media.

    (8) Procedure for recovery and invalidation.

d. If a badge exchange system is utilized for any restricted area, does the system provide for—

    (1) Comparison of badge, pass and personnel?

    (2) Physical exchange of pass for badge at time of entrance and exit?

    (3) Accounting for each badge and/or pass?

    (4) Inventory by operating personnel at the start and completion of tours of duty?

    (5) Location of personnel who have not checked out of the area at the close of the operational periods?

    (6) Security of badges not in use?

e. Are installation messengers who are required to traverse areas of varying degrees of security interest provided with special identification?

f. Are the prescribed standards for access to exclusion areas supplemented with arrangements for the following:

    (1) At least one key person is in the area at all times when work is in progress.

    (2) No other persons are permitted to enter the area until one of the key persons has entered.

    (3) The last of the key persons does not leave until all others have departed.

g. Are personnel who require infrequent access to a critical area and who have not been issued regular security-type identification for such area treated as "visitors" thereto, and issued either

(1) a visitor's badge or pass or

(2) a special pass?

h. Are all personnel, military and civilian, required to wear the security identification badge while on duty?

i. Do guards at control points compare badges to bearers both upon entry and upon exit?

j. Is supervision of personnel charged with checking identification media sufficient to insure continuing effectiveness of identification and control system.

k. Are badges recorded and controlled by rigid accountability procedures?

l. Are lost badges replaced with one bearing a different number or one that is otherwise not identical to the one lost?

m. Are procedures relative to lost, damage, and/or forgotten badges adequate?

n. Are temporary badges used?

o. Are rosters of lost badges at guard-control points?

p. Are badges of such design and appearance as to enable guards and other personnel to quickly and positively recognize the authorizations and limitations applicable to the bearers?

q. When were currently used badges originally issued?

r. Do existing procedures insure the return of identification badges upon termination of employment or assignment?

s. Are employee-type badges issued to outside contractor employees working within the installation?

t. Have local regulations governing identification and control been revised in any material respect since last reported upon? (If so, obtain copies of current regulations) .

u. Are all phases of system under supervision and control of provost marshal or security officer?

v. Do all badges bear an expiration date?

22. Visitor Control

a. Are visitors, in any instances, allowed to move about the installation unattended?

b. Do guards check on visitors' movements to assure that they do not enter areas for which they do not have required authorization?

c. Are visitors required to conspicuously display identification on outer garments at all times while on installation?

d. When visitors leave the installation, are they required to turn in their identification badges, and is the departure time in each case recorded on the visitors' register?

e. Are visitors indicating an intention to return at a later time permitted to retain their identification badges?

f. What procedures are invoked when visitor identification media are not turned in prior to departure of the visitor?

g. Is there a central receptionist? Are functions performed under supervision of provost marshal or security officer?

h. Are receptionists (or guards) stationed at different areas of security importance to implement visitor control?

i. Are visitor passes exchanged for visitor badges at any security area, and, if so, by whom is each type of identification media issued?

j. Are permanent records of visits maintained? By whom?

k. Are there special procedures applicable to visitors requiring access to classified documents and/or material?

l. Are special visitors, e.g. vendors, tradesmen, utility servicemen, special equipment servicemen, etc., issued a special or distinctive type of visitor badge?

m. What measures are employed, other than the issuance of identification badges, to control the movement of contractor personnel working within the perimeter of the installation?

n. Is the system used for identification of truck drivers and helpers in conformity with security regulations?

o. Is the provost marshal or security officer the responsible official for all aspects of visitor control?

23. Package and Material Control
   a. Is there an SOP on control of packages and materials?
   b. Are all guards conversant with the control measures?
   c. Are notices on restriction and control procedures prominently displayed at each active portal?
   d. Is there a checkroom where employees and visitors can leave their packages?
      (1) Is an adequate receipt system in effect?
      (2) Are packages inspected in the owner's presence before a receipt is issued?
      (3) Is access to checkroom restricted to authorized personnel only?
      (4) Is a policy established for disposition of items left beyond a specified period?
   e. Are shakedowns of persons and vehicles conducted and, if so, indicate frequency and scope thereof?
      (1) Regular search
      (2) Spot search

    (3) Special search

f. Are detection devices used?

g. Is DA Form 1818, Individual Property Pass, or some other equally appropriate property removal slip signed by proper authorizing official, required when property is being removed from the installation?

h. Are signature cards available in the provost marshal office for signature of officials authorizing property removals?

i. Are property removal slips surrendered to guards at exit points?

j. Is special handling established for classified packages and material?

    (1) Is material pass used to exempt from search?

        (a) Is time, date, bearer's name, using agency, description of contents, etc., properly recorded thereon?

        (b) Is preparation and issue rigidly controlled?

        (c) Is it serially numbered?

        (d) Does it provide for signature of validating official?

        (e) Is signature card readily available to guards for comparison?

        (f) Is it detached and filed properly to insure security?

    (2) Is properly cleared and identified courier used at all times?

k. Is special clothing issued for wear in installation to prevent introduction or removal of unauthorized items?

    (1) Is dressing room available for changing?

    (2) Is control procedure established to prevent transfer of items?

l. Is an effective procedure used for control and search of special vehicles?

    (1) Emergency vehicles

    (2) VIP vehicles

    (3) Special courier vehicles

    (4) Vendors' vehicles

    (5) Vehicles with loads which are impracticable to search

m. Is there close coordination between guard headquarters and those facilities and activities which handle shipments of packages and material?

    (1) Installation post office

    (2) Message center

    (3) Administration office

    (4) Packing and shipping departments

    (5) Others

n. Are new employees given appropriate instructions relative to the handling and safeguarding of classified material?

o. Are employees properly debriefed and required to sign a debriefing certificate upon termination of or transfer from sensitive duty?

24. Classified Document Security (Normally Conducted by Military Intelligence Personnel)
   a. Is a regular security education program in effect?
   b. Has a security control officer been appointed as prescribed in AR 380–5?
   c. Has a properly cleared military or civilian official been appointed as TOP SECRET control officer?
   d. Have alternate TOP SECRET control officers been designated? Does the TOP SECRET control officer receive and disseminate classified documents and/or data?
   e. Are TOP SECRET and SECRET documents covered by receipt at all times?
   f. Are TOP SECRET documents hand-carried by the TOP SECRET control officer to those individuals who are authorized access to them?
   g. Are SECRET and CONFIDENTIAL materials delivered within the installation by authorized and appropriately cleared messengers?
   h. Do containers for the storage of classified matter meet requirements set forth in AR 380–5?
   i. Are the prescribed forms properly affixed to each classified container?
   j. Is the combination padlock protected to prevent surrepititious exchange while the container is open?
   k. If a locking bar is used on a file cabinet, is it sufficiently rigid to preclude access to the drawers?
   l. Are classified containers kept locked when persons who have been authorized access are not present?
   m. Are daily security checks of classified containers made by assigned individuals?
   n. Is an up-to-date record of all combinations to classified containers maintained in the manner prescribed in AR 380–5?
   o. Are the provisions of AR 380–5, relating to changes of combinations and the exchanging or rotation of padlocks of classified containers, being complied with?
   p. Is classified material prepared for transmission and transmitted outside the installation in accordance with AR 380–5?
   q. Are rules and procedures pertinent to the safeguarding of classified material published in writing?

25. Vehicle Control
   a. Are vehicles which are allowed regular access to the installation registered with the provost marshal?
   b. Have definite procedures been established for the registration of privately owned vehicles and are they issued in writing?
   c. Do the vehicle registration requirements apply also to motor vehicles owned or operated by:
      (1) military personnel in temporary duty status in excess of 10 days
      (2) employees of any government agency physically located on the installation
      (3) employees of any individual, firm, corporation, or contractor engaged in activities on the installation
      (4) individuals, partnerships, or other business concerns whose business activities require daily or frequent use of their vehicles on the installation?
   d. Is annual registration required?
   e. Do the prescribed prerequisites for registration include a valid state registration for the vehicle and a valid state driver's license?
   f. Is mechanical inspection of vehicles and/or proof of financial responsibility required as prerequisites of registration?
   g. Are decalcomania or metal registraton tags affixed to all registered vehicles?
   h. Do registration tags bear a permanently affixed serial number and numerical designation of year of registration?
   i. Do the regulatory controls for registration tags include:
      (1) Prohibition against transfer of registration tags for use with a vehicle other than the one for which originally issued?
      (2) Replacement of lost tags at the registrant's expense?
      (3) Return of tags to the provost marshal or security officer when vehicle is no longer authorized entry into installation.
      (4) Destruction of invalidated decalcomania?
   j. What is nature and scope of registration records maintained by provost marshal or security officer?
   k. Do military police and/or gate guards make periodic checks to insure that privately owned vehicles are operated on the premises only by properly licensed persons?
   l. Is a definite system used to control the movement of commercial trucks and other goods conveyances into and out of the installation area?
   m. Are loading and unloading platforms located outside the manu-

facturing and/or operating areas and separated therefrom by controlled and guard supervised entrances?

n. Does the check at entrances cover both incoming and outgoing vehicles?

o. Are truck registers maintained?

p. Are escorts provided when vehicles are permitted access to manufacturing, operating, or restricted areas?

g. Does the supervision of loading and unloading operations insure that unauthorized goods or people do not enter or leave the installation via trucks or other conveyances?

r. Are military trip tickets examined?

s. Is a temporary tag issued to visitors' vehicles?

t. Are automobiles allowed to be parked within manufacturing, operating, or restricted areas?

u. Are parking lots provided, located away from sensitive points, and adequate for the number of vehicles parked?

v. Are interior parking areas fenced so that occupants of automobiles must pass through a pedestrian gate when entering or leaving the working area?

w. Are frequent spot searches made of automobiles?

x. Are separate parking areas provided for visitors' vehicles?

y. What is extent of guard surveillance over interior parking area?

z. Are there restrictions against employees entering parking areas during duty hours?

26. Lock Security

a. Has a key control officer been appointed?

b. Are locks and keys to all buildings and entrances supervised and controlled by a key control officer?

c. Does the key control officer have over-all authority and responsibility for issuance and replacement of locks and keys?

d. Are keys issued only to authorized personnel?

e. Are keys issued to other than installation personnel?

f. Is the removal of keys from the premises prohibited?

g. Are keys not in use secured in a locked, fireproof cabinet?

h. Are current records maintained indicating:

(1) Buildings and/or entrances for which keys are issued?

(2) Number and identification of keys issued?

(3) Location and number of duplicate keys?

(4) Location and number of master keys?

(5) Issue and turn in of keys?

(6) Location of locks and keys held in reserve?

i. Is a current key cotnrol directive in effect?

j. Are locks changed immediately upon loss or theft of keys?

k. Are frequent inventories and inspections conducted by the key control officer to insure compliance with directives?

l. If master keys are used, are they devoid of marking identifying them as such?

m. Are losses or thefts of keys promptly investigated by the key control personnel?

n. Must all requests for reproduction or duplication of keys be approved by the key control officer?

o. Are locks on inactive gates and storage facilities under seal?

p. Are locks rotated within the installation at least semiannually?

q. Where applicable, is manufacturer's serial number on combination locks obliterated?

r. Are measures in effect to prevent the unauthorized removal of locks on open cabinets, gates, or buildings?

27. Guard Forces

a. Is a guard force provided?

b. Is the guard force composed of
   (1) Civil service personnel under military direction, supervision, and control?
   (2) civilian guards of General Services Administration (GSA) or other Government agencies?
   (3) civilian employees of contractor?
   (4) military personnel assigned to the installation or activity?

c. Is present guard force strength commensurate with degree of security and economical use?

d. Is utilization of guard forces reviewed periodically to ascertain effective and economical use?

e. Is supervisory responsibility for guard force operations vested in in the provost marshal or security officer?

f. Is a guard headquarters building provided? Does the guard headquarters building contain control equipment and instruments of all alarm, warning, and guard communications systems?

g. Are guards familiar with communications equipment used?

h. Does guard headquarters have direct communication with local municipal fire and police headquarters?

i. Do members of guard force meet the minimum qualification standards?

j. Do all members of guard force have clearances equivalent to highest degree of security classification of the documents, material, etc., to which access may be required or accidentally gained during their normal duty assignments?

k. Are guards armed while on duty, and if so, with what type of weapon? Have guards fired assigned weapon for familiarization or qualification within past 12 months?

l. Are weapons kept in arms racks and adequately secured when not in use and are ammunition supplies properly secured and issued only for authorized purposes?

m. Is each member of guard force required to complete a course of basic training and thereafter take periodic courses of inservice or advanced training?

n. Are the subjects included in the various training courses adequate? Does the training cover:

  (1) Care and use of weapons?

  (2) Common forms of espionage and sabotage activity?

  (3) Types of bombs and explosives?

  (4) Orientation on the installation, with emphasis on restricted and vulnerable areas?

  (5) Location of hazardous materials and processes?

  (6) Location and use of fire protective equipment, including sprinkling control valves?

  (7) Location and operation of all important steam and gas valves and main electrical switches?

  (8) Conditions which may cause fire and explosions?

  (9) Location and use of first aid equipment?

  (10) Duties in the event of fire, explosion, natural disaster, civil disturbance, blackout, or air raid?

  (11) Use of communication system?

  (12) Proper methods of search?

  (13) Observation and description?

  (14) Patrol work?

  (15) Supervision of visitors?

  (16) Preparation of written reports?

  (17) General and special guard orders?

o. Are periodic examinations conducted to insure maintenance of guard training standards?

p. Are activities of the guard force in consonance with established policy?

q. Is supervision of the guard force adequate?

r. Are general and special orders properly posted and are they reviewed at least semiannually to insure applicability?

s. Are periodic inspections and examinations conducted to determine the degree of understanding and compliance with all guard orders?

t. Do physical, functional, or other changes at the installation indicate the necessity for or feasibility of
   (1) establishing additional guard posts or patrols?
   (2) discontinuing any existing posts or patrols?
u. Are duties other than those related to security performed by guard personnel?
v. Is two-way radio equipment installed on all guard patrol cars?
w. Are guard patrol cars equipped with spotlights?
x. Does each guard on patrol duty carry a flashlight?
y. Do guards record or report their presence at key points in the installation by means of
   (1) portable watch clocks?
   (2) central watchclock stations?
   (3) telephone?
   (4) two-way radio equipment?
z. Are guard assignments and patrol routes varied at frequent intervals to obviate an established routine?

28. Fire Prevention (In conjunction with installation fire marshal)
   a. Is a fire department authorized at the installation?
   b. If installation is within the corporate limits of a municipality or other governmental subdivision which has an organized fire department, is adequate response by the latter assured?
   c. If installation is adjacent to the corporate limits of a municipality, what is the extent of protection available from municipal or other fire departments? Are contractual arrangements in effect with contiguous municipalities?
   d. What is the estimated time lag between notification and arrival of fire fighting equipment?
   e. Are fire plans posted in conspicuous locations in all areas?
   f. Is a fire alarm system in effect? Is it adequate?
   g. Are personnel fully aware of fire prevention and protection responsibilities?
   h. Are unit personnel fully aware of the inherent fire hazards and their severity?
   i. Are regular fire-prevention inspections made to detect fire hazards?
   j. What first aid and firefighting equipment is available on the installation? Does it include an adequate amount of strategically located fire pails, sandbags, chemical extinguishers, and pumps?
   k. What types of fire extinguishers are available? Do they include carbon dioxide, carbon tetrachloride, and dry chemical types?

l. Are all extinguishers and other equipment frequently tested and inspected so as to be in perfect working order at all times?

m. Are inspections of fire extinguishers made by competent personnel, and are results of inspections carefully noted?

n. Are both first aid and firefighting equipment painted to be conspicuous? Do the personnel on the premises know the locations?

o. What type of fire alarms are installed? Are there sufficient number of alarm boxes and warning devices in the fire alarm system?

p. Is the alarm system frequently inspected and tested?

q. Has a program of fire drills been inaugurated? If so, how often are they conducted?

r. Are vulnerable or important buildings and structures on the installation equipped with sprinkler systems? Are they fed by public mains, tanks or private reservoir, or pumps?

s. Do the firefighting personnel know the location of the main control valves of the sprinkler systems?

t. Is the sprinkler system inspected periodically? Are sprinkler heads free of corrosion, paint, or whitewash?

u. Is the effectiveness of the sprinklers reduced due to obstructions, partitions, piles of material, crates or boxes?

v. Are fire hydrants accessible and in working order?

w. Is smoking discipline properly enforced?

x. Are combustible materials properly stored and safeguarded?

Total Loss Control Industrial Security*

Plan
Need
Survey
Controls

Procedures
Policy
Organization chart
Hiring practice
Job description
Duties & responsibilities
___Arrest and search
___Security of plant
___Protection of property
___Control of personnel

---

*Reprinted with permission from John A. Fletcher and Hugh M. Douglas, *Total Loss Control* (London: Associated Business Programmes Ltd., 1971) p. 88.

—Control of vehicles

—Liaison with fire control

—Accident control

—First aid

Physical Controls

Perimeter barriers

Lighting

Protection of critical areas

Supporting services

Control of openings

Personnel

Identification, admission & control

Control of parking and admission of vehicles

Classified matter

Vital records

Guard force

Equipment

Intrusion detection devices

Closed circuit television

Gates and gate houses

Two-way radio

Lock controls

Physical Security Plan†

_____

(Classification)

Map reference

Copy No.

Issuing headquarters

Place of issue

Date of issue

1. *Purpose*

State purpose of the plan.

2. *Area Security*

Define the areas, buildings, and other structures considered critical and establish priorities for their protection.

_____

†Reprinted with permission from Department of the Army Field Manual 19-30: *Physical Security.* 1965, pp. 128-131.

3. *Control Measures*

Define and establish restrictions on access and movement into critical areas. These restrictions can be categorized as to personnel, vehicles, and materials.

a. Personnel access:
  (1) Establishing controls pertinent to each area or structure.
      (a) Authority for access
      (b) Access criteria for:
          1. Unit personnel
          2. Visitors
          3. Maintenance personnel
          4. Contractor personnel
          5. National Guard
  (2) Identification and control
      (a) Describe the system to be used in each area. If a badge system is used, a complete description covering all aspects should be used in disseminating requirements for identification and control of personnel conducting business on the installation.
      (b) Application of the system.
          1. Unit personnel
          2. Visitors to restricted areas
          3. Visitors to administrative areas
          4. Vendors, tradesmen, etc.
          5. Contractor personnel
          6. Maintenance or support personnel

b. Material control
  (1) Incoming
      (a) Requirements for admission of material and supplies
      (b) Search and inspection of material for possible sabotage hazards
      (c) Special controls on delivery of supplies and/or personnel shipments in restricted areas
  (2) Outgoing
      (a) Documentation required
      (b) Controls, as outlined in (1) (a) , (b) , and (c) above
      (c) Classified shipments NOT involving nuclear material
  (3) Nuclear material
      (a) Controls on movement of warheads on the installation
      (b) Controls on shipments or movement of training warheads
      (c) Controls on pickup or delivery of warheads outside the installation

c. Vehicle control
  (1) Policy on search of military and privately owned vehicles

(2) Parking regulations
(3) Controls for entrance into restricted and administrative areas
    (a) Privately owned vehicles
    (b) Military vehicles
    (c) Emergency vehicles
d. Vehicle registration

4. *Aids to Security*

Indicate the manner in which the following listed aids to security will be implemented on the installation: .

a. Perimeter barriers
    (1) Definition
    (2) Clear zones
        (a) Criteria
        (b) Maintenance
    (3) Signs
        (a) Types
        (b) Posting
    (4) Gates
        (a) Hours of operation
        (b) Security requirements
        (c) Lock security
    (5) Maintenance and inspection

b. Protective lighting system
    (1) Use and control
    (2) Inspection
    (3) Action to be taken in the event of commercial power failure
    (4) Action to be taken in the event of a failure of alternate source of power
    (5) Emergency lighting systems
        (a) Stationary
        (b) Portable

c. Alarm systems
    (1) Security classification
    (2) Inspection
    (3) Use and monitoring
    (4) Action to be taken in event of "Alarm" conditions
    (5) Maintenance
    (6) Alarm logs or registers
    (7) Sensitivity settings

d. Communications
    (1) Locations

(2) Use

(3) Tests

(4) Authentication

5. *Guard Forces*

Include general instructions which would apply to all guards. Detailed instructions such as Special Orders and SOP should be attached as annexes.

a. Composition and organization

b. Tour of duty

c. Essential posts

d. Weapons and equipment

e. Training

f. Use of sentry dogs

g. Method of challenging with sign and countersign

h. Alert force

(1) Composition

(2) Mission

(3) Weapons and equipment

(4) Location

(5) Deployment

6. *Emergency Actions*

Indicate emergency actions of general application. Detailed plans such as disaster, fire, etc. should be attached as annexes.

a. Individual actions

b. Alert force

c. Guard force actions

7. *Coordinating Instructions*

Indicate matters which require coordination with other military and civil agencies.

a. Integration with plans of host or nearby military installations

b. Liaison and coordination

(1) Local civil authorities

(2) Federal agencies

(3) Military organizations

/s/ ———————————————

Commanding

Appendixes:

1. Installation Security Status Map

2. Special Instructions to Security Officers and Officers of the Day

3. Sergeant of the Guard Instructions

4. Special Orders for Guard Posts

Physical Security Checklist*

There is no prescribed form of checklist for making a physical security survey. Although there will be variations based upon differing missions and locations, the factors contributing to security are much the same at all installations. The checklist below may be used in making a survey. With few deletions or additions this checklist will apply to any military or industrial intsallation. (Exhibits furnished in previous surveys may be omitted unless there is substantial change.)

1. Perimeter Barriers
   a. Is the perimeter of the installation or activity defined by a fence or other type physical barrier?
      (1) Specify type and height of physical barrier and obtain (if possible) typical photograph for exhibit purposes.
      (2) Are physical barriers at perimeter lines damaged or deteriorated?
   b. If a fence is utilized as the perimeter barrier, does it meet the minimum specifications for security fencing?
      (1) Is it of chain link design?
      (2) Is it constructed of #11 gauge or heavier wire?
      (3) Is mesh opening no larger than two inches square?
      (4) Is selvage twisted and barbed at top and bottom?
      (5) Is bottom of fence within two inches of solid ground?
      (6) Is the top guard strung with barbed wire and angled outward and upward at a 45° angle?
   c. If masonry wall is used, does it meet minimum specifications for security fencing? Is it at least seven feet high with a top guard similar to that required on a chain link fence, or at least eight feet high with broken glass set on edge and cemented to top surface?
   d. If building walls, floors, and roofs form a part of the perimeter barrier, do they provide security equivalent at least to that provided by chain link fence? Are all openings properly secured? *(Note:* Openings, with an area of 96 square inches or greater, and located less than 18 feet above the level of the ground outside the perimeter barrier or less than 14 feet from uncontrolled structures outside the perimeter barrier, must be provided with security equivalent to that of the perimeter.)
   e. If a building forms a part of the perimeter barrier, does it present a hazard at the point of juncture with the perimeter fence? If so, is the fence height increased 100% at the point of juncture?
   f. If a river, lake, or other body of water forms any part of the perimeter barrier, are additional security measures provided?

---

*Reprinted with permission from Department of the Army Field Manual 19-30: *Physical Security.* 1965, pp. 140-150.

g. Are openings such as culverts, tunnels, manholes for sewers and utility access, and sidewalk elevators which permit access to the installation, properly secured?

h. List number, location, and physical characteristics of perimeter entrances.

i. Are all portals in perimeter barriers guarded or secured?

j. Do the gates and/or other entrances in perimeters exceed the number required for safe and efficient operation?

k. Are all perimeter entrances equipped with secure locking devices and are they always locked when not in active use?

l. Are all perimeter gates of such material and installation as to provide protection equivalent to the perimeter barriers of which they are a part?

m. Are gates and/or other perimeter entrances which are not in active use frequently inspected by guards or other personnel?

n. Is the provost marshal (or security officer) responsible for security of keys to perimeter entrances? If not, specify responsible individual or office.

o. Are keys to perimeter entrances issued to other than installation personnel?

p. Has any perimeter gate or entrance been activated or inactivated since the last survey? If so, give essential details.

q. Are all normally used pedestrian and vehicle gates and other perimeter entrances effectively and adequately lighted so as to assure
   (1) proper identification of individuals and examination of credentials?
   (2) that interiors of vehicles are clearly lighted?
   (3) that glare from luminaries is not in guard's eyes?

r. Are appropriate signs setting forth the provisions of entry conspicuously posted at all principal entrances?

s. Are "No Trespassing" signs posted on or adjacent to perimeter barriers at such intervals that at least one sign is visible at any approach to the barrier for a minimum distance of 50 yards?

t. Are clear zones maintained on both sides of the perimeter barrier? If clear zone requirements cannot be met, what additional security measures have been implemented?

u. Are automobiles permitted to park against or too close to perimeter barrier?

v. Are lumber, boxes, or other material allowed to be stacked against, or in close proximity to, perimeter barrier?

w. What is frequency of checks made by maintenance crews of condition of perimeter barriers?

    x. Do guards patrol perimeter areas?

    y. Do guards observe and report insecure factors related to perimeter barriers?

    z. Are reports of inadequate perimeter security immediately acted upon and the necessary repairs effected?

  aa. Is an interior all-weather perimeter road provided for the use of guard patrol cars? If so, what is its condition?

  bb. If guard patrols or other guard activities at perimeter lines have been changed since the last survey, specify the changes.

  cc. Are perimeters protected by intrusion alarm devices?

  dd. Have any additional perimeter barriers been installed or has any re-location thereof been accomplished since the last survey? If so, give. details.

  ee. Does any relocated function, newly designated restricted area, physical expansion, or other like reason indicate necessity for installation of additional perimeter barriers or additional perimeter lighting?

2. Protective Lighting

    a. Is the perimeter of the installation protected by adequate lighting?

    b. Does protective lighting provide a means of continuing during the hours of darkness the same degree of protection available during the daylight hours?

    c. Are the cones of illumination from lamps directed downward and away from the installation proper and away from guard personnel?

    d. Are lights mounted to provide a strip of light both inside and outside the fence?

    e. Is perimeter lighting utilized so that guards remain in comparative darkness?

    f. Are lights checked for proper operation prior to darkness?

    g. Are repairs to lights and replacement of inoperative lamps effected immediately?

    h. Is there a system for replacing all lamps which have been in use approximately 80% of their rated life?

    i. Do light beams overlap to provide coverage in case a bulb burns out?

    j. Is additional lighting provided at active portals and points of possible intrusion?

    k. Are gate guard boxes provided with proper illumination?

    l. Are light finishes or stripes used on lower parts of buildings and structures to aid guard observation?

  m. Does the installation have a dependable source of power for its lighting system?

    n. Does the installation have a dependable auxiliary source of power?

o. Is the protective lighting system independent of the plant lighting or power system?

p. Is the power supply for lights adequately protected? How is it protected?

q. Is there provision for standby or emergency lighting?

r. Is the standby or emergency equipment tested frequently?

s. Is emergency equipment designed to go into operation automatically when needed?

t. Is wiring tested and inspected periodically to insure proper operation?

u. Is parallel circuit used in the wiring?

v. Are multiple circuits used? If so, are proper switching arrangements provided?

w. Is a closed loop used in multiple circuits?

x. Is wiring for protective lighting properly mounted?
   (1) Is it in tamper resistant conduits?
   (2) Is it mounted underground?
   (3) If above ground, is it high enough to reduce possibility of tampering?

y. Are switches and controls properly located, controlled, and protected?
   (1) Are they weatherproof and tamper resistant?
   (2) Are they readily accessible to security personnel?
   (3) Are they located so that they are inaccessible from outside the perimeter barrier?
   (4) Is there a centrally located switch to control protective lighting?

z. Is lighting system designed and locations recorded so that repairs could be made rapidly in an emergency?

aa. Is adequate lighting for guard use provided on indoor routes?

bb. Are materials and equipment in shipping and storage areas properly arranged to provide adequate lighting?

cc. If bodies of water form a part of the perimeter, is proper and adequate lighting provided?

3. Protective Alarms

a. Is an alarm system used on the installation? What detection device is used?
   (1) Is it a local alarm system?
   (2) Is it a central station system?
      (a) Is it connected to installation guard headquarters?
      (b) Is it connected directly to a headquarters outside the installation proper? Is it a private protection service? Police station? Fire station?

b. Is there any inherent weakness in the system itself?

c. Is the system backed up by properly trained, alert guards?

d. Is the alarm system for active areas of structures turned off during operational hours?

e. Is the system tested prior to activating it for nonoperational periods?

f. Is the alarm system inspected regularly?

g. Is the system tamper resistant? Weatherproof?

h. Is an alternate alarm system provided for use in the event of failure of the primary system?

i. Is an alternate or independent source of power available for use on the system in the event of power failure?

j. Is the emergency power source designed to cut in and operate automatically?

k. Is the alarm system properly maintained by trained personnel?

l. Are properly cleared personnel utilized in maintenance of alarm systems?

m. Are frequent tests conducted to determine the adequacy and promptness of response to alarm signals?

n. Are records kept of all alarm signals received to include time, date, location, action taken, and cause for alarm?

4. Security Communications

   a. Is the security communication system adequate?

   b. What means of communication are used?

     (1) Telephone.

       (a) Is it a commercial switchboard system? Independent switchboard?

         1. Is it maintained by properly cleared personnel?

         2. Are the operators properly cleared?

       (b) Is it restricted for guard use only?

       (c) Are switchboards adequately guarded?

       (d) Are call boxes conveniently located? Weatherproof and tamper resistant?

       (e) Are open wires, terminal boxes, cables, etc., frequently inspected for damage, sabotage, and wire-tapping?

       (f) Are personnel cautioned about discussing classified matter over the telephone?

     (2) Radio

       (a) Is proper radio procedure practiced?

       (b) Is an effective routine code being used? Duress code?

       (c) Is proper authentication required?

       (d) Is the equipment maintained properly?

     (3) Messenger

(4) Telegraph

(5) Teletype

(6) Public address system

(7) Visual signals. Do all guards know the signals?

c. Is security communication equipment in use capable of transmitting instructions to all key posts simultaneously?

d. Is the equipment in use sufficient for guard to communicate with guard headquarters with minimum delay?

e. Is there more than one system of security communication available for exclusive use of security personnel?

f. Does one of these systems have an alternate or independent source of power?

g. Is there more than one system of communication restricted to security use available for communicating with outside protective agencies?

h. Does one of these systems have an alternate or independent source of power?

i. Has the communication center been provided with adequate security safeguards?

5. Personnel Identification and Control

a. Is an identification card or badge used to identify all personnel within the confines of the installation?

b. Is the identification medium designed to comply with AR 606–5 to provide the desired degree of security?

c. Does the identification and control system include arrangements for the following:

(1) Protection of coded or printed components of badges and passes with a minimum classification of CONFIDENTIAL, modified handling authorized.

(2) Designation of the various areas requring special control measures.

(3) Controlled issue of identification media.

(4) Description of the various identification media involved and the authorization and limitations placed upon the bearer.

(5) Mechanics of identification at time of entering and leaving each area, as applied to both employees and visitors.

(6) Details of where, when, and how badges shall be worn.

(7) Procedures to be followed in case of loss or damage to identification media.

(8) Procedure for recovery and invalidation.

d. If a badge exchange system is utilized for any restricted area, does the system provide for:

    (1) Comparison of badge, pass and personnel?

    (2) Physical exchange of pass for badge at time of entrance and exit?

    (3) Accounting for each badge and/or pass?

    (4) Inventory by operating personnel at the start and completion of tours of duty?

    (5) Location of personnel who have not checked out of the area at the close of the operational periods?

    (6) Security of badges not in use?

e. Are installation messengers who are required to traverse areas of varying degrees of security interest provided with special identifica-cation?

f. Are the prescribed standards for access to exclusion areas supplemented with arrangements for the following?

    (1) At least one key person is in the area at all times when work is in progress.

    (2) No other persons are permitted to enter the area until one of the key persons has entered.

    (3) The last of the key persons does not leave until all others have departed.

g. Are personnel who require infrequent access to a critical area and who have not been issued regular security type identification for such area treated as "visitors" thereto, and issued either

    (1) a visitor's badge or pass?

    (2) a special pass?

h. Are all personnel, military and civilian, required to wear the security identification badge while on duty?

i. Do guards at control points compare badges to bearers both upon entry and upon exit?

j. Is supervision of personnel charged with checking identification media sufficient to insure continuing effectiveness of identification and control system?

k. Are badges recorded and controlled by rigid accountability procedures?

l. Are lost badges replaced with one bearing a different number or one that is otherwise not identical to the one lost?

m. Are procedures relative to lost, damaged, and/or forgotten badges adequate?

n. Are temporary badges used?

o. Are rosters of lost badges posted at guard control points?

p. Are badges of such design and appearance as to enable guards and other personnel to recognize quickly and positively the authorizations and limitations applicable to the bearers?

q. When were currently used badges originally issued?

r. Do existing procedures insure the return of identification badges upon termination of employment or assignment?

s. Are employee-type badges issued to outside contractor employees working within the installation?

t. Have local regulation governing identification and control been revised in any material respect since last reported upon? (If so, obtain copies of current regulations.)

u. Are all phases of system under supervision and control of provost marshal or security officer?

v. Is an effective visitor escort procedure established?

w. Are visitors, in any instance, allowed to move about the installation unattended?

x. 'Do guards check on visitors' movements to assure that they do not enter areas for which they do not have the required authorization?

y. Are visitors required to conspicuously display identification on outer garments at all times while on installation.

z. When visitors leave the installation, are they required to turn in their identification badges, and is the departure time in each case recorded on the visitor register?

aa. Are visitors indicating an intention to return at a later time permitted to retain their identification badges?

bb. What procedures are involved when visitor identification media are not turned in prior to departure of the visitor?

cc. Is there a central receptionist?
   (1) If "yes," specify functions
   (2) Are functions performed under supervision of provost marshal or security officer?

dd. Are receptionists (or guards) stationed at different areas of security importance to implement visitor control?

ee. Are visitor passes exchanged for visitor badges at any security area, and, if so, by whom is each type of identification media issued?

ff. Are permanent records of visits maintained? By whom?

gg. Are there special procedures applicable to visitors requiring access to classified documents and/or material?

hh. Are special visitors, e.g. vendors, tradesmen, utility servicemen, special equipment servicemen, etc., issued a special or distinctive type of visitor badge?

ii. What measures are employed, other than the issuance of identification badges, to control the movement of contractor personnel working within the perimeter of the installation?

jj. Is the system used for identification of truck drivers and helpers in conformity with security regulations?

kk. Is the provost marshal or security officer the responsible official for all aspects of visitor control?

6. Package and Material Control
   a. Is there an SOP on cotnrol of package and materials?
   b. Are all guards conversant with the control measures?
   c. Are notices on restriction and control procedures prominently displayed at each active portal?
   d. Is there a checkroom where employees and visitors can leave their packages?
      (1) Is an adequate receipt system in effect?
      (2) Are packages inspected in the owner's presence before a receipt is issued?
      (3) Is access to the checkroom restricted to authorized personnel only?
      (4) Is a policy established for dispostion of items left beyond a specified period?
   e. Are spot checks of persons and vehicles conducted and, if so, indicate frequency and scope thereof?
      (1) Regular search
      (2) Spot search
      (3) Special search
   f. Are detection devices used?
      (1) Inspectoscope or other similar device
      (2) Metal detector
      (3) Other; describe and evaluate effectiveness.
   g. Is DA Form 1818, Individual Property Pass, or some other equally appropriate property removal slip signed by proper authorizing official, required when property is being removed from the installation?
   h. Are signature cards available in the provost marshal office for signature of officials authorizing property removals?
   i. Are property removal slips surrendered to guards at exit points?
   j. Is special handling established for classified package and material?
      (1) Is material pass used to exempt bearer from search?
          (a) Is time, date, bearer's name, using agency, description of contents, etc., properly recorded theron?
          (b) Is preparation and issue rigidly controlled?
          (c) Is it serially numbered?
          (d) Does it provide for signature of validating officials?
          (e) Is signature card readily available to guards for comparison?

(f) Is the pass detached and filed properly to insure security?

(2) Is properly cleared and identified courier used at all times?

k. Is special clothing issued for wear in installation to prevent introduction or removal of unauthorized items?

(1) Is dressing room available for changing?

(2) Is control procedure established to prevent transfer of items?

l. Is an effective procedure used for control and search of special vehicles?

(1) Emergency vehicles

(2) VIP vehicles

(3) Special courier vehicles

(4) Vendor's vehicles

(5) Vehicles with loads which are impracticable to search

m. Is there close coordination between guard headquarters and those facilities and activities which handle shipment of packages and material?

(1) Installation post office

(2) Message center

(3) Administration officer

(4) Packing and shipping departments

(5) Others

n. Are new employees given appropriate instructions relative to the handling and safeguarding of classified material?

o. Are employees properly debriefed and required to sign a debriefing certificate upon termination of or transfer from sensitive duty?

p. Is a regular security education program in effect?

q. Has a security control officer been appointed as prescribed in AR 380–5?

r. Has a properly cleared military or civilian official been appointed as TOP SECRET control officer?

s. Have alternate TOP SECRET control officers been designated?

t. Does the TOP SECRET control officer receive and disseminate classified documents and/or data?

u. Are TOP SECRET and SECRET documents covered by receipt at all times?

v. Are TOP SECRET document handcarried by the TOP SECRET control officer to those individuals who are authorized access to them?

w. Are SECRET and CONFIDENTIAL materials delivered within the installation by authorized and appropriately cleared messengers?

x. Do containers for the storage of classified matter meet requirements set forth in AR 380–5?

y. Are the prescribed forms properly affixed to each classified container?

z. Is the combination padlock protected to prevent surreptitious exchange while the container is open?

aa. If a locking bar is used on a file cabinet, is it sufficiently rigid to preclude access to the drawers?

bb. Are classified containers kept locked when not under observation by persons who have been authorized access?

cc. Are daily security checks of classified containers made by assigned individuals?

dd. Is an up-to-date record of all combinations to classified containers maintained in the manner prescribed in AR 380–5?

ee. Are the provisions of AR 380–5 relating to changes of combinations and the exchanging or rotation of padlocks of classified containers being complied with?

ff. Is classified material prepared for transmission and transmitted outside the installation in accordance with AR 380–5?

gg. Is classified material destroyed and recorded as required in AR 380–5?

hh. Are rules and procedures pertinent to the safeguarding of classified material published in writing?

7. Vehicle Control (AR 210–10)

a. Are vehicles which are allowed regular access to the installation registered with the provost marshal?

b. Have definite procedures been established for the registration of privately owned vehicles and are they issued in writing?

c. Do the vehicle registration requirements apply also to motor vehicles owned or operated by:

(1) military personnel in temporary duty status in excess of 10 days?

(2) employees of any governmental agency physically located on the installation?

(3) employees of any individual, firm, corporation, or contractor engaged in activities on the installation?

(4) individuals, partnerships, or other business concerns whose business activities require daily or frequent use of their vehicles on the installation?

d. Is annual registration required?

e. What information is incorporated in registration application forms?

f. Do the prescribed prerequisites for registration include a valid state registration for the vehicle and a valid state driver's license?

g. Is mechanical inspection of vehicles and/or proof of financial responsibility required as prerequisites of registration?

h. Are decalcomania or metal registration tags affixed to all registered vehicles?

i. Do registration tags bear a permanently affixed serial number and numerical designation of year of registration?

j. Do the regulatory controls for registration tags include:

(1) Prohibition against transfer of registration tags for use with a vehicle other than the one for which originally issued? .

(2) Replacement of lost tags at the registrant's expense?

(3) Return of tags to the provost marshal or security officer when vehicle is no longer authorized entry into installation?

(4) Destruction of invalidated decalcomania?

k. What is nature and scope of registration records maintained by provost marshal or security officer?

l. Do military police and/or gate guards make periodic checks to insure that privately owned vehicles are operated on the premises only by properly licensed persons?

m. Is a definite system used to control the movement of commercial trucks and other goods conveyances into and out of the installation area?

n. Are loading and unloading platforms located outside the manufacturing and/or operating areas and separated therefrom by controlled and guard-supervised entrances?

o. Are all trucks and other conveyances required to enter through service gates manned by guards?

p. If trucks are permitted direct access to manufacturing and/or operating areas, are truck drivers and vehicle contents carefully examined?

q. Does the check at entrances cover both incoming and outgoing vehicles?

r. Are truck registers maintained?

s. Are registers maintained on military vehicles entering and leaving the installation?

t. Are escorts provided when vehicles are permitted access to manufacturing, operating, or restricted areas?

u. Does the supervision of loading and unloading operations insure that unauthorized goods or people do not enter or leave the installation via trucks or other conveyances?

v. Are military trip tickets examined?

w. Is a temporary tag issued to visitors' vehicles?

x. Are automobiles allowed to be parked within manufacturing, operating, or restricted areas?

y. Are parking lots provided?

z. Are interior parking areas located away from sensitive points?

aa. Are interior parking areas fenced so that occupants of automobiles must pass through a pedestrian gate when entering or leaving the working area?

bb. Are frequent spot searches made of automobiles?

cc. Are separate parking areas provided for visitors' vehicles?

dd. What is extent of guard surveillance over interior parking area?

ee. Are there restrictions against employees entering parking areas during duty hours?

ff. Are automobiles allowed to park so close to buildings or structures that they would be a fire threat or obstruct fire fighters?

gg. Are automobiles permitted to be parked close to restricted area fences?

hh. Are parking facilities adequate?

8. Lock Security

a. Has a key control officer been appointed?

b. Are locks and keys to all buildings and entrances supervised and controlled by a key control officer?

c. Does the key control officer have overall authority and responsibility for issuance and replacement of locks and keys?

d. Are keys issued only to authorized personnel?

e. Are keys issued to other than installation personnel?

f. Is the removal of keys from the premises prohibited?

g. Are keys not in use secured in a locked, fireproof cabinet?

h. Are current records maintained indicating:

   (1) Buildings and/or entrances for which keys are issued?

   (2) Number and identification of keys issued?

   (3) Location and number of master keys?

   (4) Location and number of duplicate keys?

   (5) Issue and turn-in of keys?

   (6) Location of locks and keys held in reserve?

i. Is a current key control directive in effect?

j. Are locks changed immediately upon loss or theft of keys?

k. Are inventories and inspections conducted by the key control officer to insure compliance with directives? How often?

l. If master keys are used, are they devoid of marking identifying them as such?

m. Are losses or thefts of keys promptly investigated by the key control personnel?

n. Must all requests for reproduction or duplication of keys be approved by the key control officer?

o. Are locks on inactive gates and storage facilities under seal? Are they checked periodically by guard personnel?
p. Are locks rotated within the installation at least semiannually?
q. Where applicable, is manufacturer's serial number on combination locks obliterated?
r. Are measures in effect to prevent the unauthorized removal of locks on open cabinets, gates, or buildings?

9. Guard Forces
   a. Is a guard force provided?
   b. Is the guard force composed of civil service personnel under military direction, supervision, and control; civilian guards of general services administration (GSA) or other government agencies; civilian employees of contractor; or military personnel assigned to the installation or activity?
   c. If civilian guard force is utilized, indicate authorized and actual strength broken down numerically by positions, i.e. chief, assistant chiefs, captain, lieutenants, sergeants, basic guards, investigators, and administrative personnel.
   d. If a military guard force is utilized, indicate number of officers and enlisted men. Indicate both authorized and actual complement.
   e. Have there been changes since last survey in either the authorized or actual guard force strength?
   f. Is present guard force strength commensurate with degree of security protection required?
   g. Is utilization of guard forces reviewed periodically to ascertain effective and economical use?
   h. Is supervisory responsibility for guard force operations vested in the provost marshal or security officer?
   i. Is a guard headquarters building provided?
   j. Does the guard headquarters building contain control equipment and instruments of all alarm, warning, and guard communications systems?
   k. Are guards familiar with communications equipment used?
   l. Does guard headquarters have direct communication with local municipal fire and police headquarters?
   m. Do members of guard force meet the minimum qualification standards?
   n. Do all members of guard force have clearances equivalent to highest degree of security classification of the documents, materiel, etc., to which access may be required or accidentally gained during their normal duty assignments?

o. Are guards armed while on duty, and if so, with what type of weapon?

p. Are the weapons kept in arms racks and adequately secured when not in use?

q. Are ammunition supplies properly secured and issued only for authorized purposes?

r. Is each member of guard force required to complete a course of basic training and thereafter take periodic courses of in-service or advanced training?

s. Are the subjects included in the various training courses adequate? Does the training cover:

(1) Care and use of weapons?

(2) Common forms of espionage and sabotage activity?

(3) Types of bombs and explosives?

(4) Orientation on the installation, with emphasis of restricted and vulnerable areas?

(5) Location of hazardous materials and processes?

(6) Location and use of fire protective equipment, including spinkler control valves?

(7) Location and operation of all important steam and gas valves and main electrical switches?

(8) Conditions which may cause fire and explosions?

(9) Location and use of first aid equipment?

(10) Duties in the event of fire, explosion, natural disaster, civil disturbance, blackout, or air raid?

(11) Use of communication system?

(12) Proper methods of search?

(13) Observation and description?

(14) Patrol work?

(15) Supervision of visitors?

(16) Preparation of written reports?

(17) General and special guard orders?

(18) Authority to use force, conduct searches, and arrest or apprehend?

t. Are periodic examinations conducted to insure maintenance of guard training standards?

u. Are activities of the guard force in consonance with established policy?

v. Is supervision of the guard force adequate?

w. Are general and special orders properly posted?

x. Are guard orders reviewed at least semiannually to insure applicability?

y. Are periodic inspections and examinations conducted to determine the degree of understanding and compliance with all guard orders?

z. Do physical, functional, or other changes at the installation indicate the necessity for or feasibility of
   (1) establishing additional guard posts?
   (2) discontinuing any existing posts or patrols?

aa. Is two-way radio equipment installed on all guard patrol cars?

bb. Are duties other than those related to security performed by guard personnel?

cc. Are guard patrol cars equipped with spotlights?

dd. Does each guard on patrol duty carry a flashlight?

ee. Do guards record or report their presence at key points in the installation by means of
   (1) portable watch clocks?
   (2) central watch clock stations?
   (3) telephones?
   (4) two-way radio equipment?

ff. Are guard assignments and patrol routes varied at frequent intervals to obviate an established routine?

10. Fire Prevention
   a. Is a fire department authorized at the installation?
   b. If installation is within the corporate limits of a municipality or other governmental subdivision which has an organized fire department, is adequate response by the latter assured?
   c. If installation is adjacent to but not within the corporate limits of a municipality, what is the extent of protection available from municipal or other fire departments? Are contractual arrangements in effect with adjacent municipalities?
   d. What is the estimated time lag between notification and arrival of fire fighting equipment?
   e. If the installation is without an organized fire department, are fire prevention activities performed by technically qualified personnel?
   f. Are fire plans posted in conspicuous location in all areas?
   g. Is a fire alarm system in effect? Is it adequate?
   h. Are personnel familiar with the operation of fire extinguishers?
   i. Are unit personnel fully aware of fire prevention and protection responsibilities?
   j. Are unit personnel fully aware of the inherent fire hazards and their severity?
   k. Are regular fire prevention inspections made to detect fire hazards?
   l. What first aid and fire fighting equipment is available on the instal-

lation? Does it include an adequate amount of strategically located fire pails, sand bags, chemical extinguishers, and pumps?

m. What types of fire extinguishers are available? Do they include carbon dioxide, carbon tetrachloride, and dry chemical types?

n. Are all extinguishers and other equipment frequently tested and inspected so as to be in perfect working order at all times?

o. Are inspections of fire extinguishers made by competent personnel, and are results of inspections carefully noted?

p. Are both first aid and fire fighting painted so as to be conspicuous? Do the personnel on the premises know the locations?

q. What types of fire alarms are installed?

r. Are there sufficient alarm boxes and warning devices in the fire alarm system?

s. Is the alarm system frequently inspected and tested?

t. Has a program of fire drills been inaugurated? If so, how often are they conducted?

u. Are vulnerable or important buildings and structures on the installation equipped with sprinkler systems? Are they fed by public mains, tanks or private reservoir, or pumps?

v. Do the fire fighting personnel know the location of the main control valves of the sprinkler systems?

w. Is the sprinkler system inspected periodically? Are sprinkler heads free of corrosion, paint, or whitewash?

x. Is the effectiveness of the sprinklers reduced due to obstructions, partitions, piles of material, crates or boxes?

y. Are fire hydrants accessible and in working order?

z. Is smoking discipline properly enforced?

aa. Are combustible materials properly stored and safeguarded?

bb. Are fire barriers adequate?

cc. Are fire doors and shutters installed where needed? Are they free of obstructions and in proper working condition?

11. Recommendations for correction of observed deficiencies must be reasonable from the standpoint of cost to the government. Each recommendation must be carefully weighed to insure that the additional security obtained is worth the expense involved. In laying out the long-range security programs involving extensive construction, hiring of additional guards, installation of illumination and other protective devices, as well as specifying immediate remedial actions, primary consideration must be given to dollar value received versus dollar value spent. Whenever possible, maximum use will be made of existing facilities, supplies and equipment by renovation at minimum cost in order to reduce expenditures.

Check List for Industrial Defense Against
Civil Disturbances and Sabotage*

This check list is designed to provide a rapid inventory of the essential elements of your industrial defense plan.

Introduction

( ) Assure orderly and efficient transition from normal to emergency operations.
( ) Delegate emergency authority.
( ) Assign emergency responsibilities.
( ) Indicate authority by company executives for actions contained in plan.
( ) Vulnerability.
( ) Legal limits and liabilities.

Implementing Instructions

( ) Appoint individual(s) to implement plan.
( ) Specify conditions under which plan may be partially implemented.
( ) Specify conditions under which plan may be fully implemented.
( ) Coordinate plan among all responsible individuals to assure sequence of implementation.

Emergency Control Organization

( ) Prepare management succession list of executive and administrative personnel and key employees. Designate alternates.
( ) Assure that management continuity and emergency organization are in accord with state corporate laws and company charter or bylaws.
( ) Pre-publish company orders constituting emergency authority.

Control Center

The control center is the plant command post, the focal point for directing all emergency actions. For decentralized operations, all emergency actions should be coordinated through the central control center.

( ) Is location well protected?
( ) Can access be controlled with minimum manpower?
( ) Select alternate location.
( ) Communications, equipment, administrative supplies.

---

*Reprinted with permission from Industrial Defense Against Civil Disturbances, Bombings, Sabotage. *Check List for Industrial Defense Against Civil Disturbances and Sabotage,* Office of the Provost Marshal General—Department of the Army, pp. 43-47.

Planning Coordination (Mutual Aid)

( ) Coordinate plan with local and state officials—Civil Defense.
( ) With police departments.
( ) With fire departments.
( ) With FBI.
( ) With adjacent plants and business firms.
( ) With local utilities: Power, telephone, transportation.
( ) With employee union officials.
( ) With local news media.

Communications

( ) Adequately cover plant area.
( ) Backup primary system with two-way radios, walkie-talkies, field telephones, or megaphones (bull horns) .
( ) Monitor local and state police radios.
( ) Monitor fire department radios.
( ) Monitor hospital and ambulance radios.
( ) Establish communications with adjacent plants and businesses.
( ) Establish communications with management and key employees.
( ) Train switchboard operators in emergency procedures.
( ) Designate male operators as alternates for females who may not report.
( ) Establish emergency communications procedures.
( ) Unlisted telephone numbers at control center.

Personnel

( ) Survey secondary skills. Match with emergency requirements.
( ) Train personnel in emergency skills required, where necessary.
( ) Shelter areas.

EMERGENCY NOTIFICATION

( ) Keep switchboards open and operators available.
( ) Establish cascade system of notification for recall to work.
( ) Prepare reporting instructions.
( ) Designate reporting points, primaries and alternates out of emergency areas.
( ) Inform employees of locations and procedures.
( ) Instruct employees to report to points if normal routes to plant are closed.
( ) Plan transportation, i.e. busses, trucks, company-owned or contracted.
( ) Coordinate mutual needs with other plants.
( ) Arrange police escort for emergency repair crews.

( ) Pre-select routes from reporting points to plant.
( ) Plan for escort of female personnel; consider car pools.

TRAINING

( ) Primary or secondary emergency skills (relate to survey of secondary skills).
( ) Train for immediate internal or external emergency repairs.

SITUATION BRIEFINGS

( ) Brief employees on potential for civil disorder. Police can help.
( ) Brief employees on emergency plans. (Do this with caution. Do not create a "scare program.")
( ) During disorder, brief employees daily on impact on disorder on plant and community. Must be factual to dispel rumor and speculation.
( ) Prepare employees psychologically to remain on job: Need for loyalty, self-restraint; act only as directed by management or police; report rumors to supervisors.
( ) Plan post-emergency recognition of exemplary performance.
( ) Explain impact of emergency on plant.

EVACUATION

( ) Designate routes to evacuate buildings or plants.
( ) Inform employees of routes and procedures.
( ) Evacuate by departments (if practical).
( ) Designate primary and alternate exits away from emergency area.

Electric Power

( ) Coordinate plan with local power companies: Transmission lines, transformer banks, alternate distribution lines.
( ) Provide emergency power for lighting and other essentials (not for full production).
( ) Generators, size, location, fuel, operators.
( ) Battery-powered equipment, flashlights, lanterns, radios, batteries.

Plant Security

ORGANIZATIONAL PLANS

( ) Develop plant security organization.
( ) Write security plans and procedures.
( ) Report promptly to FBI any actual or suspected acts of sabotage or espionage.
( ) Coordinate with local and state law enforcement agencies.
( ) Have supervisory personnel attend plant protection training.

SECURITY FORCE
(′) Organize force.
( ) Prescribe qualification standards.
( ) Training.
( ) Uniforms.
( ) Arms (weapons). (Check with local officials the authority and legal liability.)
( ) Deputization, if necessary (check with local officials).
( ) Assure security force is on duty at all times.
( ) Issue written orders.
( ) Set up internal communications for exclusive use by security force.
( ) Plan auxiliary security force for emergency: Company employees, contract security.

PERIMETER BARRIERS
( ) Inspect security fence (or other barrier) regularly for proper maintenance.
( ) Post trespass warnings on all barriers.
( ) Park vehicles outside of security fence or wall, to reduce fire potential and minimize hazard of concealed explosive or incendiary devices.
( ) Light perimeter barriers and internal critical areas.
( ) Use screening to protect lighting fixtures against rocks and other objects.
( ) Insure continuous lighting in parking lots and on ground floors.
( ) Install intrusion detection devices.
( ) Install protection for glassed areas exposed to streets, i.e. windows, doors, and roof light windows.

CONTROL OF ENTRY
( ) Develop procedures for positive identification and control of employees.
( ) Give samples of identification media (photograph identification cards or badges) to local police. (Essential for crossing police lines or during curfew.)
( ) Cotnrol movement and parking of vehicles.
( ) Control movement and parking of vehicles.
( ) Procedures for control of visitors.

PROTECTING CRITICAL AREAS
( ) Identify critical areas within plant.
( ) Enclose critical areas with physical barriers.
( ) Designate specific personnel who may have access to critical areas.
( ) Control admittance to critical areas.

( ) Protect unattended critical areas with high security locks or intrusion detection devices. (Rotate locks upon notification of impending emergency.)

( ) Develop a key control system.

( ) Develop package and material control procedures.

( ) Protect gasoline pumps and other dispensers of flammables. (Disconnect power source to electrically operated pumps.)

ARMS CONTROL

( ) Keep arms room locked and under 24-hour surveillance.

( ) Store ammunition in a separate, locked location under 24-hour surveillance.

PERSONNEL SECURITY

( ) Conduct pre-employment investigations of applicants.

( ) Check personnel who are authorized access to critical areas.

( ) Brief employees on importance of plant security and vigilance.

Fire Prevention

( ) Post and enforce fire prevention regulations.

( ) Extend fire alarm system to all areas of facilities.

( ) Determine when fire department can arrive. Under conditions other than civil disorders; five minutes after report of fire? Ten minutes?

( ) Provide secondary water supply for fire protection.

( ) Install fire protection equipment on-site. Maintain properly.

( ) Install mesh wire or screening material to protect roofs of buildings immediately adjacent to the perimeter from fire bombs, molotov cocktails, or other incendiary devices, if feasible (check with local fire department).

( ) Organize employees into fire fighting brigades and rescue squads.

( ) Store combustible materials in well protected areas.

( ) Instruct employees in the use of fire extinguishers.

( ) Post signs showing location of fire hose connections.

( ) Insure that fire hose connections are compatible with local fire department equipment.

( ) Conduct fire drills periodically.

( ) Maintain good housekeeping standards.

( ) Implement recommendations in latest fire insurance inspection report.

( ) Fire department check and assist in hardening against arson.

Protect Vital Records

( ) Classify and protect vital corporate records, cash and other valuable items.

Property and Liability Insurance

( ) Review property and liability insurance against loss or obligation resulting from riots and/or other destructive acts.

Emergency Supplies

( ) Photographic equipment.

( ) Pre-stock food, water and medical supplies because conditions may not permit procurement during emergency.

( ) Designate separate sleeping quarters for male and female employees.

( ) Provide sanitation facilities.

( ) Stock administrative supplies.

( ) Stock emergency repair tools, equipment and parts.

( ) Develop procedures for employees to purchase gasoline for automobiles from plant supply in case local stations are closed.

( ) Maintain sufficient inventory of empty 55 gallon drums to be filled with water or sand for use as barricades at entrances.

( ) Have on hand enough barbed wire to form a barrier directly in front of each row of 55 gallon drums. Concertina-type wire is very effective.

( ) Maintain supply of panels or screen mesh to protect windows on ground floors.

Test the Plan

( ) Test individual parts of the plan.

( ) Test the entire plan.

( ) Test without prior announcement.

( ) Note weaknesses. Revise plan to include corrective actions.

Physical Security Inspection Checklists*

1. Unit Storage Facilities for Small Arms and Small Arms Ammunition.
2. Narcotics and Controlled Drugs.
3. Finance and Accounting Office.
4. U.S. Army Museums.
5. Quartermaster Cash Sales Store.
6. Post Exchange Activities.
7. Commissaries.
8. Open Mess Activities.
9. Warehouse Activities.

---

*Reprinted with permission from *Physical Security*, Department of the Army, FM 19-30, 1971, pp. H-1—H-28.

10. Motor Pools
11. Unit Mailrooms.
12. General.

The 12 checklists contained in this appendix are intended for use only as *guides* for physical security inspection personnel. Their most important function is to act as reminders to inspection personnel as to what to look for in each of the situations they include.

These checklists must not be viewed as entirely complete or as all-encompassing. In individual situations, there will be items of physical security interest and importance which are not included on any of the checklists. Inspection personnel must be alert for such items, and not be content merely to check off the items on the checklist.

There will also be certain facilities or installations to which none of the checklists specifically applies. In such cases, the inspection personnel should formulate their own checklists, utilizing any of the items on the attached lists as basic guidance and adding any items peculiar to the particular facility or installation.

There will also be situations in which more than one of the attached checklists will be useful. This may occur where more than one of the activities covered by the checklists is housed in a single building. Also, Checklist 12, the general checklist, will be applicable in many situations, in addition to one or more of the others.

No specific sources of reference are provided for the individual items on these checklists. Such specific references rapidly become outdated as Army Regulations, Field Manuals, and other publications are revised and republished. Further, many such references are supplemented by command publications which impose changed or additional requirements and can, where necessary, cite the sources applicable to each item. These sources may, if desired, be adapted to the locally produced checklists for convenience and ready reference.

These checklists may also, if locally desired, be adapted to the style of a locally produced form, with appropriate heading and general information spaces and columnar headings with boxes for "yes," "no," and similar checks. DA Form 2806 will serve as a basic example of such a form.

Unit Storage Facilities for Small Arms and Small Arms Ammunition

1. Arms Storage Building (Location, Floor, and Roof).
    a. Is the building used to store only small arms and not for any unrelated activity?
    b. Are the walls constructed of masonry or similar type material?
    c. Is the floor constructed of concrete?

    d. Is the roof of composition construction or a similar material that will provide an equal degree of security?

    e. Is the building posted as a restricted area?

2. Arms Storage Building (Doors and Windows).

    a. Is the number of doors limited to an essential minimum?

    b. Are all doors constructed of materials that will render access by force extremely difficult?

    c. Are large access (cargo-type) and pedestrian-type doors secured by a minimum of two locks?

    d. Are large access (cargo-type) and pedestrian-type door frames fastened in a manner that will prevent the door frame from being separated from the casing?

    e. Are all door-hinge pins spot welded or bradded to prevent removal?

    f. Are all door hinges installed so that it would be impossible to remove the closed doors without seriously damaging the door or jamb?

    g. In newly constructed facilities, are the door-hinge pins concealed or located on the inward side of the door?

    h. Is the number of windows limited to the essential minimum?

    i. Are the windows protected with steel mesh or iron bars?

    j. Is the steel mesh or bars welded or secured to a steel channel frame and fastened to the building by smooth-headed bolts or cemented into the structure?

    k. If the structural requirements for windows or small pedestrian-type doors have not been met, are intrusion-detection devices used in lieu of those requirements?

3. Building Containing an Arms Storage Room (Doors and Windows).

    a. Are exterior doors locked whenever the building ⌐ closed to normal duty traffic?

    b. Have procedures been established to insure that all doors are locked at the close of the business day?

    c. Are locking devices on exterior doors built into, and an integral part of the door?

    d. Are all exterior windows, providing unobserved access to the interior of the structure, locked?

    e. Have internal control procedures been established to insure that all windows are locked at the close of the business day?

4. Arms Storage Room Other Than Prefabricated Cages (Location, Walls, Floor, and Ceiling).

    a. Is the room posted as a restricted area?

    b. Do the walls extend from the floor to the ceiling?

    c. Are the walls of solid masonry construction or a material that will provide a similar degree of security?

    d. Is the floor constructed of solid masonry or a material that will provide a similar degree of security?

    e. Is the ceiling of solid masonry construction or a material that will provide a similar degree of security?

    f. In temporary buildings, are the exterior walls of the arms room of double wooden-wall thickness?

    g. In temporary buildings, are interior walls, ceiling, and floor constructed to insure that at least one side of the surface is 1-inch doublenailed tongue-and-groove wood sheathing or a material that will provide a similar degree of security?

    h. If the arms room is located in a facility other than troop billets, is the building locked during off-duty hours and illuminated by protective lighting?

    i. If the structural requirements for the walls, floor, or ceiling have not been met, are intrusion-detection devices used in lieu of those requirements?

5. Arms Storage Room Other Than Prefabricated Cages (Doors, Windows, and Locks) .

    a. Is the number of doors limited to the essential minimum?

    b. Is the outer door constructed of steel bars, welded to a grid with openings that do not exceed 32 square inches, or of solid wood covered on the outside with steel plates of at least 1 millimeter in thickness?

    c. Is the inner door constructed of solid wood?

    d. Are the door hinges installed so that it will be impossible to remove the closed doors without seriously damaging the door or jamb?

    e. Are all hinge pins spot welded or bradded?

    f. Are all doors locked with an approved pin-tumbler-type padlock?

    g. Is there at least one lock on each door?

    h. In newly constructed facilities, are the door-hinge pins concealed or located on the inward side of the door?

    i. Is the number of windows limited to the essential minimum?

    j. Are the windows protected with steel mesh or iron bars?

    k. Is the steel mesh or bars welded or fastened to a steel channel frame and fastened to the building by smooth-headed bolts or cemented into the structure?

    l. If the structural requirements for doors or windows have not been met, are intrusion-detection devices used in lieu of those requirements?

6. Arms Storage Room (prefabricated).
   a. If a wire-mesh cage is used for storage of small arms, is it constructed in conformance with OCE Standard Drawing 40–01–41?
   b. Is the cage posted as a restricted area?
   c. If the cage is located in a facility other than troop billets, is the building locked during off-duty hours and illuminated by protective lighting?
   d. Is the door locked with an approved pin-tumbler-type padlock?

7. Arms Rack.
   a. Are the arms racks fastened together or to the structure, and do they have adequate locking devices?
   b. Are locally fabricated arms racks constructed to insure that weapons cannot be removed from the locked rack by partially disassembling them?
   c. Are racks locked except during short periods when weapons are being removed or replaced?
   d. Are the hinge pins of the racks welded or bradded?
   e. If the racks were locally fabricated, were they built into the structure as a permanent part of the arms storage room?
   f. If lockers are being used as a substitute for racks, are they fastened to the structure?
   g. Are the lockers equipped with adequate locking devices?
   h. Are the hasps of the lockers installed so that they cannot be removed?
   i. Are the hinges of the lockers installed so that they cannot be removed?
   j. Are hinge pins of the lockers welded or bradded?

8. Key and Lock Control.
   a. Are keys to arms rooms, arms racks, and guard ammunition containers kept together in sets?
   b. Is the number of sets of keys to an essential minimum?
      (1) Arms storage room? (How many sets?)
      (2) Ammunition storage room? (How many sets?)
   c. After duty hours, are the keys stored in a locked receptacle in a place other than the storage room or in the custody of the responsible officer of the day, duty officer, duty NCO, or charge of quarters?
      (1) Arms storage room?
      (2) Ammunition storage room?
   d. Is custody of the arms room keys transferred to the relief guard only after both parties have conducted a visual inventory of

weapons, to include a total count of weapons and guard ammunition on hand?

e. Are weapons that are stored in banded crates or boxes counted as crates and boxes and not removed from the containers?

f. Is there a system of key control in effect that insures continuous custody and ready identification of the individual having possession of the keys at any given time?

   (1) Arms room?

   (2) Ammunition storage room?

g. Do the arms room and racks provide triple-lock protection?

h. Is a written record made of all key transactions?

i. Are locks replaced when keys are lost or there is a possibility of compromise?

j. Are padlocks protected against loss or compromise when not in use?

9. Guard Protection. Is the arms or ammunition storage facility checked periodically by a security or guard patrol?

10. Control of Small Arms and Ammunition.

a. Are serial numbers of all weapons assigned to the unit recorded in unit and/or station property books?

b. Is a record maintained of the serial numbers of weapons issued to individuals?

c. Are individuals who are in possession of weapons or ammunition warned of their responsibility and the inherent dangers involved in the loss of weapons and ammunition?

d. Are individuals issued weapons cards?

e. Is the weapons card turned in the arms room when the weapon is drawn?

f. Do individuals sign a weapons receipt register when weapons are removed from the arms room?

g. Have written procedures been established for issuing weapons and ammunition during emergencies or field exercises, or at other times when operational necessity dictates a need for this equipment to be issued quickly?

   (1) Weapons?

   (2) Ammunition?

h. Is an inventory, by serial number, of all unit small arms conducted by an officer at least once each month?

i. Is an inventory of ammunition, to include a physical count of all loose ammunition, conducted by an officer at least once each month?

j. Does the monthly inventory of ammunition include an inspection and count of crated ammunition to insure that bands and seals are intact?

k. Is a written record made of all weapons and ammunition trans-actions?

l. Is a written record kept of all inventories conducted?

m. How many weapons, if any, have been lost or stolen within the past 12 months?

n. How many lost or stolen weapons, if any, have been recovered during the past 12 months?

o. How many weapons, if any, have been the subject of a report of survey during the past 12 months?

p. If a loss, theft, or recovery of weapons or ammunition has oc-curred, were the local military police and higher headquarters, to include the PMG and CONARC PMO, notified promptly?

11. Ammunition Storage Facility.

a. Does the basic load ammunition storage room meet the same construction requirements as established for small-arms storage rooms?

b. Are pin-tumbler locks used for the door-locking device?

c. Is a railway car seal affixed through the locking device and stapled to protect against surreptitious entry?

d. Has a stringent system for accountability of seals been estab-lished and is a record being maintained?

e. Is the distance between fixed above-ground gasoline storage fa-cilities and the nearest ammunition storage or handling area at least 450 feet?

f. Are ammunition storage rooms free of other materials or supplies?

g. When more than one unit uses the same ammunition storage facility, are stocks separated and identified by unit?

h. When more than one unit uses a facility, is only one unit res-ponsible for the security of the storage facility?

i. Are ammunition storage areas posted as restricted areas?

j. Are fire-control measures and symbols posted?

k. Do ammunition storage facilities located outside of billeting areas have the same protective lighting and guard coverage as required for small-arms facilities?

l. Are the quantities of guard ammunition that are retained in arms rooms locked in separate containers and inventoried daily?

12. Exceptions. For each facility indicated below that does not meet prescribed standards, has a continual, visual surveillance program

of the area been established pending completion of the required modification?

    a. Arms storage building?

    b. Building that contains an arms storage room?

    c. Arms storage room?

    d. Ammunition storage room/area?

13. Privately-Owned Weapons.

    a. How many privately owned weapons, if any, are stored in the arms room?

    b. If privately owned weapons are stored in the arms room, are procedures adequate as to—

        (1) Control?

        (2) Protection?

        (3) Accountability?

Narcotics and Controlled Drugs

1. Does the location of the room/area afford adequate protection?
2. Is the room/building that houses the narcotics of permanent construction?
3. Are bulk narcotics/controlled drugs stored in a vault or similar protective storage?
4. Is there an authorized narcotics cabinet/chest (hospital ward) ?
5. Is the vault/safe/cabinet kept securely locked when not in use?
6. Are responsible personnel in close vicinity to assure protection?
7. If narcotics are stored in a small moveable safe or the like, is the safe adequately secured to a permanent part of the storage room or building?
8. Are procedures established to insure strict accountability and control of narcotics and controlled drugs?
9. Is a narcotic and controlled drug register maintained?
10. Does it contain narcotic and controlled drug inventory?
11. Does it contain a narcotic and controlled drug record?
12. Is the register maintained properly?
13. Is a separate record prepared for each drug or alcoholic content?
14. Is a joint inventory taken by the responsible person going off duty and the person coming on duty?
15. Is the balance on hand recorded in the appropriate column by both responsible persons?
16. Is the register secured and available only to authorized personnel?
17. Is the box heading of each record completed in its entirety, i.e. ward number, date correct name of the drug, accountable unit of measure, and balance on hand?

18. When a drug is dispensed, is the complete information recorded as to disposition, i.e. day, hour, patient's name, initial and last name of doctor who ordered the medication, etc.?

19. When a unit of a narcotic or controlled drug is accidently destroyed, damaged or contaminated is a record of the fact entered on the record?

20. When accountable drugs are issued to a ward, are entries made by the pharmacy representative on the appropriate form, i.e. the day, hour, amount of drugs, and new balance?

21. Are corrections of errors in the drug register in accord with current regulations?

22. Are monthly inventories and verification of records conducted by a disinterested officer?

23. Have there been any reports of a loss, theft, or unaccounted for drugs within the past 12 months?

24. Is an intrusion detection device/system installed?

Finance and Accounting Office

1. Is the Finance Office adequately guarded?

2. Have adequate precautions been taken to prevent unauthorized entrance after duty hours?

3. Have security measures been coordinated with Military Police and/ or other security forces?

4. Is the Finance Office equipped with adequate facilities for the storing and safeguarding of public funds and documents?

5. Do the safeguards employed during normal operations preclude loss, substitution, or pilferage of public funds and documents?

6. Are vaults or safes accessible at any time to unauthorized persons?

7. Are unauthorized persons excluded from the working areas of the office by means of a railing or counter?

8. Are money exchanging windows situated so as to prevent unauthorized access to funds? (If not, explain on separate sheet.)

9. Is cash in excess of current disbursing needs promptly deposited to the credit of the Treasurer of the United States?

10. Are internal office procedures established to provide controls on all undelivered and returned checks?

11. Is there a central point for their receipt, holding, and final disposition, with responsibility therefor charged to a specific individual?

12. Is the cashier provided with a separate working space or properly inclosed cage or room with a window for paying and receiving?

13. Is a cash drawer with key lock, or a field or similar safe, provided

for safeguarding funds and vouchers during temporary absence of the clerks?

14. If more than one person in the office has cash in his possession, is each person provided with a separate and secure receptacle for such monies?

15. Are receipts taken for all funds entrusted to the cashier and receipts given the cashier for all funds returned or valid vouchers accepted?

16. Is there a procedure for unannounced verfication of cash on hand?

17. Do current records indicate that such verfications are being made on an unannounced basis at least once each quarter?

18. Is a detailed record maintained of daily settlement of cash transaction between disbursing officer and cashier(s) or deputy and cashier(s) ?

19. Is positive identification of the payee made prior to any cash payments?

20. Is the cashier furnished with a list of personnel in an AWOL status, acting as impostors, or reported as receiving several casual payments?

21. Is the cashier furnished with a current list of lost or stolen financial data records folders (FDRF) ?

22. Is the cash in possession of the cashier verified daily by the Finance Officer or his deputy?

23. Is the amount of cash entrusted to a cashier always kept within the limits of his bond or otherwise within the intent of AR 37–103?

24. Has authority to keep cash on hand in a specific amount been approved by the major command?

25. Are blank checks, when not in use, kept under lock and key in the safe of the Finance and Accounting Officer or his deputy?*

26. Upon receipt of shipment of blank checks, are the cartons examined and the serial numbers checked?

27. Does the Finance and Accounting Officer or his deputy inspect the blank checks in current use at the beginning and end of each day's business to see that no blank checks have been extracted?*

28. Are cartons bearing evidence of tampering opened and checks counted individually?*

29. Does the Finance and Accounting Officer or his deputy maintain a daily record of the number of checks released, written, and returned for safekeeping?*

30. Are spoiled and voided checks properly safeguarded?*

31. When checks are voided or spoiled, are they properly marked and reported?*

---

*These questions also pertain to savings bonds.

32. Is the mailing and/or delivery of checks properly controlled to prevent loss?*
33. Is the cashier furnished with a weapon?
34. If so, is he qualified in the use of it? (Applies to TOE Division, Finance Sections.)
35. Are Class A agents furnished instruction as to their duties and responsibilities?
36. Do Class A agents account for funds promptly?
37. Do cashiers receipt for cash received for each day's business?
38. What personnel are authorized access to keys to the Finance Office?
39. Are keys to the locking devices of the meter and protection unit of check signing machines kept in the custody of the Finance and Accounting Officer or his deputy at all times?
40. Are there keys or combinations to the cashier's safe and cash drawer in the hands of any person other than the cashier?
41. Are locks replaced when keys are lost or stolen?
42. Has the cashier sealed one key and/or the combination to the safe in an envelope suitably marked so that its unauthorized opening may be detected?
43. Is this envelope in the safe of the Finance and Accounting Officer?
44. Is the combination to the Finance and Accounting Officer's vault or safe known only by such officer and his deputy?
45. Is a copy of such combination, sealed in an envelope, suitably marked so that its unauthorized opening may be detected, delivered to the installation commander for use in the event of an emergency?
46. Are procedures established to provide two disinterested persons to witness the opening, of either the cashier's or Finance and Accounting Officer's safe when those responsible persons are not present?
47. Is there a requirement that the witnesses execute an affidavit as to the contents of the safe at the time of opening?
48. When vaults or safes are opened, is the dial shielded so that the operation of the combination cannot be observed by others?
49. Are the combinations of vaults and safes changed at least every six months?
50. Are safe combinations changed when newly appointed Finance Officers, Deputies, or Cashiers open or take over an account?
51. Is there a guard post established at, in or near, the Finance Office?
52. If no such guard is furnished, is one required?
53. Do Military Police patrols check the Finance Office during the normal course of their duties?
54. If a guard is provided:
    a. Are his orders adequate?

    b. Is he fully familiar with his orders?

    c. Is he provided with a means of communication with Military Police Headquarters?

    d. Describe his duties.

55. Is there a plan establishing security requirements for funds in transit?

56. Was the plan coordinated with the installation Provost Marshal?

57. Does the plan provide for Military Police or other escort personnel?

58. Does the plan prescribe armament, communications, transportation, and equipment for escort personnel?

59. Does the plan provide for utilizing various routes to and from Finance Offices and Depositories?

60. How is route information safeguarded?

61. Is the plan adequate?

62. Is an intrusion detection device/system installed?

U.S. Army Museums

1. Are entrance doors locked with a pin tumbler dead bolt lock or by push button combination type lock fastened (not mortised) on the inside of the door?

2. Are doors containing glass or light wood panels protected by a #8 wire mesh screen with metal frame, secured to the inside of the door with $\frac{1}{4}$-inch carriage bolts?

3. Are doors containing glass or light wood panels lined on the inside with #18 gauge sheet iron, bolted on with $\frac{1}{4}$-inch carriage bolts?

4. Are double doors equipped on the inside, at the top and bottom of one of the two doors, with 5/8-inch slide bolts fitting into substantial iron sockets in the stationary framework of the door?

5. Are door hinges bolted on or fastened with lag screws wherever possible?

6. Are locks, except padlocks, affixed to the door with twist-off or one-way screws?

7. Are windows within 14 feet of the ground equipped with protective ironwork?

8. Are double hung windows protected by installing sash pins on the inside of the two upper corners of the lower sash in such a way that the pins penetrate the corresponding lower corners of the upper sash when the window is closed?

9. Are vents and similar openings having a gross area of 1 square foot or more secured by protective ironwork (unless one dimension is less than 6 inches) ?

10. Is the exterior of the building illuminated during hours of darkness?
11. Is switch for exterior lights located inside museum?
12. Is the custodian appointed by competent authority to control, issue and maintain records of all keys and combinations?
13. Are keys and combinations accessible only to personnel whose official duties require access?
14. Are keys stored in a secure locked container when not in use?
15. Are all keys inventoried at the opening and closing of the facility each day and a record thereof maintained?
16. Are locks changed or rotated immediately upon reassignment, resignation, discharge or suspension of an employee having possession of keys or combinations, or upon loss of a key or keys?
17. Does the facility have an intrusion alarm system?
18. Is the system connected to the Military Police-Security Office?
19. Is maintenance performed by Government or private concern?
20. Is secondary power source provided for the intrusion system?
21. Are small pilferable items protected in such a manner as to preclude loss or theft?
22. Are viewing surfaces of display cases constructed of at least $\frac{1}{4}$-inch plate glass?
23. Is plate glass securely fastened into frames or to the display case?
24. Are hinge butts concealed on display cases?
25. Are display cases secured with a substantial locking device?
26. Are display cases housing items of high intrinsic value equipped with an intrusion detection device?
27. Are alarm controls under the continuous supervision of the museum curator or the security force?
28. Are alarms tested before being put into operation for nonduty hours?
29. Are sidearms, rifles and small caliber crew-served weapons securely fastened to the walls or floors of the museum?
30. Are fireable weapons not secured in display cases, or by other locking devices, modified to make them inoperable?
31. Are work shops and storage areas containing historical items given the same degree of security as the museum?
32. Are security personnel specifically assigned to the museum during hours of operation?
33. Does the curator assign at least one person to act as a guard when the museum is open to the public?
34. Is the museum checked frequently by a security patrol?
35. Are museum patrol checks on an unscheduled basis?

36. Are losses or thefts of weapons reported in accordance with AR 190–11?
37. Are individuals with questionable traits employed by, or assigned to, the museum?
38. Is there a museum park; is it enclosed by an appropriate fence?
39. Is the museum park checked frequently, and on an unscheduled basis, by the security patrol?
40. Are easily moved items in museum parks anchored in place?
41. Are museum items in other exterior displays secured in place?

Quartermaster Cash Sales Store

1. Are individuals purchasing, or receiving issues of clothing and equipage, required to establish identity as an authorized purchaser?
2. Is the exchange of a clothing item for a like item of a different size permitted only within 15 days of the date of sale?
3. Are items sold to and worn by an individual exchanged for a like item because of improper fit, regardless of date of sale?
4. Are purchases made only in cash, personal check, certified check, traveler's check, or money order made payable to the Treasurer of the United States?
5. When a cash register is used, are all sales registered at the time of sale?
6. Are cash refunds given for returned merchandise?
7. Is the accounting for sales and issues in accordance with AR 710–2?
8. Are all areas of the store able to be seen by the operating personnel?
9. Is the manager of store supervisor appointed by orders?
10. Are clothing sales store cashiers appointed by formal orders?
11. Is DD Form 707 being used when depositing cash?
12. Are charge sales recorded on DA Form 3078?
13. Is DA Form 518 used for mail order purchases?

Post Exchange Activities

1. Does the manager of each activity, at the end of each business day, inspect the premises to insure that all windows, doors, safes, etc. have been closed and that no person is hidden in restrooms or elsewhere? Is an intrusion detection device/system installed?
2. Are service entrances locked from the inside when not in use for authorized movements of materials?
3. Is a strong light kept burning over the safe during nonoperational periods?
4. Is this light visible from the outside? Explain.

5. Are patrons positively identified prior to the consummation of any purchase?

6. Does any portion of the arrangement of the activity lend itself to pilferage or shoplifting? Explain.

7. Are authorized personnel available to observe patrons as a deterrent to shoplifting? Explain.

8. Are all personnel concerned familiar with procedures in handling shoplifters?

9. Is there a tally-in or tally-out system, as appropriate, for checking supplies received or shipped against shipping documents?

10. Are there any shortages in high value items such as cameras, watches, jewelry, etc.?

11. What action is taken when high value, identifiable items are missing?

12. Do sales slips indicate serial numbers of items normally possessing same?

13. If not, is such recording practical?

14. Are critical or sensitive items such as watches, cameras, etc. stored in separate secured storage in stockrooms or other areas? Describe storage of such items.

15. Are any items of comparatively high value and sensitivity displayed in such a manner that they could be readily stolen with little chance · of discovery? Describe.

16. Are issues of sensitive items to sales clerks for display and subsequent sale documented in any manner? Describe.

17. Are service doors under the security of responsible exchange employees when opened?

18. Are unauthorized personnel permitted to enter the exchange store-rooms or the kitchen serving area of an exchange food activity?

19. When it is necessary for employees of vendors, or maintenance personnel, or other individuals not directly connected with the exchange activity to enter stock or store rooms, are they always accompanied by an exchange employee?

20. Are garbage and trash inspected before removal to assure that this garbage or trash is not being used as a means of removing merchandise or material without authorization?

21. Are employees required to check all personal packages or parcels with the manager?

22. Are employees required to check with the manager prior to leaving the premises of the store?

23. Are periodic shakedown inspections conducted of employees, their

parcels and/or personal possessions prior to their departure from the premises?

24. Are female employees permitted to take their purses into the aisles of the activity?
25. Are employees required to enter and/or depart the activity through one door under the supervision of office personnel?
26. Are employees permitted to ring up their own purchases?
27. Are all sales recorded on cash registers?
28. If not, how are such sales controlled?
29. Are excessive quantities of money removed from cash registers during daily operations?
30. Are such funds immediately turned in to the cashier or branch manager?
31. Are amounts rung up on cash registers observable by the customer?
32. Are surprise counts of cash conducted?
33. Are all cash register drawers equipped with operative locks and keys?
34. Are cash register drawers kept locked when unattended?
35. Are change funds from each cash register bagged and turned in to the branch manager at the close of each business day?
36. Are personnel desiring to cash checks, money orders, or traveler's checks required to produce identification prior to cashing such instruments?
37. Are post dated checks accepted?
38. Are cashiers' cages, booths, and/or other inclosures inclosed and provided with locking devices to prevent access by persons other than the designated cashier?
39. If not, is it practicable to provide such inclosures. Explain.
40. If the activity safe(s) do not exceed 1000 pounds in weight, are they secured to the premises by being imbedded in heavy concrete bed, or steel strapped or bolted to the floor beam?
41. Can the safe be seen from the outside of the building?
42. Is such positioning of the safe possible?
43. Has the combination(s) to the safe(s) been changed when employees having access retire or are reassigned?
44. Is adequate control maintained over items taken into fitting room?
45. Are weapons/ammunition secured in compliance with regulations?
46. If so, is the control limited to the manager and assistant manager only?
47. Are frequent inventories conducted of these items? How frequently?
48. Are excessive inventory shortages promptly investigated?

49. Are armed guards provided for transfer of large sums of money to and from the activity?
50. Has the Exchange Officer developed formal training programs designed to cope with shoplifters?
51. Are employees assigned lockers or provided other containers to secure their personal property?
52. Is a list of personnel known to cash fraudulent checks available to the check cashier?
53. Are controls adequate to assure that any proceeds from old tires, batteries, used oil, etc. left by customer buying new items revert to the exchange and not to employees?
54. Are cash funds restricted to the minimum consistent with needs?
55. Are petty cash funds maintained?
56. Does the custodian count and balance the fund nightly?
57. Are signed receipts exchanged?
58. Is co-mingling of funds between salesclerks permitted?
59. Are daily cash turn-ins counted in the presence of the salesclerk?
60. Is adequate protection afforded the courier making bank deposits or change runs?
61. Is use of exchange vehicles and equipment restricted to official AAFES business? Explain.
62. When exchange vehicles are not in official use, are they parked at designated locations and properly secured?

Commissaries

1. Is door construction adequate from a security standpoint?
2. Are all first floor openings, other than doors, in excess of 96 square inches barred, grilled, or covered with chain link material?
3. If openings are not secured as such, is such securing required? (If negative, explain.)
4. Is there a crawlway beneath the building?
5. Does it provide a means of gaining unauthorized access to the building?
6. Are heating ducts so arranged that they provide an avenue for unauthorized access to the building?
7. Is the service entrance to the commissary secured so that it can be opened only from the inside?
8. Is the service door(s) kept locked at all times except during loading or unloading operation?
9. Are door hinge pins either of the lock-pin variety or welded to prevent their removal?

10. Are padlock hasps, if any, installed in such a manner as to prevent their removal?

11. Are only authorized patrons or their agents admitted to the commissary store proper?

12. Is each individual who seeks to make a purchase from the commissary store positively identified as an authorized patron or agent prior to the consummation of the sale?

13. Does the arrangement of the store lend itself to maximum observation of attempted pilferage or shoplifting?

14. Are authorized personnel available to observe patrons as a deterrent to shoplifting? (Explain on separate sheet.)

15. Is there a tally-in or tally-out system for checking supplies received or shipped against shipping documents?

16. Is the system effective?

17. Is is implemented by authorized personnel?

18. Is the system periodically checked by the commissary officer or his assistant?

19. Do inventory records indicate shortages in excess of allowable percentages?

20. Are shortages confined primarily to certain items? (If so, specify on separate sheet.)

21. If shortages are confined primarily to certain items, has corrective action been taken?

22. Is destruction of meat supplies considered unfit for human consumption witnessed by property disposal officer?

23. Were such supplies inspected by a veterinary officer prior to turn in?

24. Are reports of survey initiated when it has been determined that meat is unfit for human consumption through fault or neglect of the commissary officer?

25. Are fat trimmings that are not sold to authorized patrons, or issued to organizations subsisted on field rations, reported to the installation property disposal officer?

26. Are such trimmings turned in to the installation property disposal officer?

27. Does the amount of cash in the change fund for each cash register exceed $300.00?

28. Does each cashier receipt for such change funds?

29. Are cash register tapes and cash receipts reconciled and verified by an authorized representative of the commissary officer at the end of each business day?

30. Are checks cashed for amounts greater than the sums due with the difference returned in cash?

31. Are deposits of monies made at the close of each day's business, or as soon thereafter as practicable, whenever the cash on hand, exclusive of the change fund, exceeds $200.00?

32. Is cash retained in the commissary office overnight or during weekend or holiday periods? (If so, explain on separate sheet the method in which such funds are safeguarded.)

33. Is the security of funds held overnight, etc., considered consistent with the sum of cash held during these periods?

34. Is there any record of overages in cash receipts?

35. Are such overages, if any, turned in to the Treasurer of the United States? (Note: Check records to verify such transfer of funds.)

36. Are persons responsible for monies properly bonded?

37. Are locks and keys to all buildings and entrances under the control of the commissary officer?

38. Are keys issued to only those personnel authorized access by the commissary officer?

39. Do persons other than the commissary officer or his authorized assistant possess keys to the main entrance?

40. Are all keys to entrances or exits turned in and placed in a key locker or other secured container at the close of each business day?

41. Are locks changed immediately upon loss or theft of keys?

42. Is a record kept of the location of keys to all locks in use?

43. If master keys exist, is access to such keys restricted to the commissary officer and his assistant only?

44. Are master keys kept in a secure place when not in use?

45. If combination locks are used, has the manufacturer's serial number been obliterated?

46. Are measures in effect to prevent the unauthorized removal of opened padlocks from doors, buildings, or storage rooms?

47. Are safe combinations restricted to the minimum number of personnel necessary?

48. Is an intrusion detection device/system installed?

Open Mess Activities

1. Attach roster of mess officials to include Board of Governors.

2. Has a written "Standing Operating Procedure" (SOP), approved by the Board of Governors, been prepared?

3. Does the SOP describe each and every function of the operation of the Mess?

4. Does the SOP describe the duties of the Board of Governors, mess officials, and each employee?

5. Are mess officials and employees familiar with those parts of the SOP that pertain to them?
6. Does the Board of Governors meet at least monthly?
7. Are the proceedings of the Board of Governors meetings recorded?
8. Are the minutes of the Board of Governors meetings, signed by the President and Secretary, submitted together with financial statements and inventories to the installation commander?
9. Is a copy of the monthly financial statement displayed conspicuously on the open mess bulletin board for the preceding month?
10. Were mess funds audited in accordance with AR 36–5 and AR 36–75? (Must be audited not less frequently than annually as prescribed by AR 230–60.)
11. Are consumable supplies inventoried at least monthly by employees under the direct supervision of the secretary?
12. Are quarterly inventories of consumable supplies and a semiannual inventory of furnishings, equipment, and other property made by disinterested officers and/or noncommissioned officers appointed by the installation commander?
13. Was a physical security inspection conducted last year?
14. Has the mess entered into any type of concession agreement?
15. Is a pre-employment screening conducted on job applicants?
16. Have any losses or other type of incidents been reported during the past 12 months in connection with the operation of this open mess?
17. Are mess funds safeguarded as prescribed by AR 230–8?
18. Are employees bonded?
19. Are all alleged losses, damage or destruction of open mess funds or property investigated by a Board of Officers or an Investigating Officer?
20. Is there a guard post around the open mess? (Attach copy of Guards Special Orders.)
21. Is the open mess visited by Military Police or guard patrols? (Attach copy of Patrol Special Orders.)
22. Is there a posted fire plan for the open mess?
23. Is fire fighting equipment available at the open mess?
24. Is all cash counted before it is secured for the night?
25. Has a post central night depository been established?
26. Is it used?
27. Is the cash counted and signed for each time the responsibility for it is transferred?
28. Is a record maintained on the visits of outside workmen such as utility repairmen?

29. Are outsiders working in the mess, such as utility repairmen, plumbers, electricians, etc. kept under observation while working?
30. Are friends and relatives allowed to visit employees at work?
31. Are garbage and trash inspected before removal to assure that it is not being used as a means of removing merchandise or material without authorization?
32. Are employees required to check with the manager or steward prior to leaving the premises?
33. Are employees required to check all personal packages or parcels with the manager?
34. Are periodic shakedown inspections conducted of employees, their parcels and/or personal possessions prior to their departure from the premises.
35. Are employees required to enter and/or depart the activity through one door under the supervision of responsible personnel?
36. Has one employee been designated storekeeper with duties of receiving, storing, maintaining and issuing of all supplies?
37. Are stock records maintained on all supplies?
38. Are all supplies issued from the storeroom on some type of issue slip?
39. Are all employees, except the storekeeper, kept out of the storerooms at all times?
40. Are all sales slips numbered and accounted for?
41. Are frequent unannounced cash inventories made against sales receipts?
42. Are portable safes secured to the wall or floor of the building?
43. If beef is purchased in bulk and cut into roasts and steaks, are the roasts and steaks inventoried and entered on stock record cards?
44. Is cash over authorized limits retained at the mess overnight and over weekends?
45. Is one employee designated to make a security check of the open mess at closing time?
46. Is a light source directly over the safe?
47. Is the safe positioned so as to be visible to Military Police/Security Patrols?

Warehouse Activities

1. Is there a specific procedure in effect that assures strict accountability of all property? (On separate sheet, show value of last inventory.)
2. Are the records of this activity subjected to periodic audits?
3. Are sufficient and comprehensive physical inventories conducted?
4. Are inventories conducted by disinterested activity personnel?

5. Is fixed and real property accounted for?
6. Are stock record or bin cards maintained?
7. Are stock levels on these cards verifiable through records of incoming stock?
8. Are issues recorded on these cards indexed to specific requisitions? (Voucher No's.)
9. Are investories recorded on these cards?
10. Is there excessive use of reports of survey?
11. Is there a specific and secure procedure for the receipt of incoming property?
12. Are there any weaknesses in the present system for the physical unloading and storage of merchandise?
13. Are delivery personnel required to produce a Bill of Lading or other listing of the delivery?
14. Is an accurate tally conducted prior to acceptance?
15. Are delivery records checked against requisitions or purchase orders?
16. Is acceptance of deliveries limited to specific personnel?
17. Are incoming shipments carefully checked for signs of pilferage, damage, etc.?
18. Are shipping and receiving platforms free of trash and are shipments neatly stacked for proper observation and counting?
19. Are unauthorized persons kept from storeroom/storage areas?
20. Is a current personnel access list maintained?
21. Are supplies adequately protected against pilferage?
22. Are adequate protective measures afforded open storage?
23. Is material in open storage properly stacked, placed within, away from, and parallel to perimeter barriers, to provide unobstructed view by patrol personnel?
24. Are adequate locker and "break area" facilities provided for employees?
25. Is there a secure place to keep broken cases of damaged merchandise to prevent pilferage?
26. Is there a secure room or container for the safekeeping of sensitive items?
27. Are employees permitted to carry packages in and out of work areas?
28. Are provisions made for parking privately owned vehicles to insure that they are not parked in an area offering an opportunity to remove items from the building to the vehicle undetected?
29. Are trash collectors permitted in the building? (Janitorial help.)
30. If so, are trash containers inspected to assure no supplies are secreted in the containers?

31. Is there a specific procedure in effect for the issue and/or shipping of property?
32. Are there any weaknesses in the present system for the physical issue or shipment of property?
33. Are receivers required to receipt for the goods?
34. Are signature cards used for all authorized receptors?
35. When issues are made by shipment, is there a means to verify their arrival at the requesting facility?
36. Are shipments or deliveries receipted to the carrier or the person making the delivery?
37. Are adequate controls maintained over property prior to issue?
38. Is responsibility for items fixed?

Motor Pools

1. Is there a fire plan posted?
2. Does the plan adequately cover the evacuation of personnel, vehicles, and equipment during an emergency?
3. Is the parts room adequately secured to preclude the loss of materials?
4. Is access to the parts room controlled and limited to the essential number of personnel required to function adequately?
5. Are all tools and equipment adequately secured and marked by the unit for identification?
6. Is issue and turn-in of tools adequately controlled by means of a sign-out ledger or chit system?
7. Have there been any losses of equipment and/or tools within the last 12 months? (Attach copies of report of survey for significant losses.)
8. Is the unit POL located within the motor pool area?
9. Are all POL products such as gas, diesel, and oils adequately secured by lock during non-duty hours?
10. Are all issues controlled and checked periodically for accuracy?
11. Is the vehicle parts area under the surveillance of the night dispatcher or sentry on duty?
12. Are unit vehicles controlled by proper dispatch?
13. Are parked vehicles adequately secured during non-duty hours?
14. Is vehicle and pedestrian traffic controlled during non-duty hours?
15. Are vehicles periodically searched to preclude the loss of equipment, parts, and/or tools?
16. Are vehicle log books adequately safeguarded?
17. Are privately owned vehicles permitted in the motor pool?

18. Are driver test forms to include answer sheets adequately protected?
19. Are credit cards properly protected and accounted for?

Unit Mailrooms

1. Is a unit postal officer appointed in writing by the unit commander?
2. Is a unit mail clerk and at least one alternate mail clerk appointed by the commander of the unit?
3. Are the appointees U.S. citizens of good character?
4. Is DD Form 285 (Appointment of Unit Mail Clerk or Mail Orderly) properly prepared and carried at all times by the mail clerk and his alternate(s) ?
5. Do unit mail clerks and alternates attend courses of instruction in mail procedures at least twice each calendar year?
6. Is all mail handled ONLY by authorized mail clerks and alternates until delivery to addresses is effected?
7. Is a separate and secure mailroom provided?
8. Is the mailroom neat, clean, and free of excess equipment which could encourage possibly hiding or secreting mail?
9. Is the mailroom used exclusively for unit activities?
10. Are only authorized personnel permitted to enter the mailroom?
11. Are appropriate signs conspicuously posted which set forth the provisions for entry to unit mailroom?
12. Does the mailroom door provide a substantial degree of security?
13. Are all hinges and hasps properly mounted so as to preclude their removal?
14. Are hinge pins to all entrance doors spot welded or peened?
15. Is the mailroom door equipped with one or more secure locking devices?
16. Is the door locked when unit mail clerks are not in the mailroom?
17. Are all openings, such as trapdoors and adjoining room doors which permit access to the mailroom, properly secured or blocked?
18. Are mailroom windows barred or screened with heavy wire mesh?
19. Are all ventilators or other possible means of entrance to the mailroom covered with steel bars or adequate wire mesh?
20. Is the wire mesh anchored in such a manner so as to preclude its removal?
21. Are walls and ceilings of soft material reinforced as necessary?
22. Are all items of mail kept out of the reach of personnel standing outside the mailroom door?
23. Have locked mailboxes or other substantial receptacles been provided for deposit of outgoing mail?
24. Are mailboxes secured to fixed foundations?

25. Does the size and construction of mailboxes afford protection from the weather and security for all mail deposited therein?

26. Is one set of keys to the mailroom, mail collection boxes, safes, or other locked mail receptacles in the physical possession of the unit mail clerk or his alternate at all times?

27. Are all copies of each combination and/or duplicate keys individually sealed in separate envelopes, and are envelopes annotated as to the contents and retained by the unit postal officer in a secure manner?

28. Have the unit postal officer and the unit mail clerk written their names across the sealed portion of the envelope to facilitate the detection of tampering?

29. Is a field safe or other suitable container provided for registered and/or certified mail?

30. Is the container secured to prevent removal from mailroom?

31. If combination locks are used on containers of registered mail, is the combination known only by one mail clerk?

32. Is a security container that meets the requirements of AR 380–5 provided for overnight storage of official registered and official certified mail?

33. Are the combination and/or keys and locks to the mailrooms and mail receptacles promptly changed upon the transfer or AWOL of the mail clerk(s) or unit postal officer?

34. Has the manufacturer's serial number been obliterated on all locks and keys?

35. Are master keys and/or "SET" locks prohibited in the mailroom and on mail receptacles?

36. If individual lockboxes are used, are the combinations and/or keys and locks promptly changed upon the transfer of individuals to whom boxes were assigned?

37. If individual lockboxes are used, does only one individual have overall authority and responsibility for issuing and changing the combinations and/or keys and locks?

38. Are only U.S. mail pouches and sacks used to transport United States mail?

39. If the mail is not transported to and from the post office in a closed-body vehicle equipped with a rear door, does the unit mail clerk ride in the vehicle body with the mail, keeping it under constant surveillance at all times?

40. During periods of the postal officer's temporary absence, e.g. leave, pass, TDY, hospitalization, etc., has the unit commander appointed

in writing a temporary unit postal officer to fulfill the duties and responsibilities as outlined in AR 65–75?

41. Does the unit postal officer personally visit the unit mailroom on a daily basis to verify that all pieces of registered, numbered insured, and certified mail received are accounted for?

42. Does the unit postal officer inspect the mailroom at least once a week to insure compliance with AR 65-75?

43. Is mail delivered to only the addressee or the agent he has designated in writing?

44. Does the unit mail clerk or his alternate require positive identification of an individual address before registered, numbered insured, or certified mail is delivered?

45. Are known or suspected postal offenses such as the following reported immediately through channels: Willful destruction, loss, theft, mutilation, and the delay of mail or the mailing of obscene mail matter, chain letter, and material concerning any lottery or similar scheme?

General

1. Is perimeter of facility defined by a fence or other type physical barrier? (If possible, attach typical photograph for exhibit purposes.)

2. If a fence is utilized as the perimeter barrier, does it meet the minimum specifications for security fencing?

3. Is it of chain link design?

4. Is it constructed of #11 gauge or heavier wire?

5. Is mesh opening no larger than two inches square?

6. Is selvage twisted and barbed at top and bottom?

7. Is bottom of fence within two inches of solid ground?

8. Is the top guard strung with barbed wire and angled outward and upward at 45° angle?

9. Are physical barriers at perimeter lines damaged or deteriorated?

10. If masonry wall is used, does it meet minimum specifications for security fencing?

11. Is wall at least seven feet high with a top guard similar to that required on a chain link fence, or at least eight feet high with broken glass set on edge and cemented to top surface?

12. If building walls, floors, and roofs form a part of the perimeter barrier, do they provide security equivalent at least to that provided by chain link fence?

13. Are all openings properly secured?

14. If a building forms a part of the perimeter barrier, does it present a hazard at the point of juncture with the perimeter fence?
15. If so, is the fence height increased 100% at the point of juncture?
16. Are openings such as culverts, tunnels, manholes for sewers and utility access, and sidewalk elevators which permit access to the activity, properly secured?
17. Do the doors exceed the number required for safe and efficient operation?
18. Are doors constructed of sturdy material?
19. Are all entrances equipped with secure locking devices?
20. Are they always locked when not in active use?
21. Are hinge pins to all entrance doors spot welded or peened?
22. Are all ventilators, or other possible means of entrance to the buildings covered with steel bars or adequate wire mesh?
23. Are all windows securely fastened from the inside?
24. Are all windows not accessible from the ground adequately secured?
25. Are all openings less than 18 feet above uncontrolled ground, roofs, ledges, etc., protected by steel bars or grill?
26. Are openings less than 14 feet directly or diagonally opposite uncontrolled windows in other walls, fire escapes, roofs, etc., protected by steel bars or grills?
27. Has a key control officer been appointed?
28. Are locks and keys to all buildings and entrances supervised and controlled by a key control officer?
29. Does the key control officer have overall authority and responsibility for issuance and replacement of locks and keys?
30. Are keys issued only to authorized personnel?
31. Are keys issued to other than activity personnel?
32. Is the removal of keys from the premises prohibited?
33. Are keys not in use secured in a locked, fireproof cabinet?
34. Are records maintained indicating buildings and/or entrances for which keys are issued?
35. Are records maintained indicating number and identification of keys issued?
36. Are records maintained indicating location and number of master keys?
37. Are records maintained indicating location and number of duplicate keys?
38. Are records maintained indicating issue and turn-in of keys?
39. Are records maintained indicating location of locks and keys held in reserve?

40. Is a current key control directive in effect?
41. Are locks changed immediately upon loss or theft of keys?
42. Are inventories conducted at least annually by the key control officer to insure compliance with directives?
43. If master keys are used, are they devoid of markings identifying them as such?
44. Are losses or thefts of keys promptly investigated by control personnel?
45. Must all requests for reproduction or duplication of keys be approved by the key control officer?
46. Are locks on inactive gates and storage facilities under seal?
47. Are they checked periodically by guard personnel?
48. Are locks rotated within the activity at least semiannually?
49. Where applicable, is manufacturer's serial number on combination locks obliterated?
50. Are measures in effect to prevent the unauthorized removal of locks on open cabinets, gates, or buildings?
51. Is there a safe(s) located within the building?
52. Is safe(s) adequately secured to prevent removal?
53. Is the safe in a position where it can be observed from the outside by a security guard?
54. Is an alarm system used by the activity? (Give brief description of detection device on separate sheet.)
55. Is it a local alarm system?
56. Is it a central station system?
57. Is it a proprietary system?
58. Is it connected to activity guard headquarters?
59. Is it connected directly to a headquarters outside the activity proper?
60. Is it a private protection service?
61. Is it civil police protection service?
62. Is there any inherent weakness in the system itself?
63. Is the system backed up by properly trained, alert guards?
64. Is the system tested prior to activating it for nonoperational periods?
65. Is the alarm system inspected regularly?
66. Is the system tamper resistant?
67. Is the system weatherproof?
68. Is an alternate or independent source of power available for use on the system in the event of power failure?
69. Is the emergency power source designed to cut in and operate automatically?
70. Is the alarm system properly maintained by trained personnel?
71. Are properly cleared personnel utilized in maintenance of alarm systems?

72. Are frequent tests conducted to determine the adequate and promptness of response to alarm signals?
73. Are records kept of all alarm signals received to include time, date, location, action taken, and cause for alarm?
74. Is protective lighting provided during hours of darkness?
75. Does it provide adequate illumination for all sides of the facility?
76. Are there provisions for emergency or standby lighting?
77. Are repairs to lights and replacement of inoperative lamps effected immediately?
78. Is there an auxiliary power source?

HOME

1. How to Protect Your Home from Burglaries
2. How Burglar-proof Is Your Home?
3. How to Burglar-proof Your Home
4. Burglary Prevention Checklist for Homes
5. Home Security Checklist
6. Safety Checklist

How to Protect Your Home from Burglaries*

AT HOME

☐ Do not keep large amounts of money or other valuables at home.

☐ Lock outside doors at all times, even when you are on the premises.

☐ Do not open the door to strangers.

☐ Install slide bolts and chains on the inside of all outer doors.

☐ When you move into a new house or apartment, have new locks installed.

☐ Check door moldings for tight fit.

☐ Doors should be hinged so no pins can be removed from outside.

☐ Replace locks with the double-cylinder type (which also need keys on the inside), particularly doors with glass panels.

☐ Keep garage and tool shed locked.

☐ Remove all obstructions in your yard that could conceal a burglar breaking into your house.

AWAY FROM HOME

☐ Purchase a timer to switch lights on and off.

☐ Arrange to have mail, milk and newspaper deliveries discontinued or taken care of by a responsible neighbor.

☐ Inform neighbors and local police of your traveling plans so that special attention will be paid to your home.

HELP THE POLICE HELP YOU

☐ Write down the license numbers of vehicles used by suspicious persons in your neighborhood.

☐ Keep an inventory of valuables so you will know immediately if anything is missing. Include photographs of jewels and serial numbers of other costly items.

*Reprinted from How to Protect Your Home from Burglaries. The Seattle Post-Intelligencer.

How Burglar-proof Is Your Home?*

Are you sure your home is burglar-proof?

Whether you're at home or away, is your home "as safe as it could be" against burglary?

Here's a checklist police in Washington, D.C., are distributing to enable people to test how well their homes might foil house burglars:

Doors

YES NO

— —Do you lock all doors in your home every time you go out?

— —Do you have a chain latch on both your front and back doors?

— —Do you use the chain latch every time you answer the door?

— —Are your doors equipped with strong, pin-tumbler locks?

— —Do you have the type of hinges that cannot be forced from the outside?

— —Do you have a peep-hole in your front and back doors?

— —If your doors have a window in them, do you have the type of lock that must be opened from the inside, as well as the outside, by a key?

Windows

— —Do you close and lock every window in your home whenever you go out?

— —Do you have bars or grillwork over "out of the way" windows such as those that lead to your garage or basement?

— —Do you have pin-tumbler locks on your windows?

Keys

— —Did you have the lock tumblers changed when you moved into your new home?

— —Are you careful in giving out duplicate keys?

— —Do you always separate your home and automobile keys when you leave your car in a parking lot?

— —Have you removed all identification tags from your key ring so if you lose it, a burglar won't know where to go?

— —Are you sure that no one in your family tries to "hide" the door key in such places as the mail box or under the door mat?

— —If you lost your keys, would you have the lock tumblers changed at once?

Valuables

— —Do you keep cash, jewelry, bonds or other negotiable securities in a bank or safe deposit box?

*Reprinted from *How Burglar-Proof Is Your Home?* D and C—Washington Post.

__ __Are your checkbooks and credit cards kept under lock and key?

__ __Do you have a list of the serial numbers of such items as your radios, cameras, watches, binoculars, television and appliances?

Strangers

__ __Do you always require identification from repairmen and utility company representatives?

__ __Is the chain latch in place every time you answer the door?

__ __Are you alert for strangers who loiter in hallways, elevators and laundry rooms?

__ __Do you make a note of the license tag number of suspicious vehicles that you notice in your neighborhood?

Tell-tale Signs

__ __Do you have a mail slot in your door so that an accumulation of mail will not advertise that you are away from home?

__ __Do you stop delivery of milk and newspapers when you are going away?

__ __Do you have an automatic device that will turn on your lights and radio at dusk when you are away?

__ __Do you make arrangements to have the grass cut or the snow shoveled when you are going out of town?

__ __Do you close the garage door each time you leave?

__ __Do you always close the curtains and draw the shades after dark?

__ __If you are a woman and live alone, do you use your intials rather than your first name on your mailbox and your door and in the telephone book?

__ __Do you let the police know when you are going out of town?

__ __Do you always call police when you see or hear anything suspicious in your neighborhood?

HOW BURGLAR-PROOF IS YOUR HOME*	Check One Yes | No	Score for "YES" Answer
Do you leave a light connected to an automatic timer when you leave the house for an evening or an extended period?		20 points
Do you have Yale pin tumble cylinder locks on all exterior doors? Or, if not, have you installed Yale auxiliary night latches to protect such doors?		20 points
When leaving the house for an extended period, do you notify neighbors and local police that you are taking a trip?		5 points
When you leave your home, do you avoid leaving notes which tell where the house key can be found?		10 points
Do you wait until after your return to tell the local paper about your vacation?		5 points
Do you check the credentials of salesmen and repairmen before admitting them to your home and make certain that strange callers have no opportunity to tamper with your door lock?		5 points
When leaving your home for an extended period, do you make arrangements, by mail or phone, to have mail held for your return and daily deliveries of newspapers, milk, etc., suspended?		10 points
Before leaving your home, do you make certain that shades are left up and Venetian blinds partially open?		5 points
When you leave your home, do you check to make sure that all exterior doors and windows are securely locked and all ladders securely fastened with Yale pin tumbler padlocks?		10 points
Do you keep a record of the serial numbers and descriptions of your valuables? And do you rent a safe deposit box for storage of valuables?		10 points
My Home Protection Score is:		100 points†

*From *How to "Burglar Proof" Your Home,* Yale Lock and Hardware Division, Eaton Yale & Towne, Inc.

†A score of 100 is excellent; a score of 85 or more means you are doing a good job of foiling burglars; 70 or more means that you are doing a fair job; a score of 60 or less means that your home may become a "burglar's delight."

Burglary Prevention Checklist for Homes*

YES NO

Doors

1. Are the locks on your most used outside doors of the cylinder type?
2. Are they of either the "deadlocking" or "jimmyproof" type?
3. Can any of your door locks be opened by breaking out glass or a panel of light wood?
4. Do you use chain locks or other auxiliary locks on your most used doors
5. Do the doors without cylinder locks have a heavy bolt or some similar secure device that can be operated only from the inside?
6. Can ALL of your doors (basement, porch, French, balcony) be securely locked?
7. Do your basement doors have locks that allow you to isolate that part of your house?
8. Are your locks all in good repair?
9. Do you know everyone who has a key to your house? (Or are there some still in possession of previous owners and their servants and friends?)

Windows

10. Are your window locks properly and securely mounted?
11. Do you keep your windows locked when they are shut?
12. Do you use locks that allow you to lock a window that is partly open?
13. In high hazard locations, do you use bars or ornamental grills?
14. Are you as careful of basement and second floor windows as you are of those on the first floor?
15. Have you made it more difficult for the burglar by locking up your ladder, avoiding trellises that can be used as a ladder or similar aids to climbing?

Garage

16. Do you lock your garage at night?
17. Do you lock your garage when you are away from home?
18. Do you have good, secure locks on the garage doors and windows?
19. Do you lock your car and TAKE THE KEYS OUT even when it is parked in your garage?

---

*Reprinted with permission from Richard L. Holcomb, *Protection Against Burglary* (Iowa City: State University of Iowa, 1953) p. 54.

Miscellaneous Devices

20. If you have a fence or tight hedge, have you looked it over as a possible defense against burglars?
21. If you have a burglar alarm (is it fully approved by the Underwriters Laboratories?
22. If you have a gun, do you know the laws regarding its use?
23. If you have a gun, is it kept in perfect condition?
24. If you have a gun, is it kept where it can be found only by persons who can legally and safely use it? (The writer believes that a pistol is more of a hazard than a help because of the great danger of accidents; in almost every case, he strongly recommends against keeping one for protection.)

When You Go On a Trip

25. Do you stop ALL deliveries or arrange for neighbors to pick up papers, milk, mail, packages?
26. Do you notify a neighbor?
27. Do you notify your police if they provide extra protection for vacant homes?
28. Do you leave some shades up so the house doesn't look deserted?
29. Do you arrange to keep your lawn and garden in shape?

Safe Practices

30. Do you plan so that you do not need to "hide" a key under the door mat?
31. Do you keep as much cash as possible and other valuables in a bank (or bonded storage in the case of large items) ?
32. Do you keep a list of all valuable property?
33. Do you have a list of the serial numbers of your watches, cameras, typewriters and similar items?
34. Do you have a description of other valuable property that does not have a number?
35. Do you avoid unnecessary display or publicity of your valuables?
36. Have you told your family what to do if they discover a burglar breaking in or already in the house?
37. Have you told your family to leave the house undisturbed and call the police if they discover a burglary has been committed?
38. Do you know the phone number of the law enforcement agency that takes care of your home?

SHERIFF'S DEPARTMENT – COUNTY OF LOS ANGELES

HOME SECURITY CHECK-LIST*

NAME_____

STREET_____ PHONE_____

CITY_____ STATE_____ ZIP_____ R.D._____

S – Satisfactory   U – Unsatisfactory   Circle the appropriate condition below.

BUILDING TYPE: Residence_____ Apartment_____ Other_____

DOORS			RECOMMENDATIONS
☐ MAIN ENTRANCE	S	U	_____
☐ SIDE DOOR	S	U	_____
☐ BACK DOOR	S	U	_____
☐ BASEMENT DOOR	S	U	_____
☐ OTHER DOOR (_____)	S	U	_____
☐ OTHER DOOR (_____)	S	U	_____
☐ SLIDING DOOR (INSIDE)	S	U	_____
☐ SLIDING DOOR (OUTSIDE)	S	U	_____
WINDOWS			
☐ DOUBLE HUNG	S	U	_____
☐ SLIDING	S	U	_____
☐ CASEMENT	S	U	_____
☐ LOUVER	S	U	_____
☐ OTHER (_____)	S	U	_____
☐ LIGHTING	S	U	_____
☐ SHRUBBERY	S	U	_____
☐ ALARM SYSTEM	YES	NO	_____
☐ MISC. OPENING (_____)			_____
☐ MISC. OPENING (_____)			_____

REMARKS:_____

_____

INSPECTED BY_____ DATE_____ STATION_____

*Originally created and prepared by the Los Angeles County Sheriff's Department, Peter J. Pitchess, Sheriff.

SCHLAGE SECURITY INSTITUTE

Safety Check List*

IF YOUR ANSWER IS "NO" TO ANY OF THE QUESTIONS BELOW, YOU SHOULD IMPROVE YOUR HOME SECURITY.

YES NO Does the gate or grill of the entrance to your home have a lock?
☐ ☐

YES NO Do you use it?
☐ ☐

YES NO When you move to a new residence, do you hire a reliable locksmith to re-key all locks?
☐ ☐ (This does not necessarily require new locks but simply re-setting the cylinder to a new key.)

YES NO Do you have an apartment entrance lock capable of withstanding great force?
☐ ☐

YES NO If you have an apartment with windows opening onto a fire escape, patio or balcony, do
☐ ☐ you lock all windows when you go to bed?

YES NO Do you provide secure locks for all doors in your apartment?
☐ ☐

YES NO Do you have a double cylinder lock on all doors with glass?
☐ ☐

YES NO Do you have a night chain on your door?
☐ ☐

YES NO When you leave your home for any period of time, do you lock all windows and doors?
☐ ☐

YES NO Do you lock garage doors?
☐ ☐

YES NO Do you have a peephole or interview grill in your door?
☐ ☐

YES NO Are cabinets, closets and drawers where you keep valuables properly locked?
☐ ☐

YES NO Do you hide your spare key in a place where it cannot easily be found?
☐ ☐

YES NO When arriving home late at night are your keys ready immediately?
☐ ☐

YES NO Do you conceal your single status on your door and mailbox name plates?
☐ ☐

YES NO Do you have a "Charlie Bar" or a secondary lock for sliding glass doors?
☐ ☐

YES NO Do you lock your car when you leave it?
☐ ☐

YES NO Do you take all but ignition keys with you when a garage attendant parks your car?
☐ ☐

*Reprinted with permission from *Your Home Is Secure. . . Isn't It?* Schlage Security Institute —Safety Check List, Schlage Lock Company.

APARTMENT

If You Live in an Apartment*

1. Put a strong, short chain on your apartment door.
2. Don't leave your door unlocked even when you are home.
3. Keep the door chained when a stranger knocks until you are satisfied his purpose is legitimate.
4. Double-lock your door when you leave.
5. Put extra locks on windows facing on fire escapes.
6. When you have your car serviced, remove house keys from the key case. Keys are easily duplicated when cars are in parking lots, being repaired or serviced.
7. Urge your apartment manager to keep hallways, parking lots, laundry rooms, and all outside areas well lighted.
8. See that shrubbery that might provide an easy hiding place is kept trimmed.
9. Chcek thoroughly the reefrences of maids or service people who are given access to your apartment.

FIRE

1. Fire: Security Checklist
2. Fire Prevention Inspection

Fire: Security Checklist*

1. Has the telephone operator where employed and any deputy been instructed in the action to be taken on fire on the premises being reported?
2. Have the instructions been prepared in writing and are they immediately available to the telephonist and whoever replaces her for meal breaks and other absences?
3. Is there a full-time company fire brigade?
4. If not. are there men on each shift who will atend and deal with outbreaks of fire?
5. On an alarm is their notification procedure satisfactory?
6. Has their agreed number been maintained following leavings and tranfers?
7. What training do they receive? Check records of attendance.

---

*Reprinted with permission from *If You Live in an Apartment.* The Wichita Mayor's "Light the Night" Steering Committee.

*Reprinted with permission from Eric Oliver and John Wilson, *Practical Security in Commerce and Industry* (Great Britain: Gower, 1968) pp. 402-403.

8. Do they receive special payment for training periods, etc., and is it satisfactory?

9. Who is responsible for fire duties and supervision of any company firemen?

10. How is the fire-fighting equipment maintained?

11. When was it done last? Check records.

12. Is this satisfactory according to recommended standards of maintenance?

13. Has a Certificate of Satisfactory Means of Escape been applied for/been issued?

14. If so, have all relevant reconstuction of premises, change of usage since then been reported to the fire authority?

15. What is the type of fire alarm?

16. Can it be heard satisfactorily in every part of the premises?

17. When was the alarm last tested? Any records kept? Where applicable check General Register to ensure these have occurred at least at three monthly intervals.

18. When was a fire/evacuation drill last carried out? Have Assembly Points been designated?

19. Have supervisoros or their equivalent in offices been instructed in their duties in the event of fire being reported?

20. Have the requirements of the fire sections of the Factory Act, 1961, such as display of notices, been carried out?

Offices and Similar Buildings

21. As Number 20, with respect to the Offices, Shops and Railway Premises Act, 1963.

22. Have fire wardens/stewards been appointed in sufficient numbers and supplied with a list of their duties?

23. Have they been trained in the use of fire-fighting equipment?

24. Have staff movements of fire wardens/stewards been checked to ensure new appointments have been made where necessary?

Fire Prevention Inspection*

_____
(Name of Building)

_____
(Street & Number)

A. AUTOMATIC SPRINKLERS

1. Valves and Pressures

Valve No.	Controls	Open	Shut	Pressure with 2-inch Drain Shut	Open

2. Alarms — Any alarms inoperative?_____. Why?_____

B. FIRE DOORS

1. Did you personally close all doors, and are they in good working condition?_____

2. Are doors in good structural condition?_____

3. Are automatic closing devices in good order?_____

4. Comment on any fire door defects_____

_____

C. EXTINGUISHERS

1. Did you examine each unit?_____

2. Did you arrange for all needed refills?_____

3. Are any units exposed to freezing?_____

4. Were all units accessible?_____

5. Were all units in good condition?_____

D. HOUSEKEEPING

1. List locations where housekeeping was not satisfactory_____

_____

_____

2. Will these be cleaned up?_____. By Whom?_____
When?_____

E. ELECTRICAL

1. Are all panel boards, switch and fuse cabinets clean?_____

2. Are all outlet box covers in place?_____

3. Are all cabinet doors latched shut?_____

4. Are all motors clean?_____

5. Are any circuits overfused?_____

6. Any temporary wiring?_____. Where?_____

F. HEATING

1. Are all steam pipes and coils at least one-inch clear of woodwork (and any other combustible material) and properly supported?

_____

2. Are all stoves, stove pipes, vents and chimneys safely arranged and in good condition?

_____

G. FLAMMABLE LIQUIDS

1. Are these materials needed where found?_____

_____

*Reprinted with permission from Municipal Risk Management. *Fire Prevention Inspection*, The National Underwriters Company, Cincinnati, Ohio, pp. 211-213.

2. Were they safely stored and handled?_____
3. Are quantities limited to one day's needs inside building?

_____

4. Are safety cans used and in good condition?_____

H. *SMOKING*
1. List locations where permitted_____

_____

_____

_____

2. Is housekeeping satisfactory in these areas?_____
3. Do all personnel fully understand the rules?_____
4. Did you find any evidence of smoking in *other* areas?_____

I. *RECOMMENDATIONS*
(List here all necessary repairs, replacements, unusual conditions, suggestions for additional fire protection, or improvement of any fire hazard.)

_____

_____

_____

_____

INSPECTED BY:_____ DATE:_____
CHECKED BY:_____ POSITION:_____

Indicate below, date when reported defects were rechecked and found corrected.

_____

_____

_____

_____

Note: Reports on buildings equipped with automatic sprinkler systems should be made by properly qualified personnel.

TRANSPORTATION
Terminal Security Survey*

If available: (For terminal being inspected)

Total claims for year #_____ $_____

Shortage #_____ $_____

Theft/Pilferage #_____ $_____

Gross Annual Revenue _____

Is there a formal Security Plan? _____

Is there a security officer? _____

Name (if applicable) _____

*Courtesy of Richard G. MaCormack, Senior Transportation Security Specialist, Office Department Transportation Security, U.S. Department of Transportation, Washington, D.C.

I. *General Security*

A. PERSONNEL

	YES	NO	REMARKS
1. Are all employees screened prior to employment?	Y	N	
2. Are marked changes in the standard of living of any employee checked?	Y	N	
3. Are rumors to indicate gambling, drinking and thefts checked?	Y	N	
4. Are personnel files kept on each driver, mechanic, helper (per seniority list) and casual labor?	Y	N	
5. Are accurate records on casual employment kept to insure pre-employment checks before seniority is attained?	Y	N	
6. Is this done on a combined basis where company has one list for more than one terminal?	Y	N	

B. GUARD SERVICE

1. Is a guard service employed?	Y	N	
2. Is a guard service needed?	Y	N	
3. Is existing guard service adequate and being used effectively?	Y	N	
4. Are clock stations used?	Y	N	
5. Are all clock charts reviewed daily?	Y	N	
6. By whom?	_____		
7. Are written reports received from the guard service after each shift?	Y	N	
8. Who reviews the reports to determine if action is necessary?	_____		
9. Is the guard service performing other duties such as receiving trailers, checking seals and inspecting empties?	Y	N	
10. Do guards have an up-to-date emergency list?	Y	N	

C. LOCKS AND KEY CONTROL

1. Is there a single person designated responsible for "lock & key control"?	Y	N	
2. Is the responsibility fixed for locking the terminal during nonworking hours?	Y	N	
3. Is there a lock and key master system?	Y	N	
4. Is a tickler system maintained relative to maintenance and changing of locks or tumblers?	Y	N	
5. Is there a record of the distribution of keys?	Y	N	
6. Is it current?	Y	N	
7. Are keys obtained from terminated or transferred personnel?	Y	N	
8. Are tumblers in the locks of vital doors changed if keys are lost or missing?	Y	N	
9. Is there a lockable keyboard available for the dispatcher?	Y	N	
10. Are ignition keys controlled?	Y	N	
11. Are ignition keys removed from units when unattended?	Y	N	
12. Are gates on straight trucks making local pickups locked regardless of the value of the freight?	Y	N	
13. Is a record being kept on the dispatch sheet of padlocks given to drivers picking up high value freight?	Y	N	
14. Is a record kept on the dispatch sheet when the driver returns the key?	Y	N	

D. Money and Payrolls

	YES	NO	REMARKS
1. Is a large amount of cash maintained overnight or on weekends?	Y	N	
2. Is there an adequate safe or strongbox?	Y	N	
3. Is there a possibility that the combination has been compromised?	Y	N	
4. How long has it been since the combination was changed?			
5. Is someone responsible for night deposits?	Y	N	
6. Are deposits made daily?	Y	N	
7. Are deposits made on an irregular schedule?	Y	N	
8. Are checks kept under lock and key?	Y	N	
9. Can checks be issued by the one who made them up? Without counter-signature?	Y	N	
10. Is the Terminal Manager present when checks are distributed on a regular or spot check basis to prevent a phantom payroll?	Y	N	
11. Is there a satisfactory system in effect to establish responsibility for cash collections step by step from the freight handler through the dispatcher or warehouse foreman to the collection clerk, office manager and finally to the bank?	Y	N	
12. Does the receipt identify the waybills to which the monies apply?	Y	N	
13. Does the Terminal Manager occasionally spot check that monies received are turned in on the same day?	Y	N	
14. Is there a procedure for driver toll reimbursement?	Y	N	
15. Is someone responsible for petty cash?	Y	N	
16. How often is the petty cash box reconciled?			

E. Parking

1. Do employees have parking permits?	Y	N	
2. Is the designated parking area sufficient to accommodate all employees' cars?	Y	N	
3. Is parking permitted inside the yard?	Y	N	
4. Are there sufficient visitor parking spaces?	Y	N	
5. Are parking regulations adhered to?	Y	N	
6. Are there signs reflecting, "NO ADMITTANCE TO UN-AUTHORIZED PERSONNEL"?	Y	N	

F. Gas and Tools

1. Is company gas controlled through a ticket system?	Y	N	
2. Are there signs in maintenance office and garage reflecting, "NO ADMITTANCE TO UNAUTHORIZED PERSONNEL"?	Y	N	
3. Is all work in garage connected with business?	Y	N	
4. Is there a procedure for maintaining spare parts inventory?	Y	N	
5. Is there a method for charging out tools?	Y	N	
6. Is there someone responsible for issuing and recording the return of tools?	Y	N	
7. Are equipment and tools loaned to individuals for personal use?	Y	N	

G. Lighting

	YES	NO	REMARKS
1. Is someone responsible to turns lights on and off and check proper functioning?	Y	N	
2. Does the present lighting conform to recommended standards of 2 footcandles in vehicle, pedestrian and other sensitive areas and 1.0 footcandle in unattended parking areas?	Y	N	
3. Is there emergency lighting for power failure?	Y	N	

H. Fences

1. Is the fencing adequate and in good condition?	Y	N	
2. Are there any unnecessary gates?	Y	N	
3. Is there a program to ensure that gate locks are changed regularly?	Y	N	
4. Has responsibility been fixed to provide a weekly perimeter check of the area and maintain a record?	Y	N	
5. Are there any areas where the bottom of the fence is so high off the ground that it might permit easy entrance or exit from the terminal area?	Y	N	
6. Are there weeds and debris around the fences?	Y	N	
7. Are pallets or machinery piled against fences as to provide built-in ladders?	Y	N	

I. Thefts

1. Are thefts of interstate shipments or the revenue derived therefrom reported to the FBI as well as to the local police?	Y	N	
2. Are theft reports being prepared?	Y	N	
3. What is distribution?			
4. Are thefts of terminal property reported to local police by telephone?	Y	N	
5. Before a complaint is signed, is the Security Section notified for possible legal complications?	Y	N	
6. Are notices posted that thefts of interstate shipments are investigated by the FBI?	Y	N	
7. Are suspected thefts being investigated by the Terminal Manager prior to reporting to law enforcement agencies so as to be reasonably sure a theft has occurred?	Y	N	
8. In the case of unfounded reports, are law enforcement agencies promptly being notified the freight has been found?	Y	N	
9. Does the terminal security or loss prevention man maintain at least weekly contact with local FBI and other law enforcement agencies?	Y	N	
10. Is the cooperation of these agencies satisfactory?	Y	N	

J. Seals and Terminal Cargo Loss Prevention

1. Is one person made responsible for seal requisitioning and issuance?	Y	N	
2. Can seals issued be accounted for?	Y	N	
3. Can a continuous seal record be established inbound and			

	YES	NO	REMARKS

outbound from the time a terminal becomes responsible for a load until the burden of responsibility shifts to someone else?   Y   N

4. Does the seal record fix the time and individual responsibility at each major phase in the course of the handling of the trailer?   Y   N

5. Is there a positive program to require the shipper to acknowledge seal numbers afixed at time of shipment on the Bill of Lading even if not a shipper's load and count?   Y   N

6. Is there a positive program to require the receiver to acknowledge seal numbers on receipt especially on slipper load shipments?   Y   N

7. Have instructions for the handling of seals been posted and explained to all freight handlers?   Y   N

8. Have spot checks been made recently to see that drivers have placed seals on loads prior to leaving place of shipment?   Y   N

9. Are seals from inbound loads kept until load checks clear and, in the event of discrepancy, are these seals sent to security?   Y   N

10. Is there any record of disciplinary action taken as a result of failure to follow seal procedures?   Y   N

11. Is the Terminal Manager immediately notified of seals found broken under unusual circumstances?   Y   N

12. Are loss records kept by commodity and shipper/consignee?   Y   N

13. Are there any programs in effect to give special attention to high loss commodities and shippers?   Y   N

14. Is a Claim Prevention Bulletin being used?   Y   N

K. Entrance and Exit Control

1. Does carrier control entrance and exit?   Y   N

2. Is a log kept of all vehicles entering and leaving the terminal?   Y   N

3. Is a pass system used?   Y   N

4. Is log adequate to identify driver and vehicle?   Y   N

5. Who keeps the log?

6. Are supervisors alert for unauthorized vehicles and persons within facility?   Y   N

L. Yard Check

1. Are all loaded trailers in yard properly sealed?   Y   N

2. Are empties kept separate from loads?   Y   N

3. Are all loaded rag tops properly tied down?   Y   N

4. Make an inspection of the yard. How many trailers were found with freight and no seals?

M. Maximum Security Procedures/High Value Loads

1. Is the responsibility fixed on one person to make the decision to designate loads as requiring maximum security?   Y.   N

2. Is the shipping information relative to high value cargo kept confidential?   Y   N

3. Is the pickup of high value, theft-prone freight given special attention?   Y   N

	YES	NO	REMARKS

4. Are there receivers of high value freight who repeatedly will not take prompt delivery requiring unnecessary exposure to theft?   Y   N

5. Is any high value, theft-prone freight being picked up or delivered on a regular basis?   Y   N

6. If so, are "patterns" avoided?   Y   N

7. Are drivers specially selected for high value freight?   Y   N

8. Is a driver informed of a high value freight pickup only just prior to being dispatched for the pickup?   Y   N

9. Is the pickup driver given a seal and lock?   Y   N

10. Is the high value freight pickup early in the day and returned to the terminal promptly?   Y   N

11. Is there a special parking area designated for high value loads?   Y   N

12. Are King-Pin Locks available in the terminal?   Y   N

13. What type locks are used? _____

14. Is someone responsible for deciding on kingpin locking?   Y   N

15. Are there security procedures if King-Pin Locks are not available?   Y   N

16. Is escort service used when value or commodity calls for special care?   Y   N

II. Freight Handling Procedures

A. SOURCE DOCUMENTS

1. Are the shipping document files neat, orderly and current?   Y   N

2. Are the shipping documents properly dated, signed, number of pieces picked up, circled, etc.?   Y   N

3. Are pickup tallies attached to the shipping documents?   Y   N

4. Do the pickup tallies reflect the various commodities, sizes, quantities, etc.?   Y   N

5. Are they properly dated, signed, etc., and referenced to the shipping documents?   Y   N

6. Are cross-dock checking records shown on Shipping Documents when freight is handled at platform?   Y   N

7. Are receiving exceptions properly noted on Bills of Lading and carried forward onto the waybill set?   Y   N

8. Are shipping documents cross-referenced to OS&D reports?   Y   N

9. Is there sufficient accountability to show completely how and by whom each shipment was handled from origin to destination?   Y   N

B. DELIVERY RECEIPTS

1. Do dispatchers have an acceptable system to control return of delivery receipts by drivers and warehousemen?   Y   N

2. Is there an acceptable control to ensure that all delivery receipts are accounted for before going to permanent file?   Y   N

3. Is there a program to review both sides of all delivery receipts for OS&D exceptions prior to their going to file?   Y   N

4. When shipments have been cross-docked, is the checking record properly noted in the appropriate spaces provided on the delivery receipt?   Y   N

	YES	NO	REMARKS
5. Are drivers getting proper signatures, i.e. full name of firm, individual and date?	Y	N	
6. Is the number of pieces delivered *written and circled* on the receipt at time of delivery?	Y	N	
7. Are seal records being *written* on delivery receipts when broken on delivery?	Y	N	
8. Are drivers making a delivery tally record on delivery receipts?	Y	N	
9. Does the tally properly reflect the various commodities case sizes and quantities?	Y	N	
10. Do the drivers always phone the dispatcher before allowing an exception to be taken?	Y	N	
11. Are exceptions clearly and accurately described on the delivery receipt?	Y	N	
12. Are delivery receipt files orderly and current?	Y	N	

C. EXCEPTION REPORT

	YES	NO	REMARKS
1. Are exception reports being prepared in all cases?	Y	N	
2. Who prepares report?	Y	N	
3. Are reports sent to origin Terminal Manager for his corrective action?	Y	N	
4. Does the Terminal Manager interview the person responsible for the reported discrepancies?	Y	N	
5. Are exception reports filed at origin terminal in order of terminal issuing same with a record of the action taken?	Y	N	

D. O & S REPORTS

	YES	NO	REMARKS
1. Are all O&S incidents promptly and thoroughly investigated?	Y	N	
2. Does the O&S report record in adequate detail the results of the O&S investigation?	Y	N	
3. Does the Loss Prevention man investigate major occurrences on the spot when the situation first develops?	Y	N	
4. Does the terminal get O&S investigation from interline carriers?	Y	N	
5. Are the O&S files maintained in a neat, orderly and systematic fashion?	Y	N	

E. SECURITY CAGE

	YES	NO	REMARKS
1. Is there a satisfactory security cage available?	Y	N	
2. Is there a satisfactory control over the security of the cage?	Y	N	
3. Who has access to cage?			_____
4. Is the cage maintained in an orderly manner?	Y	N	
5. Is the cage inventory kept at a reasonable level?	Y	N	
6. What is the date of the oldest shipment in the cage?	Y	N	

F. SALVAGE

	YES	NO	REMARKS
1. Does carrier have salvage procedure?	Y	N	
2. Do employees have access to salvage?	Y	N	
3. Is salvage put out on bid?	Y	N	
4. Where are proceeds of salvage sales forwarded?			_____

GENERAL

1. Physical Security I
2. Physical Security II
3. Physical Security Surveys
4. Security Staff: Checklist
5. Gatehouse Duties: Security Checklist
6. Cash on Premises: Security Checklist
7. Cash in Transit: Security Checklist
8. Shops and Supermarkets: Security Checklist
9. Basic Security Precautions
10. Lock and Key Survey—Field of Education
11. Lock and Key Survey—Field of Business Administration
12. Lock and Key Survey—Field of Hospital Administration

Physical Security I*

SECURITY AREAS
  Types of Areas
  Control Procedures

NATURAL BARRIERS

STRUCTURAL BARRIERS
  General
  Fences
    Building Surfaces
    Building Openings

LOCKING DEVICES
  General
  Key Type Locks
  Combination Locks
  Application of Locking Devices

GUARDING SYSTEMS
  General
  Guard Forces
  Other Guarding Personnel
  Guard Dogs

PROTECTIVE LIGHTING

PROTECTIVE ALARM SYSTEMS
  General

---

*Reprinted from United States Army Special Text, *Physical Security*, S.T. 30-154 (Washington, D.C.: Government Printing Office, 1961). (Extract from the Table of Contents.)

---

†Reprinted for the Table of Contents in United States Army Special Text, 30-17-1, 1965.

Entrances
Perimeter Lighting

SECTION VII—GUARD AND GUARD SYSTEMS
Guard Personnel
Guard Supervision
Guard Employment
Guard Equipment
Guard Dogs

SECTION VIII—PERSONNEL CONTROL AND IDENTIFICATION
Identification System
Visitor Control

SECTION IX—VEHICLE CONTROL AND IDENTIFICATION
Vehicle Registration
Vehicle Control
Visitor's Vehicles
Vehicle Inspection

SECTION X—ALARM SYSTEMS
Anti-Intrusion Alarms

SECTION XI—FIRE FIGHTING FACILITIES
Fire Fighting Personnel
Fire Fighting Equipment
Fire Alarms
Water
Emergency Fire Fighting Equipment
Fire Plans
Fire Prevention Program
Sprinkler Systems

SECTION XII—COMMUNICATIONS
Communications System

SECTION XIII—UTILITIES
Electricity
Water
Heat

SECTION XIV—RECOMMENDATIONS
Recommendations
Inspections

Physical Security Surveys*

General

To assist the commander in evaluating the adequacy of existing physical security safeguards, the provost marshal or physical security officer should have surveys conducted by his military police or guard force personnel, or he may request support from higher headquarters when he has no qualified personnel available. The surveys should develop any necessary recommendations for correcting security hazards or deficiencies.

Scope of Survey

a. A survey should include a complete reconnaissance, study, and analysis of installation property and its operations, in order to insure that any physical security hazards or deficiencies are noted. The person conducting the survey should be thoroughly familiar with all physical security protective measures, in order that any recommendations made are appropriate and practicable, and in the interest of economy without sacrificing security. Recommendations should be consistent with existing conditions, such as the environment, mission, resources available to the commander, and the actual need for remedial action.

b. Surveys may be in the form of *initial, supplemental,* or *followup* surveys. Generally, the scope or areas to be covered are the same for each type. An initial survey is, as the title implies, the first survey of an installation made by the responsible surveying office. A supplementary survey is one made when there is a change in the organization, mission, or physical aspects which would affect the physical security of the installation.

c. *Special* surveys may also be scheduled. The scope should be that necessary to accomplish the specific purpose of the survey, or as directed by the commander.

Survey Personnel

a. Guard force personnel should have a clear understanding of the requirements for scheduling physical security surveys, and their role in the surveys. The guard force training program should emphasize that a conscientious guard is always alert for hazards, and does not wait for physical security surveys to discover weakness in the installation security program.

b. Where feasible and authorized, physical security survey teams should be composed of both Intelligence Corps and CID personnel. This arrangement helps to avoid duplication of effort and to insure more adequate coverage of physical security requirements. Survey personnel should be

---

*Reprinted with permission from Department of the Army Field Manual 19-30; *Physical Security.* 1965, pp. 105-109.

carefully selected since their findings have important implications for the security program.

c. Personnel conducting surveys should be well oriented in physical security techniques. They should understand that the security problem is determined by the nature of the operation, activity, or product manufactured or stored; the economic and political situation of the area; the potential danger to security; and the logistical support available. They should clearly understand that installations may vary as to requirements for protective measures. Some installations may require only a single type of protection; in others, specific internal areas may require special protection such as segregation or compartmentalization with the maximum of protection measures.

d. Arrangements should also be made for technical and administrative personnel to accompany the survey team where necessary to render assistance.

Scheduling Surveys

a. Each installation provost marshal or security officer will normally establish and maintain a survey schedule of units and activities within his installation. Survey priorities should be based on his own estimate of the situation, the personnel available to conduct surveys, and time needed to complete the surveys.

b. Activities which may benefit from annual physical security surveys are:

   (1) Finance and accounting offices
   (2) Quartermaster class I supply points, commissaries, and retail sales stores
   (3) Post exchanges
   (4) Pharmacies and other facilities handling narcotics
   (5) Unit arms rooms
   (6) Buildings and areas used for bulk storage of weapons and class V supplies
   (7) Property disposal areas
   (8) Nuclear storage sites
   (9) Storage areas
  (10) Shipping areas

c. Physical security surveys may be made any time deficiencies are noted or suspected, e.g. repeatedly short inventories, a high rate of pilferage, evidence of substandard physical security, or any other questionable practices in handling government property.

Preparatory Steps

Before conducting a physical security survey, several preliminary steps should be taken to provide an adequate and practical estimate of the security situation.

a. A preliminary contact should be made with appropriate personnel to arrange time and other details.

b. Previous surveys, if any reports are available, should be checked for background information and action taken on noted deficiencies.

c. Determine the reasons for the survey, and the type required.

d. Team personnel should be familiar with the mission and history of the installation or intended use of the area, or any changes in the mission or use since previous surveys were made.

e. Obtain installation floor and ground plans from the engineer office.

f. Review installation regulations and operating procedures.

g. Prepare a checklist for use as a guide in making the survey.

Entrance Conference

In performing the physical security survey it is recommended that survey personnel observe the following guidance:

a. The officer in charge of the survey team should report to the commander of the installation and seek his assistance and cooperation. It is important at this stage for survey personnel to make a favorable impression through their conduct and attitude in order to inspire confidence and cooperation. They should maintain high standards including proper dress, avoid use of terminology that is unfamiliar to the commander or person in charge of the activity being surveyed, and make clear that a physical security survey is performed as a means of assisting the commander in his operations and supervisory responsibilities.

b. Discuss with the commander the mission of the activity, its history, past incidents, if any, previous surveys, and any recent changes in personnel, mission, or additional buildings or areas planned.

Making the Survey

a. A physical security survey should be made of an installation to verify current data and to obtain new facts. It should be conducted not only when the installation is in operation, but also at other times, including hours of darkness. It should provide data for a true evaluation of existing hazards and the effectiveness of current protective measures.

b. The use of a survey team permits specialization by the members and develops expertness in surveying the various aspects of physical security. One member may examine the employment and training of the guard force while another surveys the perimeter barriers and the protective lighting system. Any division of duties that is expedient at a particular installation may be made.

Minimum Standards of Security

a. Security standards as developed in this field manual and appropriate security regulations should be used as a guide in evaluating a physical security program. After considering the prescribed minimum standards of security and the facts brought out by the physical security survey, a careful balance must be sought between what exists, what is desired, and what may be necessary under conditions of national emergency. Deficiencies affecting the entire installation which may be identified through physical security surveys include the following:

(1) Indications that perimeter security is inadequate.
(2) Evidence that any part of the installation is being used for unlawful or unauthorized practices.
(3) Indication that fences or lights are needed.
(4) Disclosure that control and check of persons entering or leaving the installation are inadequate.

b. Surveys of individual facilities should include, but are not limited to, inquiry into:

(1) Procedures for indoctrinating personnel in the use of internal control procedures, and their awareness of the necessity for vigilance to prevent loss of money and property.
(2) Receiving, stock control, and storage procedures.
(3) Procedures used for receiving, holding, and banking money.
(4) Identification required for persons making purchases.
(5) Structural characteristics of the buildings housing the facility.
(6) Adequacy of guard personnel and the effectiveness and enforcement of their orders.
(7) Procedures for storing and accounting for narcotics and sensitive medications.

c. Units on an installation may also be surveyed. Surveys may include, but are not limited to, inquiry into:

(1) Supply and storage room security and procedures. Special attention should be given to the security of arms and ammunition.
(2) Unit interior guard, including adequacy and application of guard orders.
(3) Safeguarding nonappropriated fund money and property.

d. Surveys of units and facilities may be expected to develop information relative to weaknesses in the security of their buildings, with respect to:

    (1) Locking devices and key control.

    (2) Pass system, if appropriate.

    (3) The adequacy of bars and/or protective screening over windows, skylights, and similar openings.

    (4) The potential of unlawful entry through attics, boiler rooms, basements, air vents, and crawl spaces under buildings.

    (5) The need for, or adequacy of, alarm systems.

    (6) Improper storage.

    (7) Lack of or inadequacy of inventories and audits.

    (8) Lack of supervision or control in the unit or activity.

    (9) Indications of changes or alterations in records.

   (10) Use of Army hospital property or facilities to perform medical examinations for personal gain, for example; receiving fees from insurance companies for physical examinations at an installation.

   (11) Excessive amounts of items on hand and their accessibility to unauthorized persons.

   (12) The refusal or failure to spot check employee work habits; the lack of internal control measures to assure honesty or to detect dishonesty, because of a mistaken belief that to do so would be poor leadership by casting suspicion upon the honesty of assigned personnel.

Evaluation

a. Security Priority List. An evaluation of the physical security survey should take into consideration the availability of materials and personnel, and evaluators should not lose sight of the mission of the installation. There will rarely be as much money, equipment, and manpower for security as is desired. When this fact is understood, the challenge for making the best of what is available must be accepted. Based on the mission and the potential security threat, a determination must be made regarding what degree of security is reasonable and necessary. One method is to make a security survey. This list will indicate under two categories the elements required for the accomplishment of the installation's mission.

b. Category I. Those elements that are considered indispensable to the mission.

c. Category II. Those elements that contribute directly but are not indispensable to the mission.

Exit Conference

Upon completion of each physical security survey, and prior to departure from the installation, survey personnel should request a meeting with the commanding officer or his representative and such staff officers as he may designate. The purpose of such meeting or exit conference will be to discuss the observations or findings of the survey personnel and their recommendations for remedial action. Frequently, what looks like a deficiency to survey personnel is not a deficiency but a measure peculiar to that installation and can be explained orally rather than through lengthy reports. During such conferences, survey personnel should present their findings in an orderly manner, and should be especially careful to discuss all security deficiencies observed during the survey.

Followup Survey Reports

The purpose of the followup survey is to insure that recommendations have been carried out. So that the initial survey record may be kept current and accurate, the same general subjects and specific points of security interest developed in the initial survey should be reexamined in subsequent followup surveys. In many instances, survey personnel will find that recommendations have not been carried out but that work orders have been submitted and/or validated. In such instances, the original deficiency is still reported as a deficiency until it is permanently corrected.

Survey Report

a. If DA Form 2800 is used, the cover sheet should reflect the required information as prescribed in AR 195–10 and FM 19–20.

b. In all other type reports, such as memorandum reports, the following information should be reflected:

(1) Synopsis

(a) The first paragraph of the synopsis should indicate circumstance surrounding the initiation of the survey. All surveys are initiated under the authority of the installation commander; however, the actual request or recommendation that the survey be conducted may come from a source subordinate to the commander.

(b) The second paragraph of the synopsis should be headed "Deficiencies noted during this survey" and should follow with a listing of deficiencies under the three headings mentioned in (2), below.

(c) The last paragraph of the synopsis should contain a remark noting that an exit interview has been conducted and that the responsible officer has been advised of noted deficiencies in the existing physical security safeguards and systems.

(2) Recommendations. The next section should contain the in-

vestigator's recommendations as to the corrective action which should be taken, based upon an analysis of all the facts in the situation in relation to other inherent factors, such as cost and feasibility, degree of security desired, and estimation of risk. In addition, recommendations which would necessitate extensive action involving the responsibilities of another staff agency should be discussed with the appropriate representative of such agency. For instance, when it has been determined that effective control of property or personnel can be enhanced by erecting a perimeter barrier in a certain area, the engineer officer should be consulted to determine the feasibility of such action from an engineering and cost viewpoint. There should be at least one recommendation for each deficiency noted in the synopsis. Recommendations may be placed under three possible headings; these may be changed or deleted as they apply to a particular situation.

(a) Security Personnel—recommendations affecting security guard utilization or employment.

(b) Administrative or operational measures—recommendations for administration or operational procedural changes.

(c) Physical security measures—recommendations regarding physical security factors, fences, lights, alarms, etc.

(3) Exhibits

(a) Survey personnel should procure and attach as exhibits to survey reports such of the following as are required for reader understanding of listed deficiencies and recommendations:

1. Documentary material in the form of current SOP, regulations, forms, maps, etc., which are pertinent to, and corroborative of the facts and findings contained in the body of the report.

2. Samples of personnel, visitor, and/or vehicular identification media.

3. Photographs and sketches, which should be used sparingly and should be meaningful. If the deficiency cannot be explained adequately in the narrative portion of the report, use a photograph or sketch marked with the deficiency on it so it can be readily identified by the reader of the report. The report should not be cluttered up with meaningless photographs and sketches.

4. Such additional evidentiary material as is deemed essential to support the points made in the report.

(b) Exhibits will be identified alphabetically and attached to the report in the order in which they are referred to in the narrative. An index of exhibits will be attached on a separate sheet of paper immediately following the body of the report.

c. Reports of completed physical security surveys may be classified in accordance with the provisions of AR 380–5, if the information contained therein is considered to warrant such classification. In other instances, the protective markings prescribed by AR 345–15 may be applied, or the report may be unclassified and unmarked. Evaluation of the information, and directives of higher headquarters, will govern the choice.

Security Staff: Checklist*

Checked by............................   Date...............

Security on Industrial Premises

SECURITY ON
1. Who is in charge of security?
2. Has a Job Description been prepared?
3. Full- or part-time? .
4. If part-time, what other duties are performed?
5. Is report on work of Security Departments submitted quarterly, half yearly, or yearly?
6. Who is the person in charge responsible to?

SECURITY STAFF (IF ANY)
7. How many are employed?
8. Is the number—
   a. under requirements,
   b. about right, or
   c. over requirements?
9. When was their status and payment reviewed and the result?
10. Is the general standard of morale: excellent, good, fair, or bad?

TRAINING
11. What form of training do they receive in—
    a. Security Duties
    b. Fire-Fighting Duties
    c. First Aid

---

*Reprinted with permission from Eric Oliver and John Wilson, *Practical Security in Commerce and Industry* (London: Gower, 1968) pp. 386-387.

    d. Accident Prevention

    e. Civil Defense

12. Does this include attendance at an outside training course? If so, which one?

DUTIES

13. Have these been embodied in a form of Standing Orders? Has each man been issued with a copy?

14. If no Standing Orders have been prepared, are the duties of the security staff described in writing?

15. When were those duties reviewed, by whom, and with what result?

16. What form of permanent record is kept of matters having a security interest?

17. Who inspects this and how often? Check.

18. What form of supervision of staff is carried out at night, at weekends, and on public holidays and by whom?

19. How is this recorded? Check.

PATROLLING

20. When is patrolling of premises carried out?

21. How often?

22. Is this excessive, satisfactory, or not often enough?

23. Are all areas given the same attention or do those more vulnerable to risk of any type receive more frequent attention?

24. Is a patrolman's clock used?

25. Are the clocking points too many, sufficient, or not enough and are they suitably placed?

26. Do the time clock records show satisfactory patrolling?

27. Is the company associated with any other in a Mutual Security Aid Scheme?

28. Are searches of company personnel and vehicles carried out? Check.

29. Are these too often, adequate, or not enough?

30. Are searches of contractors' personnel and vehicles carried out? Check.

31. Are these too often, adequate, or not enough?

32. Have any complaints been received? If so, were management informed and what were the results?

33. Are car parking arrangements and discipline of users satisfactory?

Gatehouse Duties: Security Checklist*

Checked by........................... Date..............

1. What gates are attended by security staff?
2. Are there other gates, including railway gates?
3. If so, when are they open and in what circumstances?
4. Who is responsible for opening and closing of those gates?
5. Where are the keys kept?
6. What action is taken at the gates attended by security staff—
   a. When vehicles enter—
      to collect goods,
      to collect scrap or waste materials,
      for any other purpose, for example, delivery of stores, etc.?
   b. When vehicles leave—
      after collecting goods,
      after collecting scrap or waste materials,
      after making deliveries of stores, etc.?
   c. When employees wish—
      to enter at unusual times,
      to leave at unusual times,
      to bring in large parcels and cases,
      to take borrowed tools away,
      to return borrowed tools,
      to remove purchases of company products from the premises?
   d. When requests are received for keys of premises at—
      usual times,
      unusual times?
   e. When property is reported as having been found on the premises?
   f. When property is reported lost on the premises?
   g. A fire is reported to have occurred on the premises?

Cash on Premises: Security Checklist†

Checked by........................... Date..............

1. Who collects money from bank?
   a. Company employees
   b. Cash in transit security company
2. If by the latter—

---

*Reprinted with permission from Eric Oliver and John Wilson, *Practical Security in Commerce and Industry* (London: Gower, 1968) p. 388.

†Reprinted with permission from Eric Oliver and John Wilson, *Practical Security in Commerce and Industry* (London: Gower, 1968) p. 389.

    a. Has the actual point of delivery (for example: desk in wages manager's office on third floor of Blank House) been included in the contract?

    b. Has a list of authorized receivers of the money with their specimen signatures been supplied to the security service company and acknowledged by them?

3. If there is a gate to the premises is this locked shut until the money is safely delivered?
4. Where is the money taken to on arrival?

    a. Petty cash requirements

    b. Wages money

Wages Money

1. Is the office used for making-up locked at that time?
2. Can callers outside the door be seen from inside before the door is open?
3. How many persons are present at the make-up?
4. Is any one of those permitted to leave before this is complete?
5. When make-up is complete what happens to the packets and how are they protected?
6. How are packets taken to pay-out points?
7. Is a car used where the distance requires this?
8. Are gates of premises locked when transfer of the packets is taking place on company roads?
9. How many persons are concerned in the transferral?
10. What is the physical security of pay-out points, telephone, alarm, etc.?
11. Who is present at pay-out points?
12. What happens to unpaid wage packets?
13. Who is responsible for their security?
14. When there are pay-out times outside the normal office hours, who pays out?
15. Where have the relevant packets been kept up to pay-out time? In a safe?
16. Who holds personally the key to the safe?

Safes

1. Where are safes located on premises?
2. Are they secured to the floor or wall to prevent their removal?
3. Has any of them a protective thief alarm?
4. Who has the operative key to the safe?
5. Where are any duplicates? In the bank?

6. If safe has a combination lock who has code? copies of it?
7. Who is responsible for switching on the alarm where fitted and retaining key? Preferably this should not be the safe key-holder.
8. Who is responsible for the duplicate key and where is it kept?

Cashiers/Wages Office

1. What floor is it on?
2. Is it close to stairs or lifts?
3. Can the activities of occupiers be observed from adjacent offices?
4. Can these activities be observed from other buildings?
5. Does it give an exit to a flat roof or fire escape?
6. Has the office an observation window or lens in the door?
7. Has the door a strong slam lock?
8. Has the office a counter with cash drawers fitted with slam locks?
9. Has the counter a grille or armoured glass?
10. Is an alarm fitted and tested daily?
11. Have staff been instructed on the action to be taken on hearing the alarm?

Cash in Transit: Security Checklist*

Checked by............................. Date...............

1. Is the money carried in pockets or in a bag?
2. When are the deposits and withdrawals made?
3. Do the times display a pattern of irregularity?
4. Who makes deposits and withdrawals?
5. What escort is provided?
6. Are they dressed in distinctive clothing?
7. Are those persons always the same?
8. Are they supplied with police whistles and any form of self-protection against attack?
9. How far away is the bank?
10. What transport, if any, is used?
11. Is it always the same?
12. Is the driver always the same?
13. Is a second vehicle used?
14. Has the cash vehicle any form of alarm?
15. If so, is the alarm tested immediately before going to bank?
16. Where is cash carried in the car?

---

*Reprinted with permission from Eric Oliver and John Wilson, *Practical Security in Commerce and Industry* (London: Gower, 1968) pp. 391-392.

17. If in the boot, is it locked?
18. If a container is used is it secured to the vehicle in any way?
19. Has the container any alarm fitted?
20. Are the keys of the container or any securing device carried in the car?
21. Can vehicle doors be locked from inside?
22. Is the vehicle a hired car?
23. If the driver is not known what action is taken?
24. If vehicle returning from bank with money is followed in suspicious circumstances what action would be taken?
25. Is a bank night safe used?
26. Are security arrangements satisfactory bearing in mind these observations?
27. Is route to and from bank varied and through busy streets?
28. Who decides route and when?
29. Are police informed of visits to bank?
30. If no vehicle is used, do the company employees walk against the traffic and away from the kerb edge?

Shops and Supermarkets: Security Checklist†

Staff

1. Are all references verified before employees are engaged?
2. Have Conditions of Employment been prepared?
3. Does every employee on engagement sign and receive a copy?
4. Do the Conditions refer to—
   a. Bringing parcels or cases onto the premises?
   b. Handbags, baskets in the sales area?
   c. Not leaving sales area without permission?
   d. Searching of handbags, etc.?
   e. Leaving only by front entrance?
5. Purchasing Conditions: Are these outlined in the Conditions of Employment? Do these deal with—
   a. Times of purchase?
   b. Dress when shopping?
   c. Use of wire baskets?
   d. Retention of till slips signed by checker?
   e. Sale of goods in short supply?
   f. Sale of goods reduced to clear?
   g. Amount of discount and how to claim?

---

†Reprinted with permission from Eric Oliver and John Wilson, *Practical Security in Commerce and Industry* (London: Gower, 1968) pp. 398-401.

Keys to Front Door

    6. Is keyholder registered with Police? Is information up-to-date?

    7. Who has responsibility for ensuring the premises are secure before being left?

Fire Doors

    8. Is any device fitted to activate an audible alarm if opened?

Rear or Delivery Doors

    9. Who holds the keys
       a. During time premises are open?
       b. When closed?

  10. Are doors locked between deliveries?

  11. Are delivery men admitted to sales area?

  12. Are they allowed to enter through front door?

  13. If deliveries are made to sales area are they checked there together with any collections, for example, stale bread, cakes, etc?

  14. Are composite delivery notes signed representing multiple deliveries?

  15. Deliveries—
       a. How are specially valuable and attractive goods protected?
       b. If in a separate compound, who holds key?
       c. Does the Goods Inward checker when tallying hold the delivery note at the same time?
       d. Are all over- and under-deliveries properly recorded?
       e. Are deliveries occasionally rechecked by a member of management?
       f. Is a Goods Inward Book kept? If so who makes the entries?

Rubbish and Salvage

  16. Who supervises the removal of rubbish and salvage?

  17. Are bins examined from time to time to detect stolen goods?

Cash Tills

  18. Can customers see clearly the amount rung up on the till?

  19. What pockets are there in the cashiers' overalls?

  20. Have cashiers been told they must not serve relatives?

  21. Do the cashiers—
       a. Check their floats before accepting any more money?
       b. Check the date recorder on their till?
       c. Check that the total amount previously recorded on the till has not been changed?

d. Have a key to their tills?

e. Take money, handbags, baskets or cigarettes to their check-out point?

f. Ring up on the till each item separately?

g. Shut the drawer of the till after each completed sale?

Cashing Up

22. Is an independent count taken of each till at close of business and reconciled with the registered total?

23. Is a record kept of overs and unders and brought to notice of management?

24. Is the pen record in 22 and 23 signed by the till operator and the clerk concerned?

25. Are notes above requirements collected from time to time from the till and are records made and signed by the respective cashiers?

26. Where is any spare cash and takings as in 25 kept until banked?

27. If in a safe, or other locked and satisfactory permanent container, where is key kept?

28. Are some of the day's cash takings taken to the bank during normal banking hours?

29. Is a bank safe used?

Safes

30. Where is it located?

31. Can it be seen from outside the premises?

32. Would security of the safe be improved if a light was left burning?

33. Is is secured to the floor?

34. Who holds the key?

35. Where is the duplicate? In the bank?

Shoplifters and Thefts by Staff

36. Has a policy for dealing with shoplifters and staff found stealing been decided and circulated?

37. Have "Rules for the Guidance of Managers concerned with Shoplifters" been circulated to them?

38. Are details of all employees found stealing company property and the result of any prosecutions posted in positions where they can be read by all employees?

39. Are records kept of all shoplifters whether prosecuted or not?

Security Staff (where employed)

40. Are employees told of the responsibilities and authority of such staff and that they are liable to be asked to explain their possession of company property after leaving the premises?

Basic Security Precautions*

A. *Doors, Door Frames, and Door Locks*

1. Solid core doors are preferable to panel doors or doors with glass pane.
2. Then paneled or hollow cored doors should be lined with metal sheets.
3. Glass paneled doors should be covered with closely spaced steel bars or with strong mesh on the inside of the door.
4. If there is glass in the door, the unlocking of the door from the inside should require a key and not simply a turnpiece. In the jargon of locksmiths, the lock should be "keyed from within."
5. Exterior door hinges should have non-removable hinge pins.
6. If the door is sufficiently strong but the door frame is weak, a lock should be used whose security does not depend on the door frame for mounting.
7. Door locks should have a deadbolt feature and should be used in conjunction with pick resistant key cylinder.
8. Spring latches are not effective unless fitted with a deadlocking feature.
9. If a padlock is used, it should be of a pick resistant quality and should have a hardened shackle. All identification numbers should be removed from the padlock before use.
10. Overhead doors should be locked either by electric power or slide bolts and/or a pick resistant cylinder lock.
11. Elevator doors opening directly into offices or unguarded areas should be equipped with key controlled locks.
12. Where it is necessary that "panic bars" be used on doors (like a movie theater fire door), the panic bar should have an alarm feature which will indicate when the door is opened during business hours.

B. *Windows*

1. All windows other than those providing access to fire escapes should be secured by ferry gates, bars, or mesh which cannot be removed from without or by key controlled inside locks.
2. Windows leading to fire escapes should be equipped with key controlled inside locks.
3. Outside hinged windows should have non-removable hinge pins.

C. *Hatchways*

1. Hatchways should be secured from the inside with barrel bolts, padlocks and eye or heave hook and eye.

---

*Reprinted from *Basic Security Precautions* (Rochester: Sargent & Grenleaf, Inc.) pp. 1-3.

D. Transoms

1. Transoms should be covered with metal bars or mesh which cannot be removed from without, or
2. Transoms should be secured from the inside with key controlled window locks.

E. Metal Gates

1. Accordion type gates should be equipped with top and bottom slide tracks and should be locked with a padlock which is pick resistant and which will resist the use of force. Padlocks should have identification numbers removed before use.
2. Outside hinges should have non-removable hinge pins.

F. Lighting

1. The interior of the premises should be illuminated throughout the night.
2. The safe should be well illuminated and easily visible from the street.
3. The cash register should be left open at night and should be visible from the street.
4. All outside access points, especially rear and side alley doors, should be well lighted.

G. Safes

1. When using a safe for a purpose other than the protection of records from fire, use a "chest type" safe. Such safes are designed to protect valuables against burglary.
2. If the safe is a movable type, remove the wheels and anchor the safe to the floor.

ALSO, AS GENERAL PRACTICE:
Do not leave a written copy of the combination on the premises.
When an employee resigns or is discharged, change the combination.
On locking the safe spin the dial at least 5 times in one direction.
Make bank deposits as frequently as possible and try not to rely on a safe for the overnight protection of valuables.

H. Alarms

THERE ARE SEVERAL TYPES OF ALARMS:
Central alarm systems which bring a direct response from the police and/or the alarm company are best. They are costly to install and carry a monthly rental.

Electronic alarms are available which telephone a tape recorded message to whomever you designate.

Local alarms ring a bell on the premises. If used, the neighbors should be solicited to notify the police when the alarm is activated.

1. An alarm should not be designed to be de-activated from outside the premises. Use an alarm which employs a time delay feature and de-activate by key from within.

I. Keys

AS GENERAL PRACTICE:

Keys should be possessed only by responsible personnel and by as few personnel as possible and reasonable.

Change the key cylinder whenever a key-holding employee is discharged or resigns, or when a key is lost.

Do not use a system of locks which is master keyed unless absolutely necessary.

Do not leave keys lying around during the day where some unauthorized person can take them and have copies made.

Use of a highly pick-resistant key cylinder will generally make key duplication more difficult.

Lock and Key Survey

if you are in the field of

EDUCATION

Date · · · · · · · · · · · · · · · · · · ·
Department · · · · · · · · · · · · · ·
Total Locks · · · · · · · · · · · · · ·
By ·

You may want to find out how many locks and keys you should CONTROL by distributing these survey sheets to department heads.

You may have as many copies as you wish without any obligation.

Items with Locks	Number of Locks	Items with Locks	Number of Locks	Items with Locks	Number of Locks
Access Space		Dispensers		Mail Boxes	
Air Conditioning		Sanitary Napkin		Money Bags	
Alarms		Soap			
Athletic Supplies		Towel			
Automotive				Penthouse	
		Doors (Exterior)		Plan Case	
		Entrance			
Book Cases		Exit			
Bulletin Boards		Doors (Interior)		Refrigerators	
		Cafeteria		Rolling Grills	
		Classroom		Roof Vents	
Cabinets		Closet			
Electric		Connecting			
Filing		Elevator		Safe Compartments	
Instrument		Fan Room		Safe Deposit Boxes	
Key		Fire		Screens	
Medicine		Garage		Slop Sink Closet	
Storage		Office		Switch Key	
Supply					
Wardrobe					
		Drawers		Tabernacle	
		Bench		Tanks (Oil & Gas)	
		Cash		Thermostat	
		Drafting Room		Trailers	
		Lab. Table		Trap Doors	
Camera Cases		Safe		Trucks	
Cash Boxes		Tool		Trunks	
Cash Registers					
Chute Doors		Gasoline Pump			
Clocks		Gates		Valves	
				Vaults	
		Lockers			
		Gym			
Dark Rooms		Paint		Watchman's Service Box	
Desks		Student			
Display Cases		Teachers		X-Ray	

Courtesy of P. O. Moore, Inc., Subsidiary of Sunroc Corporation, Glen Riddle, Pa.

The Moore TelKee Systems for Key Control

Lock and Key Survey

if you are in the field of
BUSINESS ADMINISTRATION

Date	
Department	
Total Locks	
By	

You may want to find out how many locks and keys you should CONTROL by distributing these survey sheets to department heads.

You may have as many copies as you wish at no cost or obligation.

Items with Locks	Number of Locks	Items with Locks	Number of Locks	Items with Locks	Number of Locks
Access Space		Dispensers		Mail Bags	
Air Conditioning		Sanitary Napkin		Mail Boxes	
Alarms		Soap		Money Bags	
Automotive		Towel			
		Doors (Exterior)		Penthouse	
Bulletin Boards		Entrance		Plan Case	
		Exit			
		Doors (Interior)			
		Cafeteria		Refrigerators	
		Closet		Rolling Grills	
		Connecting		Roof Vents	
Cabinets		Elevator			
Electric		Elevator Corridor			
Filing		Fan Room		Safe Compartments	
Key		Fire		Safe Deposit Boxes	
Medicine		Garage		Screens	
Storage		Office		Slop Sink Closet	
Supply				Switch Key	
Tool					
Wardrobe					
		Drawers		Tanks (Oil & Gas)	
		Cash		Thermostat	
		Lab. Table		Trucks & Trailers	
		Safe		Trucks	
		Tool & Bench			
Cash Boxes					
Cash Registers					
Chute Doors		Gas Pump		Valves	
Clocks		Gates		Vaults	
		Lockers		Watchman's Service Box	
Dark Rooms		Employee			
Desks		Paint			
Display Cases		Tool Room			

Courtesy of P. O. Moore, Inc., Subsidiary of Sunroc Corporation, Glen Riddle, Pa.

The Moore TelKee Systems for Key Control

Lock and Key Survey
if you are in the field of
HOSPITAL ADMINISTRATION

Date	....
Department	....
Total Locks	....
By	....

You may want to find out how many locks and keys you should CONTROL by distributing these survey sheets to department heads, such as Administrative, Nursing, Engineering, Stewards, Dietary, Housekeeping, Operating & Delivery, X-Ray, Pathological, Pharmacy, Laundry, Mortuary, Garage, and other divisions.

We will be glad to supply as many additional copies as you wish without any obligation.

Items with Locks	Number of Locks	Items with Locks	Number of Locks	Items with Locks	Number of Locks
Access Space		Dispensers		Mail Boxes	
Air Conditioning		Sanitary Napkin		Money Bags	
Alarms		Soap			
Automotive		Towel			
				Penthouse	
		Doors (Exterior)			
Book Cases		Entrance			
Blood Bank		Exit			
Bulletin Boards		Doors (Interior)		Refrigerators	
		Closet			
		Connecting			
		Elevator		Roof Vents	
Cabinets		Entrance			
Electric		Fire			
Filing		Office		Safe Compartments	
Instrument		Storage Room		Safe Deposit Boxes	
Key				Screens	
Kitchen				Slop Sink Closet	
Medicine				Switch Key	
Narcotics					
Storage		Drawers			
Supply		Bench		Tabernacle	
Suture		Cash		Tanks (Oil & Gas)	
Tool		Lab. Table		Thermostat	
Wardrobe		Safe		Trap Doors	
		Tool			
		Gas Pump		Valves	
Cash Boxes		Gates		Vaults	
Cash Registers					
Chute Doors					
Clocks		Lockers		Watchman's Service Box	
		Employee			
Dark Rooms		Patients			
Desks		Physicians		X-Ray	

Courtesy of P. O. Moore, Inc., Subsidiary of Sunroc Corporation, Glen Riddle, Pa.

The Moore TelKee Systems for Key Control

CHAPTER 5

PREPARING RECOMMENDATIONS

THE RESULTS OF any survey will only be useful if an effort is made to present clear and concise recommendations as they relate to the surveyor's findings and interpretations. Recommendations must be *realistic, feasible, easy to interpret* and will primarily serve five functions:

1. To aid in motivating the recipient of the survey to modify an existing crime risk.
2. The establishment of a frame of reference in which to act upon (set forth a plan of action).
3. Alter or reinforce a specific image of potentiality regarding crime risk. (Some individuals or organizations may have preconceived opinions of their existing safety/security.)
4. The establishing of a channel of communication. (Many personnel within an organization may not be sensitive to a problem; hence a survey may demonstrate some very important facts which should be understood by all interested parties.)
5. The creating of realistic expectations. (Establish a realistic set of aspirations which can be achieved by the recipient of the survey, i.e. be wary of overstating the problem.)

Accordingly, the influence that a surveyor exercises directly and indirectly throughout a survey will have results far beyond the scope of written recommendations. For this reason it is imperative that each survey be prepared in a professional and responsible manner.

IDENTIFYING DEFICIENCIES

All deficiencies or weaknesses within the purview of a survey should be stated in a concise and positive manner. Therefore an understanding of basic problem solving techniques should be mastered by each surveyor. For example, individual imagination, observation, and empathy in all areas that influence a security risk will enhance the surveyor's personal insight as it relates to developing and presenting recommendations.

The formulating of recommendations on a sound basis often calls for more information than is at hand in any given situation. Thus, one's ability to study changes and features of a wide variety as they relate to crime risk or deficiencies will in the long run have a far-reaching influence on any given recommendation. In this frame of reference a good surveyor should review the installation both under daylight and nighttime conditions. Finally, it is a good practice to use knowledge and research from many sources.

STATING RECOMMENDATIONS

An excellent survey may encompass a multitude of good ideas which include a variety of good suggestions, but if the written recommendations cannot be understood, little will come of the total project. Hence, it is important to illustrate each recommendation in such a manner that only *one* conclusion may be drawn from each recommendation. Therefore, state *one* specific problem and identify one solution (unless the application of two or more security processes will be needed to modify or reduce the crime risk).

The need to motivate the recipient of a survey to act upon suggested recommendations exists throughout all stages of a survey. One other aspect of the recommendations presentation process is that the final report should be typed, proofread and bound in some manner to make the document more presentable. The inclusion of drawings, photographs, etc., is a good technique to illustrate a point.

ANALYZING AND MEASURING

The measurement of the reliability of reports (recommendations) must be compared to selected responses to successive questions. In other words, compare your recommendations to your previous experience and consider the alternatives you developed from the research of existing literature. Thus, the information the surveyor prepares for any one given deficiency can be interpreted within an established framework. The key here is the analyzing of all available information and the development of an acceptable set of *averages or consistencies.* With experience and knowledge the surveyor will be able to prepare and execute an objective survey, thereupon making a final report which includes recommendations of deficiency in a concise, valid and realiable manner.

The reliability of the survey data (information about deficiencies or weaknesses) can be measured in the same way as the reliability of any other kind of research data, and that is by retesting. For this reason it is very important for a survey to *illustrate* or identify all areas of crime risks, the result being a comprehensive, reliable, valid and acceptable survey measured against any good standard of performance.

WRITTEN REPORT FORM

After all available information is collected and reviewed, the written report stage is initiated. The specific results of the inspection or survey will be prepared including deficiencies, recommendations and a general evaluation of the installation. Thus, the written report will in a practical sense describe all of the findings a surveyor had developed at any one installation.

The written report format may be different with each survey. For this reason a *general* example of a written survey form has been prepared. (Refer to Chapter 3, Model Security Survey.)

The five major categories found in most surveys include:

1. Introduction stage
2. Identification of installation or site
3. Areas of consideration
4. Specific areas
5. Conclusion

The five categories of a survey have a number of subheadings which may include:

Category 1. Introduction Stage (A brief statement of intent)

A. Authority for conducting the survey (Who initiated or requested the survey and also consider legal liability in conducting a survey)
B. Time of day or night
C. Date
D. Identify any previous surveys (date)
E. State individuals involved in survey (names)
F. State installation or site representative (name)

Category 2. Identification of Installation or Site

A. Name of organization
B. Mission/purpose (What does the organization do, e.g. drug store, food market, etc.?)
C. Identify building (site)
D. Importance of organization (Bank vs. empty warehouse)

Category 3. Areas of Consideration (Which specific area of the three processes of security will be studied)

A. Physical security
B. Information security
C. Personnel security

In some surveys all three areas may be studied, whereas in most surveys just the physical security of an installation will be surveyed.

A complete, factual, detailed, narrative report should be made on each area of consideration.

Example

Physical security: Only the physical characteristics of this building area were considered. The windows, doors, skylights and ventilations (entrances) were examined, etc.

Category 4. Specific Areas

In this part of the survey a brief detailed description of each area surveyed should be considered and a listing by categories of deficiencies and positive points made. For this reason a chronological list of areas surveyed should be made. An example would include:

1. Doors (Where located, what kind, how many, etc.; strengths or deficiencies)
2. Windows (Size, location, type, number, etc.)

Table II: AN *EXAMPLE* IN THE DEVELOPING OF SEQUENTIAL STEPS IN THE
PREPARATION OF A RECOMMENDATION

WINDOWS:

General Statement: A brief statement of the problem or situation.

Example—The only window at the rear of the store is located ten feet from the south wall of the building and is three feet from ground level.

Specific Deficiency: A detailed description of the deficiency.

Example—The window is two feet by two feet with one single pane of glass. The glass is broken in half exposing an open area of one foot by two feet.

Recommendation(s): A brief answer to the specific problem deficiency) and identifying one solution per deficiency (unless the application of two or more security processes will be needed to modify or reduce the crime risk.

Example—The window should have 20 gauge steel mesh placed on the outside of the window frame. The wire mesh should be secured by bolts with the threads and nut being located inside the window.

NOTE: A photograph or sketch of the violation and recommendation would be appropriate.

The reader can obviously perceive that more than one recommendation could be considered, e.g. alarms, steel bars, sealing up the window (bricking), etc. The example given demonstrates the broad latitude a surveyor has, while keeping in mind the financial cost of his recommendations to the recipient and the total protection plan of the organization.

Category 5. Conclusion

The conclusion should summarize the *general* objectives, deficiencies and recommendations of the survey. This is not to imply that the conclusion is a long, drawn-out section, but rather a concise narrative summation of the survey. The conclusion can generally be prepared in one or two paragraphs.

RECOMMENDATIONS

Some individuals who perform surveys prefer to have the recommendations summarized at the end of the report. Indeed this may be a good technique, but the placing of recommendations after each deficiency as described in Category 4 (Specific Areas) tends to facilitate the implementation of recommendations by the recipient.

A good practice is to summarize the weakness and recommendation on one sheet of paper prior to Category 4 (Specific Areas), which in turn tends to give the survey recipient a brief *look* at his deficiencies. This same summarization may be placed at the front of the survey (before the title page), but again the final written report form should be tailored to the individual surveyor, installation and situation. Likewise, good grammar and editorial practices should be employed throughout the survey. Again, it is stressed that a survey is a culmination of many manhours and should reflect the highest standards of professional expertise, ethics and editorial accomplishments.

PRESENTING RECOMMENDATIONS

A distinct relationship between the surveyor and survey recipient develops throughout an actual survey. Accordingly the final contribution of a surveyor's experiences will be expressed through his recommendations which will be characterized in written and verbal form. Regardless of the working relationships which existed during a survey, the final presentation of the completed survey should be rational and well organized.

In order to develop a successful system of recommendation *presentation,* the surveyor should at all times have the objectives of the survey, installation, recipient and total loss prevention program in proper perspective.

WHO RECEIVES THE SURVEY?

The surveyor has an obligation to present his findings and recommendations to the individual (or an authorized associate) who originally commissioned the survey. It is incumbent upon the surveyor to accomplish his task with the least amount of interference by both organizational and personal pressures. A certain amount of *trouble* or negative implications may arise if the final survey is not presented to the authorized authority.

HOW ARE THE SURVEY RECOMMENDATIONS PRESENTED?

This implies a method of *behavior* vs. *philosophical* action. For this reason a professional attitude should be adhered to by the surveyor. It is recommended that an office, private room, etc., be used to review all aspects of the survey. Thus a public area is not conducive to a controlled and uninterpreted presentation.

WHEN SHOULD A SET OF RECOMMENDATIONS
BE PRESENTED?

The results of a survey should be presented to the survey recipient as soon as the surveyor feels a complete and objective survey has been successfully concluded. Therefore, as soon as a survey is typed, reviewed and prepared for presentation, the final interview with the recipient should take place.

It is most important to understand that the successful presentation of recommendations to the recipient is one of the highest responsibilities a surveyor has. It is at this time that the *selling* of the recommendations will take place. Too often a surveyor tends to think the survey is completed after typing the final draft. The *failure* of many good surveys takes place during the final evaluation between the surveyor and recipient regarding recommendations and their implementation.

The possibility that a follow-up inspection may take place at a later time is no substitute for a successful description and interpretation of the defined recommendations.

Communication between the two parties (surveyor and recipient) must be specific and mutually intelligible. All conditions of the surveyed environment, including individual crime risk and recommendations, should be adequately critiqued.

CHAPTER 6

MANAGEMENT FOR CRIME PREVENTION

MANAGEMENT FOR CRIME prevention has been extracted from the publication *Crime Against Small Business*, to form a reference base for the security surveyor. The need to understand problems of the small businessman is a major concern for any surveying team.

Essentially, this section will aid the surveyor in understanding and developing a total protection plan as it relates to the survey. A systematic approach to any type of survey will necessitate a comprehensive understanding of many and varied security topics. Within this framework of knowledge the surveyor can establish good practices in preparing, implementing and evaluating a security survey. All too often a poor survey is effected because the surveyor does not have a real understanding of his subject.

The concept of protection may have far-reaching implications both to the individual and organization. The investment of time and money, if not instituted in a prudent manner, may in the long run be very costly. In this connection the reduction of crime should be systematically studied prior to the actual implementation of loss controls. As has been outlined in previous chapters, the security survey should be considered the cornerstone or starting place for any security program. In this light the information for Chapter 6 has been included to aid the surveyor in his *total* security education program. The Selected Bibliography may also be of great value to the individual who seeks a better understanding of the total security environment concept.

BUSINESS MANAGEMENT FOR CRIME PREVENTION*

Introduction

Every small businessman is confronted with the problem of protecting his business against some phase of crime. It thus becomes his responsibility to establish policies and rules and to weigh the value of different protective devices, as measures to reduce the impact of crime on his business.

Among the courses of action open to the businessman for more effective protection against crime are (a) use of physical means such as alarm systems,

---

*Reprinted with permission from *Crime Against Small Business*, Document No. 91-14 (Washington, D.C.: Government Printing Office, 1969).

antitheft devices, door and window guards, and firearms; (b) training of employees to cope with shoplifting, armed robbery, burglary, employee pilferage, and embezzlement; (c) reorganization of business practices and procedures; (d) modification of the physical features and layout of the place of business; (e) rethinking of the attitude of management in coping with the problem of crime, leading perhaps to a stronger stand on prosecution of persons committing crimes against the firm, including shoplifters and the small minority of dishonest employees.

The Cost of Crime and of Crime Prevention

Established management practices to combat crime are notably lacking among small firms. As a result, losses through crime may not be detected early or may not be known at all. Shoplifting and employee pilferage, two costly sources of losses, are poorly controlled in small businesses. Because they do not lend themselves to precise cost analysis, the small businessman does not generally know the cost to him of these crimes. Thus, the value of losses in burglary also may be hard to determine if control measures are inadequate.

Any investment the businessman makes in crime prevention should be considered in relation to (a) the immediate cost of crime and the savings to be realized, and (b) the effect of his investment in discouraging future crimes against him.

Immediate investments whose value management would need to appraise might include protective devices such as antitheft mirrors to cut down on shoplifting, or photographic equipment to take pictures of checkpassers, or antiburglary devices.

Investments of a more general nature, spread over a longer period, would include training employees on how to detect shoplifting and actions in the case of a robbery.

It is entirely possible that certain kinds of investments may reduce other costs. For example, the installation of a central burglar alarm system may reduce insurance costs enough to offset the alarm cost. The businessman should explore all possibilities of cost reduction in connection with his expenditures to reduce his crime losses.

The Need for a More Positive Attitude

Research into the problem of crime against small business has brought out the fact that, while small businesses may appear concerned over the problem, little action is being taken. The smaller the store and the smaller the community, the less the effort is being applied. Most small businesses are not security conscious. Yet, ironically, a single crime such as a burglary, or a series of small, continuous losses as by pilferage may so sap the firm that failure ultimately occurs.

A part of the problem is lack of knowledge by the small businessman about how to cope with the kinds of crime discussed in this study, combined with sidestepping or procrastination. He finds it hard to accept the possibility that one or two of his employees might be dishonest or that his business could be burglarized. It may take a burglary or a robbery or significant employee theft losses to jar the businessman into positive action.

Ignorance of the law adds to the businessman's frustration. Many times, he is unaware of the legal protection afforded him. Many states have laws protecting the businessman from suit for false arrest for shoplifting, providing the suspect is detailed in a reasonable manner for a reasonable period of time and if the businessman is reasonably sure that he has taken merchandise with no intention of paying for it. Since the businessman is often not sure of his rights, he is reluctant to take any action, thus permitting the offender to go free to practice on other, equally unwary businessmen.

The need for a positive, direct approach by the businessman is obvious. In spite of the efforts of law enforcement agencies, the primary responsibility rests with the individual to protect his firm through appropriate devices, through indoctrination and training of employees, through cooperation with other area businessmen, and through establishing appropriate liaison with his local police.

Resources Available to the Small Businesseman

Most metropolitan police departments are in an excellent position to help small businessmen through training, counseling, and publications.

Procedures for Controlling Crime in Business

The remainder of this appendix deals with five separate areas of crime. In each, a brief narrative is presented, describing the problem. This is followed by a checklist of possible remedies. Thus, the businessman can identify the kind of problems with which he is confronted and then read about courses of action to meet these problems.

The five areas are:
1. Burglary
2. Robbery
3. Shoplifting
4. Bad checks
5. Employee theft

I. Burglary

The General Problem. From the management point of view, protection against burglary is a matter of attitude and housekeeping. It is the responsibility of the businessman to discourage burglary by maintaining the highest level of protection for his establishment.

To begin with, the businessman must accept the fact that burglary is entirely possible and no business is immune from it. While certain types of crimes are more directly related to the kind of business (shoplifting in retail stores), burglary is more likely to affect all small businesses. FBI reports show that nonresidence daytime burglaries are up 83 percent between 1960 and 1967. Nonresidence nighttime burglaries are up 47 percent for the same period.

Protection of the obvious points of entry is not sufficient. The businessman must anticipate every conceivable method by which a burglar could gain entry into the building—through doors, windows, roofs, sidewalk openings, and all other possibilities.

There are certain managerial decisions that must be reached with respect to burglary. It is advisable that the businessman counsel with all sources of assistance. These might include his local police department, his insurance agent, representatives of burglar alarm companies, safe companies, cash register companies, and building architects.

The businessman should know as much as possible about the alternatives available to him in burglary protection. Basically, he needs to make decisions relating to the following:

1. The kind of an alarm system, if any, best suited to his kind of business. The cost of maintaining an alarm system must be measured against the expected savings in insurance and the average cost of a typical burglary for his kind of business.

2. The adequacy of locks on entrances to the building. This includes locks on windows, sidewalk entrances, roof openings, as well as doors. Too often locks are not changed for long periods of time and the businessman may not actually know all who have keys to the building. He should make it a practice to change locks or tumblers on locks as often as he feels necessary to give adequate protection. Further, the types of locks should be such as to give maximum protection. Window locks should be given the same thorough inspection as door locks. Counseling with a competent locksmith will eliminate many unforeseen problems.

3. The establishment of a routine for total protection, with assigned responsibility to others in the owner's absence. There is no substitute for good housekeeping in burglary protection. The owner should establish a fixed daily routine to assure that every precaution is being taken. This includes such measures as:

   a. Leaving the cash register open at night.
   b. Turning on lights inside and outside the building before leaving.

   c. Checking to see that no one is hiding in the building at closing time.

   d. Doublechecking all doors and windows.

   e. Checking to see that the alarm is turned on and is operating properly.

Essentially, the businessman's function in burglary is to increase the time needed to gain entry. The individual businessman's effort is the most important part of prevention. By installing adequate lights, locks, alarms, and other devices, the physical security of the business will deter at best or delay at least the efforts of even the most determined burglar.

But the business is not secure unless it is totally protected. The most intricate alarm system is of no use if it fails to cover even the smallest roof opening. The strongest door will do little good if the burglar can quickly enter an unlocked window. Anything short of total protection means inadequate protection.

Appendix C of this report contains a detailed listing of the kinds of burglary problems the small businessman may face and suggested courses of action he may take to improve his level of protection. The type of business, its location, age, and architecture of the building are all factors which govern burglary protection.

Like other matters of crime, however, protection against burglary begins with a positive attitude on the part of the owner that protection of the individual business is *his* responsibility.

A. Lighting

The Problem. The majority of burglaries occur at night, and naturally the criminal welcomes darkness to conceal his presence and his actions. Three out of four commercial burglaries are committed against buildings that have either no lights or inadequate lights. The would-be burglar can be discouraged and perhaps thwarted by adequate lighting inside and outside a building.

   Preventive actions:

1. Place a night light over the safe.
2. Alleys and rear of business should be well lighted.
3. Illuminate all entry points well.
4. Keep night light on inside the building.
5. Night lights should be wired so that the alarm is set to go if they go out.
6. Install inside lights to the rear so that an intruder's silhouette can be seen from the street.

B. Locks

The Problem. The easier the method of entry, the greater the chance of burglary. Locks that can be forced, duplicated, or easily opened increase the likelihood of burglary. Experienced would-be burglers can quickly size up the ease of entry by casual observation of locks on doors, storage, windows, etc. The burglar-proof lock has not yet been invented, but adequate locks are available and will deter even the most determined.

Preventive actions:

1. Modern, cylinder-type locks are preferable.
2. Proper installation should prevent prying, cutting, twisting.
3. Lock bolts should be protected against being pushed back with a thin instrument.
4. Control of keys is important.
5. Hinge pins and hasps should be installed to prevent removal of pins and screws.
6. High grade steel hasps will prevent prying, twisting, cutting.
7. Padlocks should be locked in place at all times to prevent key duplicating.
8. Lock bolts should be flush and point inward.

C. Doors

The Problem. Most burglaries occur by forcing a natural opening in the building, such as a door or a window. Inadequate doors offer the burglar easy access to the premises. Doors too fragile for adequate protection, improper fit of doors in jambs, antiquated locking mechanisms—all add to the problem. Strength and security can be had without sacrificing looks. Protection, however, should overweigh appearance.

Preventive actions:

1. Panels and glass should be protected against being kicked or knocked out.
2. Put bars on the inside to prevent breaking the entire door.
3. Double doors should be flush-locked with long bolt.
4. If the door has glass that can be broken, install double-cylinder lock requiring key both inside and out.
5. Install sheet metal on inside and outside of basement doors.
6. Install door frames that cannot be pried off hinges or removed.
7. Cylinder ring of lock should be recessed to discourage use of lock puller.

D. Windows

The Problem. Windows offer easy access to the building unless adequately protected. Display windows in retail stores are susceptible to hit-and-run tactics. Other windows, poorly protected, permit the burglar to enter the building, oftentimes undetected, particularly when the windows are poorly lighted. Windows should offer light, ventilation, and visibility, but *not* easy access.

Preventive actions:

1. Properly installed grates give maximum security.
2. Glass bricks are highly effective on windows not needed for ventilation.
3. Locks must be designed and located so they cannot be reached and opened by breaking the glass.
4. Heavy merchandise and equipment piled in front of unused windows will give some protection.
5. Cleaning windowsills periodically will assure that fingerprints are more likely to be left by a burglar.
6. Avoid, wherever possible, window displays that obstruct view into the building.
7. Expensive or small items left in the windows overnight invite burglaries.

E. Safes

The Problem. Given the alternative, the burglar prefers cash to other property. Far too many businesses have safes that are inadequate to company needs, have not had combinations changed for years, or are easily opened or removed by a skilled burglar. Hiding the safe will serve only to give the burglar better working conditions. Money needs more protection than records.

Preventive actions:

1. The safe should be easily visible from the outside of the building.
2. Lightweight safes should be secured to the structure to prevent being carried away.
3. Cash should be kept at a minimum by frequent banking.
4. Never leave the combination written where it can be found.
5. When you change employees, change the combination of the safe.
6. Keep a light burning over the safe at night.
7. Lock safe securely when leaving the premises by turning the dial several times in the same direction.

F. Building Exteriors

The Problem. The enterprising burglar will take every advantage to gain entry into the building, especially if entry points are poorly protected. The alert businessman needs to ask himself, "If I were determined to gain entry to this building, what are *all* the possible ways *I* could do it?" The outward appearance and security of the building will often determine whether or not it will be attacked. Every opening represents a hazard—inspect and correct wherever possible.

Preventive actions:

1. Fences should be strong, in good repair, and kept free of debris and boxes.
2. Weeds around the outside of the building or fence provide a good hiding place.
3. Ladders should be kept locked up.
4. Blind alleys afford protection for the burglar.
5. Sidewalks openings and their frames should be securely and properly locked.
6. Skylights and ventilators on the roof are easy access points unless protected.
7. Fire escapes and exits should be designed for quick exit but difficult entry.
8. Utility poles offer easy access to roofs.

G. Alarms

The Problem. Twenty-four hour vigilance by the businessman is not practicable; consequently, he must rely on other means of detecting any real or attempted burglary. An adequate alarm system may give *constant* protection, whether the businessman is on or off the premises.

Preventive actions:

1. All openings should be covered by alarms.
2. Periodic tests will insure that the alarm is in proper working order at all times.
3. Power sources should be hidden, protected, checked, and tested regularly.
4. Designate employee who is to notify authorities if alarm goes off.
5. Properly installed alarms can result in lower insurance premiums.
6. The type of alarm should be adequate to the needs of the business.

H. Other Safeguards

The Problem. Poor general housekeeping or lack of controls are invitations to burglary. The businessman should establish basic policies and operational routine to reduce the risk of burglary. Responsible employees should be able to carry out the functions in the owner's absence.

Preventive actions:
1. Keep a record of serial numbers of all merchandise and equipment.
2. Policy numbers and serial numbers of large denominations of bills, should be recorded.
3. Before locking up each night, check to see that no one is hiding in the building.
4. Leave the cash register open at night to prevent unnecessary damage.
5. All checks should be logged and marked "For Deposit in Account of _____" as soon as they are received.

Burglary—Summary Considerations

How a Burglar Enters a Place of Business
(According to Police Statistics)

Break front windows: 22 percent
Break front door glass: 16 percent
Break rear or side windows: 14 percent
Enter through basements, coal chutes, or other openings: 14 percent
Force rear door locks. 13 percent
Break rear door glass: 10 percent
Force front door locks: 9 percent
Enter roof or skylight: 2 percent

What to Do If Burglary Occurs

1. Do not disturb anything at the scene. The chances of apprehension are greatly increased if the scene is left completely intact.
2. Preserve all clues.
3. Call the police immediately.
4. Be prepared to assist the police in every way.
5. Be prepared to provide information as to items missing.

II. Robbery

In the order of magnitude of ordinary crimes, robbery represents the smallest monetary loss, falling significantly below shoplifting, employee theft, fraudulent checks, and burglary. The one outstanding factor about robbery, however, is the personal danger the businessman and his employees are likely to face from violence.

Some sort of a weapon is used in nine out of 10 robberies, with firearms used in about two out of three armed robberies. There appears to be a growing tendency for robbers to shoot or otherwise injure their victims.

Because of the sudden, often violent action of a robbery, the victims are often taken by surprise and off their guard. The typical robbery occurs in a very short period of time—less than a minute. The victim generally finds it difficult to relate details of the robbery accurately and reliably to the police.

Almost universally, police departments counsel against the victim of a robbery taking any action which might antagonize the robber. Instead, he is cautioned to cooperate fully with the robber's wishes, but, at the same time, noting factors relating to the robbery that will be useful to the police —description, escape route, property taken, etc.

The businessman needs to prepare himself in advance by reaching certain basic decisions about the possibility of a robbery, in order to give himself and his employees maximum protection against the actual occurrence. These include:

1. Admission that a robbery is possible. Few businesses are immune from the attention of the would-be robber. Businesses that maintain cash and/or high value items on the premises are likely targets for robbers. For this reason, all businesses are advised to maintain the least possible level of cash exposure, to make bank deposits often but not regularly, i.e. predictably, and to give merchandise subject to robbery maximum protection. Jewelry stores are preferred targets of robbery. So are pharmaceutical departments of drug stores. Any business with cash on the premises is a prospective target and the amount of cash does not necessarily have to be large. Banks represent a special case and are not dealt with specifically here.

2. The establishment of a definite plan to be followed in the event of a robbery. The manager and employees should be prepared to make careful mental observations and to write them down as soon as possible. Provision needs to be made for relaying information the police will need, particularly for suspicious persons noted on or near the premises.

3. The kinds of protective devices to be maintained on the premises. Many businesses have worked out systems with adjoining businesses in the event of a robbery. A signal or light is flashed to alert the adjoining firms that a robbery is in process so that the police can be notified.

4. A decision on whether or not to use force to thwart an attempted robbery. Increasingly, businessmen are arming themselves as a precautionary measure against a possible robbery. Most police departments caution against businessmen using firearms to prevent a robbery. The typical businessman is neither adequately trained nor prepared mentally to face up to a would-be robber.

There is a growing feeling among police departments however, that if the business owner is insistent on using guns, then he should know how to use firearms, have a gun that is safe and operable, and have an understanding of his responsibility for using a gun. The Kansas City (Mo.) Metropolitan Police Department has conducted several programs on proper and legal firearms use. A detailed study of this program is attached to this appendix.

In the final analysis, the businessman's best protection is to take no action that would provoke the robber. He should cooperate to the extent demanded, making a careful note of all details of the robbery and robber and reporting to the police at the first opportunity. There follows below an action plan for the businessman in establishing a program for dealing with robbery.

A. General Preventive Measures

The Problem. Robberies will occur because the businessman has made it easy and convenient for the robber because of poor housekeeping, poor cash-handling methods, and a general lack of planning toward the possibility of robbery. While it is impossible to eliminate robberies completely, it is the businessman's responsibility to deter the would-be robber as much as possible through good operational practices.

Preventive actions:

1. Keep the interior and front and rear entrances well lighted.
2. Keep advertising and merchandise out of the windows as much as possible. This will permit a clear view into the building.
3. Keep the rear and/or side doors locked at all times.
4. Maintain a record of decoy currency (bait money) by serial number and series in the cash register, to be given to a robber.
5. Be sure alarms are in working order at all times.
6. Do not open the place of business *before* or *after* regular business hours, as far as possible.
7. Avoid routine procedures that can be observed and used to advantage by would-be robbers.
8. Call the police if a request is received to open the place of business after regular hours.
9. Keep cash exposure and cash on the premises at the lowest possible level.
10. Keep checks separate from cash, even when making the bank deposit.
11. When making bank deposits:
    a. Go directly to the bank.
    b. Conceal the money, if possible.
    c. Do not leave deposits or withdrawals unattended in an automobile.
    d. Do not go to the bank alone.
    e. Vary time and routine of bank trips.
    f. If possible, make deposits in daylight hours.

12. Do not keep large sums of money on the premises—bank as often as possible.
13. Do not keep large sums in the cash register or where it may be exposed to the view of others.
14. Beware of till tapping—the procedure whereby one person distracts the attention of the cashier while an accomplice steals from the cash register.

B. *Anticipating a Possible Robbery*

The Problem. The speed with which a robbery normally takes place makes it difficult for the businessman or his employees to give helpful information to the police. Be prepared for the possibility of a robbery by deciding in advance what is to be done and who is to do it.

Preventive actions:

1. Be alert for persons attempting to hide on the premises near closing time.
2. Instruct all employees on the use of the alarm system.
3. Call the police if a suspicious person is observed on or near the premises. If he is driving a car, get the license number.
4. Make plans in advance as to who will take certain actions if a robbery occurs:
   a. Who calls the police;
   b. Who makes observations;
   c. Who protects the evidence at the scene;
   d. Who detains witnesses.
5. Some employees are gifted in the art of observation. These persons should be alerted to make observations during a holdup.
6. Practice identification with coworkers.
7. If possible, install height markers, e.g. black plastic tape, at varying heights on door frame to identify approximate height.
8. Discuss with employees what they might do if a robbery occurs.

C. *What to Do if Robbed*

The Problem. Most robberies take place in approximately 1 minute. During that time, the victim must do the robber's bidding, yet be observant enough to give the police useful information. To the average person, however, a robbery is a frightening experience. The robber is generally armed and should be considered capable of committing bodily harm.

Preventive actions:

1. Take no action which would jeopardize personal safety.
2. If the robber displays a firearm, consider it to be loaded.

3. If possible, activates the silent alarm.
4. Attempt to alert other employees by use of prearranged signals.
5. Attempt to delay the robber if at all possible, but without sacrificing personal safety.
6. Try to maintain possession of the holdup note, if one is used.

D. Observation

The Problem. The chances of apprehending a robber are considerably enhanced if the victim is able to give an accurate description of the person or persons. The victim must be prepared to observe the robber, usually within a minute or less. By remaining calm during a robbery, the victim's powers of observation will increase and danger of injury will be minimized.

Preventive actions:
1. Observe physical characteristics of the robber:
   a. Race, age, height;
   b. Facial characteristics, complexion and hair;
   c. Clothing worn, head to foot;
   d. Physical carriage;
   e. Speech;
   f. Marks, scars, deformities;
   g. Robber's method of operation.
2. Look for accomplices.
3. Note method of escape.
4. Describe escape car, model, make, year, license number.
5. Ascertain direction of travel.
6. Describe type of weapon used.
7. If more than one robber is involved, study the nearest one. Don't try to observe all in detail.
8. Comparison of the robber with someone the victim knows aids in recalling details.

E. After the Robbery

The Problem. The ability of the police to apprehend the robber is dependent on the speed of notification by the victim and the clarity with which he describes the circumstances of the robbery. It is essential that the victim remain calm and collected so that he can take positive and proper action in notifying the police.

Preventive actions:
1. Notify police as soon as robbers leave the premises.
2. Give the exact time the robbers left.

3. Protect the scene of the crime; stop others from disturbing the premises.
4. Hold all witnesses until police arrive.
5. Lock the doors if possible—allow no one in except the police.
6. Don't trust to memory, jot down all information immediately.
7. Do not discuss the holdup with anyone until questioned by the police.
8. Do not touch any articles that may have been touched or left by the robber.
9. Once the police are called, stay on the line so that other vital information can be obtained.
10. The following are kinds of information generally asked by the police radio dispatcher:
    a. Location of the armed robbery;
    b. Whether anyone was injured;
    c. When the robbery occurred;
    d. The weapon used by the robber;
    e. Direction in which the robber went;
    f. Description of the vehicle;
    g. Description of the robber;
    h. Description of clothing;
    i. Description of money or article taken;
    j. How the robber carried the loot.

III. Shoplifting

The General Problem. Although the average shoplifting loss is small (estimated at $3 average per theft in supermarkets), the cumulative effect is quite high. SBA's field survey shows shoplifting losses to all business for the year 1967–68 of $504 million.

While no store, large or small, is entirely immune to the effects of shoplifting, certain types are particularly susceptible. Stores that trade in relatively small, high-priced merchandise experience high total dollar losses and a high average loss per theft. Many convenience goods stores, such as variety stores, experience individually small but numerous losses.

Modern merchandising techniques have contributed substantially to the increasing shoplifting problem. Self-service methods, while cutting costs and increasing sales, have also made shoplifting easier. The merchant should be aware that self-service displays, large areas, and limited sales personnel facilitate shoplifting.

A factor reducing the risk to the shoplifter has been retailer hesitance to prosecute those caught. Fear of suit for false arrest, time-consuming involvement in court proceedings and concern for retaliation are among reasons for unwillingness to prosecute.

Provable figures on the cost of shoplifting can only be derived from the value of merchandise in the hands of those caught in the act. SBA's estimate of $504 million is based on reports from merchants in a scientifically representative sample of all businesses. However, the total is at best an estimate, since it may be impossible to know the separate components of total shrinkage, which includes recordkeeping errors, unrecorded markdowns, lag in markups, and employee theft.

Another situation, which adds to the difficulty of studying the nature and extent of the shoplifting problem and its cost, is the apparent tendency to ignore the problem, especially among small firms.

It is essential that the merchant take certain specific actions to combat shoplifting. There are six major areas of action:

1. Establish a system of controls that will help to measure shoplifting. Inventory control procedures are not well set up in many stores. Without such controls, pinpointing merchandise losses is virtually impossible.

2. Study types of shoplifters. By numbers alone, amateur shoplifters far exceed professionals. Yet dollar losses to professionals may exceed those to amateurs. The retailer must make intelligent decisions on how to deal with the juvenile, the vagrant, the narcotics addict, the professional and other types. The greatest increase in shoplifting is among juveniles, both in number of incidents and amount stolen. In the past, retailers have been reluctant to sign complaints against juveniles for fear of alienating their parents, who may be customers of the store. However, storekeepers are being forced to change their position, sometimes for basic survival.

3. Become aware of how shoplifters operate. The amazing variety of methods is limited only by the ingenuity of those stealing.

4. Alert the sales force and give them training in a program to detect shoplifting and apprehend offenders. The smaller business cannot ordinarily afford its own security staff. The owner, even if knowledgeable about shoplifting methods, is generally not in a position to do much observing. His primary hope lies in an alert and observant sales force, at least minimally trained in defense against shoplifting.

5. Adopt a physical layout for the store which will discourage shoplifting. Avoid too many entrances and exits, merchandise too near doors, crowded aisles, display counters that obstruct the view, incorrect placement of cash registers, and other mistakes.

6. Adopt definite policies for dealing with apprehended shoplifting suspects.

Many states now have some form of "merchant protective act" which permits the retailer to detain a person in reasonable manner for a reasonable period of time if the retailer has reason to believe that the person has taken an item without the intention to pay for it.

Large retail stores generally maintain security personnel, and apprehensions can be made only by these persons. Smaller stores usually lack security personnel and must rely on regular employees to carry out their functions. Most law enforcement agencies recommend that authority to detain a suspect be limited to a select few, possibly the owner and manager.

The pages which follow give a detailed analysis of shoplifting problems the retailer may encounter, and make recommendations on reducing losses to this source.

A. Types of Shoplifters

The Problem. Shoplifters come from all walks of life. However, they fall into two broad categories—ordinary customers and professionals who steal for a living. Shoplifting can be impulsive, compulsive, deliberate or desperate. It will be helpful to the businessman if he knows and understands the various types and subtypes who may patronize his store.

The Various Types. The following is a checklist of the more important shoplifter types:

1. *The amateur.* Steals impulsively, a simple desire for an item being the most important motive. Generally is nervous and self-conscious, but exercises caution. Takes food, clothing and many other items for actual use.

2. *The kleptomaniac.* Steals compulsively whenever he or she has the urge. Repeats whenever the urge recurs. Usually nervous and shy. There are very few true kleptomaniacs.

3. *The juvenile.* The majority of the teenage thieves are girls. Usually work in groups, but not necessarily in a formally organized gang. Steal partly for thrills, or to gain status within their group. Usually take merchandise they can use, such as records, clothing, or recreational items.

4. *The professional.* He is skillful operator and knows all the tricks of the trade in his chosen profession. Dresses, talks and acts so as to avoid suspicion. Interested in small, high-value items for which he can find an easy resale market. Usually very cautious and does not take unnecessary chances. Generally steals for a living.

5. *The narcotics addict.* Needs money to procure narcotics. Will take in a brazen manner when desperate. Is sometimes frantic beyond reason, and can be dangerous when an attempt is made to apprehend him.

6. *The vagrant.* Takes from need. Usually steals food, alcoholic beverages, tobacco, and articles of clothing needed for personal use. Often is under influence of alcohol. Is almost always the hit-and-run type.

B. *Shoplifter Signs to Watch For*

The Problem. The skilled shoplifter operates with speed and deftness. The typical employee, however, is not trained to observe and recognize the telltale signs that a shoplifter is at work.

A Few Typical Shoplifter Telltale Actions. Persons observed in the following actions and modes of behavior may be suspected as possible shoplifters:

1. A person who leaves the area with undue haste.
2. A person who frequents washrooms.
3. People who enter the store carrying bundles, bags, boxes, topcoats over arms, briefcases, newspapers, umbrellas, or have an arm in a sling. All these can provide opportunities for concealment of merchandise.
4. People who come in wearing heavy outer garments out of season, baggy clothes, full or pleated skirts.
5. Individuals who have unusual walks, others who tug at a sleeve, adjust socks, rub the back of neck, or are noted in various other unusual actions which might assist in hiding articles.
6. Customers who reach into display counters or walk behind sales counters.
7. The fussy customer who doesn't seem to know what she wants and interchanges articles frequently.
8. Those who don't appear to be interested in articles about which they have inquired.
9. The disinterested roamer who waits for a friend or mate to shop.
10. The nervous, flush-faced, or dry-lipped person, or the perspirer in a room with normal temperature.
11. The person who keeps one hand constantly in an outer coat pocket.

C. *Common Methods Used by Shoplifters*

The Problem. Professional shoplifters adopt methods of operation that fit their unique talents and the kind of merchandise they steal. They make use of sophisticated schemes and often employ special devices to aid in stealing. By contrast, the amateur uses crude and obvious procedures such as simply putting the item in his pocket. Employees need to be trained particularly to detect the more skillful operators.

Shoplifter Methods. The following is a checklist of some of the more important methods that may be employed by a shoplifter:

1. Palms small articles. Packages, newspapers, coats, gloves, and other things carried in the hand may be used as aids.
2. Uses umbrellas, knitting bags, diaper bags, large purses, briefcases,

paper sacks, booster boxes, and similar devices to conceal merchandise.

3. Has a slit in pocket of his outer garment. Places hand through slit as though hand is in pocket, and carries stolen merchandise in hand which is concealed by the outer garment.

4. Wears a skirt, trousers, or other garment with elastic waistband—or wears "shoplifter bloomers."

5. Tries on a garment, places outer garment over the stolen one, and wears it out of the store.

6. Has hooks on inside of coat, pants, dress, or slip, and uses them in much the same way as a magician.

7. Enters store without jewelry or accessories and wears or carries items of this type out of the store in the conventional manner.

8. Wears a long outercoat and conceals articles between legs.

9. Walks to an unattended section, or one near a convenient exit, grabs merchandise and hastily departs from the store.

10. Two or more shoplifters may work together as a team. One or more occupy the attention of the clerks; the others, who appear to be just waiting, actually are shoplifting.

D. Combating the Shoplifter

The Problem. Even with the best policies and practices, some shoplifting is bound to occur in any store. However, there should be an effort to hold it to the minimum. The businessman must depend on his employees and on himself to detect shoplifting. All should be trained in alertness and effective detection.

Preventive Actions to Take. The following is a checklist of policies and practices to curb shoplifting:

1. Serve all customers as promptly as possible. Customers approached immediately will appreciate the service. Shoplifters will be served notice that this is not the time or place to attempt theft.

2. When busy with a customer and another enters the store or department, the salesperson should acknowledge his presence by saying something like, "I'll be with you in a moment."

3. The salesperson should never turn his back on the customer. This is an open invitation to shoplifting, if the customer is so inclined.

4. Keep an eye on people loitering or wandering in the store.

5. Never leave the store or department unattended. This offers a golden opportunity for theft.

6. If possible, give each customer a receipt for every purchase. This will help prevent shoplifters from obtaining cash refunds for stolen merchandise.

7. Develop a warning system so that all employees can be alerted when presence of shoplifters is suspected. In a small store, this might be a code word.
8. Also develop a procedure for employees to notify the office or some clerical location when they suspect thieves are present.
9. Lock up expensive merchandise that is attractive to shoplifters in a showcase displayed in a position where it can be viewed by more than one salesperson.
10. Do not stack merchandise so high on counters or in aisles that it blocks the view of salespeople.
11. Arrange merchandise so customers must pick it up. If not, a thief can push it off the counter into some type of container.
12. When merchandise is made up of pairs, display only one of a pair.
13. Whenever possible, attach merchandise in some way to make its removal difficult.
14. Keep counters and tables neat and orderly.
15. Place telephone so that salespeople can view their sales area while using the telephone.
16. Return to stock any merchandise which was taken out for customer's inspection and was not sold.
17. As a deterrent to shoplifting, keep service fast and efficient, especially when waiting on juveniles.
18. Keep each area clear of discarded saleschecks. Shoplifters may use them as apparent evidence of purchase.
19. To deter till-tappers, establish definite cash register procedures:
    (a) Keep register open while it is actually being used to ring up a sale;
    (b) close the drawer before wrapping the merchandise;
    (c) do not allow any customer to distract the cashier while another person is being waited on;
    (d) keep registers locked when not in use.

IV. Fraudulent Checks

It has often been said that fraudulent checkwriting is the safest crime the individual can engage in—all he has to carry is a loaded pen. It is also one of the most difficult to control.

Check cashing is a service provided by a wide range of businesses, but not necessarily associated with the purchase of merchandise. Checks are cashed as a convenience to customers, whether or not the person has made a purchase and whether or not he even intends to make a purchase. It is this "service" that has made fraudulent checks the widespread problem it is today. Laxity on the part of the businessman, combined with the desire to increase sales volume has been a principal cause of the problem.

As a matter of management, the businessman must make some very basic decisions about permitting the cashing of checks at his place of business:

1. Whether checks will be cashed for more than the amount of purchase. In certain kinds of stores, especially food stores, there is a tendency to permit checks to be cashed for more than the amount of purchase. Knowing this, checkpassers make small purchases as a ruse to cash a check. There is no assurance, however, that exact payment will guarantee the check's genuineness. This is particularly true for items that can be easily disposed of at a price satisfactory to the "purchaser." It must be remembered that several days may elapse before discovery that a bad check has been accepted. In the meantime, the person passing the check may have departed the area.

2. The extent to which checks will be cashed as a service to the store's customers. It is not uncommon for certain types of stores to cash checks for amounts totaling considerably more than the gross sales of the business. These will include payroll, pension, social security, welfare, and allotment checks. It is uncertain whether the increase in sales resulting from the check cashing service is sufficient to offset the losses experienced by accepting uncollectable checks.

3. The kind of a procedure the business institutes to insure that the check is genuine and collectable. Insistence on certain kinds of identification, care in examining the check for accuracy in all detail, and other pertinent factors are essential to reduce the chances of accepting a bad check. The businessman is admonished to exercise all due caution in cases where he is not personally acquainted with the person desiring to cash a check. If he is not totally satisfied that the check is authentic, he should refuse to cash the check. There is a common fear among many businesses that a stringent check cashing policy will serve to alienate that store's customers, causing a greater loss of business than that experienced through bad checks. No substantive data has as yet been advanced to prove this claim, however.

4. Whether or not to use protective devices in cashing checks. There are numerous devices available to the firm cashing checks, based on the principal of photographing the check and the person simultaneously. Firms that produce this equipment assert that the device has a strong deterrent effect on professional checkpassers. Thus, the cost of the equipment is more than offset by the reduction in number of fraudulent checks presented for payment. It is this deterrent quality, more than the possibility of apprehension, that gives the device its sales appeal.

5. A decision on the action to take when an uncollectable check has been accepted. Technically, uncollectable checks can be classified as due to

(a) insufficient fund checks, or (b) defraud. The former category suggests a significantly different treatment from the latter, yet from the business-man's point of view, both represent a loss of revenue.

In the case of fraudulent checks, the businessman must decide the course of action that he will take and the extent to which he will pursue it. This includes notifying the proper law-enforcement agency, signing a complaint, and prosecuting the checkpasser if and when he is caught.

One of the common complaints among merchants is on the complications arising from bringing a checkpasser to trial: testifying in court, only to have the person acquitted; the case set aside or postponed, causing undue delay and expense on the part of the merchant. In those areas, however, where a firm stand has been taken by the merchants and the courts, reduction in fraudulent check passing has been noticeable. Laws governing fraudulent checks and strict prosecution of offenders, however, will not arbitrarily reduce bad check losses unless the business that accepts checks establishes a firm policy and adheres to it.

For every careful merchant who refuses to accept a check because it is improperly written, contains abbreviated information, or lacks sufficient identification, many other merchants will cash the same check without hesitation.

1. Principal causes of losses:
   a. The lack of a check-cashing procedure.
   b. Failure to examine every check.
   c. Failure to record certain information on the check.
   d. Indiscriminate cashing of checks.
   e. Fear that a sale would be lost unless checks are cashed without undue complication.

A. Establishing a Check-Cashing Procedure

The Problem. Most small businesses have no set policy for doing business by check. It is essential that the businessman establish a procedure that will give him the greatest possible protection against bad checks and then hold to that policy without deviation.

Preventive actions:

1. Establish a firm policy regarding the cashing of checks for amounts over the cost of the merchandise (or service) .
2. Assign the responsibility of cashing checks for amounts higher than the purchase only to certain employees.
3. Examine *every* check carefully.
4. *Require* a suitable amount of identification.

5. *Require* an address and telephone number of the *maker* and *endorser* of every check.
6. Record identification numbers on the check.
7. Assign the cashing of checks to new or young employees only when under the supervision of experienced employees.

B. Identification

The Problem. Most checks are cashed in situations where the passer is not personally, known to the businessman. He must rely on some form of proof presented that the passer is the legitimate owner of the check. Usually this decision must be reached quickly under hurried conditions and often by someone not skilled in detecting fraudulent checks. It is doubtful if foolproof identification exists anywhere in the world since all types now in use can be counterfeited.

Preventive actions:
1. Be sure to ask for identification.
2. Identification should be requested if the passer is not *personally* known.
3. The best types of identification now being used include:
   a. Driver's license.
   b. Military or government identification.
   c. Some airline and national credit cards.
4. Always require *at least one* type of physical description identification, such as a driver's license.
5. Never accept social security cards, lodge cards, hunting and fishing licenses, employment records, or birth certificates alone.
6. Compare the physical description on the identification to the person presenting the check.
7. Compare the signature on the identification to that on the check.
8. Record the identification number somewhere on the check.
9. Require just as much identification with certified checks, cashier's checks, money orders, Government checks, and State warrants as on personal checks.
10. Try not to give the impression of suspicion when asking for identification.
11. A good customer will not object to the need to ask for identification.
12. Be sure all identification used is current.
13. In the absence of a sufficient amount of good identification or none at all, do not cash the check.
14. Be cautious if the person presenting the checks becomes angry when asked for his identification.

15. If an out-of-State driver's license is used as identification, be sure to record the name of the state issuing the license.

16. Never cash a check for a stranger until positive identification is established. Insist on local references, then check them carefully.

17. Don't accept a combination of identification that is too readily offered.

18. Ask for identification that is not ordinarily carried, such as paid utility bills, a tax statement, statement from a retail store.

C. *Examining the Check*

The Problem. Most fraudulent checks are passed because the businessman does not take the time to examine the check thoroughly. Establishment of identification is not enough. Care must be taken to be sure the check is correct in *all* respects. Examine every check before it is cashed.

Preventive actions:

1. Examine the dateline.
   a. The check must be dated.
   b. The check must not be postdated.
   c. Establish a policy regarding the cashing of checks over 30 days old.

2. Examine the payee line.
   a. Be sure name of the payee and the endorsement can be read, that the endorsement is written exactly as appears on the front and includes address and telephone number.
   b. Be sure payee/endorser identification establishes his identity.
   c. Do not accept checks with second endorsements from strangers (two-party checks).

3. Examine the digit and written amounts.
   a. These amounts should correspond exactly.
   b. Do not accept the check if either shows signs of alteration.
   c. Do not accept the check if *any* part has been altered.

4. Examine the maker.
   a. The maker's name should be legible and should include his address and telephone number.
   b. If the maker's name cannot be read, ask him to write it again.
   c. Beware of checks if any part of the maker's name extends past the space allotted.
   d. Beware of titles preceding the maker's name. These are often meant to distract attention from the check, the passer, or his identification.

5. Examine the name of the bank section.
   a. It should be imprinted on the check. If not, be sure the name of the bank and city of location are written out completely—not abbreviated.
   b. Be sure it is a bank and not a savings and loan association or some other kind of business.
6. Examine the endorsement.
   a. The endorsement should be written exactly as it appears on the payee line on the front of the check.
   b. The endorsement should be legible and include an address and telephone number.
   c. If already endorsed, ask that the check be endorsed again in the receiver's presence.

D. Additional Precautionary Measures

The Problem. Losses, in merchandising, to bad check artists are a serious and costly problem. Carelessness causes most of them. The best way to keep bad check losses to a minimum is to follow sound and sensible practices, and always use caution and common sense whenever a check is accepted. The cashing of a check for a stranger should be treated in the same way an unsecured loan would be made to him. Take nothing for granted.

Preventive actions:

1. Beware of checks that have a company name stamped with a rubber stamp or typewritten.
2. Refuse to cash a check that has the word "HOLD" written anywhere on it.
3. Watch out for the "I'm an old customer" routine.
4. Don't be misled if the passer waves to someone, particularly if it is another employee.
5. Beware of the bigname dropper.
6. It is not good business to cash a check for an intoxicated person.
7. If a check is cashed for a juvenile, be sure he or his parents are well known to the person cashing the check.
8. Never assume a check is good because it *looks* good.
9. Beware of personal checks bearing unusually high sequence numbers.
10. Beware of checks far in excess of the amount of purchase.
11. The person cashing the check should mark it with his initials so that it can later be identified in court, if necessary.
12. Report all check law violators to the proper local law enforcement agency.

13. Follow through with prosecution on all check cases after a complaint has been signed.
14. The businessman should protect his own blank checks, canceled checks, bank statements, and check protector from theft.
15. Review own canceled checks for unauthorized signatures or altered amounts.
16. Every businessman who cashes checks should be familiar with the laws in his state governing fraudulent checks.

V. Employee Theft

The General Problem. The great majority of employees are honest and therefore have a stake in minimizing dishonesty by other employees. Furthermore, among those who may be potentially dishonest, a great part will have no opportunity for theft. Nevertheless, there will be employees who succeed in stealing, and it may never be possible to eliminate this leakage entirely. Except in very small stores, merchandise and cash may pass through the hands of several employees, affording temptations and opportunities to steal. The discussion which follows provides checklists of methods of employee theft and proven actions to meet the problem. It must be emphasized that these are not directed against honest employees, but will serve to protect them and their jobs from the debilitating effects of inside theft.

A. Theft of Cash

The Problem. Cash is handled by sales personnel, cashiers, bookkeepers, and credit department personnel. Employee theft can be discouraged by a management which is alert and enforces a good system or rules.

Methods of Theft. The following is a checklist of some of the principal methods of employee cash theft:

1. "Underring" the cash register. The clerk does not give the customer a sales receipt and pockets the money later.
2. Failing to ring up sales. The clerk leaves the register drawer open, puts money directly into the register without ringing up certain sales and takes out the stolen money later.
3. Ringing up "no sale" on the register, voiding the sales check after the customer has left and pocketing the money.
4. Overcharging customers so that cash overages can be stolen.
5. Taking cash from a "common drawer" register.
6. Cashing bad checks for accomplices.
7. Making false entries in store's records and books to conceal thefts.
8. Giving fraudulent refunds to accomplices or putting through fictitious refunds.

9. Stealing checks made payable to cash.
10. Pocketing unclaimed wages.
11. Paying creditor's invoice twice and appropriating the second check.
12. Failing to record returned purchases and stealing an equal amount of cash.
13. Padding payrolls as to rates, time worked, or number of employees.
14. Forging checks and destroying them when returned by the bank.
15. Pocketing collections made on presumably uncollectible accounts.
16. Issuing checks on "returned" purchases not actually returned.
17. Raising the amount on checks, invoices or vouchers after they have been officially approved.
18. Invoicing goods above the established prices and getting a kickback from the supplier.

B. *Theft of Merchandise*

The Problem. Thefts of merchandise may range from simple pocketing of an item to larger-scale stealing concealed by intricate accounting manipulations. The problem becomes more difficult when there are weaknesses in stock control systems.

Methods of Theft. The more frequent methods of merchandise theft are included in the following checklist:

1. Passing out merchandise across the counter to accomplices.
2. Trading stolen merchandise with friends employed in other departments.
3. Hiding merchandise on person, in a handbag or in a parcel, and taking it out of store at lunchtime, on relief breaks, or at the end of the day.
4. Hiding goods in stairways, public lockers, and corridors for later theft.
5. Taking unlisted packages from delivery truck.
6. Stealing from warehouse with cooperation of warehouse employees.
7. Stealing from stockroom by putting goods on person or in packages.
8. Stealing from returned-goods room, layaway, and similar places where goods are kept.
9. Making false entries to pad inventories so shortages will not be noticed.
10. Giving employee discounts to friends.
11. Putting on jewelry, scarves, or jackets to model; then wearing them home and keeping them.
12. Shoplifting during lunch hour or relief periods.
13. Stealing special "property passes" to get stolen articles out of store.

14. Taking sales slips from training room or supply area to put on stolen goods.
15. Stealing trading stamps.
16. Getting stolen goods through the mailroom by slapping on "customer's own" label normally used to ship out altered goods.
17. Putting "return to manufacturer" label on goods and sending them instead to the employee's own address.
18. Picking up by sales clerk of a receipt discarded by customer and putting it on stolen goods which the clerk keeps or turns in for refund.
19. Intentional soiling of garments or damaging of merchandise so employees can buy them at reduced prices.
20. Printing of own tickets for stolen goods by marking-room employees.
21. Clerks spurring sales with unauthorized markdowns, in order to get kickback from manufacturers.
22. Employees stamping own mail with store postage meter.
23. Shipping clerks sending out stolen goods to their own disguised post office boxes.
24. Smuggling out stolen goods in trash and refuse containers.

C. Curbing Employee Thefts Through Preventive Measures and an Action Plan

The Problem. The turnover rate in retail stores is high under normal conditions, and increases on a seasonal basis when additional personnel are required. This rapid turnover accentuates the need for well-developed policies to curb employee thefts. Honest employees will not be outraged by efforts to prevent thievery. Meanwhile, the small group of potentially dishonest employees will find it more difficult to steal if they are confronted with an effective system of control and detection.

Preventive Actions to Take. The following is a checklist of actions and policies suggested for curbing employee thefts:

1. Screen new employees carefully, insisting on references that can be checked.
2. See that supervisors set a good leadership example, alerting them to the employee theft possibility.
3. Give special attention to employees who appear to have financial or other personal problems which might increase the temptation to be dishonest.
4. Set up retraining classes for employees who make numerous sales check errors.
5. Check employees who arrive early or stay late when there is no need to do so. (When losses by theft appear very high, consider setting up

afterhour "plants." Use honest shopping, for example, Wilmark—for testing salespeople.)

6. Permit no employee to make sales to himself.
7. Require all employee purchases to be checked in the package room.
8. Restrict all employees to a single exit if possible.
9. Give each sales person his own cash drawer, but permit no one to do final tally on his own cash register.
10. Use care about allowing employees free access to storerooms.
11. If confronted with a theft problem, do not completely eliminate the possibility that relatives of management are involved. They, too, may have personal problems and resentments which will provoke them to dishonesty.
12. Beware of "theft contamination." Dishonesty, once it gains a foothold in a business, can spread.
13. Have fixed policies about discipline for dishonesty. Failure to take decisive action, or failure to be consistent can have an adverse effect on other employees.
14. Have a good system of controls, including an effective internal audit system.
15. Have a tight control of employee packages. Also check packages found on delivery platforms, loading docks and similar locations, to see if they have correct shipping labels.
16. Use tamper-proof packaging with all price tags inside the wrapping.
17. Have a sound refund system, and be sure it is being followed.
18. Keep valuable items locked up, with the manager in possession of the keys. Also keep all storerooms locked.
19. Keep interchangeable items, such as butter and margarine, in separate cases.
20. Have employees sign for all tools and equipment issued to them.
21. Make all deliveries through the store.
22. Double check all merchandise received at docks to assure that everything paid for is there.
23. Investigate carefully all inventory shortages, remembering it is possible that thieving employees will attribute these losses to shoplifters.
24. Probe all losses, even minor ones, at once, bearing in mind that most embezzlers start with small thefts.
25. Inventory all supplies, equipment, and merchandise systematically.
26. Change all locks and combinations when you change custodial personnel.

D. *Special Theft Problems of Small Businesses*

The Problem. In small stores, one person frequently combines all the functions of bookkeeping with the collection and disbursement of funds. Moreover, in a small business, the owner's time is so often taken up with nonsupervisory activities that he is unaware of the extent to which stealing is taking place.

Preventive Actions to Take. Good internal control requires that work be divided, so that there is little opportunity for inside theft without collusion. The following are suggestions for small businesses, especially.

1. All cash receipts should be deposited intact daily.
2. All disbursements should be by check, countersigned by the manager.
3. Each month, the manager should personally reconcile the bank accounts.
4. During the first few days of each month, the manager should receive and open all the incoming mail.
5. The manager should compare all cash receipts with the deposits shown on his bank statement.
6. Someone other than the bookkeeper should do all of the receiving and shipping of merchandise.
7. The mail should be opened by someone other than the cashier or cash receivable bookkeeper.
8. Cash registers should be locked so that employees cannot read the totals.
9. All refunds and sales checks should be numbered.
10. A control should be kept of all salesbooks and all refund books.
11. Rigid control should be maintained on petty cash disbursements.

APPENDICES

Part A. PHYSICAL PROCEDURES

Part B. INTERNAL AND EXTERNAL SECURITY PROGRAMS

Part C. GUIDELINES TO DEVELOP SECURITY POLICY

PART A

PHYSICAL PROCEDURES

INFORMATION REGARDING *specific* recommendations as they relate to security violations or areas of loss have been developed by the British Home Office, Crime Prevention Center (Stafford, England), to be used as lecture notes for students. Extracts from these excellent procedures have been prepared for use by security and crime prevention personnel.

The important aspect of this section to the *surveyor* would be the *choice* of recommendations to be implemented in certain stituations. Thus, an innovative and creative security *surveyor* would use this list as a guide and modify sections to meet his needs.

The individual who has security surveying responsibilities is encouraged to develop detailed recommendations, preferably on a separate sheet of paper so as to be used as an addendum to the original surveys. As was stated earlier, the initial survey would not depict an in-depth recommendation as found in this section.

Procedural information as it applies to:
1. Protection of windows
2. Safes and strongrooms
3. Vehicle security
4. Security of cash and valuables in transit
5. Thefts from offices, shops and warehouses

(Lecture notes prepared by the Crime Prevention Center, Stafford, for use by students.)

APPENDIX A-1
PROTECTION OF WINDOWS*

The modern architectural trend is towards an ever-increasing use of large areas of glass in order to provide a maximum of light or display. The problem of its protection is one with which we are faced in a large proportion of surveys.

Broadly speaking there are five main ways in which protection can be achieved, namely by the use of:
1. Bars

---

*Reprinted with permission from the Home Office Crime Prevention Center Lecture Notes, Stafford, England.

2. Grilles
3. Fastenings
4. Special glass
5. Alarm installations

Window Bars

Method One

Where possible, bars should be fitted internally and set back not less than two inches from the external surface of the wall. Each window bar should be grouted into masonry at the top and bottom (or sides, for horizontal bars) to a minimum depth of three inches. When bars are longer than two feet, cross-ties of mild steel, two by three-eighths inches, should be provided at intervals of not more than eighteen to twenty inches and welded at the intersections or otherwise made immovable, e.g. by flattening the window bars above and below the cross ties.

Alternatively, the cross ties can be fitted separately into the masonry to a depth of at least three inches at each end, and welded at the intersections.

The bars should be of mild steel, not less than three-fourths inch in diameter or section (square section is stronger), and fitted at not more than five-inch centers.

Method Two

Where it is not possible to sink the individual bars into masonry, they should be threaded through the cross ties. The ragged, or fish-tail, ends of the ties should then be fixed into the surrounding masonry at each end, and the bars should again be welded or otherwise secured at the intersections.

Method Three

This involves the manufacture of the bars and cross ties as a complete unit, to the above specification. The unit, where possible, should be fitted internally and the fixing ends sunk to at least three inches and fixed not less than two inches from the exterior surface of the wall. It should not be secured by screws or bolts into woodwork.

In all cases, the use of lengths of iron piping in the place of solid bars should be discouraged. Piping is easily and silently cut with a special wheel cutter, but this tool will cut only part way through solid bars. The bolt-croppers needed to sever a three-fourths inch bar are very heavy and unwieldy. Of course, bars of any thickness can be cut with a hacksaw or a pocket chain saw, but this is a noisier process.

It should be remembered that hollow tubing is widely used in burglar alarm systems to give protection to windows.

Roller Bars

Roller bars, consisting of a steel tube holding a revolving hardened steel bar, resist cutting by hacksaw and offer good protection.

Wooden Window Frames

With wooden window frames, where sinking into the masonry is not practicable, bars should be welded to a cross-member which is then drilled between each bar and secured to the woodwork with substantial coach-bolts, fitted with nuts and burred over. The external heads of the coach-bolts can be countersunk and the cavities filled and painted.

Metal Window Frames

Difficulties may occasionally be experienced in using metal window bars to protect metal frame windows, where the methods outlined above cannot be followed. In these cases it is usually possible to secure the bars to the window frames but, because of the variety of such frames now in use, it is impossible to lay down any standard specifications, although the requirements as to strength and spacing of bars will, of course, apply.

Fanlights

If fanlights are not required for ventilation, they should be screwed up and the appropriate protection bars fitted. If ventilation is required, cradle bars should be used. An illustration of these bars appears in *Burglary Protection and Insurance Surveys* by D. E. Bugg.

Roof Windows

Roof windows are called by different names, e.g. lantern lights, dome lights, skylights and roof lights. It is generally very difficult to obtain even a reasonable degree of security in the windows themselves and, where possible, the only worthwhile form of protection is the fitting of substantial bars in accordance with the specifications already mentioned.

Window Grilles

Display Windows

Display windows can be protected by grilles, of which there are several types, e.g. collapsible, expanded metal, welded mesh, etc. The type of grille to be recommended will depend upon the nature of the premises concerned and the type and value of the goods on display. As a general rule, it is preferable for such grilles to be fitted internally, but where they are of necessity erected externally, care must be taken to ensure that they are adequately secured against easy removal.

Display windows are often the target of the *Smash and Grab* thief and, where possible, shopkeepers should be encouraged to remove valuable items from display or alternatively, where such property as transistor radios, tape recorders, etc. are on show, every effort must be made to secure these or site them at the back of the window. In the case of double display windows of the type separated by a small arcade, the suggestion may be accepted that easily transportable goods be transferred to one window which may then be protected by a collapsible grille in conjuction with roller shutters or collapsible metal gates on the arcade entrance. These measures have already proved successful.

It should be borne in mind that rarely is it necessary for collapsible grilles to be of full window length, and as the cost of grilling can be expensive this point is important.

Other Windows

In certain premises, permanent window bars may not be acceptable as a means of providing security and it may, therefore, be necessary to advise protection by a grille made up from expanded metal or welded mesh of substantial gauge affixed in a frame which fits the dimensions of the window. The grille can be secured by means of permanently fixed coach-bolts drilled through the window frame. The heads of the bolts should be countersunk and the cavities filled and painted over. The framed grille can then be fitted internally over the threaded ends of the bolts and secured by wing-nuts and washers.

Alternative fixing methods can be used, e.g. by the use of close-shackle padlocks fastened through staples over which the grille is fitted, or by fitting hinges to one side of the grille and securing by padlock (s) at the opening edge.

It should be noted that welded mesh and expanded metal can be bought cut to the required size, but local labour will be necessary to make up the frames. The grille materials can be obtained in several finishes, including aluminium, galvanised an P.V.C., or they may be painted after assembly.

It should be understood that in removable grilles, there are inherent weaknesses which must not be overlooked. One has already been mentioned, namely, the gauge of metal used—this should always be commensurate with the risk and should generally be capable of withstanding a determined attack. Secondly, with either expanded metal or welded mesh, the framing is important. In the main, grilles will be more effective against attack if contained in the substantial flat steel frame which protects the ends of the metal. Thirdly, with regard to heavy woven wire meshes which are not welded, if they are bent and tooped, as so often happens, solely to a frame of round section metal rod, the ends of the mesh can very easily be opened sufficiently to allow access to the window. Cases have occurred where wire grilles framed in this way have been bent upwards from one corner sufficiently to allow access. It is suggested that where frames are of the metal rod variety, the ends of the mesh be spot welded where they are fastened to the frame.

Note: Expanded metal grilles are made from a solid sheet of steel which is cut and expanded usually whilst in the cold state. It is not welded or joined and is consequently very strong.

Ornamental Grilles

Ornamental grilles, made of wrought iron or other metals, can be obtained. They are usually made to order by local craftsmen and their cost is fairly high. It should be remembered that, generally, they are produced more for decoration than for security, but they do offer a measure of protection.

Shutters

Wooden window-shutters, fitted internally, provide a good standard of security, and where they are available, their use is to be recommended. These should be of plywood, not less than five-eighths inch thick. Additional strength can be obtained by plating with sheet metal, not less than 16 gauge, and the shutters should be secured by a crossbar and padlock.

A peephole in the shutter is desired to allow police supervision at appropriate premises.

Glass

Although glass has many security applications, *unbreakable* glass does not exist. Several methods have been devised by manufacturers to ensure that an expanse of glass will not shatter when subjected to violence. The most common of these is the introduction of a wire mesh into the glass and this product is widely used, because of the improved safety it affords, as a fire protection medium, i.e. in smoke-doors, and to provide extensive glazing in schools and industry. Manufacturers do not claim any special *security* properties for glass of this kind, although it does offer greater resistance to criminal attack than *plate* or *float* glass of normal thickness.

Toughened glass, with a strength about five times that of plate glass of comparable thickness, is being widely used for security purposes in windows, as *protective* glass screened and in the form of external doors. It should be remembered, however, that this glass depends for its strength upon the maintenance of an intact surface. If the surface is punctured, internal forces will cause the *entire* piece of glass to disintegrate completely.

Increasing security use is being made today of laminated glass. This usually takes the form of a sheet of transparent plastic sandwiched between two layers of glass and gives a high level of resistance against attack. Special adhesives must be used for glazing with laminated glass.

Bullet resistant glass is constructed of several sheets of glass—each sheet bonded with a layer of sandwich of plastic (vinyl butyral or similar plastic). Bullets are stopped by the energy absorption of the plastic.

In the use of these protective glasses, the thickness of the element must be chosen according to the required protection, and the advice of the various manufacturers should be sought for each risk.

The manufacturers instructions for fitting must be strictly followed or the full protection afforded by the installation could be considerably lessened.

Barrier glasses in which a welded steel mesh is incorporated between two sheets of glass bonded by a plastic interlayer, is readily available and affords excellent protection in premises where a high degree of security is required.

Whenever possible, all glazing should be done from inside, as with outside glazing covered by wooden beading, the beading can easily be removed and the pane of glass taken out.

Display Windows

Additional protection can be given to display windows by reglazing with a laminated glass, or by suspending a sheet or sheets of laminated or toughened glass about six-inches behind the existing plate glass window. The suspension chains should be substantial and the ceiling fixture should be very secure. The lower edge of the suspended glass should be allowed *limited* movement to absorb the shock of any object thrown at the window, but precautions should be taken to prevent the glass being lifted by the thief, e.g. by clips and chain. Where two or more sheets are so suspended, each sheet should be very securely attached to its neighbour so that it cannot be moved aside.

Some occupiers have installed suspended perspex shields in place of laminated or toughened glass. Although perspex is cheaper, its use has been criticised on the grounds that after prolonged exposure to light and heat it tends to become brittle, thereby reducing its effectiveness as a crime prevention measure.

Sliding Glass Panels

The securing of sliding glass panels in show cases and in newspaper or cigarette kiosks can present problems, and there is available a ratchet lock which is clipped to the rear sliding panel. The ratchet is then closed and secured by means of a cylinder lock. Other locks, using a metal plunger which is attached to the lock on the front panel and which passes into a recess in the rear panel, are available for wooden sliding panels.

Glass in Doors

Many offences are committed by breaking glass panels in doors and releasing the door lock. In dwelling houses, the appropriate advice will be to fit locks which cannot be manipulated without a key. In business premises, however, whilst a similar proposition applies, it may well be found that the use of toughened glass panels, bandit glass or barrier glass will be acceptable. Again, it is worthwhile to mention that toughened glass depends for its strength on an intact surface.

Glass Blocks

Where viewing is not required, the use of glass blocks will give a higher degree of security. Ventilation blocks are available if necessary.

Alarm Installations

The protection of windows by means of alarm devices can be very effective and there are numerous types of contacts which may be used. One of the most common is the metal or plastic tube protecting the wiring. Skylights are frequently protected by laced wire, metal framed windows by magnetic contacts and sash windows by plunger contacts (micro-switches). Others in use are infrared rays, and the use of taut wire which gives the alarm when touched. Vibrator contacts (impact switches) and metal foil are often used on the windows of jewellers premises and more recently the laser beam, still in the experimental stage, when used as a *curtain* may well supersede other types of conventional protection for large areas of glass.

The use of alarm devices—usually vibrator contacts—on jewellers' windows is very limited in its application against the *Smash and Grab* raider due to the critical time element involved in this class of crime. They are also the cause of many false alarms.

Alarm Glass

There are two types of alarm glass. One type has ultra thin wires embedded in the plastic interlayer that bonds two sheets of glass. The wires which are closely spaced must be connected to an electrical alarm. Any attempt to break through the laminated glass breaks the fine wire and initiates the alarm.

The other type is a vacuum glass which is a unitized panel consisting of an exterior facing sheet of glass, a thin air space which is under partial vacuum, and an interior barrier of laminated (burglar) glass. If the outer glass is penetrated, air enters and the pressure change sets off the alarm via the air valve which is connected to an electrical alarm system.

One-way Vision Glass

It is not practicable to produce a glass which will only allow vision in a specified direction in all lighting conditions, but considerable success can be achieved under controlled conditions. The direction of vision is always from the darker side to the lighter side and, therefore, the illumination must be less on the observer's side.

Three types of glass can be referred to under the heading of one way glass:

Neutral Tinted. A tinted, polished plate glass which, when looked at from the brighter side appears black, but when looked through from the darker side has a dark smoky tint which preserves the relative colour values of objects seen through it. It is available in three-sixteenths inch thickness only.

Transparent Mirror. A polished plate glass to which a thin metallic film has been applied. By this treatment the glass is made to reflect the major proportion of the light which falls upon it. This works in the same way as the neutral tinted glasses, and needs the same lighting conditions.

Venetian Strip Silvering. A polished plate glass on which broad silvered strips alternate with narrow clear lines. The relative width of the strips and lines can be varied according to the particular application.

APPENDIX A-2
SAFES AND STRONGROOMS*
Siting and Installation

Siting

CONVENTIONAL SAFES

Wherever possible, it is desirable for safes to be sited in positions visible to patrolling police officers, security staffs, night watchmen and, in suitable cases, to members of the public, e.g. post offices, banks, supermarkets, cooperative stores, etc. The longer the breaker can work unseen, the better the quality of the safe needed to defeat him.

Such siting may require the provision of means to permit examination of safes, such as clear-view panels in glass through which there is no direct

---

*Reprinted with permission from the Home Office Crime Prevention Center Lecture Notes, Stafford, England.

view, peepholes in doors and walls. Mirrors may be sited to allow inspection of safes and their immediate vicinity, where it is not possible to obtain a direct view.

It is vitally important that patrolling officers are thoroughly briefed on the location of safes and observation aids so that the additional protection afforded by such siting is fully maintained.

Siting requires the most careful thought. Considerations of space and office layout may demand that a safe is located against an inner or party wall. Since such walls are likely to be insubstantial, siting in this way may afford an opportunity to the thief to work unobserved *through the wall* on the side or back of the safe. The question of the weight of the safe and the strength of the floor must also be considered.

WALL SAFES

With few exceptions, wall safes will not afford adequate protection to more than about $120. The protective value lies in their concealment and the well-known *hiding-places*, e.g. behind pictures, in built-in wardrobes, etc., should be avoided. While it may be difficult to advise on siting, wherever possible the safe should be installed in a brick cavity wall, in accordance with the fixing instructions laid down by the manufacturer.

Occupiers should be warned of the dangers of overloading their security.

FLOOR SAFES

Models of floor safes are available for all floorings at ground level. Again, good concealment is essential and may be achieved by floor coverings in everyday use, furniture, etc. The installation should always comply to the fixing instructions of the manufacturer.

Although floor safes may be more robust than wall safes, there is, again, the danger that occupiers will overload their security. In up-to-date models, their efficiency has been increased by the inclusion in the safe door of drill-resistant material and an anti-explosive device in the form of a captive steel bolt which is triggered off by the force of the explosion.

Some models have been designed to accept notes through the door without unlocking and these are especially suitable for garages, kiosks and cafes, to enable assistants to keep unprotected holdings to a minimum, thereby reducing the risk of loss. In this case, the considerations of siting will vary with the type and layout of the premises, since the safe must be immediately available to the staff on duty. Care should be taken to ensure that keys are not held by attendants.

OFFERTORY BOXES

Wall safes, designed or modified for use as offertory boxes, should be firmly embedded in masonry and not attached to pews or other wooden fixtures. Clearly, to fulfill their purpose, they are usually sited in conspicuous positions and, to reduce the risk of loss, responsible persons should be advised to empty them frequently.

ILLUMINATION

In every case where a safe is positioned to facilitate inspection by the Police and others, occupiers should be urged to install observation lights, preferably in duplicate, thereby obviating unnecessary calling out of key-holders in the event of a bulb failure.

Installation

ANCHORAGE OF SAFES

A leading company of safe manufacturers recommends that *any safe* weighing less than one ton and sited on a ground floor should be secured against bodily removal or manipulation to facilitate attack. We accept this as a reasonable standard.

Anchorage of safes sited on floors which are above or below ground level will depend upon the facilities available for their removal or manipulations, e.g. lifts, ramps, hoists, etc. It is recommended that *any safe* weighing less than 12 cwt. and sited not at ground level should be suitably fastened to the fabric of the building. The weight factor for safes on *upper floors* will very often limit (a) the size of the safe, and (b) the amount of additional protection which can be afforded to it, both of which may operate to the advantage of the criminal.

FIXING TO FLOOR

The main consideration in deciding the method of anchoring safes to floors is the material of which the floor is made. Because of the nature of the construction of many safes, the fixing methods described below may not be suitable in all cases.

Floors of stone, concrete or composition provide the best material for anchorage. An excellent method is to use four substantial rag-bolts (or similar bolts) which are sunk into the floor and grouted in position, or, if the safe is to be placed in a concrete plinth, longer bolts will be needed to project from the floor surface, through the plinth, into the base of the safe.

Four holes are drilled in the base of the safe to coincide with the positions of the bolts, metal sleeves can be inserted (to prevent the loss of filling material), and the safe is placed over the threaded ends. Mild steel locking-plates, not less than one-fourth inch thick, linking each pair of bolts, are fitted before the nuts are put on, with the object of spreading the force if an attack is made on the safe, thus reducing the likelihood of the safe being levered over the nuts.

A similar method can be used for fixing safes to wooden floors, but in these cases, the bolts should be wrapped round the joists and secured by screws. Where substantial joists are available, the use of bolts can be considered.

Another acceptable method is to weld two substantial girder sections across the base of the safe. The site is prepared by taking out sufficient depth of floor material to allow the safe and girders to be dropped into the opening into which a hard mix concrete is poured. Care must be taken to allow clearance for the opening door and lower hinge.

It is common to fasten down safes by the use of metal straps around the body. Invariably, the metal used for the straps is easily dealt with by oxy-acetylene cutting or by hacksaw and has the disadvantage of holding the safe stationary, thereby facilitating the use of ripping tools on the body. It is known, too, that in some cases the final anchoring of metal strapping has been by means of bolts through the floor, nutted over on top, and instances have come to notice where, merely by removing the nuts, the strapping has been removed, and the safe carried away or manipulated for attack. For these reasons, this method has limitations.

It should be borne in mind that some of the methods described can, with suitable modifications, be utilised to anchor safes to walls through the back and/or side instead of through the base, although this is likely to be possible only with older safes or with the lower grades of modern safes. Further, because of the insubstantial nature of many walls, this method is not likely to prove so secure.

Manufacturers will supply safes already equipped with base-fixing devices and safes can be purchased with holes and sleeves to accept floor-bolts.

Additional Protection of Safes

Safes can be made less vulnerable to attack by encasing in reinforced concrete. This increases the weight, thereby making the removal of the safe more difficult, and protects the weakest parts of the body from direct attack. Experience has shown that the use of housebricks, blue bricks or concrete without reinforcement, adds little protection. Since such protection adds nothing to the strength of the safe door, care should be taken to ensure that safe limits of cash holdings are not exceeded.

METHOD

The most efficient cladding is obtained by the use of strongly reinforced concrete. If the concrete is not reinforced, it is possible for it to be peeled off in complete slabs, like the shell from a hard boiled egg. The reinforcing fabric, e.g. steel rods, $9'' \times \frac{1}{4}''$, welded mesh or expanded metal, should be secured to the safe at four inch centres in all directions, normally by welding.

Before cladding begins, the safe should be anchored by one of the methods already described.

A hard mix of aggregate and cement should be recommended (1 of cement to 1½ of sand to 3 of aggregate). This will give a cube crushing strength of 3,750 pounds per square inch after twenty-eight days.

The concrete surround should be at least nine inches thick and should be consolidated on all sides of the safe and must also be bonded to the floor. Where there is a base plinth, this must also be bonded to the floor.

Where a safe is hidden in a specially built cupboard, it is still advisable to anchor the safe and concrete it in, and the cupboard should be sited, if possible, where it can be observed from outside the building.

WELDING

Certain safes contain fire resisting materials which release moisture when heated. Such safes should not be subjected to welding operations because the heat may activate the materials and render them less resistant to fire.

Where it is necessary to anchor a safe of this type, the manufacturers should be asked to supply the safe with reinforcing fabric or girder-sections already fixed in position.

ELECTRIC PROTECTION

In premises where a burglar alarm system is installed or is under consideration, care should be taken to ensure that any safes are sited, or re-sited, so that they are within the protected area, or that the protection afforded by the burglar alarm installation is extended to give protection to safes that cannot be re-sited.

Strongrooms

The considerations for the siting of safes apply, in general, to the siting of strongrooms. The ideal is an island site so that all sides and the roof may be inspected. A good, modern strongroom will resist criminal attack for several hours and it is only common sense that it should be sited where inspections can be carried out to observe whether all is in order so that thieves are denied the time to carry out their objectives.

Advice on the erection of a strongroom is a job for the expert, but the Crime Prevention Officer can advise on siting. Obviously, the best time to give this advice is at the drawing-board stage. During the construction period, before the completed strongroom is taken into use, precautions should be taken to ensure that no unauthorised persons have access to security fittings and that no opportunity is afforded to make long-term preparations for future crime.

It is difficult to modify existing structures to the level of security commensurate with present-day requirements. Many strongrooms are sited in basements where an attack could be carried out unobserved, and many of the more successful attacks have been possible because the thieves have been able to work for up to two days without danger of being observed. It should be borne in mind however, that considerable strengthening of existing strongrooms may be effected by the use of precast concrete blocks and a *modern* strongroom door. It is true that there will be a loss of cubic capacity, but in the smaller room, this can often be allowed for by a re-arrangement of the contents.

Many cases are on record where entry to strongrooms has been effected through party walls and consideration must be given to this danger when police advice is sought, particularly where adjoining premises are easily accessible or have ben vacated. Ventilators and apertures made to accommo-date door-stops, etc., give opportunity for attack by explosives. High grade strongrooms should have no opening other than the doors.

ELECTRIC PROTECTION

As for safes, a practical answer to some of the problems of strongroom security is the installation of an efficient burglar alarm system or systems which can be designed to give warning of attacks by any of the methods known to be used by criminals, including the thermic lance. Using the defence-in-depth technique, all probable approaches to the strongroom area should be included in the protection of the burglar alarm system.

SECURITY CHECKS

To supplement the protection of a burglar alarm installation, a system of security checks at night and at week-ends by the staff, at irregular times, should be considered. Such a scheme would reduce the time available to thieves to gain entry into a strongroom. At least one Bank has already instituted a system of security checks and the police are always informed that such checks are being made.

KEY SECURITY

The value of security afforded by safes and strongrooms will be lost without high key-security. Keys left on premises, or in the doors of safes or strongrooms, can easily become compromised. They can be copied or photo-graphed, and duplicates produced.

In the same way, details of the combinations of keyless locks should be carefully protected. To avoid the embarrassment and inconvenience of a "lockout," it is advisable to deposit these details, and any duplicate keys, at a bank.

APPENDIX A-3
VEHICLE SECURITY

Vehicle security consists of three problems:

the theft or taking of vehicles;

---

*Reprinted with permission from the Home Office Crime Prevention Center Lecture Notes, Stafford, England.

the theft from within vehicles;
the theft of components and accessoried from vehicles.

How then can the problems be tackled? In the first instance the ordinary commonsense advice must apply. The motorist should be encouraged to use supervised car parks and, in any event, he should be advised when parking, to avoid where possible, dimly lit side streets. Next, he should be reminded always to remove the ignition key and to lock his car, having first removed any valuable property, or if this is not practicable, having concealed it, preferably under lock and key. As a precautionary measure, the serial numbers of property such as cameras, transistor radios, etc., should be separately recorded.

Having taken these elementary precautions, the motorist will have provided himself with initial security, but the locked car generally presents little difficulty to the thief, provided he is given the time and is able to work unobserved. The next step, therefore, is to encourage the use of vehicle protection devices and, to ensure his co-operation, adequate work must be undertaken in the field of propaganda.

The most fertile ground is usually found during talks. Organised bodies, and motoring organisations should be encouraged to seek the advice of the Crime Prevention Officer. Posters, press articles, articles in motoring publications, radio and television features, stickers on windows, and leaflets have all proved their usefulness, as indeed has the use of closed circuit television in crime prone areas, or the use of binoculars from vantage points on high buildings, in conjunction with personal radios and special patrols.

Printed publicity, however, is no substitute for personal contact between the police and the motoring public, and every endeavour should be made to point this out to beat officers.

Vehicle Immobilisation and Alarm Devices

Vehicles may be protected with immobilisers, alarmed immobilisers, alarms, or combined alarms and immobilisers.

An immobilisation device can be divided into three component parts: the controlling device, or the means by which the vehicle is remobilised; the setting system, or the means by which the device is made effective; and the mechanism or actual means by which immobilisation is achieved. Similarly, alarm devices can be divided into four component parts: the controlling device, or the means for switching the alarm on or off; the setting system, or means by which the alarm is primed; the actuating device, or means by which the device is triggered into action; and the mechanism, or means used to create an alarm.

Therefore, a vehicle protection device must firstly incorporate control equipment. This may take the form of:

a key lock,
a combination lock,
a removable cap,
a removable screw insert,
a concealed switch
or simply clip-on leads

The control equipment may use two forms of control as in the Alarmatic system, i.e. key control and dial control. Some of these forms may be sub-divided.

The key control systems may be common keys with the disadvantage of a limited number of differs and may have the key code stamped on the control lock, or the control system may use registered keys obtainable only under carefully checked conditions. The Sidleen, Yale and Ingersoll keys are examples. Concealed switches too can take varying forms, push-pull, tumbler and rotary. Whilst the use of concealed switches housed within the car for actuating immobilisers is practicable, the use of the same sort of switch sited on the vehicle exterior is not a recommended practice.

Combination locks have largely given way to electronic pulse code locks offering sophisticated security. Removable caps offer effective methods of control provided:

1. the manufacturer produces sufficient differs
2. the cap or insert is not lost
3. the wires to the device are protected

Clip-on leads are the simplest form of control and are only used in conjunction with portable, hi-jack alarm systems.

All vehicle protection devices must be set. The setting systems fall into the broad groups, manual or automatic. Manual systems are often the cheaper of the two systems. They usually take the form of a key switch or a push button. Automatic systems, on the other hand, are invaluable when an employee has custody of a vehicle as it may be the only means of ensuring that the device is properly set. Automatic systems are usually set when the ignition switch is turned off, or, in the case of diesel vehicles, when the engine strangler is operated. Such setting systems, in the case of alarms, may have a time-lapse device or a sensing device to enable the user to quit the vehicle having previously set the alarm. Key controlled by-pass switches are also sometimes used.

Vehicle alarm systems must have a device, or devices, to activate the alarm in the event of an attack. These may be switches, electrical detectors, car movement detectors or manual systems. Switches are used to detect interference with doors, boot-lids, bonnets, flaps, covers and even hand-brakes. Such switches protect only a portion of the vehicle. Electrical detectors can detect the presence or absence of electricity in a circuit. Car movement systems are usually pendulums, horizontal spring balances, or mercury switches. The latter system is perhaps the crudest and the pendulum can be prone to interference, when transversely mounted, by strong winds or passing vehicles. All such systems can produce false alarms by accidental activation. Consequently, they usually incorporate a time limitation device in the circuit. Manually activated systems take the form of hi-jack buttons.

All vehicle protection devices employ a mechanism. Alarm mechanisms can be divided into audible and visual systems, and immobiliser mechanisms can be divided into electrical and mechanical systems.

The audible alarm systems can produce a continuous or pulsating signal and can take the form of a horn, armoured horn, klaxon or siren. The visual systems usually activate the obligatory lights, direction indicators, or the head lights. Obviously, audible signals attract attention and visual signals identify the source of the signal. Pulsating circuitry is often used in conjunction with normal car horns since these are usually incapable of producing a sustained note without damage. Armoured horns are obviously more difficult to overcome.

Electrical immobilisers take the form of interrupted ignition circuits, earthed ignition circuits, general isolation of electrical circuits (but such systems mean that clocks and side lights cannot be used when the device is set), starter motor circuit cut-outs, and fuel pump circuit cut-outs. All such electrical circuit systems are effective only if the wiring is concealed or, at vulnerable points, armoured. Electrical immobilisers of the simpler kind can often be overcome by the persistent thief with some knowledge of car mechanics.

Mechanical immobilisers act as locking devices upon the clutch, leaving the vehicle still free to move; on the gear lever, usually retained in the reverse position; on the hydraulic brakes; on the handbrake, a less effective way of immobilisation; on the steering column, an effective method but one that may involve high fitting charges; and as a fuel line intercepter, thought by some to be the cause of air locks in the fuel pipe line.

No one system is perfect. A crime prevention officer should consider what can be afforded, the type of vehicle to be protected, the nature of the valuables carried in the vehicle, the use made of the vehicle and the places in which it is normally parked, and, finally, the nature of the driver. He should bear in mind that some systems are permanently fixed in position, some can be transferred only to identical vehicles, some can be changed with difficulty and some are easily interchangeable.

In addition to the foregoing, vehicles can be protected by fitting special locks to doors, bonnets, windows, quarter lights, petrol filler caps, and car radio aerials. Items such as trailers and grille-protected compartments can be linked into the alarm.

Finally, the person who can afford to spend very little can make or have made a simple, concealed switch to isolate the fuel pump or the ignition, circuit, or to earth the coil, preferably through a resistance such as the car horn.

The precaution of changing the plug leads is not recommended, since drivers will rarely continue the precaution for long, and there may be a risk of engine damage. Similarly, the removal of the rotor-arm, while effective in preventing starting, is also not likely to appeal to drivers as a long-term precaution.

The use of protection devices has been mentioned and, broadly speaking, these are classified in a separate hand-out.

Commercial Vehicles

Commercial vehicles pose special problems. They are often used by company servants or employees and an element of trust is involved. They often carry high value loads. High value loads are not necessarily items such as tobacco, spirits and TV sets. The value of a load of TV sets can be exceeded by the value of a load of, say, meat cubes.

Such factors mean that operators must take into account the irresponsibility that exists in the world today. To minimise this factor, operators should use vehicle security devices which present difficulties to the dishonest and combat the indifference of the driver, i.e. alarms which are automatically set.

Optional Extras

Steering locks are now offered by some manufacturers as optional extras on new vehicles but vehicle operators buying from most of these manufacturers must remember to specify a steering lock at the time of ordering since, once the vehicle has left the production line, the steering column has then to be dismantled to fit a lock.

For higher risks it must always be remembered that immobilisers and alarms relying upon electricity for power MUST have such a supply and its essential circuitry wiring protected against attack.

Immobilisation Not Enough

It has often been said that "If it is worth transporting it is worth stealing," and all vehicles should, therefore, be equipped with an efficient immobiliser but it is also obvious that the greater the value of the load the more comprehensive the protection required. In addition to the danger of the theft of a complete load, there are those vehicles employed on local deliveries which are subjected to the attentions of petty thieves who steal packages from temporarily unattended vans. Van boys/mates or guard dogs immediately jump to mind as obvious deterrents but, for various reasons, are not always available and substitutions, such as self-locking doors, locking roller shutters, grille partitions and doors and/or alarms have to be used.

Motor Cycles and Scooters

Certain models have steering locks fitted as standard equipment. In addition to locks and chains, throttle locks to secure the twist grip controls are available.

There is also the alarm designed by the Lander Equipment Company, which utilises a mercury switch. Tilting the machine will disturb the mercury switch, thereby causing the alarm to operate. The horn will sound continuously until switched off at the concealed master switch.

Outboard Motors

Many locks are available, designed to secure the clamp handles used to secure the motor to the transom. More comprehensive forms of boat protection can be obtained by using a Sea-Bell alarm, or Aqualert, which provides wanderlead protection for loose equipment and a flashing mast head light.

APPENDIX A-4
SECURITY OF CASH AND VALUABLES IN TRANSIT*

Recommendations

If recommendations are to be made to, and adopted by, management or supervisors, it is important to ensure that employees, in turn, are made conversant with them and that this situation is periodically.

Movement on Foot

1. New employees whose references have not been authenticated should NEVER be used for the transpart or handling of money.
2. Women, elderly or infirm men, or immature youths, should not be used.
3. The first and last hundred yards (or so) of any journey, including those parts that lie within a building to which thieves may have access, when cash is carried are the most likely places for an attack,

---

*Reprinted with permission from the Home Office Crime Prevention Center Lecture Notes, Stafford, England.

and it is during these parts of the movement that special vigilance should be excerised.

4. Frequent changes of times, routes and collection or delivery points may offer security advantages. Where the choice lies between a busy route and a quiet route, the busy one should be used. Alternative routes should be surveyed before use for likely danger spots.

5. There is often an advantage to be gained by carrying small amounts of cash on the person rather than in a bag or case; alternatively, notes only may be carried on the person and the coin in a bag or case. The use of cash-carrying garments, alarm bags or cases, or dummy bags, should be considered.

6. The person carrying the cash should walk facing oncoming traffic in order to reduce the risk of a surprise attack from behind, by persons using a vehicle.

7. An escort of able-bodied male (s) should be considered in all cases and strongly recommended when large amounts of money are being moved. The escort should be the first to leave the cash collection point, e.g. bank and should survey the immediate approaches before the cash is brought on to the street.

8. The escort should walk a few yards behind the person carrying the money and should have means of raising the alarm. He should know the location of public telephones and police boxes along the route. A knowledge of local residents and trades-people would be of value.

9. Consideration should be given to a policy of dividing the risk by using two or more persons or vehicles for the conveyance of the money. A decoy is of value.

10. Special care is needed in the use of a night safe. Money should never be exposed to view until the night safe door has been opened. Rent collectors, football pools collectors, cinema managers or cashiers, because of their regular use of night safes, often at fixed times, have been the special "targets" of criminals. Escorts should stand with their backs to the safe, rather than watch the movements of their companion.

11. The practice of fastening cash-cases to the body is the subject of controversy. It prevents the surprise snatch, but does not find favour with all employers because of the risk of injury to employees. Where this method is used, the bag or case should be fastened to a harness or to a waist-strap and not to the wrist, so that the hands remain free.

12. Avoid regular or rigid procedures. Whatever scheme is adopted, it should not be slavishly adhered to over a protracted period, but

should be constantly reviewed and varied to meet changing circumstances.

Movement by Vehicle

1. Where practicable, a closed vehicle should always be used for the conveyance of moderate to large sums of money.

2. The times of collection and deposit (or transfer) should be varied. To allow latitude, Bank Managers may approve out-of-hour transactions.

3. Vary the routes whenever possible, bearing in mind that a busy route is safer and should be used in preference to a quiet alternative. To provide greater variation, it is often possible to arrange for transactions to be carried out at different branches of Banks. Consider the survey of a route before the movement of an unusually large consignment.

4. Advantage is gained by varying the vehicle(s) used, if no loss of security will result. Consider the use of decoy vehicle(s) of similar type.

5. A vehicle which is to be used regularly for the transport of money should be:
   a. Maintained in good mechanical condition,
   b. Fitted with separate internal door fastenings,
   c. Fitted with an immobiliser,
   d. Fitted with a distinctive siren or alarm,
   e. Fitted with an additional internal mirror for the observer,
   f. Checked for fuel, etc., before each journey.

6. Within the vehicle, additional safeguards should be provided for the protection of the cash. These can take the form of:
   a. A vehicle-safe secured to a substantial part of the structure. The most convenient place for a safe is usually in the boot of a car and, by fitting additional locks, good security is obtained. The disadvantage is that the cash-carrying personnel can be held within the vehicle while the thieves attack the boot. Preferably codes and safe-keys should be carried in the vehicle;
   b. Ring-bolts, welded to the chasis, through which may be threaded cable or steel chain secured to the cash-container;
   c. Alarm bag;
   d. Additional, weighted, decoy containers.

7. The following security procedure should be considered and, where appropriate, recommended:

a. The driver to remain in the vehicle *at all times,* with doors *locked* and, when stationary, with immobiliser and alarm set.

b. The driver to be given route instructions only when the money and personnel are safely inside the vehicle with the doors locked.

c. The person in charge should decide the route immediately prior to departure. He should carry a record of police telephone numbers and should know the location of public telephones along the route. His equipment should include a pencil and pad to enable him to record details of suspected vehicles for report to the police.

d. Routes should be timed and, in the event of non-arrival at the destination within an agreed tolerance period, enquiries should be started to trace the vehicle.

e. An escort should be provided and its strength will depend on the amount of money to be moved. For substantial sums, at least two able-bodied men, in addition to the driver, are recommended. Each should be allotted specific duties during loading and unloading and in the event of an attack. Only trusted employees should be used.

f. Ideally, a separate vehicle should be used for transporting the escort. If such a vehicle is used, it should always travel at a convenient distance behind the cash-carrying vehicle, taking care not to become separated in traffic. When the cash-carrying vehicle is stationary at its destination, the escort vehicle should be parked in front and the driver should remain at the wheel;

g. Consideration should be given to the use of radio-telephone or radio in cash-carrying vehicles where such facilities are available, and, when an escort vehicle is used, in this vehicle also.

h. In the absence of very special reasons, hired taxis and public transport should not be used for the transport of cash and valuables.

General

SECRECY OF CASH MOVEMENTS IS ESSENTIAL. The knowledge of such movements must be restricted to the smallest number of people necessary for their safe completion.

Close attention should be given to security precautions within premises. There is little point in safeguarding cash in transit if it is exposed to criminal attack at departure or arrival points.

Specialist Cash-in-transit Services

A number of private companies offer services for the transit of cash. Specially constructed and adapted vehicles are used for the movement of money on a contract basis. The companies undertake full responsibility for cash movements from the time the cheque is obtained from the cashier until the money is safely delivered. Some of the organisations now offer overnight holding facilities and will put wages into packets, delivering them at an appointed place and time.

The main points in favour of these organisations are:

1. Removal of risk of attack on employees;
2. Certainty of delivery of cash, even if a successful attack is carried out;
3. Saving in employee's time and the provision of transport. It is often cheaper, and usually more convenient, to use such a service than it is to use employees and company vehicles;
4. The standard of security afforded is greater than most companies can reasonably be expected to provide for themselves.

APPENDIX A-5
THEFTS FROM OFFICES, SHOPS AND WAREHOUSES*

Over the years certain problems relating to particular classes of premises have been found to occur quite frequently. Below, these are dealt with briefly as a guide to the type of problems which often require attention and at the same time a method is suggested by which that problem may be overcome.

1. Offices

a. *Offices left temporarily unattended:* Create the opportunity for sneak-in thefts. Visitors should be left in no doubt as to where the enquiry office or reception desk is located. These positions should be provided with a warning bell. Unknown persons found wandering should be challenged and directed to the correct office.

b. *Board Rooms left unlocked:* When not in use they should be locked and items of value removed and secured.

c. *Care of personal property of staff:* There is general lack of care on the part of the employees with regard to their personal property. Lockers should be provided and their use encouraged. Warning notices in wash rooms, etc., will serve to remind them of the dangers of leaving items of value in wash-rooms and on desks, i.e. handbags, brief-cases, watches and rings.

---

*Reprinted with permission from the Home Office Crime Prevention Center Lecture Notes, Stafford, England.

d. *Making up wages:* Provision of an appropriate room the door of which is fitted with a viewer lens, good quality locks and door chains. Staff should be warned to suspect all "callers."

e. *Key Security:* Adoption of a strict system of key security, if necessary, using a code or similar system. Warn of dangers of labelling keys showing office names and functions.

Give constant publicity by visits, leaflets, posters, and stickers of the dangers of leaving safe keys in desks or "hiding places."

f. *Housekeepers and cleaners:* Point out the danger of all doors being unlocked by the housekeeper to facilitate the movements of cleaners, and the subsequent failure to re-lock.

g. *Concealment on premises:* Prior to closure there should be a methodical search against concealment of persons on premises. Incorporation of a pressure mat into an alarm system discloses the presence of a previously concealed intruder.

2. Shop

a. *Dishonest employees:* The need to check the character references of new employees cannot be over-emphasised. Warn of the dangers of entrusting cash to new or junior employees. Advise a system of "bonding" wherever appropriate.

b. *False or duplicate key:* Fitting of the best possible locks under the circumstances should be advised. Where chain stores are involved, encourage a system where the manager has a high quality personal padlock.

c. *Displays:* Can obstruct examination of premises by police after business hours. This can be remedied by varying the position of articles on display and providing observation lights at vulnerable points.

d. *Theft by smashing windows:* This offence, often committed at night, can be obstructed by the use of Bandit glass, suspended toughened glass, removal of display at night, or the items moved out of reach.

Grilles or shutters provide not only protection against theft from windows but prevent entry through the window.

e. *Lunchtime larcenies:* Check whether meal-time rota provides the best possible supervision under the circumstances.

f. *Shoplifting in Supermarkets:* Measures which can prove effective include encouraging press publicity about convictions combined with frequent use of store detectives. Closed circuit television can be of assistance in large establishments and thought must be given to whether there should be publicity in connection with its use. Supervision by staff or detectives can also be carried out by the use of venetian striped mirror or "one-way" mirrors.

g. *Thefts from displays inside shops:* It is an accepted fact in the retail industry that goods placed in a position where they can easily be handled by customers attract better sales than those which are out of reach. This of course leads to easier theft. Security may be improved by the use of light, attractive chains which will allow handling. A male/female jointed electrical thread connected to an alarm in the shop can be effective.

Small articles can be screened by a glass shield.

h. *Damage to cash registers and tills:* To avoid damage by thieves in the course of breaking offences it is recommended that the cash register or till be emptied each night and left open.

i. *Snatches from tills:* Encourage design of tills or arrangement of cash so that notes of high denomination are difficult to reach.

j. *Snatches from inside jewellers shops:* Encourage the following:

(1) Adoption wherever possible of a system of one assistant to one customer where purchases over a certain amount are likely.

(2) Layout of counters so that a snatch of valuable property cannot be accomplished with a clear means of escape.

(3) Shoppers should not be allowed to handle a pad of rings, but should indicate one ring while it is under glass and be given this to examine. Pads should always be left in display cases. Watch those who wish to compare a number of rings at one time.

(4) Goods should not be taken outside the shop for viewing purposes, but to a suitable window.

(5) Fitting of a bandit alarm which is readily audible from outside the shop, and ensuring that the staff receive instruction in its use and are warned of the dangers of false alarms. Staff should be instructed to operate the alarm at once if attacked.

(6) It is possible to obtain clamps into which pads of rings may be placed if brought out of display cases.

k. *Losses from bad cheques:* Advise on the precautions which can be taken.

l. *Rear entrances:* Should be kept locked, especially during peak business hours to prevent "sneak in" thefts.

3. Warehouses

a. *Opening time attacks:* Use two sets of keys so that at least two persons must be present in order to open up.

b. *Alarm weaknesses:* Point out the possibility of entries via ceiling, adjoining premises and outer walls, and ensure that these points are incorporated in the alarm system. In extensive premises alarming only a valuable section may be a solution. The control equipment must always be within the protected area.

  c. *Bogus workmen:* There should be a systematic check of the identity of all callers, and if possible the provision of a register to record all visits (especially in bank premises).

  d. *Vulnerable windows:* If not required, brick in; if required, consider the use of glass bricks.

  e. *Cellar flaps and hoists:* Ensure that these are not a weak link.

  f. *Lifts:* These should be immobilized when the premises are vacant.

4. *General Considerations*

  a. Where possible, liaison with architects and builders at an early stage.

  b. In case of premises to be fitted with a mastered system of locks, ensure a correct start otherwise whole system may be frustrated. Remember that master-keying reduces security.

  c. Regular checks on security matters wherever possible.

  d. Encourage the appointment in business premises of a person to be specifically responsible for security and passing on information regarding the premises involving such things as workmen on premises or when temporary weaknesses arise in the security, change of key-holders, etc.

  e. Necessity in office blocks for some system whereby premises are systematically searched at the close of business to lessen the risk of persons concealing themselves thereon.

  f. Liaison between person responsible for adjoining premises wherever possible.

  g. Ensure that the problem of opening up for, and supervision of, the cleaning staff is fully covered from the security point of view. There should be one manned point of entry and exit only.

  h. Let it be known that the police know and the thief knows that it is a common practice to hide keys on premises. Do everything to discourage the practice.

  i. When visiting, pay attention to the caretaker's lodge or the reception area. It is there that weaknesses in key security, etc., often become apparent.

  j. When contacting persons by letter ensure that the letters, wherever possible, are individual and not stereotyped.

  k. Information regarding security over holiday periods or when stock is abnormally high is valuable. Encourage concerns to pass this information to Police.

In all cases, occupiers should be encouraged to maintain contact with the police Crime Prevention Department on all matters affecting the security of people, property, and premises.

PART B

INTERNAL AND EXTERNAL SECURITY PROGRAMS

THE FOLLOWING MATERIALS afford examples of the kind that may be prepared for an addendum to a survey and are presented as a guide for security and crime prevention survey specialists. Many of the aids can be obtained free of charge from local Small Business Administration field offices or related sources.

Procedural information as it applies to:

1. Insuring Entrance Door Lock Security
2. Preventing Burglary and Robbery Loss
3. Preventing Employee Pilferage
4. Reducing Shoplifting Losses
5. Preventing Retail Theft
6. Control of Expendable Tools I
7. Control of Expendable Tools II
8. Outwitting Bad Check-passers
9. Forgery and Check Alteration—Prevention
10. Cash Handling Procedures
11. Security of Records
12. Protecting Your Records Against Disaster

APPENDIX B-1
INSURING ENTRANCE DOOR LOCK SECURITY*

EDWIN F. TOEPFER†

While technological advances have made building security "easier" for architects in one sense, these advances have, in another sense, made the problem of building security more complex than ever. Not only must the architect be aware of the various types and special functions of door locks, for example, but he must also be cognizant of the correct attachment methods as well.

---

*Reprinted with permission from Edwin F. Toepfer, Insuring Entrance Door Lock Security. In *Architectural Record* (New York: McGraw-Hill, 1964).

†President, Toepfer Safe and Lock Co., Milwaukee, Wisconsin.

Developing Security Standards

Recognizing the need for an impartial source of qualified knowledge of lock security, the Associated Locksmiths of America recently appointed a committee to study the problem. This Security Standards Committee is at work conferring with law enforcement personnel, insurance underwriters, lock manufacturers, builders, contract hardware men, and architects in an effort to arrange a meeting of the minds between these groups to adopt practical standards for entrance door security. Their recommendations will be available to city building code authorities who are working on such additions to building codes. In addition to door locks and methods of attachment to doors and frames, the committee is also concerned with proper reinforcement of door and window jambs to prevent ripping, peeling and spreading. At least one lock manufacturer has anticipated future demands and made available both a case-hardened cylinder guard and a steel reinforcing insert to properly support their lock strike plate in "soft" metal frames.

Entrance Door Security

While door locks do not constitute the total solution to the problem of building security by any means, they warrant thorough discussion for two reasons. First, the most popular means of illegal entry by nonprofessional burglars is the main entrance. Secondly, door locks of all types require a new evaluation, due to the revolution in design and functions, and the lessening concern for security among some manufacturers. Let us, therefore, first consider the basic requirements for entrance door security.

Lock cylinders should be of solid brass construction with a full .051 diameter cylinder plug, with a full complement of no less than five pin tumblers and preferably six pins. Master keying should be kept as simple as possible, as each split of tumblers created by master and submaster functions reduces security against picking and interchange of keys. The following key change table of a major lock manufacturer is typical:

1. 1,000,000 theoretical mathematical key changes on a 6 pin tumbler cylinder (not master keyed).
2. 15,625 secure, practical and useable key changes on a 6 pin tumbler cylinder (not master keyed).
3. 2,000 maximum secure changes on a simple master keyed system with one key section.

The number of secure changes is further reduced by complex master keying. The maison keying system common on apartment and office buildings, which provides for all keys to open a common entrance, prevents the establishment of a highly secure master key system. Use of several sections of key blanks in a large master key system presumably increases maximum key changes, and in effect it does. However, it also leads to a reduction in security by the promiscuous use of master section key blanks by key cutters who do not stock all sectional types of key blanks. Individual keys duplicated on master blanks cause them to become sub-master keys of a sort.

Mechanical Functions Decisive

Appearance is no guide to the reliability of locks. This fact was dramatized recently by the experience of the security superviser of a major public utility company. For years, the security of these buildings had been taken for granted, as the company had always specified quality hardware in all construction work. A security survey for the entrance doors of 45 of the firm's buildings exposed, however, the fallacy that cast bronze screwless shank knobs and trim were synonymous with security since mechanical functions of the lock must also be considered. Using wire coat hangers and celluloid rulers during the survey, the security superviser was able to surreptitiously enter 31 of the 45 buildings, as many of the impressive-looking locks were found to be improper for the purpose. They did not possess automatic deadlatch features to prevent "case knifing" of the latch, and in some cases the deadlatch did not operate due to malfunction. The glaring deficiency of these locks would no doubt have been magnified if certain other tests had been made to attempt to defeat them.

Methods of Increasing Lock Cylinder Security

1. The complexities of master keying can best be resolved by a competent hardware consultant who many times will confer with the client's locksmith, who is often familiar with the special problems of the business. Security in master keyed lock systems may be maintained by sound planning with the client, who often should be discouraged from insisting on "single key" performance for executive personnel. This single master key to fit "everything" in complex systems advocated by some suppliers results in much cross keying and resulting loss of security.

2. If removable core cylinders are used, the architect should emphasize the importance of tight control of the core removal key, as this key, in effect, is a grand master key, providing access to the inner mechanism of all of the locks. This fact is often unknown or overlooked.

Inasmuch as key blanks for the many special sectional key types are usually not readily available from lock supply sources, provisions should be made in advance to have the building occupant's locksmith supplied with the proper types of key blanks in sufficient quantities to take care of the demands for additional keys. Failure to make this advance provision often results in the duplication of keys on master section key blanks, which breaks down the cylinder security, as such keys become sub-master keys which will pass many of the locks for which they are not intended.

The fact that security starts with key control cannot be overemphasized. It is within the power of the hardware specification writer to insure security for the future of a building or project by the manner in which he specifies key control. Regardless of the size of a building, a key control system is a necessary part of the security story. The system should be a complete type, including key gathering and identification envelopes, proper pattern key markers, temporary markers, signature receipt forms and cross index records. The storage cabinet should be secured by a tamper-resistant combination (safe type) lock of the built-in type, as this lock becomes the guardian of the complete lock system.

Additional Lock Security Measures

Armored face plates should be specified to prevent the advance loosening of cylinder set screws by burglars planning a later entry.

Automatic dead latch should be specified on all locks not having a dead bolt function, as a protection against release of the latch with a "case knife."

Double cylinder locks should be used whenever possible. When fire codes or convenience consideration requires an emergency handle or push-bar release from the inside, it becomes possible for a burglar to release the lock from the outside by "hooking" the handle or bar with a wire coat hanger through the space between pairs of doors, mail slots, transoms or other openings. Therefore, auxiliary double cylinder locks should be specified for protection during the "unoccupied" hours. When such added protection is not possible, an automatic astragal may be used to close the opening between pairs of doors.

Cylinder protector rings should be specified to prevent "pulling" of lock cylinders, which is very common in some areas. This simple process of removal of the cylinder by burglars, permitting release of the lock with a finger, is rapidly increasing in scope. Some manufacturers now supply hardened, non-pullable cylinder protection rings for their locks as an added security feature.

Extra long lock bolts are required to meet the growing burglary technique of spreading of the door jamb to by-pass the lock bolt. Bolts, 1-in. long and longer, with hardened steel inserts are available. An additional vertical bolt which locks into the threshold, provides added protection.

Reinforced strike plate mountings are required, especially on metal frames, to prevent ripping of the metal around the strike plate. This recently identified burglary technique was developed to circumvent the secure types of locks now available for narrow style metal doors. A section of steel angle or channel inserted in the area of the strike plate will prevent the peeling or ripping of the soft metal, and properly anchor the strike. On wood jambs a sub-base of plywood under the door frame in the area of the strike plate and hinges will supply proper anchor facility for the full length of the wood screws. This reinforcing will also serve to prevent spreading of the door jamb. The extensive use of hollow metal doors and frames has resulted in the use of metal too light for security purposes on entrance doors. Such doors should be of 16 gauge construction and frames, of 14 gauge construction. When possible, channel iron or structural steel frames should be used.

Locks for Safety Control

In addition to locks designed to keep burglars out, there are the more intriguing types of locks developed for safety, especially concerning the invisible dangers of the "atomic age." Research and developmental laboratories require personnel safety locks which will allow emergency entrance and exit, and simultaneously alert the control office, and prevent entry into danger areas, even by persons possessing a key, until a control station authorizes such entry by remote electrical means. Such foundations are incorporated in single unit electromechanical locks with "cheat-proof" protection features. Closed-circuit television and intercom systems combine with such locks to create the ultimate in remote control safety supervision.

Data processing areas, laboratories and dark rooms require air-lock and light-lock doors. The increased demand for such interlock devices has created certain mechanical and safety problems. The all-important factor is safety, and therefore such interlocks should incorporate a "fail-safe" feature to prevent trapping of personnel due to power failures resulting from emergencies.

Safes and Vaults

Location of safes and vaults and proper lighting of them is an important part of interior planning. Placement of such equipment within unobstructed view from public streets is an important factor in discouraging burglars. Not one, but a pair of lights assures an uninterrupted source of light for the safe area.

While on the subject of safes, it is well to point out the misunderstanding regarding the difference between insulated vault doors and fire doors. Fire doors are essentially non-combustible doors intended primarily to help prevent the spread of flames from one section to another. They will, however, permit the passage of heat in temperature ranges far too high to be considered safe for the protection of papers. Furthermore. the absence of the conventional combination lock prevents the owner from obtaining burglary insurance on vaults equipped with fire doors. On the other hand, insulated vault or file storage room doors are intended to prevent, for a specified period of time, the influx of heat into an enclosed area of fire-resistive vault-like construction. These doors contain insulation of a type that actively dissipates heat to prevent the buildup of destructive temperatures inside the vault for the period for which the doors are labeled (one to six hours). Vault door rating requirements allow a maximum temperature of 300°F. at a distance of 2 in. inside the door. Fire doors are permitted to pass much more heat than this.

APPENDIX B-2
PREVENTING BURGLARY AND ROBBERY LOSS*

S. J. (Bob) Curtis†

Summary

Small stores are prime targets for burglars and holdup men. Seeking dark and easy-to-enter stores, burglars usually operate at night. Attracted by careless displays of cash, *holdup men* often strike at opening or closing time or when customer traffic is light.

Because you may be the next victim of a *robbery or a burglary* in your area, you should be aware of the precautionary measures that are available to lessen the impact of these two crimes. This *Aid* discusses some of them for both types of crime.

Burglary

Burglary is any unlawful entry to commit a felony or a theft, even though no force was used to gain entrance.

Retailers whose stores have been broken into know that burglaries are costly. What these business owners may not be aware of is that the number of burglaries has doubled in the past several years and, therefore, they may be two-, three-, or four-time losers if the trend is not reversed.

Moreover, few burglars are caught. Almost 80 percent of all burglaries go unsolved. Police prevention and detection are difficult because of lack of witnesses or evidence to identify the criminal.

Prevention must start with the small merchant himself. He can use a combination of measures to protect his store from burglars. Among the things he can use are: (a) suitable locks, (b) an appropriate alarm system, (c) adequate indoor and outside lighting, and (d) a secure store safe.

In addition, the owners of high-risk stores—ones in areas with a reputa-

---

*Reprinted with permission from Small Business Administration S.M.A. No. 134, Washington, D.C., 1972.

†Management consultant in Dayton, Ohio.

tion for rampant crime—should also consider using: (a) heavy window screens, (b) burglar-resistant windows, (c) private police patrols, and (d) watchdogs.

Locks

Be sure to use the right kind of lock on your doors. In addition to being an obstacle to unwanted entry, a strong lock requires a burglar to force his way into the store. Under standard burglary insurance policies, a forced entry is necessary to collect on burglary insurance.

Most experts on locks agree that the *pin-tumbler cylinder lock* provides the best security. It may have from 3 to 7 pins. Locksmiths caution, however, that a burglar can easily pick a lock with less than 5 pins. (There are a few non-pin tumbler locks that give high security, but you should check with a locksmith before you use one.)

Dead bolt locks should be used. They cannot be opened by sliding a piece of flexible material between the door edge and door jamb. (Dead bolt is a lock bolt that is moved positively by turning the knob or key without action of a spring.)

When you use a double cylinder dead lock, the door cannot be opened without a key on either side. This fact means that on a glass door there is no handle for a burglar to reach by merely breaking the glass. Such a lock also provides protection against "break-outs"—a thief concealing himself before closing time and breaking out with stolen goods.

Safeguarding entrance ways, especially the rear door, cannot be over emphasized. Bar the rear door, in addition to locking it, because many burglars favor back doors.

INSTALLING LOCKS. The best lock is ineffective if it is not properly installed. For example, if a lock with a $5/8''$ long latch bolt is installed in a door that is separated from the door-jamb by $1/2''$, the effective length of the bolt is cut to only $1/8''$. Have a locksmith check the locks on your exterior doors to be sure that your locks give you the right protection.

KEY-CONTROL. To keep keys from falling into the hands of burglars, issue as few keys as possible. Keep a record on the keys you issue. Exercise the same care with keys as you would a thousand dollar bill by doing the following:

1. Avoid the danger of key duplication. Caution employees not to leave store keys with parking lot attendants, or in a topcoat hanging in a restaurant, or lying about the office or stockroom.
2. Keep your records on key distribution up-to-date so that you know what keys have been issued and to whom.

3. Whenever a key is lost or an employee leaves the firm, without turning in his key, re-key your store.
4. Take special care to protect the *master key* used to remove cylinders from locks.
5. Have one key and lock for outside doors and a different key and lock for your office. Don't master-key because it weakens your security.
6. Have a code for each key so that it does not have to be visibly tagged and only an authorized person can know the specific lock that key fits. Don't use a key chain with a tag carrying the store's address.
7. Take a periodic inventory of keys. Have employees show you each key so you will know it has not been lost, mislaid, or loaned.

Burglar Alarms

The silent central-station burglary alarm system gives your store the best protection. The reason: It does not notify the burglar as does a local alarm —such as a siren or bell—outside the store. A silent alarm alerts only the specialists who know how to handle burglaries.

In large cities, central alarm systems are available on a rental basis from private firms in this business; in small cities, they are often tied directly into police headquarters. Part of the cost for installing a silent alarm system will sometimes be defrayed by a reduction in your burglary insurance premium.

Although a building-type local alarm is cheaper and easier to install, it too often only warns the thief and is not considered by specialists to be as effective as a central stations alarm. Of course, if no central alarm service system is available, or such an alarm is not economically feasible, then by all means install a building alarm.

Whether your alarm is central or local, you have a wide choice of alarm sensing devices. Among them are radar motion detectors, invisible photo beams, detectors that work on ultrasonic sound, and vibration detectors. Also there is supplemental equipment, such as an automatic phone dialer. This phones the police and the store owner, and gives them verbal warning when an alarm is breached.

Each type of alarm has advantages in certain situations. For example, proximity alarms are often used on safe cabinets. You should seek professional guidance to get the best alarm for your needs.

Flood Your Store with Lights

Outdoor lighting is another way to shield the store from burglary. Almost all store break-ins occur at night. Darkness cenceals the burglar and gives him time to work.

Light frustrates his intent. By floodlighting the outside of your store on all sides you can defeat many burglars. All sides include alley entrances and side passageways between buildings where entry might be made.

Mercury and metallic vapor lamps are good for illuminating the exterior walls of a store. They are designed to withstand vandalism and weather—wind velocities up to 100 miles per hour. Some have a heat-tempered lens that cannot be broken with less than a 22 calibre rifle.

Some stores control their floodlights automatically with a photo electric eye system. It turns on the lights at dusk and turns them off at dawn.

Indoor lighting is also important. When a store is lighted inside, police officers or patrol cars can see persons in the store or notice the disorder which burglars usually cause. When the store is left dark, a burglar can see the police approaching, but they can't see him.

Policemen get to know the lighted stores and will check the premises when, and if, the light is off.

It is also important to arrange window displays so police patrols can see into the store.

Your Safe

Be sure the safe in which you keep your money and other valuables is strong enough to deter burglars. Police remind merchants that a file cabinet with a combination lock is *not* a money safe. Store money should be protected in a *burglar-resistant money chest*—as such safes are properly called.

Insurance companies recognize the *E safe* as adequate for most merchant risks (except, in a few cities, where torch and explosive attacks on safes are common). Insurance companies give a sizeable reduction in premiums for use of the *E safe*. Over the years, the saving can pay the added cost of an *E safe*.

Locating Your Safe. Putting a safe in the back of the store or where it is not visible from the street, invites burglary. Police recommend that the safe be visible to the outside street. Also the safe area should be well-lighted all night.

But visibility and lighting will be wasted effort if your safe can be carted off by a burglar. Weight is no guarantee that the safe can't be stolen. Safes weighing 2,000 pounds have been taken out of stores.

No matter what the safe weighs, bolt it to the building structure.

Leave The "Cupboard Bare." Even when you use an *E* rated burglar-resistant money box, it is a good idea to keep on hand the barest minimum of cash. Bank all excess cash each day.

Leave your cash register drawer empty and open at night. A burglar will break into a closed one, and the damage to your register can be costly.

In addition to leaving the "cupboard" as bare as possible, use a silent central station alarm on your safe cabinet. When closing your safe at night, be sure to do the following:

1. Check to see that everything has been put into safe.
2. Make a note of the serial numbers on large bills taken in after your daily deposit.
3. Check to be sure that your safe is locked.
4. Activate the burglar alarm.

Make is a practice never to leave the combination of your safe on store premises. Change the combination when an employee who knows it leaves your firm.

High-risk Locations

Some stores are in high-risk locations. These areas have a reputation for crime. Night after night, people break display windows and help themselves or force their way into stores.

Because many windows are smashed on impulse, you should minimize the chance of loss. If possible, remove attractive and expensive merchandise from the window at night. Many jewelry stores protect items left in the display window by secondary glass—a piece of heavy glass hanging on chains from the window's ceiling. Being non-fixed, the secondary glass is difficult to break even if the burglar smashes the display window.

If your store is in a high-risk location, you need to consider using heavy window screens, burglar-resistant glass, watch dogs, or private police patrols.

HEAVY WINDOW SCREENS. Heavy metal window screens or grating are an inexpensive way for protecting show windows. You store them during business hours. At closing time, you put the screens up and lock them in place.

BURGLAR-RESISTANT GLASS. When used in exterior doors, windows, display windows, and in interior showcases, this type of glass deters burglars. It has a high tensile strength that allows it to take considerable beating. It is useful in areas with riot problems.

Burglar-resistant glass is a laminated sandwich with a sheet of invisible plastic compressed between two sheets of glass. It mounts like ordinary plate glass and comes in clear, tinted, and opaque.

Of course, this type of glass can be broken with continual hammering—as with a baseball bat or sledge hammer. But it will not shatter. The burglar who is patient enough to bang a hole in the glass will find it bordered by a barrier of jagged glass icicles.

Even in prestige locations, burglar-resistant glass offers protection. It can be used in stores selling high value merchandise, such as cameras, furs, and jewelry.

WATCHDOGS. In larger cities, agencies offer watch dog service on a nominal hourly basis. An owner-manager can use these dogs on a spot check basis one or two nights a weak to deter burglars. Word soon gets around that a store is using watchdogs, and burglars cross the store off their list. The sight and sound of an angry watchdog makes them afraid.

PRIVATE POLICE PATROLS. A private police patrolman can be used to supplement the public police force when it is undermanned and overworked. A private patrolman can discourage burglars by checking the store during the night. Sometimes he may catch a burglar in the act; othertimes, he can discover the breakin shortly after it occurs. In either case, his prompt notice to the police increases the likelihood of catching the culprit and recovering your merchandise and money.

A private patrolman is also qualified to testify on the store conditions prior to a crime. This sort of testimony expedites the payment of insurance claims. In disasters, such as a flood or riot, he can initiate emergency measures.

He can also help you train your employees. His checks may reveal unlocked doors, open windows, and other signs of employee carelessness which he can help you correct.

Robbery

ROBBERY is stealing or taking anything of value by force, or violence, or by use of fear.

Retailers who have been robbed several times are not surprised to learn that police call robbery the fastest growing crime in the Nation. Moreover, the greatest increase is in retail stores. Holdups there have increased 75 percent in the past several years.

Only about one third of the robberies in the United States are solved by identification and arrest. Even when robbers are caught almost none of the cash property is recovered.

Robbery is a *violent* crime. The robber always uses force or the threat of force, and the victims are often hurt. In 65 percent of store holdups, he uses a weapon.

What can you do to reduce losses from robbery in your store?

Your first line of defense is training your people. How you handle your cash is also important. Two other vital defensive actions are: (a) you should use care in opening and closing your store and (b) you should use care when answering after-hours emergency calls.

Training to Reduce Risk

You should let each of your employees know what may happen if a robbery occurs. Train them on how to act during a holdup.

Emphasize the protection of lives as well as money. Warn each person that you want no "heroes." The heroic action by an employee or customer may end as a deadly mistake. The holdup man is as volatile as a bottle of nitro-glycerine. Handle him with the same care you would use with any explosive.

Instruct your people to do the following when, and if, they face a holdup man:

1. Reassure him that they will cooperate in every way.
2. Stay as calm as possible.
3. Spend their time making mental notes on the criminal's build, hair-color, complexion, voice, what he is wearing, and anything that would make it possible to identify him. A calm accurate description of the thief can help bring him to justice. (Police advise that employees should not discuss or compare descriptions with each other but wait until the police arrive.)

You can provide a reference point to make descriptions accurate. Mark the wall or the edge of the door jamb in such a way that later the employee will be able to give a more accurate estimate of the holdup man's height. Often the person who has been held up compares the criminal's height with that of another person in the store. The clerk ends up unconsciously describing this innocent person used for comparison, rather than the holdup man.

Instruct your employees not to disclose the amount of loss. The police and news reporters should receive such information only from you. When talking to reporters, play down the theft. Don't picture your store as being an easy mark with a great deal of cash on hand.

Don't Build Up Cash

Cash on hand is the lure that attracts a holdup man. The best deterrent is to keep as little cash in the store as possible. Another deterrent is camera equipment that photographs robbers.

Make bank deposits daily. During selling hours, check the amount of cash in your register or registers. Remove all excess cash from each register several times a day.

Do not set up cashier operations so that they are visible to outsiders. The sight of money can trigger crime. Balance your register an hour or two before closing—not at closing time. Make it a rule to keep your safe locked even during business hours.

When making bank deposits, use an armored car service, if practical. If not, you should take a different route to the bank each day and vary the time of the deposit. Obviously, the best time to make deposits is during daylight hours.

You should also vary the route you travel between the store and your home. Keep your store keys on a separate key ring. At least then, you won't be stranded by the loss of your car and personal keys.

Opening and Closing Routine

Opening or closing the store is a two-man job. When opening your store, station one person—an employee or your assistant—outside where he can observe your actions. You enter the store, check the burglar alarm to be sure it is still properly set, then move around in the store and look for any signs of unwanted callers.

You and your assistant should have an agreement on the length of time this pre-opening check is to take. Then if you do not reappear at the scheduled time, your assistant should phone the police.

The outside man should always know where the nearest phone is located. He should have a card in his wallet with the police phone number typed on it and coins taped to the back side of the card so that he has the right change to make the call.

When he calls the police he should calmly:
1. Give his name.
2. Give the name and address of the store.
3. Report that a holdup is in progress at the store.

Under normal conditions, the owner-manager would return to the entrance after finishing his store inspection and give the outside man a predetermined "all clear" signal.

Your night closing should be a similar routine. A few minutes before closing, you make a routine check of stockrooms, furnace room, storeroom, and other places where a thief might hide. A second employee should wait just outside the store until you have finished your inspection. If you drive to work, he should bring your car to a location near the exit door. He should watch while you set the burglar alarm and lock the door.

Be Cautious on Night Calls

Whenever you receive an emergency call to return to the store at night, be careful.

First, never return to the store without first notifying someone that you are returning.

Second, if it is a burglar-alarm break, phone the police department and ask that a police car meet you at the store.

Third, if it is a repair problem, phone the repair company and have the service truck sent out before you leave home.

Fourth, if you arrive at the store and do not see the police car, or the repair truck, do not park near the store. And do not enter the store.

Fifth, make it a habit to certify *all* phone calls you receive after store hours, no matter where they originate. A careless slip on your part may be all the criminal is waiting for.

Following these precautions can mean the difference between life and death.

APPENDIX B-3
PREVENTING EMPLOYEE PILFERAGE*

SAUL D. ASTOR†

Summary

Not all crooks roam the streets of the Nation's cities. Many spend their time in the manufacturing plants of small companies. There, disguised as honest citizens, they pilfer whatever comes to hand, often tampering with records to cover up their thefts.

To prevent pilferage, an owner-manager must recognize that some employees cannot be trusted and make all employees aware that he is taking steps to thwart dishonest personnel. Such steps include setting up a system of loss prevention (devices and procedures), administering the system rigidly, and auditing it often to discourage dishonest employees who try to bypass the system.

To steal, or not to steal? That is the question that faces employees in small plants. Many employees answer that question almost unconsciously. They see items lying around and pick them up for their own use. They slip small hand tools into their pockets, for example. Or they dip into the bin for a fistful of nuts and bolts or snip off a few feet of wire for a home repair job.

But not all the employees who pilfer are nickel-and-dime thieves. Some are professionals who carry off hundreds and thousands of dollars worth of equipment and materials.

Misplaced Trust

One reason for pilferage is misplaced trust. Many owner-managers of small companies feel close to their employees. Some regard their employees as partners. These owner-managers trust their people with keys, safe combinations, cash, and records.

---

*Reprinted with permission from Small Business Administration S.M.A. No. 209, Washington, D.C., 1970.

†President, Management Safeguards, Inc., New York, N.Y.

Thus, these employees have at hand the tools which a thief or embezzler needs for a successful crime.

Unfortunately, some of the "trusted" employees in many small businesses are larger partners than their bosses anticipate. Unless you're taking active steps to prevent loss from inplant pilferage, some are probably trying to steal your business, little by little, right under your nose. Few indeed are the businesses in which dishonest employees are not busily at work. Usually, these employees are protected by management's indifference or ineptitude as they steal a little, steal a lot, but nevertheless, steal first the profit, and then the business itself.

One of the first steps in preventing pilferage is for the owner-manager to examine the trust he puts in his employees. Is it blind trust that grew from close friendships? Or is it trust that is built on an accountability that reduces opportunities for thefts?

A Climate for Dishonesty

In addition to misplacing trust, it is easy for an owner-manager to create an environment in which dishonesty takes root and thrives. Just relax your accounting and inventory control procedures. Nothing deters would-be thieves like the knowledge that inventory is so closely controlled that stolen goods will be missed quickly.

And what about the plant where it's common practice for the boss's brother-in-law to help himself from the stockroom without signing for the items he takes? Soon such a plant becomes a place where inventory shrinkage soars as employees get the message that record-keeping is loose and controls are lax.

In a manufacturing plant, no materials and no finished goods should be taken without a requisition or a removal record being made. Exceptions? Absolutely none.

Similarly, the owner-manager who does not exercise tight control over invoices, purchase orders, removals (for example, tools, materials, and finished goods), and credits is asking for embezzlement, fraud, and unbridled theft. Crooked office workers and production and maintenance personnel dream about sloppily kept records and unwatched inventory. Why make their dreams come true?

One shipping platform employee's dream came true to the tune of $30,000—the amount of goods he stole from his company. When caught, he said, "It was so easy, I really didn't think anyone cared."

Let your people know that you care. Make them aware of the stress you place on loss-prevention.

This point must be driven home again and again. And with every restatement of it—whether by a security check, a change of locks, the testing of alarms, a systems audit, a notice on the bulletin board—you can be assured that *you are influencing that moment of decision when an employee finds himself faced with the choice of whether to steal or not to steal.*

Haphazard Physical Security

Also high on the list of invitations to theft is haphazard physical security. Owner-managers who are casual about issuing keys, locking doors, and changing locks are, in effect, inviting the dishonest employee into the plant or office after work. But intelligent key control and installation of timelocks and alarms are ways of serving notice to crooked workers to play it straight.

Sometimes profits go out the window—literally. For example, one distributor caught "trusted" employees lowering TV sets and tape recorders out of a third-story warehouse window to confederates below. Unfortunately they were not caught until they had milked their boss of thousands of dollars worth of merchandise.

But more often, the industrial thief uses a door rather than a window. And the more doors a plant has, the more avenues of theft it offers.

The plant that's designed for maximum security will have a minimum number of active doors with a supervisor or guard, if warranted, stationed near each door. Moreover, a supervisor should be present when materials or finished goods are being received or shipped and when trash is being removed. As long as a door stays open, a responsible employee, a supervisor, or a guard should be there.

Central station alarm systems should be used to protect a plant after hours. Their purpose is to record door openings and closings and to investigate unexpected openings. Time-locks are also designed to record all openings.

"Breaking-out"

A record of door openings can be important because the dishonest employee is often a specialist at "breaking-out" (hiding and leaving the plant after closing hours). If your plant is not protected against break-out, you can be hurt badly because this method of operation allows a thief to work pretty much at his own speed.

An after-hours thief puts out of commission the alarm system that works beautifully against break-in. He can often leave by a door equipped with a snap-type lock—a door that does not require a key from the inside. Quickly and easily, he can pass goods outside and then snap the door closed behind him. Thus, he leaves no evidence.

A motion detector, electric eye, or central station alarm will deter such a thief. You can also discourage break-outs with a lock that needs a key on both sides, provided that local or State fire regulations do not prohibit such a lock. When goods, materials, or money are missing and evidence of forced entry is lacking, begin to look immediately for the inside thief, the dishonest employee.

Audit Control Methods

Loss-prevention controls and procedures by themselves are not enough to protect your assets. Controls and procedures must be audited from time to time or they will break down. No loss-preventive control is stronger than its audit.

One effective auditing method is the input of deliberate errors. What will your people do if, for example, you see that more finished goods than the shipping order calls for reaches the platform? Will the shipping clerk return the excess to stock? Will he try to divert it for his own use (perhaps in collusion with a truck driver)? Or will he simply ship the order without checking the amount, without ever knowing that the excess existed? Such a check is well worth making.

If the bookkeeper and the accounts receivable clerk are not dependable, alert and honest, disaster can result. Check them by withholding an invoice from each of them and watching to see what they do. Will they miss the invoice? Will they realize that a missing invoice means lost revenue and call it to your attention?

Unannounced inspections are another excellent method of checking your preventive procedures. Such inspections are most effective during overtime periods or when the second or third shift is working. For example, one owner-manager popped up on the shipping platform after the second shift had left. He noticed a loaded truck parked at the platform and ordered it unloaded. The cartons in the rear were legitimate deliveries, but he found the front half of the truck crammed with stolen goods. The checker, who was hired to see that such stealing did not happen, had gone to sleep and let the accommodating driver load his own truck.

Influence Employees

You should never underestimate your ability to influence your employees in the direction of honesty. Your use of good controls, stiff loss-prevention procedures, and cleverly located physical security devices are powerful reminders to employees that the boss does indeed care.

But controls and devices can be wasted if the owner-manager fails to set a personal example of honesty and conscienciousness. A personal example of high integrity by the boss is the most important step in demonstrating to employees that dishonesty is intolerable.

Such an example includes following the same loss-prevention rules that apply to employees. For instance, the owner-manager should sign for items he takes from the stockroom just like any other person.

Keep Crooks Off Balance

The crooked employee who is the most successful at his "second trade" is the one who tests the system and is convinced that he can beat it. He can steal you blind. With every "score," his confidence increases and along with it his danger to the company. The best way to stop such a crook is to keep him off balance—keep him from developing the feeling that he .can beat your system.

Here's an example of how one owner-manager keeps crooks off balance. When inventory shrinkage became a major problem, he made a loss-prevention survey. To help keep employees honest, he tightened certain existing controls and put in some new ones. He reduced the number of exits employees could use by half. He scheduled "unscheduled" locker inspections for the unlikeliest possible moments. Employees were no longer allowed to take lunch boxes or bags of any kind to their work stations. Package inspection procedures were tightened.

To date, this owner-manager has caught no thieves. But simply by tightening controls and adding a number of surprise elements to his loss-prevention maintenance system, he reduced his inventory loss drastically.

Don't Play Detective

Dishonest employees, working alone or in collusion with others, can find ways to beat the system no matter how theft-proof you try to make it. "Smart cookies" can devise ways to get away with substantial amounts of money, materials, or goods.

When an owner-manager suspects theft, he should not attempt to turn detective and try to solve the crime himself. Even the best businessman may botch a criminal investigation because it's an area in which the average businessman is an amateur.

When you suspect theft, bring the police or a reliable firm of professional security consultants into the picture without delay. Where dishonest employees are bonded by insurance companies, ironclad evidence of theft has to be uncovered before you can file a claim with the insurance company to recover your losses. Professional undercover investigation is among the most effective ways to secure such evidence.

APPENDIX B-4
REDUCING SHOPLIFTING LOSSES*

Addison H. Verrill†

Summary

Shoplifters and magicians have one thing in common. Both rely on sleight-of-hand. However, amusement turns to anguish when individuals who·pretend to be customers come into a small store and prove that "the hand is quicker than the eye."

The methods which shoplifters use are discussed in this *Aid,* and the types of persons who practice this form of thievery are described. The *Aid* also gives practical suggestions on using protective devices, on what employees must do, and on apprehending and arresting shoplifters.

Shoplifters are stealing me blind, is a complaint made by many retailers. And rightly so, because in some localities the shortages caused by nimble-fingered artists are the greatest percentage of a retailer's inventory shrinkage.

Unfortunately, there is no easy way to break up such thievery. It is a constant battle in which you must fight individual engagements. One difficulty is identifying your opponent. Challenging an innocent person can be costly as well as embarrassing.

A key to reducing shoplifting losses is knowing your man and catching him in the act. What methods are used by the shoplifter? What kind of person is he?

Methods of Shoplifters

Professional shoplifters are sleight-of-hand experts. Under ordinary circumstances, they can, and do, snatch items from counters and pass these items to confederates without detection.

The best protection a retailer has is a sales force trained to watch for such things. In stores where clerks are not wide awake, shoplifters can literally take over. These thieves have been known to step behind counters, pose as sales clerks, and collect money from customers.

As for the hand-is-quicker-than-the-eye techniques, shoplifters come equipped with coats and capes which have hidden pockets and slits or zippered hiding places. Hands emerge unseen from slits to snatch up articles directly from open displays. Many times, such performances are blocked from view by the open coat itself. These shoplifters are also adept at palming small items with the cover-up aid of loose handkerchiefs and gloves.

Sometimes shoplifters have special hooks or belts on the insides of their

---

*Reprinted with permission from Small Business Administration S.M.A. No. 129, Washington, D.C., 1968.

†President, Dale System Incorporated, New York, N.Y.

coats or tricky aprons and undergarments designed to hold innumerable articles. Some sleight-of-hand thieves slip merchandise into packages or into boxes that have a hinged top, bottom, or end. Salesclerks should know how to spot such devices. Employees should also be suspicious of and watch shoppers who carry bulky packages, knitting bags, shopping bags, and umbrellas. These are handy receptacles for items which a shoplifter *purposely* knocks off counters.

Some shoplifters do not confine their activity to shopowners. They even steal from customers. They pick up packages or handbags which store patrons carelessly lay aside in their preoccupation with shopping.

Ticket switching is another method used by shoplifters. It is an especially vexing problem for owner-managers of a store. It is almost impossible to prove the guilt of a ticket switcher, for one thing. Also there is the hazard of false arrest countercharges.

Types of Shoplifters

Fortunately for the owner-manager of a small store, the majority of shoplifters are amateurs rather than professionals. A breakdown of various types should help you to understand the motives which causes these individuals to steal and the methods they use.

Juvenile Offenders. The young make up about 50 percent of all shoplifters, and indications are that this type of offender is on the increase. Sometimes youngsters steal "for kicks" or because they have been "dared" to do so. They may enter stores in gangs. In order to discourage these rebellious and unsupervised juveniles, retailers should "get tough." Youth is no excuse for crime. It should be prosecuted and made to pay through the proper legal channels.

Housewives. Many retailers report that the majority of adults who are apprehended are women, and a significant number of them are housewives. They steal because they have given in to momentary impulse and temptation. Many of them are first offenders and by catching them, you may help prevent them from becoming habitual shoplifters.

Kleptomaniacs. Thefts by kleptomaniacs stem from psychological compulsions. The term is a combination of the Greek word for thief, "kleptes," and the word "maniac." Often kleptomaniacs do not need the items they pick up. But even so their behavior is no less costly to you.

Drunkards and Vagrants. Drunkards and vagrants are probably the most clumsy shoplifters and the easiest to detect. They often steal because they desperately need money and food.

Narcotics Addicts. Drug addicts are, of course, more desperate than vagrants. Also addicts may be armed. They should be handled by the police.

PROFESSIONAL SHOPLIFTERS. The professional is the most difficult type to detect and apprehend. He is clever at his craft. When he comes into the store, he often pretends that he is shopping for something to buy for his wife.

The professional shoplifter is "in business" for money. He usually steals to resell his loot to established fences. He often has a police record. Indeed, he may belong to an underworld organization which will supply bail and help him in court.

The professional can be discouraged from stealing if he sees that store personnel are really alert.

Call the Police

Regardless of the type of shoplifter, the common answer that most shoplifters give when caught is: "I have never done this before."

Failure to prosecute "first offenders" encourages shoplifting. It is best to operate on the premise that he who steals will also lie. Call the police when you catch a shoplifter.

When every merchant in town follows the policy of prosecuting each shoplifter, the word gets around. Hardened professionals will avoid the town. Amateurs will think twice before yielding to the temptation to pocket a choice item.

Protective Personnel and Devices

In reducing shoplifting losses, the deterrent factor is all important. Protective devices help you to discourage borderline shoplifters—ones who don't steal unless the coast is clear—and to trap bold ones. Among these devices are two-way mirrors, peepholes, closed-circuit television, radio communication, and detectives posing as customers.

Some large stores use uniformed guards and plainclothes personnel who serve as a reminder to patrons that only legally purchased merchandise may be removed from the premises. One way to identify such merchandise is to use stapled packages with receipts attached outside.

When you have no guards and rely solely on your own people, convex wall mirrors can be helpful. They allow store personnel to see around corners and keep several aisles under observation from regular work stations.

Anti-shoplifting signs prominently displayed warn potential thieves and deter some. Various uses of public address systems have also been employed to discourage shoplifters. When a suspect has been observed, a "walkie-talkie" radio can be used for speedy communication between you and those employees who handle such situations.

Electronic devices which expose the shoplifter are also on the market.

One example of such a device is an electronic pellet or wafer attached usually to an expensive garment so that it cannot be removed without tearing the merchandise. If a shopper tries to remove the garment from the store, the pellet or wafer sends out signals. The cashier removes the pellet with special shears when the customer purchases the garment.

You should keep in mind that there is a legal danger in using electronic devices. If the cashier forgets to remove the pellet device, an innocent shopper may be stopped outside and falsely detained.

When shoplifters use ticket switching to gain their ends, you can use the following alternatives:

1. *Tamper-proof gummed labels* which rip apart when attempt is made to remove labels.
2. Hard-to-break *plastic string* for softgoods tickets.
3. When tickets are stapled on, *special staple patterns* are used which are recognizable to store personnel.
4. *Extra price tickets* are *concealed* elsewhere on merchandise.

If you use simple and basic pricing methods, don't ticket prices in pencil. Use a rubber stamp or pricing machine.

Physical Layout of Stores

A store's layout can discourage or encourage shoplifting. For example, high fixtures and tall displays which give visual protection to the shoplifter will encourage his practices. To destroy such protection, set your display cases in broken sequences. If possible, run them for short lengths with spaces in between.

Keep small, high-priced items out of reach, preferably in locked cases. Keep valuable and easy-to-hide items at counters where clerks are in continuous attendance. Or better yet, let the customer ask a salesman to show him such items.

If fire safety regulations allow it, lock all exits not to be used by customers. In addition, attach noise alarms to the exits which must be kept unlocked. Always close and block off unused checkout aisles.

What Employees Must Do

Employees must watch merchandise and people if you are to prevent shoplifting. Generally, your salesclerks should be alert to persons who wear loose coats or capes or bulky dresses. They should also watch persons who carry large purses, packages, umbrellas, and shopping bags. Those who push baby strollers and collapsible carts also bear watching as well as individuals who walk with short steps. The latter may be carrying stolen goods between their legs.

In clothing stores, clerks should beware of the "try-on" shoplifters. They try on an item for size, as it were, and then, if they feel no one has seen them, walk out wearing the garment. Salespeople should keep a check on the number of garments carried into the fitting rooms. Thieves often try to sneak in extra garments beyond the number permitted.

You and your people should be especially alerted for "teams"—thieves who pretend not to know each other. One of the team will attract the clerk's attention away from the partner. He will cause a fuss, ask unreasonable questions, create an argument, even stage fainting fits while his partner picks up the merchandise and makes a quick exit.

Sales persons should keep in mind that ordinary customers want attention while shoplifters do not. When busy with one customer, the salesman should acknowledge other customers with polite remarks such as, "I'll be with you in a minute." It can make a shoplifter feel uneasy. Such attention pleases ordinary customers.

Salesclerks should not give the impression that they distrust customers, but they must always be alert to their movements. If possible, they never should turn their backs to customers even when fetching merchandise for them. They should display merchandise neatly because missing items are easily detected when orderly arranged.

You should schedule your employees' working hours with floor coverage in mind. An adequate number of clerks should be on duty during your store's busy periods. These periods are most conducive to theft.

Finally, and most important, you should instruct employees about what they are to do when they observe a theft by a shoplifter. This training should be done periodically, at least once every three months. Such knowledge helps prevent legal problems in addition to catching offenders.

Apprehension and Arrests

Be certain or risk a false arrest suit is a good rule to follow when catching a shoplifter.

In pursuing this rule, salespersons should not accuse patrons of stealing. Nor should they try in any way to apprehend shoplifters. When a salesperson sees what appears to be a theft, he should keep the suspect in sight and alert you immediately. The police or the store detective should be notified if you use one. In fact, salespersons should alert you about any suspicious loiterers.

If your refund desk clerk receives a returned item and recognizes it as a stolen or suspicious item, she should delay the person and call you. Ask the person for identification and have him sign his name and address. If the item is stolen, he will usually give a wrong name and have no identification.

Some organizations in large cities have control files on shoplifters who have been caught. Your retail merchant's association can inform you about the services available in your area. You can check these files to see whether the person you catch has a record. Usually a shoplifter claims to be a first offender. He is apt to remain a "first offender" if the merchant allows him to leave without positive identification and without filing his name with the police and local retail merchant association.

You should also check to see what the law is in your State. Many States have passed "shoplifting laws" which, among other things, deal with apprehending shoplifters. Check with your lawyer or the police in your area.

GENERAL RECOMMENDATIONS. It is best to apprehend shoplifters outside of the store. For one thing, apprehension of this kind strengthens the store's case against a shoplifter. Then, too, scenes or any type of commotion which a shoplifter precipitates interferes with store operation.

You should recognize that apprehension in many States does not necessarily have to be initiated outside of the store. Sometimes, it suffices if a shoplifter is observed concealing merchandise on his or her person. A shoplifter is generally apprehended in the store if the merchandise involved is of substantial value, and if you feel that he may get away with the stolen goods if you allow him to get beyond the store premises.

If the shoplifter is an elderly person, treat him or her with extra gentleness lest he be "shocked." If you don't, he may have a heart attack. A good approach to stopping a suspect is to speak to him and identify yourself. Then say: "I believe you have some merchandise on your person or in your bag which you have forgotten to pay for. Would you mind coming back to the store to straighten out this matter?" Never touch the suspect because the contact could be construed as roughness.

APPENDIX B-5
PREVENTING RETAIL THEFT*
SAUL D. ASTOR†

Summary

Theft, especially employee theft, is more serious than some small marketers might think. Dishonest employees account for about two thirds of retail stealing.

Positive steps can be taken to curb theft. Some are outlined in this *Aid*. They include safeguards against employee dishonesty and ways to control shoplifting. In addition, key theft hazards are spelled out, and preventive

---

*Reprinted with permission from Small Business Administration S.M.A. No. 119, Washington, D.C., 1972.

†President, Management Safeguards, Inc., New York, N.Y.

measures are detailed. The advantages of undercover investigation are also described.

Retail theft loss estimates vary by the type of operation and the efficiency of management. They range, for example, from about 0.7 percent of sales for the well-managed department store to about 4.5 percent for the loosely controlled operation. Dishonest employees account for about two thirds of the retail theft, according to one estimate. You can blame another one-third on shoplifting.

The encouraging thing is that even though you cannot eliminate stealing entirely, you can take positive steps to keep it to a minimum. The key lies in the proper mix of the right controls.

Thieving Personnel

The best profit-safeguard you can provide in a store is the employee whose integrity is beyond question. The trouble is too many retailers take integrity for granted. "Innocent until proven guilty" is a meaningful and deep-rooted American principle. But it doesn't preclude the need to install effective theft deterrents and to take measures to track down dishonesty.

Case after case points up this need. All too often, the biggest crook turns out to be the most trusted employee, the hard worker who has been with the company "umpteen" years, the one about whom you are most likely to exclaim, "Not Charley! Anyone but Charley!"

The problem is that Charley, with his long experience, knows store procedures backwards. Because he is so knowledgeable and well trusted, he is in a better position to steal than anyone else. And all it takes to get him started is one weak moment, one time of need, one dishonest friend, or one temptation that is too hard to resist. And once he's started—it's like being on dope.

An example is a trusted store manager, who was on the payroll for years and had often been a guest in the owner's home. Undercover investigation to determine the reason for inventory shortages revealed the following: The store manager had altered reports to indicate that the store received more goods than was actually delivered. He was in collusion with a vendor who split the extra payments with him. Also he stole merchandise and carried it away from the store in his automobile on Sundays.

Steps to Take

One fact is obvious. The store with the greatest proportion of honest employees suffers the least from theft loss. The trick is to take every precaution to ensure that the people you hire are honest to begin with. Then, take pains to maintain the kind of store climate that will encourage them to stay honest.

Improving the Level of Personnel

Upgrading the level of retail personnel is largely a matter of careful personnel screening and selection, including careful reference checks, credit checks, psychological tests, and personal character examinations. Doing these things and sticking to the basic tenets of employee motivation can help you to generate a store atmosphere which discourages employee theft.

Screening Applicants

Just like a book, a job applicant can't be judged by his outward appearance alone. Don't let the "front" he puts on dull your caution. His appearance, experience, and personality may all be striking points in his favor. And he may still be a thief. Or he may be an alcoholic drug addict, or other high security risk. Remember that the man you easily pick may just be looking for easy pickings.

One hiring mistake could prove to be a devastating profit drain for months or years to come. No matter how urgently you may need additional personnel, it does not pay to loosen your screening and hiring procedures. When you compromise your standards of character and integrity, you also compromise your profit position.

Don't take chances. Run a conscientious reference check on *every* new employee. No security measure is more important than this.

Lack of knowledge about the store's routine usually restricts a new employee's stealing to what he can slip from the cash register or conceal on his person. You can detect either by close watch of daily receipts and a personal scrutiny of the new employee until you are satisfied that you can trust him.

Set the Tone

Checking out new employees is only the beginning of upgrading your personnel. Another important step is setting a tone or atmosphere which will encourage honesty in your store.

In doing it, *shoot for excellence of conduct and performance.* Because people respect high standards, you should not settle for less. They also tend to copy the individuals who set such standards and require that they be met.

It is important to adopt a *"Zero Shortage"* attitude. If you feel that a "reasonable writeoff" due to pilferage is all right, keep it a secret and hammer away at shortage control, even when losses diminish.

The owner-manager should also *avoid setting a double standard of moral and ethical conduct.* If an employee sees a supervisor in even a minor dishonest act, he is encouraged in the same direction. Return overshipments, or overpayments, promptly. When you set rules, have them apply to *everyone.* The owner-manager cannot expect his people to set standards that are any higher than those he sets for himself.

Preserving the dignity of employees is essential if you expect your people to respect you and the store. Employees should be treated with courtesy and consideration. Show an interest in them as individuals. Then back that interest—to mention an example or two—by keeping restrooms and other areas clean and attractive and by providing fresh uniforms, if your business uses them. Respecting employees may not reform the hard-core thief. But it will help keep many others from straying.

Finally, the owner-manager should not *expect his people to achieve the impossible*. Giving an employee an unrealistic goal is an invitation to cheat. When you do, you give no alternative. It is either cheat or admit failure and losing his job.

Provide the Incentives

A third step in upgrading personnel is to enable employees to live up to your expectations. The following practices can be helpful.

Make certain each person is matched to his job. An employee should not be put in a position where he is forced to lie or cheat about his performance because he is unable to do his work. Lying and cheating, even on a small scale, is just a step away from theft.

Set reasonable rules, and enforce them rigidly. Loosely administered rules are more harmful than no rules at all. The quickest way to undermine employee respect for you and for the store's assets is to show softness and permissiveness.

Set clear lines of authority and responsibility. Each employee needs a yardstick by which to measure his progress and improve his performance. To fulfill this basic, human need, his duties should be spelled out—preferably in writing. When he does not know who does what, there will be error, waste, and the kind of indifferent performance that breeds dishonesty.

Employees should be given the resources they need to achieve success. Whether he is a buyer, a salesperson, or a stock boy, nothing is more frustrating to any employee than to see his goal blocked by circumstances beyond his control. To perform well, an employee needs the proper tools, the right information, and guidance when it is required. Denying such support and expecting him to produce is a sure way to weaken morale.

Be fair in rewarding outstanding performance. The top producing salesperson who receives the same treatment as the mediocre employee is apt to become resentful. Individuals who make a worthwhile profit contribution are entitled to, and expect, a fair share of ego and financial satisfaction. Honest recognition of merit by the owner-manager triggers more honest effort on the part of the employee.

Finally, you should remove the temptation to steal. One organization of counter service restaurants is noted for its good employee relations. It treats people fairly. It displays faith in their integrity and ability. But it also provides uniforms *without pockets*.

Remove the opportunity to steal and half the battle is won. There is no substitute for rigid, well-implemented preventive measures and controls.

In addition, the owner-manager should use a continuing program of investigation and training. He should train employees on ways to eliminate stock shortage and shrinkage. One small retailer, for example, trains his employees to record items, such as floor cleaner, which they take out of stock for use in the store. "Otherwise, it's an inventory loss," he says, "even though it's a legitimate store expense." Above all, never stop letting your people know that you are always aware and that you always care.

Retail Theft Hazards

In preventing theft, you should be aware of certain hazards. Some of them, along with anti-theft pointers, are discussed in this section.

Pricing

Loosely controlled pricing procedures constitute a major cause of inventory "shrinkage."

Case in Point: Items in a thrift store were ticketed in pencil. Moreover, some tickets were unmarked. Since the store was inadequately staffed, many customers marked down prices, switched tickets, or wrote in their own prices.

Anti-theft Pointers. Price items by machine or rubber stamp, not by handwriting.

Permit only authorized employees to set prices and mark merchandise.

Make *unannounced* spot checks to be sure that actual prices agree with authorized prices and price-charge records.

Refunds

Refunds provide the dishonest employee an easy means to ply his trade. There are more ways to lose money on returns or refunds than the average retailer dreams possible.

Case in Point. In one store, many returned items were marked down to a fraction of cost because of damage. It was easy for clerks to get authorization to buy "as is" merchandise. When they were armed with an okay, they substituted first-grade items for "as is" stock.

Anti-theft Pointers. Insist on a merchandise inspection by someone other than the person who made the sale.

Match items to the return vouchers and then return the merchandise back into stock as quickly as possible.

Keep a tight control on all credit documents. Spot check customers by mail or telephone to make sure they got their refunds.

Popular Salespeople

The popular salesperson is a great asset—*providing* he is popular for the right reasons. However, many salespeople win "fans" because of the deals they swing and the favors they grant.

Case in Point. Customers stood in line to wait for one veteran saleswoman. They refused to be served by anyone else. And no wonder! She switched tickets for many "special" customers, giving them substantial markdowns. Store losses amounted to about $300 a week—not including $25 a week in increased commissions for the crook.

Anti-theft Pointers. The popular salesperson may be your biggest asset. But don't take it for granted. Find out for yourself *why* he is so well liked.

Pay special attention to the salesperson who is visited by too many personal friends. To discourage such socializing, some retailers hire people who live outside the immediate store vicinity.

Cash Handling

The cashier's post is particularly vulnerable to theft. The experienced cash handler with larceny on her mind can rob a store blind in a hundred-and-one ways.

Case in Point. A store owner's sales were high, but his profits were dragging. The cause was traced to a cashier who rang up only some of the items bought by his "customers." In most cases, he didn't ring "put-downs" at all. (A "put-down" is the right amount of cash which a customer leaves on the counter when he rushes out without waiting for his tape.)

Anti-theft Pointers. Keep a sharp eye open for signals—nods, winks, and so on—between cashiers and customers.

Pay special attention to cashiers when they are surrounded by clusters of people.

Be alert to the use of over-ring slips to cover up shortages.

Watch for items bypassed when ringing up sales.

Check personal checks to make sure they are not being used to cover up shortages.

Use a professional shopper to check for violations of cash register and related procedures.

Backdoor Thefts

Large scale theft is carried on more often through the back than the front door. Hundreds, even thousands, of dollars worth of merchandise can be stolen within a few seconds.

Case in Point. A stockboy parked his car at the receiving dock. He kept his trunk closed but unlocked. At 12:30 P.M. when the shipping-receiving manager was at lunch, the stockboy threw full cartons of shoes into his trunk and then slammed it locked. Elapsed time: 18 seconds.

Anti-theft Pointers. Have a secondary check by a worker or salesperson on all incoming shipments.

Insist on flattening all trash cartons and make spot checks of trash after hours.

Prohibit employees from parking near receiving door or dock.

Keep receiving door *locked* when not in use. Make sure locked door cannot be raised a few inches. A receiving door should be opened only by a supervisor who remains in area until it is relocked.

Alarm on door should ring until turned off with key held by store manager.

Distribute door keys carefully and change lock cylinders periodically.

Shoplifting

Shoplifting is greatest in the self-service store located in a low-income metropolitan fringe area. But regardless of location, no retailer can afford to leave himself unprotected against shoplifters. The following actions can help to cut down on shoplifting losses:

Keep tight checks and controls on washrooms and fitting rooms.

Keep unused checkout aisles closed.

Schedule working hours to assure adequate personnel coverage during peak periods.

Keep doors that are used infrequently locked.

Post anti-shoplifting signs.

Display small inexpensive items behind the checkout counter.

Keep small expensive items in locked display cabinets.

Use plainclothes patrols in larger stores.

Make sure employees know what to do when they spot a shoplifter.

Turn over apprehended shoplifters to the police.

Investigation and Detection

Most people are basically honest. Remove the temptation to steal, and there is every chance that they will remain honest. But unfortunately, the retailer must also protect himself against the minority who are basically dishonest—the hard-core thieves.

The only way to stop an employee who is a chronic thief is to uncover his method of operation and put an end to both it and his employment before your loss is great. Undercover investigation is the most effective way to do it because the chronic thief is adept at working around anti-theft procedures such as package examinations at employee exits.

Such investigation can be done by: (a) developing your own informants or (b) hiring professional investigators.

Although home-grown informants might appear to be less expensive, working with a qualified, reputable investigative firm has advantages. For one thing, the well-trained professional does the job in an objective, impersonal way. He knows what to look for, where to look, and what steps to take to trip up the hard-core thief.

The investigator's function is clear-cut—to investigate and to uncover employee and customer theft as quickly as he can. He reports his findings to the owner-manager with documented evidence.

You can also get advice, assistance, and information from a merchants' protective association, a retail credit bureau, a better business bureau, the police department, and the district attorney's office.

APPENDIX B-6
CONTROL OF EXPENDABLE TOOLS*
Jack Hawley†

The Value of Control

The value of the tangible benefits which will accrue to the small manufacturer through a system of expendable tool control cannot be overestimated.

First of all, it is possible to reduce materially expendable tool inventories, by culling out those tools which show no usage over an extended period and by reducing the stock of tools which show only a slight usage. Frequently inventories can be reduced by as much as 50 percent. More important, this reduction can be maintained by the use of statistics which will prevent the repurchase of such tools through habit. Losses of tools issued to production workers, and arguments over reasons for such losses and who was responsible, are practically eliminated. Breakage or damage to tools can be reduced by as much as half, and the time required for issuing and reclaiming of tools is also considerably reduced. The availability of usable tools is increased without additional purchases through more systematic and improved tool maintenance procedures. Finally, the fact that a perpetual inventory is being maintained, makes taking the annual inventory a much quicker and easier job.

---

*Reprinted with permission from Small Business Administration. Technical Aids for Small Manufacturers, No. 49, Washington, D.C., 1957.
†President, Management Control Systems, Incorporated, Washington, D.C.

Control and proper care of expendable tools can bring substantial reductions in production costs.

Interestingly enough, it has only been in recent years that this important function has begun to receive proper recognition by manufacturers, large and small alike. The enormous productive demands of World War II provided the greatest single impetus to this recognition by spotlighting the improper care and losses of small tools and the consequent serious drain on production. Even in view of this practical lesson, however, many firms were reluctant to consider the control of expendable tools as anything more than a necessary evil, a "grudged" cost factor in production whose primary purpose was to guard against pilferage and inventory losses other than the usual wear through usage.

More recently, though, an ever-increasing number of manufacturers are installing plans for expendable tool control, not only to guard against "lost-strayed-stolen" tools, but also to provide an important factor in production planning and accounting. These companies have found that expendable tool control systems will protect them against nonconsuming inventory shrinkage and offer additional advantages. The extent of these advantages is shown by the major points of expendable tool control.

What Is an Expendable Tool?

In general an expendable tool may be defined as a consumable, semiconsumable, or nonconsumable production requisite which is charged off, either as a cost on a specific job or as an overhead manufacturing expense. This is the kind of tool being considered as opposed to a depreciable capital asset item.

Consumable tools represent the bulk of this class and, in addition, the bulk of repetitive procurement. These are such items as drills, cutters, reamers, broaches, taps, dies, and so on, which require frequent sharpening and dressing. Semiconsumable tools constitute the bulk of the remaining items in the class, such as wrenches, hammers, pliers, and the like, which are subject to breakage or eventual deterioration and obsolescence. Nonconsumable tools can generally be repaired through replacement of parts and correct maintenance. Although they will usually represent a much higher dollar value, these gauges, measuring devices, hand power tools, and others, represent the smallest portion to the class.

Control Is a Must

It is no secret to the average small manufacturer that his expendable tools represent a substantial item of expense. As a matter of fact, this cost will frequently equal, if not exceed, the investment in closely-controlled major equipment when the two costs are considered over the life of the major equipment. This single fact alone is sufficient reason for giving special attention to close control of expendable tools when planning for production.

Inventory shrinkage due to loss and pilferage will certainly be minimized by adoption of a comprehensive program for the control of expendable tools, but this saving is only a small part of the potential reward. A much greater saving will be found in terms of the tools themselves. Correct maintenance control and proper preservation procedures will do much to guarantee a longer tool life, avoiding early breakage, deterioration, and obsolescence.

But the biggest advantage of all in the well-planned and correctly operated expendable tool control system is its effect on the production process. Improperly maintained tools can cause delays in production. Not only can time be lost, but valuable, partially completed products can be spoiled as well. Expendable tools, as a production cost factor, are either difficult or impossible to assess if there is no systematic plan to provide such information. All of these undesirable features can be translated directly into lost dollars in the absence of an effective plan for expendable tool control.

By the same token, the existence of such a control system can turn this loss into a saving. It must, however, incorporate certain fundamental features if it is to provide such a benefit.

Basic Points of Expendable Tool Control

In order to obtain the minimum advantages for the small manufacturer, the control of expendable tools requires a place, a person, and a plan. The place will be, of course, the tool room or tool crib. The person will be the crib tool attendant. And the plan will provide for the issue and receipt of expendable tools, their care, and maintenance, inventory records, and accountability.

Location of the Toolroom

The toolroom or crib must be considered as a production unit inasmuch as it supplies an essential service in the production cycle. As such, its location should be planned carefully rather than decided on a haphazard basis.

The room should be located in a position which will facilitate the easy withdrawal and return of tools by production workers. Another factor affecting the location is the type of manufacturing operation; tool-crib location will vary in job shops as opposed to strictly production shops. But regardless of these considerations, it is not (generally) economically sound to permit each department to run its own tool service and control operation, although there may be a few minor advantages in such a system. There should be a single point for service and control.

An undesirable building arrangement might well be responsible for operations conducted on more than a single floor or in adjacent buildings. The operation may be a job or short-run production shop which calls for frequent use of tools for short periods. Whatever the reason, the temptation to set up separate points for the control of expendable tools should be resisted. If necessary, one or more sub-cribs may be set up but they should all be controlled and serviced by the main tool crib.

The mere existence of a centralized service and control location will automatically avoid many of the costly abuses which lead to the loss of tools. For example, small tools which are left on machines, benches, or in improvised tool racks on the production floor may frequently fall to the floor, become mixed with chips, turnings, and other debris, and be swept up and consigned to the scrap heap. These same tools, when they are exposed to dirt, dust, oil, humidity, acid fumes and many other corroding elements, can easily become unsatisfactory and even harmful to production operations.

When tools remain in the possession of production employees, even though they may be stored in boxes, cans, or drawers, they are still subject to severe damage to cutting edges, alignment, measuring points, gauging, and overall accuracy. Regardless of the efficiency of the capital equipment employed, an attempt to use such tools in production is likely to increase operating costs through damaging a partially completed product or causing its rejection in quality inspection.

Once the location of the tool crib has been selected, the next point for consideration will be its internal arrangement and the facilities for handling and storing the tools.

Expendable Tool Storage

The tool crib should be kept immaculately clean and frequently painted. This will add indirectly to tool life, since it will have an important psychological effect on workers who use the tools. A poorly run or sloppy tool crib will always be a constant source of expense and annoyance. It is not difficult to avoid this unfortunate situation if certain basic principles and practices are given proper attention.

First of all, tool storage racks, regardless of their weight, should be provided with casters. This is an important point in good housekeeping but there is an addition advantage in rapid tool issue in cases where the demand for a type of tool is subject to change—a change which might be temporary or even semi-permanent. In view of this requirement, steel shelving on casters will provide the best storage of expendable tools.

The method of storing the individual tools within the tool storage racks is most important because it has a direct bearing on the effectiveness of the effort to protect and preserve the tools.

Shanked tools, for the most part, are best protected when they are arranged upright in baseboards, which serve to separate them individually. If they are to be stored in trays or on shelves, separate niches should be provided. Niches should be lined with some "soft" material, much as wood or cork, in order to further protect the tool.

The cutting edges of such tools as drills, reamers, broaches, and the like, should be protected from contact with each other to prevent dulling. The same thing is true of all hard surfaces where contact with such a surface can also damage the cutting edges of these tools.

Milling cutters, grinding wheels, and other similar tools, which have a central bore are best stored on horizontal or vertical pegs. The pegs should have an outside diameter which is just slightly less than the shaft bore of the tools.

One of the simplest methods for the storage of sensitive instruments, such as gauges, micrometers, and the like, is to keep them in the original boxes in which they were packed. The same type of protection can be provided through an arrangement of special trays, containing recesses cut to fit the outline of the instrument.

In addition to the specific methods of storage for expendable tools with sensitive features, there are several general practices which can add to the effectiveness of the tool crib's internal arrangement.

Less sensitive tools may be grouped in trays or on shelves according to type, kind, or size. Tools which are applicable to a single tool equipment or a group of such equipments should be arranged separately from general purpose tools. The bins or storage racks of the tools which are most in demand, and therefore most frequently used, should be placed in the most practical position adjacent to the issue point.

The Tool Crib Attendant

In the past, too many manufacturers have left the control and maintenance of expendable tools up to the men who actually use them, the production workers themselves. This is a particularly great temptation for the smaller manufacturer with his very real concern over costs. Because his labor force is usually not large and he knows most, if not all, of his men, he is apt to feel that the establishment of a system for the control of expendable tools is unnecessary and a waste of money. This approach can offer only one advantage—simplicity. But as time goes by it will become more and more expensive, because it is a makeshift method in which the production worker is expected to do a good job with something in which he has little interest and for which he may lack the necessary qualifications and equipment. When assigned to a production worker, care and maintenance of tools will always be delayed until the last possible moment or not be done at all. As a result the proper tool may not be available, or may be dull or improperly sharpened. The obvious result is inventory shrinkage and wasted production time.

In order to achieve the maximum benefits from a system of control of expendable tools, it is necessary to assign responsibility for the function to a single, well-qualified individual. In smaller shops, it might not be necessary for the tool attendant to have an assistant. Further, he might have other duties as well as his responsibility for the tool crib. Whatever the case, this important function must be assigned to an individual who is fully experienced in the methods and procedures for the control and maintenance of small tools.

Thus the ideal tool-crib attendant should be a toolmaker or tool maintenance man who is thoroughly familiar with all types and kinds of tools, their use and application, and the approved techniques for their maintenance. In many cases, he will be able to offer assistance in the selection of the proper tool to do a particular job by virtue of his experience.

The well-qualified tool attendant will also be able to lend advice and counsel on procurement problems which involve expendable tools. He will understand the tools with which he works and will thus be in a position to take the best possible care of them, not only in terms of regular maintenance but from the standpoint of repairs as well. Such an individual will fill the second requirement of the place-person-plan triangle.

Since many of the tool attendant's duties involve maintenance, the subject of expendable tool maintenance will provide a good lead into the third and last requirement—a plan for the control of expendable tools. This subject will be covered in a later Technical Aid.

APPENDIX B-7
CONTROL OF EXPENDABLE TOOLS—II*

JACK HAWLEY†

Adequate control of expendable tools, as outlined in "Control of Expendable Tools—I", includes a person, a place, and a plan. The first two of these have been covered in Technical Aid No. 49. This Aid will enumerate the factors essential to a successful plan.

Maintenance and Preservation of Expendable Tools

In order to provide for sound application of an effective system of maintenance, the tool crib attendant or attendants must have the necessary

*Reprinted with permision from Small Business Administration. Technical Aids for Small Manufacturers, No. 51, Washington, D.C., 1957.
†President, Management Control Systems, Inc., Washington, D.C.

equipment to carry out routine maintenance tasks as well as to make certain minor repairs.

The available equipment for tool maintenance should permit the performance of a variety of simple operations, such as sharpening cutting tools, refacing grinding wheels, and so on. In addition, it should be possible, for the tool attendant to make simple repairs to dies and small power hand tools, and to perform the host of similar maintenance and repair operations which do not require heavy or special equipment.

The tool maintenance equipment which is installed in the tool crib should also be equipped with the jigs and fixtures which make possible automatic positioning of tools for accurate maintenance work. Holders should be provided for the positioning of cutting tools so that the required angles and clearances will be obtained automatically.

It is obvious that such jigs and fixtures will make for faster and more efficient performance of tool maintenance operations. However, it is also important to note that their use will have a direct and substantial bearing on tool life. It has been demonstrated conclusively that careful maintenance of tools under the controlled conditions provided by these jigs and fixtures can increase tool life by as much as 100 percent over hand maintenance methods. This is particularly true in the case of cutting tools.

Cleanliness of the tool crib was previously mentioned as a major consideration in the maintenance and preservation of tools. The importance of this requirement makes it desirable to maintain a small hand vacuum cleaner for use in the tool crib. The cleaner is excellent for removing dust and dirt from tool locations where other types of cleaning are impractical.

Inevitably, there will be repair jobs which are beyond the capabilities of the tool-crib attendant or which exceed the limitations of the maintenance and repair equipment available to him. When such a repair is required, identifying data about the tool and the repair to be made should be carefully recorded as an important item of tool-crib inventory data. In the case of most smaller manufacturers, inability of the tool-crib attendant to make the repair will mean that the repair cannot be made within the plant. Where this is true, the broken or damaged tool will, of course, be sent to a qualified toolmaker for repair.

Expendable Tool Charge-out

It is necessary to establish methods and procedures for issuing tools, a tool charge-out system, and the tool-crib records which these functions involve.

Tool loan or charge-out is the initial step in the cycle through which the tool crib serves the production effort. As such, it is the logical starting point for an examination of the methods of accounting for expendable tools. Such control, which can be found in any well-planned system for the maintenance and preservation of expendable tools, will start with an adequate and accurate method of charge-out. There are, generally speaking, two such methods in use today.

The Check System

This system, which was practically in universal use just a few years ago, features the use of a brass or plastic check or tag as the medium of exchange between the production worker and the tool crib.

This check carries the individual employee's identification stamped upon it, usually his clock or employee number. When the employee withdraws a tool, he surrenders his check for it and the check is placed in the position from which the tool was removed. When the tool is returned, the employee receives his check back from the tool-crib attendant. Sometimes, rather than identifying the employee, the check carries a number which identifies the production job on which the tool is to be used. In either case, the system provides information as to the current location of the tool but provides little else.

For example, the system offers nothing in the way of an accounting medium; the maintenance of some additional type of record is necessary if an accounting is to be made of the use of the tools. In spite of this disadvantage, however, the system is still in use in many shops.

The Charge-out Slip System

On the other hand, those organizations which studied the potential economies resulting from a well-planned expendable tool accounting system, have adopted a method which goes far beyond that of merely assuring return of the tool to the tool crib. The results have been so rewarding that the systems, even when started with "tongue-in-cheek" acceptance, have gained ever-increasing interest and support from management. These systems are based upon the use of charge-out slips in place of the brass or plastic checks.

Charge-out slips for the withdrawal of expendable tools from the tool crib are usually multiple-copy forms. The complete form consists of an original and one copy since this is normally sufficient to satisfy all phases of control. Refinements in statistical analysis of tool usage or a requirement for additional information copies can add one or more copies to the pack. For pure control purposes, however, an original and one copy should be enough. Where a greater number of copies is required, the reverse side of all but the last copy of the form carries spot carbon, automatically transferring to the other copies those entries made on the original.

The charge-out slip should be so designed as to guarantee that it will meet all requirements of the individual shop. As a minimum, however, it should always include:

1. The employee's identification, usually by means of a number;
2. The tool's identification, also by means of a number, as an essential to speedy statistical sorting. The number should be based upon a classification system which will provide positive identification of the class, size, and other limitations of the tool;
3. Date upon which the tool is issued;
4. Quantity in which the tool is issued;
5. Alphabetical name of tool, its size and other limitations;
6. Signature of the workman withdrawing the tool.

In the case of production shops which require preparation of production operations sheets for each production unit in advance of the scheduled starting date of the job, the charge-out slips are normally prepared at the same time the operation instructions are written. These slips are forwarded to the tool crib, where the tools are picked and segregated in advance for delivery to the workmen on the date that production is scheduled to begin. The signatures of the individual workmen are obtained at the time the tools are delivered. Once these tools have been issued to the workmen, they are retained by them until completion of the production cycle. Of course, if a tool is damaged or needs sharpening or repair, it is returned to the tool crib for the necessary work and replaced by another tool of the same type and size.

In shops doing job work, experimental manufacture, or short-run production operations, tools are withdrawn frequently and are retained for relatively short periods. The workers withdraw the tools as needed, preparing a charge-out slip for each tool required. The charge-out slips should be available in a handy receptacle at or near the tool-crib issue window and a shelf-type writing surface should be provided for the convenience of the workman who will be listing his tool requirements there. Upon presentation of the charge-out slip to the tool-crib attendant, the tool is located and issued to the workman.

The tool-crib attendant separates the original of the charge-out slip from its duplicate copy and files it by the employee's identification number. The duplicate copy may be placed on a hook or in a clamp at the location from which the tool was removed. If a bin storage system is being used, the copy may be placed with the record showing the tool's location in the bin, if the physical size of this record is sufficient to allow it. In either case, the duplicate copy is, at this point, performing the same function as the brass or plastic check. It is serving as a notice that the tool has been issued and, further it identifies the individual to whom it was issued.

The fact that the charge-out slip is dated at the time of issue tends to prevent a worker's retaining a new or favored tool after the immediate need for it has been satisfied—a practice which not only deprives other workers of the use of the tool, but also requires maintenance of an excessive inventory to satisfy workers' needs.

When the workman returns a tool, the original of the charge-out slip is removed from the employee file, the date of return indicated and initialed by the workman, and the slip then placed with the returned tool pending inspection of the tool. If this inspection shows that the tool is in satisfactory condition and can be reissued, it is returned to the bin from which it was drawn. The duplicate copy of the charge-out slip is then destroyed, unless some other record will be served by its retention. The original of the charge-out slip is placed in a file by tool number. Thus all slips relating to the same tools are kept together for purposes of future statistical accounting.

In some plants a slight variation of the foregoing, as outlined in the following paragraph, will be more suitable.

When the workman returns the tool, the original of the charge-out slip is returned to him and the duplicate is placed with the returned tool pending an inspection of the tool prior to its return to the bin from which it was drawn. If this inspection shows that the tool is in satisfactory condition and can be reissued, it is returned to its bin and the duplicate of the charge-out slip is placed in a file by tool number, thus putting it with other slips carrying the same tool number for purposes of future statistical accounting.

The simple procedure outlined above will cover the majority of transactions. However, in those cases in which the tool was broken or damaged during its period of use, there is a variation in the procedure.

Broken or Damaged Tools

If a tool is broken or damaged while in the possession of a workman, he should be held responsible for reporting that fact to the tool-crib attendant at the time he returns the tool. For this purpose a damaged tool report should be used which is similar in design to the charge-out slip.

In addition to identifying the workman and department returning the tool as well as showing the tool identification number and description, this form should provide space for an explanation of the damage and reason for it. Further, space should be available for a notation as to the disposition of the tool, such as scrap, salvage, or repair.

The foreman of the department in which the tool was used and damaged should be responsible for determining the cause of damage—whether it was due to carelessness or neglect on the part of the workman or else was unavoidable due to the nature of the operation or the design of the tool. The workman should place his signature on the damaged tool report before returning the tool to the tool crib. When the tool and damaged tool report are received, they should be put to one side until time permits a complete inspection of the tool to determine what disposition should be made of it.

Occasionally a broken or damaged tool will be turned in without a damaged tool report. However, the regular inspection of a returned tool prior to its replacement in the storage bin should reveal that the tool has been damaged and the tool-crib attendant should then fill out a damaged tool report. After recording as much of the required information as may be available to him, he can send the damaged tool report back to the foreman of the department in question for verification and, in addition, an explanation of the cause of the damage.

As in the case of the charge-out slip, the duplicate copy of the damaged tool report is primarily for use as a control copy. Once the facts of the damage have been collected and the cost of any repairs posted to the original of the damaged tool report, the copy may be destroyed, unless its retention will serve some other record-keeping purpose. Just as the original or duplicate of the charge-out slip was filed by tool identification number for future statistical accounting purposes, the original of the damaged tool report is also filed by the same number for the same future use.

Expendable Tool Accounting

The charge-out slips and the damaged tool reports should be analyzed on a periodic basis. The interval between analyses should be based upon usage of the tools. It is the total number of pieces of paper which will determine the size of the job of analysis.

This analysis will provide a picture of the usage of each tool for the period covered and, when compared with usage data for preceding periods, will also indicate whether the usage is increasing or decreasing. Damaged tool reports will provide information for the adjustment of inventory as well as data on repair costs, losses, and value of scrap accumulated, due to damaged tools. In addition to this statistical information, which is useful for the expendable tool record-keeping function, the data on causes of tool damage can point the way to corrective measures and thus serve to reduce the amount of future damage.

This is all very valuable and worthwhile information, but it must be collected at some central point if its maximum potential is to be realized. That point is the perpetual inventory record of expendable tools.

Perpetual Inventory for Expendable Tools

The perpetual inventory record for expendable tools should be maintained by means of one of the many excellent commercial systems available to the small manufacturer. No attempt will be made here to describe such a record in detail. However, certain basic features of any well-conceived plan of inventory control for expendable tools should be pointed out.

First of all, the record should contain a card for each class of tool and for each type, kind, or size of tool within that class. In addition to the description of the tool which is used as the "title" of the card, the card should include information as to the aisle, shelf, and bin number where the tool is stored, sources of supply, cost, usage rate (turnover), and so on. The record is established through a physical inventory count. Thereafter it should show increases through purchase, salvage of similar tools to meet the specifications of the tool in question, and additions from any other sources. By the same token it should show decreases through loss, breakage, scrap, or any other withdrawal process. Since the inventory control record is maintained in the tool crib, it is a ready source of reference as to the location of tools as well as a possible physical location for the filing of original charge-out slips and damaged tool reports.

When such an inventory control record is maintained on an up-to-date and accurate basis, effective control of expendable tools is brought within easy reach.

APPENDIX B-8
OUTWITTING BAD CHECK-PASSERS*

LEONARD KOLODNY†

Summary

Time was when a man's word was as good as his bond. But nowadays, even the signatures of many persons are worthless—especially to retailers who are stuck with bad checks.

This *Aid* offers suggestions that should be helpful in keeping bad checks out of the cash registers of small stores. For example, the key items on a check should be examined closely because they can tip off the owner-manager to a worthless check. His procedures should also include a dollar limit on the size of checks he will accept and the type of identification necessary to back up the signature or endorsement. In addition, it is profitable to review with employees the checks which the bank refuses to honor.

A neatly dressed stranger pays for his groceries with a payroll check issued by a company in a nearby city. In the next few hours, he does the same thing in several other food stores.

*Reprinted with permission from Small Business Administration S.M.A. No. 137, Washington, D.C., 1971.

†Manager of the Retail Bureau of the Metropolitan Washington Board of Trade, Washington, D.C.

In another community, a middle-aged man pays for a pair of shoes with a Government check. He moves to other stores and cashes several more Government checks.

In a third city, a well-dressed woman pays for an expensive dress with a blank check. "I need a little pocket cash," she says. "May I make the check for $20 more?" The salesclerk agrees, never suspecting that the customer does not have an account in any bank.

Tomorrow, these three con artists will work in other communities.

The specialist in payroll checks will fill out blank ones which he has stolen. The passer of Government checks is also a thief. He steals Social Security checks, tax refund checks, and so on from individual mail boxes. "Blank Check" Bessie will hit her victim after the banks have closed.

These three, and others who pass worthless checks, are clever. They live by their wits and are often glib talkers. But they are not so clever that you can't outwit them.

Types of Checks

Winning the battle of wits against worthless check-passers is largely a matter of knowledge and vigilance. You have to know what you're up against, pass the information on to your employees, and be constantly on guard when accepting checks.

You are apt to get seven different kinds of checks: personal, two-party, payroll, Government, blank, counter, and traveler. And some customers may offer money orders.

A *personal check* is written and signed by the individual offering it. He makes it out to you or your firm.

A *two-party* check is issued by one person to a second person who endorses it so that it may be cashed by a third person. This type of check is most susceptible to fraud because, for one thing, the maker can stop payment at the bank.

A *payroll check* is issued to an employee for services performed. Usually the name of the employer is printed on it, and it has a number and is signed. In most instances, "payroll" is also printed on the check. The employee's name is printed by a check writing machine or typed. In metropolitan areas, you should not cash a payroll check that is handprinted, rubber stamped or typewritten as a payroll check, even if it appears to be issued by a local business and drawn on a local bank. It may be a different story in a small community where you know the company officials and the employee personally.

A *government check* can be issued by the Federal Government, a State, a county, or a local government. Such checks cover salaries, tax refunds, pensions, welfare allotments, and veterans benefits, to mention a few examples.

You should be particularly cautious with government checks. Often they are stolen, and the endorsement has been forged.

In some areas, such thievery is so great that some banks refuse to cash Social Security, welfare, relief, or income tax checks, unless they know the customer or he has an account with the bank. You should follow this procedure also. In short, know your endorser.

A *blank check* is a form not issued by a bank and not carrying its name. It may be bought at variety and stationery stores. In the proper spaces, the maker writes the name, address, account number, and branch designation of his bank. The risk in cashing such checks is great. Also some banks do not honor them.

A *counter check* is one which a bank issues to depositors when they are withdrawing funds from their accounts. It is not good anywhere else. Sometimes, a store has its own counter checks for the convenience of its customers. A counter check is *not* negotiable and is so marked.

You should check local bank practices on blank checks and counter checks because of the coded magnetic tape imprints which many banks use for computer processing. Personal printed checks often have the individual's bank account number in magnetic code.

A *traveler's check* is a check sold with a preprinted amount (usually in round figures) to travelers who do not want to carry large amounts of cash. The traveler signs the checks at the time of purchase. He should countersign them only in the presence of the person who cashes them.

In addition, a *money order* can be passed as a check. However, a money order is usually bought to send in the mail. Most stores should not accept money orders in face-to-face transactions.

Some small stores sell money orders. If yours does, never accept a personal check in payment for money orders. If the purchaser has a valid checking account, he does not need a money order. He can send a check in the mail.

Look for Key Items

A check carries several key items such as name and location of bank, date, amount (in figures and spelled out), and signature. Close examination of such key items can sometimes tip you off to a worthless check. Before accepting a check, look for:

NONLOCAL BANKS. Use extra care in examining a check that is drawn on a nonlocal bank and require the best type of identification. List the customer's local and out-of-town address and phone number on the back of the check.

DATE. Examine the date for accuracy of day, month, and year. Do not accept the check if it's not dated, if it's post-dated, or if it's more than 30 days old.

LOCATION. Look first to be sure that the check shows the name, branch, town and State where the bank is located.

AMOUNT. Be sure that the numerical amount agrees with the written amount.

LEGIBILITY. Do not accept a check that is not written legibly. It should be written and signed in ink and must not have any erasures or written-over amounts.

PAYEE. When you take a personal check on your selling floor, have the customer make it payable to your firm. Special care should be used in taking a two-party personal check.

AMOUNT OF PURCHASE. Personal checks should be for the exact amount of the purchase. The customer should receive no change.

CHECKS OVER YOUR LIMIT. Set a limit on the amount—depending on the amount of your average sale—you will accept on a check. When a customer wants to go beyond that limit, your salesclerk should refer him to you.

Require Identification

Once you are satisfied that the check is okay, the question is, "Is the person holding the check the right person?" Requiring identification helps you to answer the question.

But keep in mind that no identification is foolproof. A crook is a crook no matter what type of identification you ask him to show. If he wants to forge identification, he can.

Some stores demand at least two pieces of identification. It is important to get enough identification so the person presenting the check can be identified and located if, and when, the check turns out to be worthless.

The following types of identification should be useful in determining the type to use in your store.

CURRENT AUTOMOBILE OPERATORS LICENSE. If licenses in your State do not carry a photograph of the customer, you may want to ask for a second identification.

AUTOMOBILE REGISTRATION CARD. Be sure the name of the State agrees with the location of the bank. If it doesn't, the customer must have a plausible reason. Also make sure that the signatures on the registration and check agree.

SHOPPING PLATES. If they bear a signature or laminated photograph, shopping plates and other credit cards can be used as identification. The retail merchants' organization in some communities issues lists of stolen shopping plates to which you should always refer when identifying the check-passer.

GOVERNMENT PASSES can also be used for identification in cashing checks. Picture passes should carry the name of the department and a serial number. Building passes should also carry a signature.

IDENTIFICATION CARDS, such as those issued by the armed services, police departments, and companies, should carry a photo, a description, and a signature. Police cards should also carry a badge number.

Several types of cards and documents are not good identification. Some of them (for example, club cards) are easily forged, and others (for example, customer's duplicate saleschecks) were never intended for identification. Unless they are presented with a current automobile operator's license, do not accept the following:

Social Security Cards	Letters
Business Cards	Birth Certificates
Club or Organization Cards	Library Cards
Bank Books	Initialed Jewelry
Work Permits	Unsigned Credit Cards
Insurance Cards	Voter's Registration Cards
Learner's Permits	Customer's Duplicate Cards

Some large stores photograph each person who cashes a check along with his identification. This procedure is a deterrent because bad check passers don't want to be photographed.

Compare Signatures

Regardless of the type identification you require, it is essential that you and your employees compare the signature on the check with the one on the identification.

You should also compare the person standing before you with the photograph and/or description on the identification.

"His writing did not compare with his character and age," the owner-manager of a store in the Midwest said. He was referring to a forger he helped catch. The forger was a tall, athletic-looking man, but his writing was like a woman's. It was small and precise. Moreover, he wrote very slowly and carefully.

Set a Policy

You should set a policy on cashing checks, write it down, and instruct your employees in its use. Your policy might require your approval before a salesclerk can cash a check. When all check-cashers are treated alike, customers have no cause to feel that they are being treated unfairly.

Your procedure might include the use of a rubber stamp. Many stores stamp the lower reverse side of a check and write in the appropriate information. Here is a sample of such a stamp.

Your policy might also include using a bad check list, if one is available. Such a list helps you to spot persons who are known, or suspected, as bad check-passers. Your better business bureau, local trade organization, or police may have such a list. In the Washington, D.C. area, for example, the Mutual Protective Association exchanges bad check information with its members. In other cities, local authorities may provide such current information on forgers, "hot check" rings, and so on who may be operating in those areas.

You should frequently review your policy and procedure on check cashing with your employees. Remind them about what to watch for in spotting bad checks.

Employee apathy toward accepting checks is a big reason why stores get stuck with bad checks. The bigger the store, the more difficult it is to keep employees interested in catching bad checks. One effective way is to show employees your bad checks.

Refusing a Check

You are not obligated to take anyone's check. Even when a stranger presents satisfactory identification, you do not have to take his check.

In most cases, you will accept a check when the customer has met your identification requirements. You want to make the sale. But never accept a check if the person presenting it appears to be intoxicated.

Never take a check if the customer acts suspiciously. For example, he may try to rush you or your employees while you are checking his identification. Or he may appear nervous and be over-attentive to the people about him.

Never take a check that has an old date.

Never take a check that is dated in advance.

What Can You Recover?

Whether you can recover a bad check depends on the person who gave it to you and his circumstances. He may be one of your best customers who inadvertantly gave you a check when the funds in his bank account were insufficient. On the other end of the scale, he may be a forger.

INSUFFICIENT FUNDS. Most checks returned because of insufficient funds clear the second time you deposit them. Notify the customer that he has overdrawn his account and that you are redepositing his check. But if the check is returned a second time, in some localities, it is the retailer's collection item. He must notify the maker and ask for immediate payment.

You should check the practices of your bank. In the Washington, D.C. area, for example, after a second return for insufficient funds, the bank will not let you re-deposit the check. It is your collection item. Some stores prosecute if the customer does not redeem such a check within a week of the second return. Stores with a reputation for being easy-going about insufficient funds checks usually receive plenty of them.

The procedure on prosecution depends on the State. In one jurisdiction, for example, a merchant must send the check writer a certified or registered letter and give him 5 days from date of receipt of that notice to comply before the merchant can prosecute. In another jurisdiction, the maker has 5 days after the date of notice to make the check good. In a third, a resident has 10 days to make good his check.

No Account. Usually you've lost when the bank returns a check marked "no account." Such a check is evidence of a swindle or a fraud unless there has been an extraordinary error. In *rare* instances, a customer may issue a check on the wrong bank or on a discontinued account. You should quickly determine what the circumstances are. If the person is known in the community, proceed with your collection efforts. If you find yourself "stuck" with the check, call your police department.

Closed Account. A check marked "closed account" is a warning of extreme carelessness or fraud. Accounts are closed by both individuals and by banks. The latter may close an account because of too many overdrafts. An individual may open a new account by removing funds from his old account. In such case, he may forget that he has issued a check that is still outstanding against the old account.

If you don't get your money back within a reasonable time, you should consider prosecuting the check writer.

Forgery. Forged checks are worthless.

Any alteration, illegal signature (s) of the maker of the check, a forgery of the endorsement, an erasure or an obliteration on a genuine check is a *crime*.

Watch out for smudged checks, misspelled words, poor spacing of letters or numbers indicating that changes may have been made. Payroll checks with the company's name and address typed in could be fraudulent. Most payroll checks are printed.

When you suspect forgery, call the police. Thus, you help protect yourself and others against further forgery.

You should refer a forged U.S. Government check to the field office of U.S. Secret Service.

A forged check transported in interstate commerce is a Federal offense.

You should check with your lawyer about local practices on collecting through the courts on a bad check which a customer used to pay on his account. In the Washington, D.C. area, for example, merchants cannot collect through the courts on such a bad check. The reason is: **The merchant still has the account and no injury was suffered through the issuance of the check. The account may be collectible through the usual civil procedures used for collection purposes.**

A bad check issued to pay for merchandise taken is not a theft but a misdemeanor. It is an exchange——the checks for goods. A misdemeanor carries a lighter penalty than a theft since a check may be collectible through civil procedures. Criminal action may be taken through signing a formal charge with the police.

GET EVIDENCE. You cannot prosecute bad check passers without good evidence. The person who cashed the bad check should be positively identified and connected with the receiving of money for it.

Teach Employees by Pointing Out Errors

One way to keep employees aware of what to look for is by showing them the bad checks which the bank returns. Hopefully, you don't have as many as one large city store that received 28 worthless checks in less than a week.

When they were analyzed, the following common mistakes were highlighted for employees:

On three, the written and the numerical **amounts** differed.

Two were not **endorsed** at all.

One was endorsed **improperly.**

Two were made out to a **different** store.

One had **no signature** where the maker should sign.

Two were **dated incorrectly.**

Ten were **counter** checks and were unacceptable.

Four had either **improper** or **no identification.**

Two had **no address.**

One was **post-dated.**

To avoid such mistakes, impress on your employees the necessity to read, compare, and think.

APPENDIX B-9
FORGERY AND CHECK ALTERATION-PREVENTION*

	Yes	No	*Does Not Apply*	*COMMENTS*
1. Does teller request adequate identification from members regarding withdrawals?	Y	N	N/A	

---

*Reprinted with permission from Loss Prevention Program Operational Security Analysis, *Forgery and Check Alteration-Prevention*. Developed by the Risk Management Department of CUNA International, Inc., Filene Houes, Madison, Wisconsin.

	Yes	No	Does Not Apply	COMMENTS
2. Credit union check drawn payable to the credit union's bank (for purpose of replenishing change fund)?	Y	N	N/A	
3. Are all checks, money orders, and traveler's checks stamped "FOR DEPOSIT ONLY" *immediately* upon receipt?	Y	N	N/A	
4. If a member (especially a new member) deposits a check (drawn on an out-of-town bank) in his share account, are tellers instructed to "flag" the account (not grant a share withdrawal request) until the check has cleared the bank?	Y	N	N/A	

Preparation of Credit Union Checks

	Yes	No	Does Not Apply	COMMENTS
5. Is there space between $ sign and first figure?	Y	N	N/A	
6. Is the "dollar line" written in longhand?	Y	N	N/A	
7. Is the payee line adequate?	Y	N	N/A	
8. Are "voided" checks cancelled properly?	Y	N	N/A	
9. Are words or payee names abbreviated on the payee line?	Y	N	N/A	
10. Are checks signed in the checkbook with a ballpoint pen?	Y	N	N/A	
11. Are all used and unused checks maintained under lock and key (especially during non-business hours)?	Y	N	N/A	
12. Are signatures placed on checks before checks have been filled in completely?	Y	N	N/A	
13. Is checkwriter safeguarded during non-business hours?	Y	N	N/A	
14. Is checkwriter locked (key removed) and signature plate removed (locked in safe or vault) during non-business hours?	Y	N	N/A	
15. Are all built-in control features used on the checkwriter?	Y	N	N/A	
16. Is the inking mechanism of the checkwriter too light?	Y	N	N/A	
17. Do authorized "check signers" sign letters, etc., the same way they sign credit union checks? ..	Y	N	N/A	
18. Are checks ever presigned?	Y	N	N/A	
19. Are all checks prenumbered in sequence by a printer?	Y	N	N/A	
20. Is the checkwriter used for ALL checks?	Y	N	N/A	
21. Does the credit union have a voucher check system?	Y	N	N/A	
22. Does an individual (who is not authorized to sign or disburse checks) receive bank statements (and cancelled checks) DIRECTLY from the bank and prepare reconciliations?	Y	N	N/A	
23. Are invoices and other supporting documents attached to checks before checks are signed?	Y	N	N/A	

APPENDIX B-10
CASH HANDLING PROCEDURES*

	Yes	No	Does Not Apply	COMMENTS
1. Cash received from bank and verified IMMEDIATELY by two or more employees acting jointly?	Y	N	N/A	
2. Central cash fund turned over BY RECEIPT to a single credit union employee?	Y	N	N/A	
3. Central cash fund locked in a compartment in safe under EXCLUSIVE control of individual responsible?	Y	N	N/A	
4. Currency distributed to tellers by RECEIPT?	Y	N	N/A	
5. Currency counted IMMEDIATELY by tellers in presence of individual in charge of central cash fund?	Y	N	N/A	
6. Only one individual has access to a specific fund or cash drawer?	Y	N	N/A	
7. Each teller has lockable cash drawers or cash trays?	Y	N	N/A	
8. Are they locked when they leave their stations?	Y	N	N/A	
9. Key to teller cash compartments (at counter and safe) under teller control at all times?	Y	N	N/A	
10. Spare keys under proper control?	Y	N	N/A	
11. Tellers balance daily?	Y	N	N/A	
12. Does teller receive receipt for cash turned in?	Y	N	N/A	
13. Periodic surprise cash counts conducted by supervisor?	Y	N	N/A	
14. Cash disbursements handled properly?	Y	N	N/A.	
15. Interchange of funds among tellers by receipt (other than change making)?	Y	N	N/A	
16. Teller over and short records maintained?	Y	N	N/A	
17. Teller change fund liquidated when teller takes vacation or leave of absence?	Y	N	N/A	

APPENDIX B-11
SECURITY OF RECORDS*

	Yes	No	Does Not Apply	COMMENTS
1. General ledger placed in fire-resistive container?	Y	N	N/A	
2. Ledger cards stored in fire-resistive container?	Y	N	N/A	
3. Notes stored in fire-resistive container?	Y	N	N/A	
4. Is the construction of the vault adequate?	Y	N	N/A	
5. Is the vault door adequate?	Y	N	N/A	
6. Member ledger cards, general ledger, and notes microfilmed on periodic basis?	Y	N	N/A	

*Reprinted with permission from Loss Prevention Program Operational Security Analysis, *Cash Handling Procedures*. Developed by the Risk Management Department of CUNA International, Inc., Filene House, Madison, Wisconsin.

*Reprinted with permission from Loss Prevention Program Operational Security Analysis, *Security of Records*. Developed by the Risk Management Department of CUNA International, Inc., Filene House, Madison, Wisconsin.

7. Is the frequency of microfilming
   of vital records adequate? .... Y   N   N/A
8. Is a copy of the microfilm stored in a recommended
   location away from the credit union office? ...... Y   N   N/A
9. Are duplicate records maintained
   at the Record Preservation Center
   (Bureau of Federal Credit Unions)? .... Y   N   N/A
10. Is a copy of the bank deposit slip retained in the
    credit union office as evidence of money in transit? Y   N   N/A
11. Does credit union office have a sprinkler system? .. Y   N   N/A
12. Are appropriate fire extinguishers
    located in credit union office? .... Y   N   N/A
13. Is personnel adequately trained to
    effectively use fire prevention equipment? .... Y   N   N/A

APPENDIX B-12
PROTECTING YOUR RECORDS AGAINST DISASTER*

EDWARD J. STEWART†

Summary

Disaster is no respecter of small business. Recently, a typical small concern in a disaster area lost everything—including all records. It was a striking example of what lack of important documents and information can mean to a business establishment in time of disaster. An appeal was made to the American Red Cross and Small Business Administration for funds with which to restore the business. Both agencies were badly hampered by the lack of proper records of earnings. If the businessman had taken proper advance precautions to protect his valuable records, there would have been less delay and little chance of his not obtaining the funds he needed.

During the past 2 years, various U. S. regions have been the scenes of major disasters. These have ranged from tornadoes and hurricanes to saltwater floods and high winds with torrential rainfall. In addition, while business buildings are often located above the flood line, many of them do not have adequate protection from cyclones and tornadoes.

In situations like these, one of the gravest management problems derives from the loss of business records. The problem is grave because any evaluation of the extent of damage, to be acceptable, must be supported by accurate figures and descriptive information. Virtually every organization providing financial assistance covering losses due to a disaster—a bank, an

*Reprinted with permission from Small Business Administration, Management Aids for Small Manufacturers, No. 75, Washington, D.C., 1956.

†Regional Director, Small Business Administration, Region I, Boston, Massachusetts.

insurance company, the Red Cross, or the Small Business Administration—must have dependable proof as to the size of the loss and the fact that relief is justified. To provide this proof, correct and current records should be maintained and should be protected against destruction.

Where business records are concerned, carelessness and lack of foresight by owners and managers is all too common. Often, important ledgers and irreplaceable legal documents are lost forever. As a result, there have been many cases where disaster-struck concerns, seeking financial assistance for rehabilitation, have met serious obstacles. Such difficulties could have been avoided had essential information been protected systematically in advance. Moreover, the fact remains that in large companies, as well as in small concerns and among individual proprietors, most regular records are vulnerable to loss or destruction.

Here is the experience of one firm. This concern was operated in a one-story, wooden-frame building located in a low area at the foot of two hills. A flood swept through the building damaging the flooring, electric motors, and inventory. The operator stated that he "kept the books under the counter, and they were so badly damaged that they were thrown out with all of the other debris." When the owner applied for a loan, he could not give any figures to substantiate his loss, nor could he submit any figures which would enable an investigator to determine what the past business experience of the concern had been. The inability of the applicant to substantiate any claims resulted in his loan application being declined. In fact, he could not be helped in any tangible way.

Floods, winds, and fire can strike anywhere and cause key documents to be destroyed or rendered completely useless. How would your concern make out if your office were demolished? Do you have an alternative, immediate source of information as to inventory, receivables, finances, and similar items? Could you prove how much a disaster cost you? Could you back up your tax returns?

Tax Considerations

Continuity of records—and hence the safeguarding of them—is important from the tax standpoint. Some records (like employee withholding statements) are required by law, others (like unusual business expenses) are dictated by commonsense. All of them help to document earnings statements and avoid mistakes on tax returns. What you need, of course, is sufficient evidence to support the figures you claim. The burden of proof lies with you. If appropriate records are not available, due to a disaster, expensive confusion and even tax penalties may result. Here again, carefully protected duplicate information is usually the best answer.

If your return is questioned and the treasury agent finds upon inspection that you haven't appropriate records to justify what you claim, you are told both orally and by letter to keep permanent books of account plus the following original records: invoices, bills, vouchers, tapes (such as for cash register), and receipts. These items, therefore, should be added to your list of records which should be protected against disaster.

In fact, if a follow-up investigation shows that a businessman has consistently failed to maintain proper records, the Internal Revenue Service may hale him into court on the charge of willful negligence. The penalty for this misdemeanor is a fine of $10,000 or one year's imprisonment, or both, plus the court costs.

Four specialized types of records which are important to safeguard for tax purposes are depreciation, tax withholding statements, unusual business expenses, and business losses.

Depreciation. To substantiate depreciation figures on capital assets (like machinery and equipment), you should safeguard records on date of purchase, cost, estimated useful life, estimated salvage value; and depreciation already taken in past years.

Tax Withholding Statements. As an employer, you are required by law to maintain records on (a) income taxes withheld from employees' wages, (b) taxes withheld from employees' wages under the Federal Insurance Contributions Act for old age and survivors insurance, and (c) taxes on employers under the Federal Unemployment Tax Act for unemployment insurance. Hence, these documents, too, should be protected.

Unusual Business Expenses. If you want to take the full deduction for unusual expenses such as entertainment and travel which are incurred on behalf of your firm, they should be fully documented to show that they are both accurate and allowable. These records, therefore, have lasting value.

Business Losses. There may also be legitimate deductions for losses sustained in the course of regular operations. For example, a marketing innovation may not work out, a manufacturing experiment may fail—or a disaster may strike. Such situations may produce sizable losses which are quite properly deductible—if suitably recorded.

Here is a case in point. One businessman, engaged in the manufacture of automotive devices, was the victim of a severe flood. A substantial part of his loss was destroyed or damaged inventory ($35,000) and records. An outside financial specialist had to be brought in to make estimates and analyses of the company's sales and normal inventories—with the usual ratios in effect in the automotive trade. If the owner had been able to produce proper inventory records, he would have been able easily to substantiate his inventory losses. Failure to maintain these records and store them in a safe place required that the financial specialist devote much high-priced time to his estimated verifications of the flood loss.

Government Contract Records

If you have a supply contract with the Federal Government you have still another series of documents to protect. They can range from invitations to bid and requests for proposals, through your actual bids or proposals, to the contract itself with the specifications, drawings, reports, correspondence, invoices and payments relating to it.

Essentially, you want to be able to reconstruct the terms, history and status of your contract. Details about what you agreed to do, how far you have progressed, and what remains to be accomplished can be of cardinal significance in working out with your contracting officer arrangements for completing work and avoiding delinquency.

For example, an aircraft company sustained heavy loss as a result of floods. Unfortunately, master blueprints and specifications for plane production were lost and serious interruption of operations resulted. The cost of reproducing the necessary thousands of drawings and specification records was very high. Moreover, only a rough estimate of their replaced value could be made. The loss on account of production problems, and delays in delivery of finished units was extremely heavy. However, if a second set of prints and specifications had been deposited in a safe, dry vault located on high ground out of reach of floods, the company could have been back in production almost immediately—and could have saved much goodwill and thousands of dollars.

In the same way, you also need to take care of records relating to any Government work you may be doing under subcontract to a larger prime contractor. Remember that the prime has schedules and prices to meet, which, in part, depend upon you. If disaster strikes you, the prime will want to know as soon as possible what the effect will be upon him and how soon he can expect you "back on the team" productionwise.

You may also need detailed records on costs and pricing in connection with the renegotiation procedure. If your Government-contract work during a fiscal year totaled $250,000 or more, and involved renegotiable contracts, you can be renegotiated. If you are, and can offer proof of having priced closely and of having accepted risks, you stand a better chance for a favorable settlement than if your operating statements show apparently excessive profits with no background facts to justify them. Such background facts can come only from good records.

Constructive Action Possible

The cases of lost records mentioned in this Aid point to a serious situation. Nevertheless, it is one in which constructive action is possible—even for the small enterprise.

A good place for a firm to start is to collect all its valuable papers which are not frequently used for reference. They should be placed in a safe-deposit vault (for example, a bank or other safekeeping institution) where they will be adequately protected from fire, wind and from water damage in case of flood. Such vaults are available for rent in most cities; the cost is low when compared to the potential loss.

Current records of accounts payable and receivable should be reproduced regularly and preserved in a safe place. Similar precautions should be taken for sets of tracings, blueprints, drawings, and important specifications, as well as for models and prototype mechanisms. Special care should be taken of items for which it is not feasible to make and store a duplicate. Insurance policies and related data also deserve special care. The settling of claims can be greatly accelerated when adequate information is available. Then, too, if a dispute arises between the businessman and the insurance company, proof of loss through accurate documentary evidence may save thousands of dollars for the insured.

Remember, however, that such safety measures are worth very little if the material you store and safeguard is out of date. Unless all documents are maintained on a reasonably current basis or have a long-term value, you are missing the point of the whole procedure.

Four Steps to Take

What kind of action, then, should be taken once you have decided to put this program into effect? Basically, there are three steps:

Analyze the Records. All your operating executives should be told of the plan, and asked to make a complete survey and listing of all their valuable records—reports, drawings, and other material—which are vital to the full operation of the activities they supervise.

Copy Key Items. Make arrangements to reproduce all of these key items. Then accumulate all of the duplicates, carefully indexed or identified, and properly packed and protected for storage.

Arrange for Safe Storage. After assembling this material, contact the warehouse, bank, or other safekeeping institution and describe your space needs. When you have arranged adequate storage, you should provide the executives of the storing company with the names of the persons representing your firm who have authority for access to these valuable documents.

Keep Things Current. Once you have your system of safe storage in operation, check up on it regularly to see that the right material is stored, that it is up to date, and that material which is no longer useful is extracted and destroyed.

A Word About Microfilm

In connection with copying key records, the question of microfilm may well come to mind. Basically you can use microfilming in any one of three ways: (a) have it done for you on contract, (b) do it yourself with rented equipment, (c) do it internally with purchased equipment. The main deciding factors are cost, volume of work, and control requirements.

The great advantage of microfilm is space saving. This can be very important if the protected storage space you plan to use is relatively expensive. Obviously, when reduced to microfilm, a great many documents can be fitted into a space the size of an ordinary desk drawer. If, however, you can get well-protected storage space at relatively low cost, be very careful to compare the cost of storing duplicate, full-sized documents with the cost of microfilming. According to the National Records Management Council, full-sized records can sometimes be stored for several years at less expense than the initial cost of microfilming.

The classified pages of your local telephone directory should help you find both contract microfilming services if you want them, or concerns which rent or sell the equipment. Naturally, costs will vary a good deal, but rental charges for a microfilm recorder run typically from around $35 to $80 per month. To buy a recorder would cost anywhere from about $450 to $3,300 and the reader to go with it would involve some $165 to $800 more.

Note to Individual Proprietors and Partners

In the case of individual proprietorships, it is important to recognize that the person and the business are more closely identified than is true of corporations. As a consequence, it is imperative in guarding against disaster that a will, insurance policies, copies of income tax returns, deeds for property, and other essential records and legal instruments, be placed in a safe depository. In this way they can be preserved for reference—not only by the individual himself, but also by those who will have to take over the management of the estate in the event of the owner's death or incompetency.

The matter of protecting a will is particularly important. History demonstrates that healthy businesses can be forced to the wall because there is no owner's will. The fact that the will was destroyed in a disaster doesn't help.

Through the specific instructions in a will a proprietor can provide for executors to carry out plans he made during his lifetime for the management or sale of his business interests. Conversely, the lack of specific authorization to continue operations can result in immediate liquidation of the business—as ordered by the court having jurisdiction over the administration of the estate.

In partnerships, too, the preservation of business records can be essential. If, for example, key agreements and similar documents are destroyed at a time when the partnership has to be dissolved, management and legal problems can arise very quickly. For this reason, the wisest policy is often for the partners to provide individually for the safeguarding of records. When this is done, each has available the material he needs for his own use and protection.

Getting a Program Started

Many small business owners will be inclined to say: "Fine! I agree with all that's been said. Something should be done. I'll get at it just as soon as my regular work lightens up a bit."

But then they get involved with other things. Memory dims, enthusiasm slackens, and the whole idea is forgotten. Or they put off positive action on the grounds that their "affairs are not in order."

These are natural tendencies, but they are also dangerous. For instance, a small manufacturer of a patented, food-packing machine experienced a heavy loss by fire. Unfortunately, no precaution had been taken to keep a complete duplicate set of drawings and specifications in a safe place. The delay in preparing a new set of dimensional drawings—secured by actually dismantling a complete machine in a customer's plant—was expensive. The problem could have been avoided if another set had been printed in the beginning and put away for safekeeping. The cost of such protective storage in a suitable vault would be only a few dollars a year.

However, an important word of caution is appropriate at this point. All changes, additions, or other information concerning these drawings and specifications should be made in the secondary source immediately after such changes take place in order to keep stored records constantly current.

The threat and risks of disaster exist whether you forget them or not. You seldom, if ever, get all your affairs in prefect shape. Furthermore, your business needs to have its important records protected more when the risks are not evident, and when affairs are not in "apple-pie order," than when they are. Procrastination increases the risks of loss and waste—and competitive disadvantages.

Putting off the start of a constructive program is a major reason for being caught short when misfortune occurs. Intelligent plans and positive action are essential if you are to give your business a reasonable chance of survival and recovery. Just as you insure a home and personal property against loss, so also you should protect your business against disaster by safeguarding its vital records. The time to begin is now.

PART C

GUIDELINES FOR THE DEVELOPMENT OF SECURITY POLICY

Outlined example of polices and disaster plan formation:

1. Bomb Threat Policies (Example: large manufacturing company)
2. Riot and Sabotage Policies (Example: large manufacturing company)
3. Industrial Defense Plan Against Civil Disturbance, Bombings, Sabotage. (Example)

Part C appendices are presented to guide the surveyor in preparing examples of *written policy* as they relate to security. The following guidelines for the development of security policies should be referred to prior to the actual writing of a specific operating procedure. (The survey depicts recommendations and not policy but a survey may aid the appropriate administrator in preparing security policy.)

Guidelines for the Development of Security Policy*

1. Essential of security policy formation
   a. Definite, positive policy formation
   b. Translate into practice
   c. Flexible yet highly permanent
   d. Cover all foreseeable situations
   e. Founded on facts and sound judgment
   f. Conform to laws and organizational interest
   g. General statement rather than detailed procedure
2. Why policy should be reduced to writing (S.O.P.)
   a. Lessens misinterpretations and error
   b. Provides a checklist
   c. Constitutes useful instructional device
   d. Failure to write is admission of weakness
3. Who is responsible for formulating policy?
   a. Control must lie at top management level.
   b. Policymaker seeks staff aid and guidance.
   c. Security not only a concern of security officer
4. Steps in the development of security policies

---

*Richard S. Post and Arthur Kingsbury, *Security Administration* (Springfield, C C Thomas, 1970) pp. 118-119.

a. Determine objectives.
b. Outline problems.
c. Consider practical aspects.
d. Test and analyze.

5. Prescribing procedures and rules
   a. Consider objectives, problems, and policies.
   b. Make it a job analysis.
   c. Make it extensive enough to maintain uniformity.
   d. Be brief as possible with clarity.
   e. Follow standard pattern.

6. Examples of operational areas needing policy formulation
   a. Visitor control
   b. Loading dock area
   c. Document control
   d. Political activities
   e. Disbursement of funds
   f. Check cashing

APPENDIX C-1
BOMB THREAT POLICIES*

Procedure for Handling Bomb Threats

Instruct personnel, especially those at the telephone switch board, of a sequence of actions to be followed in the event a bomb threat call is received as indicated below.

1. Keep the caller on the line as long as possible. Ask the caller to repeat the message. Record every word spoken by the person making the call.
2. If the caller does not indicate the location of the bomb or the time of possible detonation, the person receiving the call should ask the caller to provide this information.
3. Inform the caller that the building or area is or may be occupied and the detonation of a bomb could result in death or serious injury to innocent people.
4. Pay particular attention for any strange or peculiar background noises such as: motors running, background music and the type music and any other noises which might give even a remote clue as to the place from which the call is being made.
5. Listen closely to the voice (male—female), voice quality, accents and

---

*Reproduced by special permission from the Bulletin to Management, copyright 1972, by the Bureau of National Affairs, Inc., Washington, D.C., pp. 11-13.

speech impediments. Immediately after the caller hangs up, the person receiving the call should report this information immediately to the Plant Superintendent—Safety and Plant Protection.

6. The Superintendent—Safety and Plant Protection should report this Information immediately to the Local Police Department, Fire Department, FBI and other agencies as deemed necessary. The sequence of notification should be determined after consultation with such local agencies.

7. The Superintendent—Safety and Plant Protection shall notify the Plant Manager, Director—Corporate Safety and Public Relations in accordance with the Corporation Accident Communications Policy under Section C, Serious Public Liability and Civil Incidents. The Plant Industrial Relations Superintendent should also be notified of any bomb threats. The Plant Manager, General Manager and Director—Corporate Safety shall follow this established reporting procedure also in notifying the Vice President—Operations.

8. In order to obtain an Army Bomb Disposal Unit, the Local Police must first find and identify the bomb and then notify the proper Army Disposal Unit for the particular plant involved according to locality. The Army Bomb Disposal Unit for the Pennsylvania and West Virginia Plants is located in _____, Pennsylvania, and the Disposal Unit for the Ohio Plants is located in _____, Ohio. None of the Police Departments in Ohio, Pennsylvania or West Virginia have bomb disposal units.

Procedure for Evacuation in Bomb Threat Situations

The decision whether to evacuate or not to evacuate a plant is the responsibility of the Plant Manager in consultation with the Vice President Operations and/or General Manager _____ Plants in the event a _____ Plant is involved. If a determination to evacuate is made, the following procedure is recommended for evacuation.

1. The signal for evacuating the building in the event of a bomb threat should be similar or the same as that used for evacuation in the event of a fire, if such system exists. The use of a different signal for a bomb threat may tend to create unnecessary excitement and confusion during the process of evacuation. It may be necessary to walk through the areas with portable loud speakers to inform the employees of the evacuation. Emergency shut-down procedures already in existence should be utilized if evacuation is determined necessary. All electricity, gas and fuel lines should be cut off at the main switch or valve.

2. Priority of evacuation would be determined by suspected location of

the bomb, i.e. whether in a building, outside, etc. It is recommended to evacuate the floor levels above the danger area in order to remove those personnel from the extremes of danger as quickly as possible. Training in this type evacuation should be available from police or fire units within the plant community.

3. When the Police and Fire Departments arrive at the plant, the contents, operation, floor plan, etc., will be strange to them unless they have been through the area at some previous date. Thus, it is extremely important that the evacuation unit be thoroughly trained and thoroughly familiar with the areas being evacuated.

4. If the area or building is evacuated, controls must be established immediately to prevent unauthorized access to the building. If proper coordination has been effected with the Local Police and other agencies, they may assist in establishing controls to prevent re-entry into the area or building until the danger has passed.

5. Remove the personnel a safe distance from the building to protect them against debris and other flying objects in the event there is an explosion.

6. Pre-emergency plans should include a temporary relocation in the event an explosion materializes and the area or building is rendered untenable for a considerable period of time.

Procedure for Search in Bomb Threat Situations

The evacuation unit or a separate unit should be trained in bomb search techniques, but not in the techniques of neutralizing, removing or otherwise having contact with the device. The search unit should be thoroughly familiar with area, floor plan of the building, etc. To be proficient in searching a building, they must be thoroughly familiar with all walkways, hallways, restrooms, locker rooms, false ceiling areas and every conceivable location in the building where an explosive or incendiary device might be concealed. Guidelines for the search are listed below.

1. During the period of search, a rapid two-way communication system is a must. The existing telephone system would probably be the most efficient. The use of radios during the search can be dangerous because the radio beam could cause a premature detonation of an electric initiator (blasting cap).

2. During the search particular attention should be given to such areas as elevator shafts, all ceiling areas, restrooms, locker rooms, access doors and crawl spaces in restrooms and other areas which are used as a means of immediate access to plumbing fixtures, electrical fixtures, etc., utility and other closet areas, areas under stairwells, boiler or

furnace rooms, flammable storage areas, main switches and valves, e.g. electric, gas, and fuel, indoor trash receptacles, record storage areas, mail rooms, ceiling lights with easily removable panels, and fire hose racks.

Although this list is not totally complete, it does put emphasis on the areas where a time-delayed explosive or incendiary device might be concealed. Each plant should review the possible areas of concealment and have a listing for the search units use.

3. *If a strange or suspicious object is encountered it should not be touched.* Its location and a description as can best be provided should be reported to the Superintendent Safety and Plant Protection immediately.

4. If the danger zone is identified as located, the area should be blocked off or barricaded with a clear zone of three hundred feet until the object has been removed or disarmed or danger has otherwise passed.

5. During the search the medical personnel should be alerted to stand by in the event of an accident involving an explosion of the device.

6. Pre-emergency plans should include a temporary relocation in the event an explosion materializes and the area or building is rendered untenable for a considerable period of time.

Instructions to Floor Captains

TO: FLOOR CAPTAINS

FLOOR CAPTAINS

A. Assist employees to the EXITS of the floor they are on. (Elevators are *NOT* used during a bomb threat, stairways only.)

B. Be on the alert for suspicious packages. (DO NOT TOUCH)

C. Open windows if a bomb threat. Close windows and doors for Fire.

D. Stay Calm.

Employees

A. When an alarm is sounded, *WALK* to nearest exit, and continue to the outside of the building. (Follow Floor Captains instructions.)

B. *Walk* to at least 1 block from the building. This will keep the exits open for others coming out and protect you from injury.

C. Use stairway only. (NO ELEVATORS).

D. Don't touch any packages during evacuation.

E. Remain outside until given the order to return.

The phone in the lobby will be the emergency number to call to report any emergency, or suspicious objects.

APPENDIX C-2
RIOT AND SABOTAGE POLICIES*

"Guidelines for Defense Against Civil Disturbances and Sabotage"

I. Introduction

This is an extremely hard area to define, and impossible to make hard and fast rules applicable to all types of business. Even legislators have been caught up in the problem of trying to define riot, insurrection or whatever you wish to call it. However, for our purposes in this guide, we will talk about the types of trouble to expect and what our defensive actions should be.

II. Types of Trouble and Your Actions

A. Hit and Run Period of Unrest: This is the most prevalent and something that most cities have already experienced more than once in varying degrees—sometimes publicized and sometimes not. Youthful vandals move fast, avoid police contact, are unprofessional in their efforts, throw fire bombs at will but keep gun play to a minimum, loot what is readily accessible, generally do not congregate except at disaster scenes, attack individuals when they have superior strength, seek darkness and cover, and operate, at least in initial stages, in core city areas, sometimes eventually spreading to include suburban commercial centers and isolated installations such as restaurants, gas stations, taverns and the like. Industries removed from the core area and in operation are not primary targets generally in this period. Warehouses, supply yards, and retailers are susceptible in all areas because of the mobility of vandals.

B. Full Scale Riot: This is different in that crowds gather and do not attempt to shield themselves from police. Burning and looting is general. All businesses are vulnerable. There is a total lack of respect for authority, and often a disregard for personal safety by the rioters themselves. Initially, the same core areas are the start, but outlying commercial centers are in great danger of mass infiltration. Gun play may be prevalent. Virtually no business in any location is exempt from attack. Hit and run attacks are frequent in outlying areas. Police may find that their initial efforts are essentially containment rather than enforcement.

*Reprinted with permission from ASPA-BNA SURVEY: Industrial Security. *Riot and Sabotage Policies,* Bulletin to Management, Washington, D.C., Bureau of National Affairs, 1972, pp. 13-16.

They will be unable to answer all calls. Many businesses in the primary riot area will be on their own for protection.

Obviously, your location, and your definition as to *which of the two conditions exists,* will affect your plans and actions.

A boarded up, abandoned business in a *riot zone* will have no defense because looters have plenty of time to break the barriers. On the other hand, during *hit and run* conditions, the same business might be fairly effectively safeguarded by its barriers because vandals are in a hurry and wish to avoid police. With no quick entry possible and no openings for fire bombs, they will often select another target. Conversely, a business in a *riot zone* where maximum interior and exterior lighting is provided, and armed guards are safe but visible, may have a chance of survival. The same would apply to *hit and run* conditions. While the chance of minimizing loss is often better under this system, the risk of injury or death to personnel is great.

III. *Purpose of the Plan*
  A. Assure orderly and efficient transition from normal to emergency operations.
  B. Delegate emergency authority.
  C. Assign emergency responsibilities.
  D. Indicate authority by management for actions contained in plan.
  E. Decide vulnerability.

IV. *Implementation*
  Each plant manager or facility supervisor should:
  A. Appoint individual (s) to implement plan.
  B. Specify conditions under which plan may be partially implemented.
  C. Specify conditions under which plan may be fully implemented.
  D. Coordinate plan among all responsible individuals to assure sequence of implementation.

V. *Emergency Control Organization*
  A. Prepare management succession list of executive and administrative personnel and key employees. Designate alternates.
  B. Pre-publish company orders constituting emergency authority.

VI. *Control Center*
  Establish control center or plan command post, the focal point for directing all emergency actions. For decentralized operations, all

emergency actions should be coordinated through the central control center. Assure that the following criteria is followed:

A. Location is well protected.
B. Access can be controlled with minimum manpower.
C. Alternate location is selected.
D. Command post is adequately provided with communications equipment, administrative supplies and written procedures and information lists.

VII. Planning Coordination (Mutual Aid)

A. Coordinate plan with local and state officials, Fire Departments, Police Departments, Civil Defense, Hospitals.
B. With adjacent plants and business firms.
C. With local utilities: Power, telephone, transportation.
D. With employee union officials.
E. With local news media.

VIII. Communications

A. Provide adequate communications to cover plant areas.
B. Back-up primary system with two-way radios, walkie-talkies, field telephones, or megaphones (bull horns).
C. Monitor local and state police radios.
D. Establish communications with adjacent plants and business, and within management.
E. Train switchboard operators in emergency procedures.
F. Designate male operators as alternates for females who may not report to work.
G. Establish emergency communications procedures.

IX. Provide for Emergency Notification of Employees

A. Keep switchboards open and operators available.
B. Establish cascade system of notification for recall to work.
C. Prepare reporting instructions.
D. Designate reporting points, primaries and alternates out of emergency areas.
E. Plan transportation, i.e. busses, trucks, company-owned or contracted.
F. Coordinate mutual needs with other plants.
G. Arrange police escort for emergency repair crews.
H. Pre-select routes from reporting points to plant.
I. Plan for escort of female personnel: consider car pools.

    J. Brief employees on emergency plans. (Do this with caution. Do not create a "scare program.")

    K. During disorder, brief employees daily on impact of disorder on plant and community. Must be factual to dispel rumor and speculation.

    L. Prepare employees psychologically to remain on job; Need for loyalty, self-restraint; act only as directed by management or police; reporting rumors to supervisors.

    M. Explain impact of emergency on plant.

    N. Designate shelters for employees in the event evacuation it not possible.

X. Evacuation

    A. Designate routes to evacuate buildings or plants.

    B. Inform employees of routes and procedures.

    C. Evacuate by departments (if practical).

    D. Designate primary and alternate exits away from emergency area.

XI. Electric Power

    A. Coordinate plan with local power companies: Transmission lines, transformer, former banks, alternate distribution lines.

    B. Provide emergency power for lighting and other essentials (not for full production).

    C. Generators, size, location, fuel, operators.

    D. Battery-powered equipment, flashlights, lanterns, radios, batteries.

XII. Plant Security

    A. Organizational Plans

        1. Develop plant security organization and identify the security force by uniform or other easily recognized badge of authority.

        2. Write security plans and procedures. (Include training requirement, assignment of auxiliary force, duty roster, and weapons policy).

        3. Equip the security force with personal protection equipment such as face shield, helmet, gas mask, and chest protector.

        4. Report promptly to local and state law enforcement agencies any actual or suspected acts of sabotage.

        5. Inspect security fence (or other barrier) regularly for proper maintenance.

6. Post trespass warnings on all barriers.
7. Park employee vehicles outside of inner security fence or wall, to reduce fire potential and minimize hazard of concealed explosive or incendiary devices. These vehicles must be protected against sabotage.
8. Light perimeter barriers and internal critical areas.
9. Use screening to protect lighting fixtures against rocks and other objects.
10. Insure continuous lighting in parking lots, yard areas, and on ground floor.
11. Install protection for glassed areas exposed to streets, i.e. windows, doors and roof light windows.
12. Develop procedures for positive identification and control of employees.
13. Control movement and parking of company vehicles.
14. Procedures for control of visitors.
15. Lock all doors, windows, roof latches and means of entrance to buildings.

B. Protecting Critical Areas
1. Identify critical areas within plant.
2. Enclose critical areas with physical barriers.
3. Designate specific personnel who may have access to critical areas.
4. Develop a key control system.
5. Develop package and material control procedures.
6. Protect gasoline pumps and other dispensers of flammables. (Disconnect power source to electrically operated pumps.)
7. Post watchmen at strategic locations, the roof area is a vulnerable spot. Be careful watchmen are not mistaken for snipers or vandals.

XIII. Fire Protection

A. Post and enforce fire prevention regulations.
B. Extend fire alarm system to all areas of facilities.
C. Determine when fire department can arrive. Under conditions other than civil disorders; five minutes after report of fire?
D. Provide secondary water supply for fire protection.
E. Install mesh wire or screening material to protect roofs of buildings immediately adjacent to the perimeter from fire bombs, molotov cocktails, or other incendiary devices, if feasible.
F. Organize employees into fire fighting brigades and rescue squads and train these groups to work efficiently.

    G. Store combustible materials in well-protected areas.

    H. Instruct employees in the use of fire extinguishers and place extra extinguishers at strategic locations.

    I. Post signs showing location of fire hose connections.

    J. Insure that fire hose connections are compatible with local fire department equipment.

    K. Check sprinkler systems to assure their operation and remove control handles in exposed areas.

XIV. *Protect Vital Records*

    A. Protect vital records, cash and other valuable items.

    B. Remove those records which cannot be replaced to a remote location if time permits.

XV. *Emergency Supplies*

    A. Photographic equipment.

    B. Pre-stock food, water, and medical supplies because conditions may not permit procurement during emergency.

    C. Provide sanitation facilities.

    D. Stock administrative supplies.

    E. Stock emergency repair tools, equipment and parts.

    F. Develop procedures for employees to purchase gasoline for automobiles from plant supply in case local stations are closed.

    G. Maintain sufficient inventory of empty 55 gallon drums to be filled with water or sand for use as barricades at entrances.

    H. Have on hand enough barbed wire to form a barrier directly in front of each row of 55 gallon drums. Concertina type wire is very effective.

    I. Maintain supply of panels or screen mesh to protect windows on ground floors.

    J. Place in a strategic location, emergency pumps and other supplies which can be used to supply emergency service.

    K. Provide emergency feeding service for employees.

    L. Provide emergency sleeping quarters.

    M. Develop plans for a secondary sanitary water supply.

XVI. *Medical Requirements*

    A. Organize first-aid teams.

    B. Set up emergency first-aid stations; if professional medical staff personnel are available, have them man stations; if not, designate a first-aid team to assume the duties.

XVII. *Test the Plan*

Test the entire plan.

APPENDIX C-3
INDUSTRIAL DEFENSE PLAN AGAINST
CIVIL DISTURBANCES — BOMBINGS — SABOTAGE*

Copy Number _____

Issued to: _____

_____

Date of Issue: _____

Introduction to the Plan

This presents the foundation on which the plan is based.

1. *Purpose:* (This paragraph should include a statement or statements comparable in scope to the following: "To establish a continuing program of preparation for protection against civil disturbances and sabotage, and to insure the continuation or restoration of essential operations in the event of other hostile or destructive acts.")

2. *Assumptions:* (Assumptions stating in substance the premises shown below should appear in this paragraph.)

    a. National

    (1) Potential civil disturbances in the United States could, with little or no warning, seriously endanger selected areas within the U.S. industrial base.

    (2) Widespread sabotage against U.S. industry is not inconceivable.

    b. Local: Each facility is vulnerable and subject to sabotage, bombings, civil disturbances, and other hostile or destructive acts.

3. *Basic Planning Data:* (This paragraph should include information as listed below.)

    a. Maps: (Attach as appendix a topographical map showing the facility and surrounding areas, including the road and rail nets, the locations of neighboring industrial facilities, power plants, pumping stations, etc. Indicate on the map the location of residence of key employees residing in each area. Indicate the distance most of the employees live from the plant, i.e. 11-25 miles or whether there is no general pattern.)

    b. Vulnerability: (The degree of vulnerability to civil disturbances is contingent primarily upon sociological, environmental, and geographic factors. Vulnerability to sabotage bombings, and arson may in addition to these factors include criticality of the plant, criticality of the product and accessibility to the plant. Answers to the following questions should provide indicators to the relative degree of vulnerability.)

---

*Reprinted with permission from Industrial Defense Against Civil Disturbances, Bombings, Sabotage. Office of the Provost Marshal General—Department of the Army, pp. 1-3.

(1) Is the facility located in an urban area?

(2) Is the facility located in close proximity, 5-10 miles, to an urban area?

(3) Is the facility located near other industries or near military installations?

(4) Is the facility in a remote location?

(5) Have there been previous incidents of civil disturbances, fire bombing or similar acts by dissident groups? At what frequency? To what degree of destruction?

(6) Are environmental and sociological conditions conducive to incidents which might erupt into a riot situation?

(7) Are there good plant/police/community relations?

(8) Is there good plant management-employee relations?

(9) Has a determination been made whether hostile factors exist among plant employees?

(10) Is the plant producing "war materials" under defense contract and has there been employee opposition to this endeavor?

(11) Have there been incidents of employee disfavor to the U.S. involvement in Vietnam, or other areas?

(12) If producing war materials, are they "critical" to the defense effort?

(13) Have there been unexplained incidents of production stoppage? Slowdown? Defective end items?

(14) Have there been incidents of unexplained small fires in the plant?

(15) Have there been internal labor disputes which have not been completely reconciled?

c. Physical layout: (Maps, blueprints, and schematic drawings of production and or assembly lines.)

b Operational data

(1) Personnel: (Indicate the total number of employees and specify the number of contractual or vendor personnel present daily.)

(2) Shift operation: (Indicate the total number of employees and contractual personnel, male and female, assigned to each shift.)

4. *Legal Considerations*

(The resort to legal remedies should be a major consideration in industrial defense planning. All potential criminal acts or violations should be considered to assure adequate preparation for legal remedy. Advance consideration of the leadtimes and processing factors of legal recourse could mean the difference in pursuing a successful legal remedy.)

a. Essential considerations of protecting life and property under various contingencies.

b. Advance coordination with legal authorities and courts to determine methods of invoking legal options to avoid adverse reactions.

c. Thorough review of laws, statutes, codes, court decisions and common forms of preliminary legal action such as restraining orders and injunctions.

d. Maintain complete and accurate records of all incidents.

e. Document and preserve all evidence for possible legal action. This may be accomplished by:

    (1) Photographs of the incident.

    (2) Statements from witnesses.

    (3) Physical evidence, e.g. explosives, incendiaries, weapons, etc.

    (4) Copies of dissident literature/handouts.

    (5) Other admissible evidence and useful information.

f. Liability for injury/death to employees of other persons on plant property.

g. Liability for damage to property of others in your possession or on your premises.

h. Insurance coverage against injury to persons or damage to property resulting from civil disturbances and bombings.

5. *Employee Transportation:* (Indicate the mode of transportation used by employees for getting to and from work, i.e. 60 percent bus, 30 percent private auto, 10 percent subway.)

6. *Training and Tests:* (This paragraph should contain instructions for training and rehearsing personnel and testing the plan.)

7. *Implementing Instructions:* (Include a statement to the effect—this plan is effective immediately for training purposes. It will be effective for emergency actions when ordered by [specify the job title (s) of the person (s) with authority to partially or completely implement the plan under emergency conditions].)

SIGNATURE
(Senior Executive)

ANNEXES	APPENDIXES
I Emergency Organization	I Bomb Threats
II Personnel Protection	II Industrial Sabotage
III Fire Prevention	III Check List
IV Plant Security	IV General Planning
V Utilities and Services	
VI Planning Coordination and Liaison	
VII Records Protection	
VIII Damage Reduction	
IX Restoration	
X Emergency Requirements	
XI Testing	

SELECTED BIBLIOGRAPHY

BOOKS

Brodie, Thomas G: *Bombs and Bombings: A Handbook to Detection, Disposal and Investigation for Police and Fire Departments.* Springfield, C C Thomas, 1971.

Brown, Ralph S.: *Loyalty and Security: Employment Tests in the United States.* New Haven, Yale, 1958.

Cole, Richard B.: *The Application of Security Systems and Hardware.* Springfield, C C Thomas, 1970.

Cole, Richard B.: *Protect Your Property: The Applications of Burglar Alarm Hardware.* Springfield, C C Thomas, 1971.

Criminal Law. Gardena, Calif., Gilbert Law Summaries, 1970.

Criminal Procedure. Gardena, Calif., Gilbert Law Summaries, 1971.

Currer-Briggs, Noel (Ed.): *Security Attitudes and Techniques for Management.* London, Hutchinson, 1968.

Curtis, S.J.: *Modern Retail Security.* Springfield, C C Thomas, 1960.

Curtis, S.J.: *Security Control—External Theft.* New York, Chain Store Age Publishing Corp., 1971.

Davis, John Richelieu: *Industrial Plant Protection.* Springfield, C C Thomas, 1957.

Gocke, B.W.: *Practical Plant Protection and Policing.* Springfield, C C Thomas, 1957.

Green, Richard: *Business Intelligence and Espionage.* Homewood, Ill., Dow Jones—Irwin, 1966.

Hamilton, Peter: *Espionage and Subversion in an Industrial Society.* London, Hutchinson, 1967.

Healy, Richard J.: *Design for Security.* New York, Wiley, 1968.

Hemphill, Charles E.: *Security for Business and Industry.* Homewood, Ill., Dow Jones—Irwin, 1971.

Jacobs, Paul; and Landau, Saul: *The New Radicals.* New York, Vintage, 1966.

Momboisse, Raymond M.: *Industrial Security for Strikes, Riots and Disasters.* Springfield, C C Thomas, 1968.

National Fire Protection Association: *Fire Protection Handbook.* National Fire Protection Association, 1969.

National Industrial Conference Board: *Industrial Security: Combating Subversion and Sabotage,* Part 1, No. 60. New York, Nat. Indust. Conf. Board, 1953.

Oliver, Eric; and Wilson, John: *Practical Security in Commerce and Industry.* London, Gower, 1968.

Oliver, Eric; and Wilson, John: *Security Manual.* London, Gower, 1969.

Post, Richard S.; and Kingsbury, Arthur A.: *Security Administration: An Introduction.* Springfield, C C Thomas, 1970.

Tobias, Marc Weber: *Locks, Safes, and Security: A Handbook for Law Enforcement Personnel.* Springfield, C C Thomas, 1971.

United States Government: *Guide to Subversive Organizations and Publications.*

U.S. Office of Defense Mobilization: *Standards for Physical Security of Industrial and Government Facilities.* Washington, D.C., Gov. Print. Off., 1958.

Wade, Worth: *Industrial Espionage and Misuse of Trade Secrets.* Ardmore, Advance House, 1965.

Wilensky, Harold L.: *Organizational Intelligence.* New York, Basic Books, 1967.

PUBLICATIONS OF THE GOVERNMENT, LEARNED SOCIETIES, AND OTHER ORGANIZATIONS

Academic Guidelines for Security and Loss Prevention Programs in Community and Junior Colleges. The American Society for Industrial Security, in Cooperation with the American Association of Junior Colleges, 1972.

Department of the Army Field Manual: *Physical Security FM 19-30.* Washington, D.C., Gov. Print. Off., 1972.

Howington, Jon R.; and Kingsbury, Arthur A.: *A Bibliographical Manual for Criminal Justice, Crime Prevention, and Security for the Community College.* Detroit, M & L Associates, 1972.

National Industrial Conference Board: *Industrial Security: Plant Guard Handbook* Part 11, No. 64. New York, Nat. Indust. Conf. Board, 1953.

National Investigations Committee: *A Guide to Security Investigations.* Washington, D.C., The American Society for Industrial Security, 1970.

Rykert, Wilbur: *Reduction of Criminal Opportunity.* Pittsburgh, National Crime Deterrence Council, Inc., 1971.

U.S. Department of Justice: *The Nature, Impact, and Prosecution of White-Collar Crime.* Washington, D.C., Gov. Print. Off., 1970.

PERIODICALS

Canadian Security Gazette. Canadian Security Gazette Limited. 2792 Yonge Street, Toronto, Ontario, Canada.

Environmental Control and Safety Management. A.M. Best Company, Park Avenue, Morristown, New Jersey 07960.

Government Security and Loyalty Report. Bureau of National Affairs Inc., 1231 25th Street, N.W., Washington, D.C. 20037.

Occupational Hazards. Occupational Hazards, 614 Superior Avenue, Cleveland, Ohio 44113.

Security and Protection. The Industrial Police and Security Association by Trade News LTD., Drummed House 203.209 North Gower Street, London. N.W.I.

Security Gazette Limited. Security Gazette Limited, 3 Clement's Inn, London WC2, England.

Security Management. American Society for Industrial Security, 404 NADA Building, Washington, D.C. 20006.

Security News. Security News, Jamaica, New York.

Security Systems Digest. Security Systems Digest, National Press Building, Washington, D.C. 20004.

Security World. Security World, 2639 South La Cienega Boulevard, Los Angeles, Calif. 90034.

Systems Technology and Science for Law Enforcement and Security. Lomond Systems, Inc., Mt. Airy, Maryland 21771.

MICROFILM SERVICES

Industrial Security Microfilm. American Society for Industrial Security, 404 NADA Building, Washington, D.C. 20006.

Security Infobank. Micro Photo Division, Micro Publishers, Bell & Howell, Old Mansfield Road, Wooster, Ohio 44691.

INDEX

The Ethics of Immigration